COBB

COBB

A Biography

by Al Stump

with a foreword by Jimmie Reese

Algonquin Books of Chapel Hill
1994

For their support and assistance in numerous ways, I want to thank:

From baseball—Jimmie Reese; Lew Matlin of the Detroit Tigers; Tigers' manager Sparky Anderson; Charlie Gehringer; Casey Stengel; Fred Haney; Frank "Lefty" O'Doul; Tris Speaker; Davy Jones; Herold "Muddy" Ruel; Branch Rickey; Mickey Cochrane; Heinie Manush; Ted Williams; Joe DiMaggio.

Also, Buddy Dyer and Wayne Wilson at the Amateur Athletic Foundation in Los Angeles, the Baseball Museum and Hall of Fame at Cooperstown, N.Y., the Burton Historical Collection at the Detroit Public Library, the *Detroit News*, the *Detroit Free Press*, the *Los Angeles Times*.

Also, at the *Los Angeles Times*—Jim Murray, Bill Dwyer, Earl Gustkey, and Larry Stewart.

And, Will Fowler; Gene Fowler; Elmer Griffin; Bill Henry; Arthur Sohikian; A. C. Ginn; Joe Cunningham; John Schouweiler; Ron Shelton—and, from Shelton's office, Kellie Davis and Karin Freud—Robert Wuhl; Ron Birnbach.

And finally, for long-term help and support, Col. Barney Oldfield; Grace Buscher Guslander; Dr. Alan Herman; the Watermans—Sherry, Bobby, and Kylie; Shannon McVicar; Robyn Harper; my editor, Louis D. Rubin, Jr.; my agent, Michael Siegel; and for their helpful efforts, Jennifer Decker and my wife, Jo Mosher.

Published by
ALGONQUIN BOOKS OF CHAPEL HILL
Post Office Box 2225
Chapel Hill, North Carolina 27515-2225

a division of
WORKMAN PUBLISHING COMPANY, INC.
708 Broadway
New York, New York 10003

LIBRARY OF CONGRESS CATALOGING-IN-PUBLICATION DATA
Stump, Al.
Cobb:a biography/by Al Stump:with a foreword by Jimmie Reese.—1st ed.
p.   cm.
Includes bibliographical references and index.
ISBN 0-945575-64-5
1. Cobb, Ty, 1886–1961.   2. Baseball players—United States—Biography.   I. Title.
GV865.C6S78   1994
796.357'092—dc20
[B]   94-26122
CIP

1   3   5   7   9   10   8   6   4   2
First Edition

To my wife, Jo

"The honorable and honest Cobb blood . . . never will be subjected. It bows to no wrong nor to any man . . . the Cobbs have their ideals and God help anyone who strives to bend a Cobb away from such."

—Ty Cobb, 1927

"Ty Cobb, the greatest of all ballplayers — and an absolute shit."

—Ernest Hemingway, 1948

CONTENTS

ILLUSTRATIONS

FOLLOWING PAGE 204

TWO EARLY PHOTOGRAPHS OF COBB

COBB IN EARLY YEARS WITH DETROIT TIGERS

THE TIGER OUTFIELD, 1907–1912:
DAVY JONES, COBB, SAM CRAWFORD

HUGH JENNINGS

COBB AND NAP LAJOIE IN 1910 CHALMERS AUTO

COBB SLIDES INTO THIRD AGAINST JIMMY AUSTIN

SLIDE INTO HOME RUN BAKER
THAT TOUCHED OFF NEAR-RIOT

COBB AT BAT IN 1915

CHRISTY MATHEWSON AND COBB IN ARMY UNIFORM, 1918

PORTRAIT SHOT OF COBB

COBB AND YOUTHFUL FANS

TY COBB, HERSCHEL COBB, BOBBY JONES, AND BIRD DOG

COBB AT 1925 WORLD SERIES, PITTSBURGH

COBB AND O. B. KEELER

WITH PHILADELPHIA ATHLETICS

EDDIE COLLINS, COBB, TRIS SPEAKER ON 1928 A'S

BABE RUTH AND COBB WITH YOUTH BASEBALLERS

COBB AND TED WILLIAMS, 1961

FOREWORD

BY JIMMIE REESE

B abe Ruth had it right about his greatest rival, Ty Cobb, when he told me, "Cobb's the meanest, toughest——— who ever walked onto a field. He gave everybody hell— me included—because he couldn't stand to lose. All he wanted was to beat you on Saturday and twice on Sunday. Otherwise he was miserable."

I'm a former New York Yankee infielder and, at age ninety-three, the oldest surviving major-leaguer in the Association of Professional Ballplayers. I serve now as a coach with the California Angels. Not many are left who saw Ty Cobb on the rampage in the years 1905–28. None of us can ever forget him. At bat, his eyes blazed at pitchers. He was the only ballplayer I can remember who started each game with a snarl and ended it the same way. What a wildcat he was. Cobb was so shrewd and talented in every aspect of the game that he didn't need to make baseball a war, but he was always in a battle. In a day when the game was already a tough enough fight, Cobb added a new dimension. He'd force errors time and again by his wild offensive play, such as stealing home base against a veteran battery. We called him "Jack Dempsey in spikes." The story is quite true that Cobb filed his spikes to razor sharpness to first intimidate opponents and then gore them. I don't know how he stood twenty-four years of punishment from the players who retaliated. Call it another Cobb "incredible."

Here's a typical story about him: One day a Yankee rookie pitcher threw a beanball at Cobb and it nicked his ear. Big Ty didn't say a thing then, but next time up he drag-bunted down the first-base line. The pitcher went to handle the bunt, and the next thing he knew he was flying through the air, halfway knocked out. Cobb's spikes had actually cut the pants and part of the shirt right off him. The man was left bloody, ragged, and permanently scarred. Lou Gehrig of the Yankees, a sweet guy, became angry enough to say, "Cobb is about as welcome in American League parks as a rattlesnake." Another true fact was that far fewer beaners and dusters were aimed at Cobb than at any other hitter, because of fear. I can't tell you where he studied psychology, but he was a master at it.

Babe Ruth, my roommate on the Yankees, once went on a hunting trip with Cobb, and Ty wouldn't share the same tent with Babe. He refused to get friendly with anyone on another club even while relaxing in the off-season.

Babe, of course, became baseball's biggest box-office figure; Cobb was growing old when Ruth's home-run output had the country going crazy. Ruth was all power and Cobb was mostly science, with some power added. They broke fairly even in statistics. Ty Cobb's .367 lifetime batting average is still the best ever recorded, whereas Babe averaged .342. Cobb remains tops today in runs scored, with 2,244 to Babe's 2,174. Ruth edged over Cobb in slugging average, runs batted in, and by far in homers. So the spoils were fairly even. Which of them was the greatest player of all time? Who contributed most to his team? They'll be arguing that one well into the next century. I guess you know whom I favor—the one they never called a "rattlesnake" in the dugouts, the one with a big belly. But what a wonderful player was the Detroit Tiger, as you'll learn in reading this book by a savvy baseball writer, Al Stump, who knew Ty Cobb well.

Editor's Note: Jimmie Reese, who wrote this foreword early in 1994, died while this book was in the final stages of production in July 1994.

PREFACE

Ty Cobb always was a taciturn man; he grew more and more reclusive with advancing age, and upon reaching seventy-three in 1960 he was holed up in a pair of dreary homes worth $5 million in Atherton, California, and at Lake Tahoe, Nevada. Baseball's greatest, most thoroughly disliked player of this century lived without electric lights (candles only in one of his hideouts) and without telephone service (in both). The multimillionaire had been estranged from his five children decades earlier. Two wives had charged extreme cruelty in divorces, each deposing that the Georgia Peach was uncontrollable when crossed or drunk, or whenever he was reminded of how he had regularly bloodied opponents with his spikes—"Cobb's kiss," as one victim, Frank "Home Run" Baker, called his slashing.

Cobb chose me to ghostwrite his memoirs early in 1960 largely on the recommendation of New York editor, biographer, and Hollywood screenwriter Gene Fowler, and of Grantland Rice, dean of sportswriters. He had fired several previous ghosts who had displeased him in one way or another. Various other autobiographical projects had fallen through.

As a U.S. Navy combat correspondent in World War II, I had met

General Douglas MacArthur. "Take the writing job," counseled MacArthur, an old West Point shortstop, who was Cobb's number-one fan and close friend. "The world has known only one like him."

So began a turbulent period of close to one year with the most brilliant player who ever lived. Cobb's competitiveness and truculence remain unmatched in American sport. His compulsion to win was awesome. As Paul Gallico wrote, "There was a burning rage in Ty Cobb never far from the surface. He brought a fury, cruelty and a viciousness heretofore unencountered even in the roughest kind of play." Gallico, a longtime sports editor at the New York *Daily News* who closely studied Cobb in his late career, felt that Cobb's weird conduct, both on and off the field, could have been signs of significant mental illness.

It was to be expected that a man as abidingly competitive as Cobb, as emotionally wrapped up in what his career was and wasn't, would not be able to maintain a detached objectivity about that career. Too, the memories of elderly men are notoriously fallible. Therefore his version of long-ago events is not to be taken as unvarnished fact— although his recall was often striking—so much as an index of the way he saw things as having happened.

What resulted from our collaboration was *My Life in Baseball: The True Record*, which was finished and at the publishers before Cobb died in July of 1961. We first conceived the book in January of 1960, traveling together to various parts of the country, including New York, Detroit, Georgia, Arizona, his home in Atherton, California, his lodge at Lake Tahoe, and my beach house in Santa Barbara, California.

It was the Georgia Peach's combination of acute intelligence and powerful, sometimes uncontrollable passions, placed in the service of his remarkable physical abilities, that made him the embodiment of baseball excellence as the game was played in his day. Precisely that personality is demonstrated in the way that he could shape his recall of what actually took place into something closer to his heart's desire.

One reason for the tediously slow going on the first book was that the records of his 24 seasons, 3,033 games, and 11,429 at-bats were badly jumbled, out of sequence, and fading in clarity. He had set more than ninety major-league records at various points in his incredible, unequalled run from 1905 through 1928. He was the original baseball Hall of Famer, the first named to the shrine, and we were enmeshed in yellowing game descriptions, photos by the hundreds, statistics, correspondence, old contract copies, and sporting journals published before the turn of the twentieth century.

That 1961 autobiography was very self-serving. Cobb had the final say in its contents, accorded him by the publisher. And when we did not agree, which was often, it was his word that was accepted by Doubleday. The book sold moderately well and was called by some one of the finest books of its kind. But it was a subsequent article I wrote for *True Magazine*, which Bob Considine called "possibly the best sports story I have ever read," that won sports awards and, finally, a contract for a movie based on the relationship between Cobb and myself, which is scheduled for release in late 1994.

During the long stretches of time we spent together, my feelings for Ty Cobb were often in flux. My respect for his greatness, my contempt for his vile temper and mistreatment of others, my pity for his deteriorating health, and my admiration for his stubbornness and persistence produced a frustrating mix of emotions. With so much material left over, there was need for another manuscript, but it wasn't until three decades later that I finally felt compelled to put the real Ty Cobb to rest. Since much of the material is presented in the first person, as Cobb told it to me, the reader is invited to watch not merely Ty Cobb in action on the diamond, but his memory at work as well.

—Al Stump
Southern California
July 4, 1994

COBB

PROLOGUE

"I never saw anyone like Ty Cobb. No one even close to him as the greatest all-time ballplayer. That guy was superhuman, amazing."

Casey Stengel, 1975

"Few names have left a firmer imprint upon the pages of the history of American times than has that of Ty Cobb. For a quarter of a century his aggressive exploits on the diamond, while inviting opposition as well as acclaim, brought high drama . . . This great athlete seems to have understood from early in his professional career that in the competition of baseball, just as in war, defensive strategy never has produced ultimate victory."

General Douglas MacArthur, 1961

"Fans and the sporting press are always trying to compare Ty Cobb and Babe Ruth. This is absurd since they are incomparable, like trying to draw a comparison between an elephant and a wolf. Beloved Babe was a man of simple makeup, savage Cobb was a mass of paradoxes with a life that reads like a Gothic horror tale."

Paul Gallico, 1975

"Crowds jeered Cobb and stoned him, but they came in great numbers to see him. He was undoubtedly the greatest competitor any sport has ever known. For his brilliant hour, a Napoleon, he dominated his world."

The Sporting News, 1951

"A Columbia University professor, lecturing on Ty Cobb, said that if he'd entered banking he'd have been a leading American banker; if he'd gone into politics he'd have become president . . . He'd have been number one at whatever field he chose."

Harry Golden, 1959

"He threw me more curves in money negotiations than a whole tribe of Arabs. He'd hold out until hell froze over until he got what he demanded."

Frank Navin, President, Detroit Tigers, 1926

"The great trouble with baseball today is that most players are in the game for the money that's in it—not for the love of it, the excitement and thrill of it."

Ty Cobb, 1960

"After World War I, there were more than 20 newspapers published in New York—and not one of them knew Ty Cobb's terrible personal secret."

Marshall Hunt, New York Daily News, 1973

"Cobb's first wife, a charming Augusta girl, started divorce proceedings against Cobb three times and went through with it on the fourth attempt, saying, 'I simply can't live with the man any longer.'"

Fred Lieb, 1977

"Once, on a golf course, I was about to putt on the fifth green when I heard a voice yelling, 'Get out of my way, I'm coming through!' Then came the demand again. So I made way and Ty Cobb played right through me without apology. I guess nobody but the great Cobb would dare to do that to a president."

Dwight Eisenhower, 1964

"Every time I hear of this guy again—I wonder how he was possible."

Joe DiMaggio, 1990

The Lifetime Record of Ty Cobb

No small part of the charm of our National Game consists of the validity of its statistical record as an index of comparative performance across the years. Research by baseball statisticians in recent years has produced extensive and often valuable revision in the lifetime records compiled by Ty Cobb and other early diamond stars. Depending upon which revision one consults, the totals can vary considerably. The narrative that follows, however, is a biography centered on Cobb's own memories, and Cobb's assumptions about his career were based on records as they were posted and credited to him for more than a half-dozen decades of baseball history. It has seemed appropriate, therefore, to use those figures throughout as they were published and generally accepted by baseball fans prior to the appearance of recent revisions. The following is the remarkable lifetime record of Tyrus Raymond Cobb, as drawn from the *Baseball Register* for 1942:

Year Club	League	G	AB	R	H	HR	SB	RBI	BA	PO	A	E	FA
1904—Augusta	So. Atl.	37	135	14	32	1	4	—	.237	62	9	4	.946
1904—Anniston	S. E.	22	—	—	—	0	6	—	.370	—	—	—	—
1905—Augusta	So. Atl.	104	411	60	134	0	40	—	.326	149	15	13	.927
1905—Detroit	Amer.	41	150	19	36	1	2	—	.240	85	6	4	.958
1906—Detroit	Amer.	97	350	44	112	1	23	—	.320	107	14	9	.931
1907—Detroit	Amer.	150	605	97	212	5	49	116	.350	238	30	11	.961
1908—Detroit	Amer.	150	531	88	188	4	39	101	.324	212	23	14	.944
1909—Detroit	Amer.	156	573	116	216	9	76	115	.377	222	24	14	.946
1910—Detroit	Amer.	140	509	106	196	8	65	88	.385	305	18	14	.958
1911—Detroit	Amer.	146	591	147	248	8	83	144	.420	376	24	18	.957
1912—Detroit	Amer.	140	553	119	227	7	61	90	.410	324	21	22	.940
1913—Detroit	Amer.	122	428	70	167	4	52	65	.390	262	22	16	.947
1914—Detroit	Amer.	97	345	69	127	2	35	57	.368	177	8	10	.949
1915—Detroit	Amer.	156	563	144	208	3	96	95	.369	328	22	18	.951
1916—Detroit	Amer.	145	542	113	201	5	68	67	.371	325	18	17	.953
1917—Detroit	Amer.	152	588	107	225	7	55	108	.383	273	27	11	.973
1918—Detroit	Amer.	111	421	83	161	3	34	64	.382	359	26	9	.977
1919—Detroit	Amer.	124	497	92	191	1	28	69	.384	272	19	8	.973
1920—Detroit	Amer.	112	428	86	143	2	14	63	.334	246	8	9	.966
1921—Detroit	Amer.	128	507	124	197	12	22	101	.389	301	27	10	.970
1922—Detroit	Amer.	137	526	99	211	4	9	99	.401	330	14	7	.980
1923—Detroit	Amer.	145	556	103	189	6	9	88	.340	362	14	12	.969
1924—Detroit	Amer.	155	625	115	211	4	23	74	.338	417	12	6	.986
1925—Detroit	Amer.	121	415	97	157	12	13	102	.378	267	9	15	.948
1926—Detroit*	Amer.	79	233	48	79	4	9	62	.339	109	4	6	.950
1927—Philadelphia	Amer.	134	490	104	175	5	22	93	.357	243	9	8	.969
1928—Philadelphia	Amer.	95	353	54	114	1	5	40	.323	154	7	6	.964
Major League Totals		3,033	11,429	2,244	4,191	118	892	1,901	.367	6,294	406	274	.961

*Released, November 2, 1926, and signed with Athletics, February 1927.

WORLD SERIES RECORD

Year Club	League	G	AB	R	H	HR	SB	RBI	BA	PO	A	E	FA
1907—Detroit	Amer.	5	20	1	4	0	0	0	.200	9	0	0	1.000
1908—Detroit	Amer.	5	19	3	7	0	2	3	.368	3	0	2	.600
1909—Detroit	Amer.	7	26	3	6	0	2	5	.231	8	0	1	.889
World Series Totals		17	65	7	17	0	4	8	.262	20	0	3	.870

EXTRA INNINGS

"To get along with me — **don't increase my tension."**

—Ty Cobb

E ver since sundown in the Sierra range, Nevada inter-mountain radio had been crackling warnings: "Route 50 now highly dangerous. Motorists stay off. Repeat: AVOID ROUTE 50."

By 1:00 A.M. the twenty-one-mile, steep-pitched passage from Lake Tahoe's sixty-eight-hundred-foot altitude into Carson City, a snaky grade most of the way, was snow-struck, ice-sheeted, thick with rock slides, and declared unfit for all transport vehicles by the State Highway Patrol.

It was right down Ty Cobb's alley. Anything that smacked of the apparently impossible brought an unholy gleam to his eye. The gleam had been there in 1959 when a series of lawyers advised Cobb that he stood no chance in court against the Sovereign State of California in a dispute over income taxes, whereupon he bellowed defiance and sued the state for sixty thousand dollars plus damages. It had been there more recently when doctors warned that liquor would kill him. From a pint of whiskey per day he upped his consumption to a quart and more.

Sticking out his grizzled chin, he had told me, "I think we'll take a little run into town tonight."

A blizzard rattled the windows of Cobb's luxurious hunting lodge on the eastern crest of Lake Tahoe, but to forbid him anything—even at the age of seventy-three—was to tell an ancient tiger not to snarl. Cobb was both the greatest of all ballplayers and a multimillionaire whose monthly income from stock dividends, rents, and interest ran to twelve thousand dollars. And he was a man contemptuous of any law other than his own.

"We'll drive in," he announced, "and shoot some craps, see a show, and say hello to Joe DiMaggio—he's in Reno at the Riverside Hotel."

I looked at him and felt a chill. Cobb, sitting there haggard and unshaven in his pajamas and a fuzzy old green bathrobe at one o'clock in the morning, wasn't fooling.

"Let's not," I said. "You shouldn't be anywhere but in bed."

"Don't argue with me!" he barked. "There are fee-simple sons of bitches all over the country who've tried it and wished they hadn't." He glared at me, flaring the whites of his eyes the way he'd done for twenty-four years at quaking pitchers, basemen, umpires, fans, and sportswriters.

"If you and I are going to get along," he went on ominously, "*don't increase my tension.*"

It was the winter of 1960. We were alone in his isolated, ten-room lakeside lodge—bearskin floor rugs, mounted game trophies on walls—with a lot of work to do. We'd arrived six days earlier, loaded with a large smoked ham, a twenty-pound turkey, a case of scotch, and another of champagne, for the purpose of collaborating on Ty's autobiography, a book that he'd refused to write for more than thirty years but had suddenly decided to publish before he died. In almost a week's time we hadn't accomplished thirty minutes' worth of work.

The reason: Cobb didn't need a high-risk auto trip into Reno, but immediate hospitalization, and through the emergency-room entrance. He was desperately ill, and had been so even before we left California.

We had traveled 250 miles to Tahoe in Cobb's black Imperial limousine, carrying with us a virtual drugstore of medicines. These included digoxin (for his leaky heart), Darvon (for his aching back), Tace (for a recently operated-upon malignancy of the pelvic area), Fleet's Compound (for his impacted bowels), Librium (for his "tension"—that is, his violent rages), codeine (for his pain), and an insulin needle-and-syringe kit (for his diabetes), among a dozen other panaceas that he'd substituted for ongoing medical care. Cobb hated doctors. "When they meet an undertaker on the street," he said, "the boys wink at each other."

His sense of balance was precarious. He tottered about the lodge, moving from place to place by grasping the furniture. On a public street, he couldn't navigate twenty feet without clutching my shoulder, leaning most of his 208 pounds upon me and shuffling along with a spraddle-legged gait. His bowels wouldn't work, a near-total stoppage that brought groans of agony from Cobb when he sought relief. He was feverish. There was no one at the Tahoe hideaway but the two of us to treat his critical condition.

Everything that hurts had caught up with his six-foot, one-inch body at once, and he plied himself with pink, green, orange, yellow, and purple pills—often guessing at the amounts, since labels had peeled off some of the bottles. But he wouldn't hear of hospitalizing himself.

"The hacksaw artists have taken fifty thousand dollars from me," he said, "and they'll get no more." He spoke of a "quack" who'd treated him a few years earlier. "The joker got funny and said he found urine in my whiskey. I fired him."

His diabetes required a precise food-insulin balance. Cobb's needle wouldn't work. He misplaced the directions for his daily insulin dosage and his hands shook uncontrollably when he went to plunge the needle into his abdominal wall. He spilled more of the stuff than he injected.

He'd been warned by experts, from Johns Hopkins to California's Scripps Clinic, that liquor was deadly for him. Tyrus snorted and began each day with several gin and orange juices, then switched to "buzzers" of Old Rarity scotch, which held him until the night hours when sleep was impossible, and he tossed down cognac, champagne, or "Cobb cocktails"—Southern Comfort stirred into hot water and honey.

A careful diet was essential. Cobb wouldn't eat. The lodge was without a cook or other help—in the previous six months, he had fired two cooks, a male nurse, and a handyman in fits of anger—and any food I prepared for him he nibbled at, then pushed away. As of the night of the blizzard, the failing, splenetic old monarch of baseball hadn't touched solid food in three days, existing almost solely on quarts of booze and mixers.

My reluctance to prepare the car for the Reno trip burned him up. He beat his fists on the arms of his easy chair. "I'll go alone!" he threatened.

I was certain he'd try. The storm had worsened, but once Cobb set his mind on an idea, nothing could alter it. Beyond that, I'd already found that to oppose or annoy him was to risk a fierce explosion. An event of a week earlier had proved that point. It was then that I discovered he carried a loaded Luger wherever he went, looking for opportunities to use it.

En route to Lake Tahoe, we'd stopped overnight at a motel near Hangtown, California. During the night a party of drunks made a loud commotion in the parking lot. In my room adjacent to Cobb's I heard him cursing and then his voice, booming out the window.

"Get out of here, you——heads!"

The drunks replied in kind. Groping his way to the door, Cobb fired three shots into the dark that resounded like cannon claps. Screams and yells followed. Reaching my door, I saw the drunks climbing one another's backs in their rush to flee. The frightened motel manager, and others, arrived. Before anyone could think of calling the police, the manager was cut down by the most caustic tongue ever heard in a baseball clubhouse.

"What kind of pesthouse is this!" roared Cobb. "Who gave you a license, you mugwump? Get the hell out of here and see that I'm not disturbed! I'm a sick man and I want it quiet!"

"B-b-beg your pardon, Mr. Cobb," the manager said feebly. He apparently felt so honored to have as a customer the national game's most exalted figure that no cops were called. When we drove away the next morning, a crowd gathered and stood gawking with expressions of disbelief.

Down the highway, with me driving, Cobb checked the Luger and reloaded its nine-shell clip. "Two of those shots were in the air," he remarked. "The third kicked up gravel. I've got permits for this gun from governors of three states. I'm honorary deputy sheriff of California and a Texas Ranger. So we won't be getting any complaints."

He saw nothing strange in his behavior. Ty Cobb's rest had been disturbed; therefore, he had every right to shoot up the neighborhood.

At about that moment I began to develop a nervous twitch, which grew worse in about the time it takes to say Grover Cleveland Alexander of the Philadelphia Phillies. I'd heard reports of Cobb's weird and violent ways without giving them much credence. Until early 1960 my own experience with the legendary Georgia Peach had been slight, amounting mainly to meetings in Scottsdale, Arizona, and New York to discuss book-writing arrangements and to sign the contract.

Locker-room stories of Ty's eccentricities, wild temper, wars with his own teammates, egotism, and miserliness sounded like the usual scandalmongering you get in sports. I'd heard that Cobb had flattened a heckler in San Francisco's Domino Club with one punch; that he had been sued by Elbie Felts, an ex–Coast League player, after assaulting him; that he boobytrapped his main home, a Spanish-mission villa at Atherton, California, with high-voltage wires; that he'd walloped his ex-wives; that he'd been jailed in Placerville, California, at the age of sixty-eight for speeding, abusing a traffic cop, and then inviting the judge to return to law school at his, Cobb's, expense.

I passed these things off. The one and only Ty Cobb wished to write his memoirs, and I felt distinctly honored to be named his collaborator. As the poet Cowper reflected, "The innocents are gay." I was eager to start. Then a few weeks before the book work began, I was taken aside and tipped off by an in-law of Cobb's and by one of Cobb's former teammates on the Detroit Tigers that I hadn't heard the half of it. "Back out of this book deal," they urged. "You'll never finish it and you might get hurt."

They went on: "Nobody can live with Ty. Nobody ever has. That includes two wives who left him, butlers, housekeepers, chauffeurs, nurses, and a few mistresses. He drove off all his friends long ago. Max Fleischmann, the yeast-cake heir, was a pal of Ty's until the night a house guest of Fleischmann's made a remark about Cobb spiking other players when he ran bases. The man only asked if it was true. Cobb knocked the guy into a fishpond and never spoke to him again. Another time, a member of Cobb's family crossed him—a woman, mind you. He broke her nose with a ball bat.

"Do you know about the butcher? Ty didn't like some fish he bought. In the fight, he broke up the butcher shop. Had to settle fifteen hundred dollars on the butcher out of court after going to jail. He had a gun in his possession at the time."

"But I'm dealing with him strictly on business," I said.

"So was the butcher," replied my informants.

"In baseball," the ex-teammate said, "a few of us who really knew him well realized that he was wrong in the head—unbalanced. He played like a demon and had everybody hating him because he *was* a demon. That's how he set all those records that nobody has come close to since 1928. It's why he was always in a brawl, on the field, in the clubhouse, behind the stands, in the stands, on the street. The public's never known it, but Cobb's always been off the beam where other people are concerned. Sure, he made millions in the stock market—but that's only cold dollars. He carried a gun wherever he went in the big league and scared hell out of us. He's mean, tricky, and dangerous. Look out he doesn't blow up some night and clip you with a bottle. He specializes in throwing bottles.

"Now that he's sick he's worse than ever. And you've signed up to stay with him for months. The time will come when you'll want to write in his book about the scandals and wild brannigans he was in—and he'll chop you down. Don't be a sucker."

Taken aback, but still skeptical, I launched the job. My first task was to drive Cobb to his Lake Tahoe retreat, where, he declared, we could work uninterrupted.

Everything went wrong from the start. The Hangtown gunplay incident was an eye-opener. Next came a series of events, among them Cobb's determination to set forth in a blizzard to Reno, which were too strange to explain away. Everything had to suit his pleasure, or else he threw a tantrum. He prowled about the lodge at night with the Luger in hand, suspecting trespassers (there had once been a break-in at the place). I slept with one eye open, ready to move fast if necessary.

Well past midnight that evening, full of pain and ninety-proof, he took out the Luger, letting it casually rest between his knees. I had continued to object to a Reno excursion in such weather.

He looked at me with tight fury and said, biting out the words, "In 1912—and you can write this down—I killed a man in Detroit. He and two other hoodlums jumped me on the street early one morning with a knife. I was carrying something that came in handy in my early days—a Belgian-made pistol with a heavy raised sight at the barrel end.

"Well, the damned gun wouldn't fire and they cut me up the back."

Making notes as fast as he talked, I asked, "Where in the back?"

"WELL, DAMMIT ALL TO HELL, IF YOU DON'T BELIEVE ME, COME AND LOOK!" Cobb flared, jerking up his shirt. When I protested that I believed him implicitly but only wanted a story detail, he picked up a half-full whiskey glass and smashed it against the brick fireplace. So I gingerly took a look. A faint whitish scar ran about six inches up his lower left back.

"Satisfied?" jeered Cobb.

He described how, after a battle, the men fled before his fists.

"What with you wounded and the odds three to one," I said, "that must have been a relief."

"Relief? Do you think they could pull that on *me*? I WENT AFTER THEM!"

Anyone else would have felt lucky to be out of it, but Cobb had chased one of the mugs into a dead-end alley. "I used that gun sight to rip and slash and tear him for about ten minutes until he had no face left," related Ty with relish. "Left him there, not breathing, in his own rotten blood."

"What was the situation—where were you going when it happened?"

"To catch a train to a ball game."

"You saw a doctor instead?"

"I DID NOTHING OF THE SORT, DAMMIT. I PLAYED THE NEXT DAY AND GOT THREE BASE HITS."

Records I later inspected bore out every word of it: on August 3, 1912, in a blood-soaked, makeshift bandage, Ty Cobb hit 2 doubles and a triple for Detroit, and only then was treated for the painful knife slash. He was that kind of ballplayer, through a record 3,033 games. No other pro athlete burned with Cobb's flame. Boze Bulger, a great old-time baseball critic, said, "He was possessed by the Furies."

Finishing his tale, Cobb looked me straight in the eye.

"*You are driving me into Reno tonight*," he said softly. The Luger in his hand was dangling floorward.

Even before I opened my mouth, Cobb knew he'd won. He had an extra sense about the emotions he produced in others—in this case, fear. As far as I could see (lacking expert diagnosis and as a layman understands the symptoms), he wasn't merely erratic and trigger tempered, but suffering from megalomania, or acute self-worship, delusions of persecution, and more than a touch of dipsomania.

Although I'm not proud of it, he scared hell out of me most of the time I was around him.

And now Cobb gave me the first smile of our association. "To get along with me," he repeated softly, "*don't increase my tension.*"

Before describing the Reno expedition, I would like to say, in this frank view of a mighty man, that the most spectacular, enigmatic, and troubled of all American sport figures had his good side, which he tried his best to conceal. During the final ten months of his life I was his constant companion. Eventually I put him to bed, prepared his insulin, picked him up when he fell down, warded off irate taxi drivers, bill collectors, bartenders, waiters, clerks, and private citizens whom Cobb was inclined to punch, cooked what food he could digest, drew his bath, got drunk with him, and knelt with him in prayer on black nights when he knew death was near. I ducked a few bottles he threw, too.

I think, because he forced upon me a confession of his most private thoughts, along with details of his life, that I know the answer to the central, overriding secret of his life. Was Ty Cobb psychotic throughout his baseball career? The answer is yes.

KIDS, DOGS, and sick people flocked to him and he returned their instinctive liking. Money was his idol, but from his approximate $12 million fortune he assigned large sums to create the Cobb Educational Fund, which financed hundreds of needy youngsters through college. He built and endowed a first-class hospital for the poor of his backwater hometown, Royston, Georgia. When Ty's spinster sister, Florence, was crippled, he tenderly cared for her until her last days. The widow of a one-time American League batting champion would have lived in want but for Ty's steady financial support. A Hall of Fame catcher, beaned by a pitched ball and enfeebled, came under Cobb's wing for years. Regularly he mailed dozens of anonymous checks to indigent old ballplayers (relayed by a third party)—a rare act among retired tycoons in other lines of business.

If you believe such acts didn't come hard for Cobb, table the thought. He was the world's champion pinchpenny.

Some 150 fan letters reached him monthly, requesting his autograph. Many letters enclosed return-mail stamps. Cobb used the stamps for his own outgoing mail. The fan letters he burned. "Saves on firewood," he muttered.

In December of 1960, Ty hired a one-armed "gentleman's gentleman" named E. Anthony Brown. Although steadily criticized, poor Brownie worked hard as cook and butler. But when he mixed up a grocery order one day, he was fired, given a check for the week's pay—forty-five dollars—and sent packing.

Came the middle of that night and Cobb awakened me.

"We're driving into town *right now*," he stated, "to stop payment on Brownie's check. The bastard talked back to me when I discharged him. He'll get no more of my money."

All remonstrations were futile. There was no phone, so we had to drive from Cobb's Tahoe lodge into Carson City, where he woke up the president of the First National Bank of Nevada and arranged for a stop-pay on a piddling check. The president tried to conceal his irritation; Cobb was a big depositor in his bank.

"Yes, sir, Ty," he said. "I'll take care of it first thing in the morning."

"You goddamn well better," snorted Cobb. And then we drove through the 3:00 A.M. darkness back to the lake.

But this jaunt was a light workout compared to the treacherous Reno trip he now directed we make.

Two cars were available at the lodge. Cobb's 1956 Imperial had no tire chains; the other buggy was equipped for snow driving.

"We'll need both cars for this operation," he ordered. "One car might break down. I'll drive mine, you take the one with chains. You go first. I'll follow your chain marks."

For Cobb to tackle precipitous Route 50 was unthinkable. The Tahoe road, with its two-hundred-foot drop-offs, had killed a record eighty motorists. Along with his illness, drunkenness, and no chains, he had weak eyes and was without a driver's license. California had turned him down at his last test; he hadn't bothered to apply in Nevada.

Urging him to ride with me was a waste of breath, however.

A howling wind hit my Buick a solid blow as we shoved off. Sleet stuck to the windshield faster than the wipers could clear it. For the first three miles, snowplows had been active, and at fifteen miles per hour, in second gear, I managed to hold the road. But then came

Spooner's Summit, 6,900 feet high, and beyond it a steep descent of nine miles. Behind me, headlamps blinking, Cobb honked his horn, demanding more speed. Chainless, he wasn't getting traction. *The hell with him*, I thought. Slowing to low gear, fighting to hold a roadbed I couldn't see even with my head stuck out the window, I skidded along. No other traffic was on the road that night as we did our crazy tandem around icy curves, at times brushing the guardrails. Cobb was blaring his horn steadily now.

And then here came Cobb.

Tiring of my creeping pace, he gunned the Imperial around me in one big skid. I caught a glimpse of an angry face under a big Stetson hat and a waving fist. He was doing a good thirty miles per hour when he'd gained twenty-five yards on me, fishtailing right and left, but straightening as he slid out of sight in the thick sleet.

I let him go. Suicide wasn't in my contract.

The next six miles was a matter of feeling the way and praying. Near a curve I saw taillights to the left. Pulling up, I found Ty's car swung sideways and buried, nose down, in a snowbank, the hind wheels two feet in the air. Twenty yards away was a sheer drop-off into a canyon.

"You hurt?" I asked.

"Bumped my———head," he muttered. He lit a cigar and gave four-letter regards to the highway department for not illuminating the "danger" spot. His forehead was bruised and he'd broken his glasses.

In my car, we groped our way down-mountain, a nightmare ride, with Cobb alternately taking in scotch from a thermos jug and telling me to step on it. At 4:00 A.M. in Carson City, an all-night garageman used a broom to clean the car of snow and agreed to pick up the Imperial—"when the road's passable."

"It's passable," said Ty. "I just opened it."

With dawn breaking, we reached Reno. All I wanted was a bed, and all Cobb wanted was a craps table.

He was rolling now, pretending he wasn't ill; with the scotch bracing him, Ty was able to walk into the Riverside Hotel casino with a hand on my shoulder and without staggering as obviously as usual. Everybody present wanted to meet him. Starlets from a film unit on location in Reno flocked around, and comedian Joe E. Lewis had the band play *"Sweet Georgia Brown"*—Ty's favorite tune.

"Hope your dice are still honest," he told Riverside co-owner Bill Miller. "Last time I was here I won twelve thousand dollars in three hours."

"How I remember, Ty," said Miller. "How I remember."

A scientific craps player who'd won and lost hefty sums in Nevada in the past, Cobb bet hundred-dollar chips, his eyes alert, not missing a play around the board. He soon decided that the table was cold and we moved to another casino, then a third. At the last stop, Cobb's legs grew shaky. Holding himself up by leaning on the table edge with his forearms, he dropped three hundred dollars, then had a hot streak in which he won eight hundred. His voice was a croak as he told the other players, "Watch 'em and weep."

But then suddenly his voice came back. When the stickman raked the dice his way, Cobb loudly said, "You touched the dice with your hand."

"No, sir," said the stickman. "I did not."

"I don't lie!" snarled Cobb.

"I don't lie, either," insisted the stickman.

"Nobody touches my dice!" Cobb, swaying on his feet, eyes blazing, worked his way around the table toward the croupier. It was a weird tableau. In his crumpled Stetson and expensive camel's-hair coat, stained and charred with cigarette burns, a three-day beard grizzling his face, the fuming old giant of baseball towered over the dapper gambler.

"You fouled the dice, I saw you," growled Cobb, and then he swung.

The blow missed as the stickman dodged, but, cursing and almost falling, Cobb seized the wooden rake and smashed it across the table. I jumped in and caught him under the arms as he sagged.

And then, as quickly as possible, we were put out into the street by two large uniformed guards. "Sorry, Mr. Cobb," they said unhappily, "but we can't have this."

A crowd had gathered, and as we started down the street, Cobb swearing and stumbling, clinging to me, I couldn't have felt more conspicuous if I'd been strung naked from the neon arch across Virginia Street, Reno's main drag. At the corner, Ty was struck by an attack of breathlessness. "Got to stop," he gasped. Feeling him going limp on me, I turned his big body against a lamppost, braced my legs, and with an underarm grip held him there until he caught his breath. He panted and gasped for air.

His face gray, he murmured, "Reach into my left-hand coat pocket." Thinking he wanted his bottle of heart pills, I did. But instead I pulled out a six-inch-thick wad of currency, secured by a rubber band. "Couple of thousand there," he said weakly. "Don't let it out of sight."

At the nearest motel, where I hired a single room with two twin beds, he collapsed on the bed in his coat and hat and slept. After finding myself some breakfast, I turned in.

Hours later I heard him stirring. "What's this place?" he muttered.

I told him the name of the motel—TraveLodge.

"Where's the bankroll?"

"In your coat. You're wearing it."

Then he was quiet.

After a night's sleep, Cobb felt well enough to resume his gambling. In the next few days, he won more than three thousand dollars at the tables, and then we went sightseeing in historic Virginia City. There, as in all places, he stopped traffic. And had the usual altercation. This one was at the Bucket of Blood, where Cobb accused the bartender of serving watered scotch. The bartender denied it. Crash! Another drink went flying.

Back at the lodge a week later, looking like the wrath of John Barleycorn and having refused medical aid in Reno, he began to suffer new and excruciating pains in his hips and lower back. But between groans he forced himself to work an hour a day on his autobiography. He told inside baseball stories, never published:

"Frank Navin, who owned the Detroit club for years, faked his turnstile count to cheat the visiting team and Uncle Sam. So did Big Bill Devery and Frank Farrell, who owned the New York Highlanders—later called the Yankees.

"Walter Johnson, 'the Big Train,' tried to kill himself when his wife died.

"Grover Cleveland Alexander wasn't drunk out there on the mound, the way people thought. He was an epileptic. Old Pete would fall down with a seizure between innings, then go back and pitch another shutout.

"John McGraw hated me because I tweaked his nose in broad daylight in the lobby of the Oriental Hotel, in Dallas, after earlier beating the hell out of his second baseman, Buck Herzog, upstairs in my room."

But before we were well started, Cobb suddenly announced we'd go riding in his twenty-three-foot Chris-Craft speedboat, tied up in a boathouse below the lodge. When I went down to warm it up, I found the boat on the bottom of Lake Tahoe, sunk in fifteen feet of water.

My host broke all records for blowing his stack when he heard the news. He saw in this a sinister plot: "I told you I've got enemies all around here! It's sabotage as sure as I'm alive!"

A sheriff's investigation turned up no clues. Cobb sat up for three nights with his Luger. "I'll salivate the first dirty skunk who steps foot around here after dark."

(Parenthetically, Cobb had a vocabulary all his own. To "salivate" something meant to destroy it. Anything easy was "softy boiled," to outsmart someone was to "slip him the oskafagus," and all doctors were "truss-fixers." People who displeased him—and this included a high percentage of those he met—were "fee-simple sons of bitches," "mugwumps," "lead-heads," or, if female, "lousy slits.")

Lake Tahoe friends of Cobb's had stopped visiting him long before, but one morning an attractive blonde of about fifty came calling. She was an old chum—in a romantic way, I was given to understand, in bygone years—but Ty greeted her coldly. "Lost my sexual powers when I was sixty-nine," he said when she was out of the room. "What the hell use to me is a woman?"

The lady had brought along a three-section electric vibrator bed, which she claimed would relieve Ty's back pains. We helped him mount it. He took a twenty-minute treatment. Attempting to dismount, he lost his balance and fell backward. The contraption jack-knifed and Cobb was pinned, yelling and swearing, under a pile of machinery.

After we freed him and helped him to a chair, he told the lady— in the choicest gutter language—where she could put the bed. She left, sobbing.

"That's no way to talk to an old friend, Ty," I said. "She was trying to do you a favor."

"And you're a hell of a poor guest around here, too!" he thundered.

"You can leave any old time!" He quickly grabbed a bottle and heaved it in my direction.

"Thought you could throw straighter than that!" I yelled back. Fed up with him, I started to pack my bags.

Before I'd finished, Cobb broke out a bottle of vintage malt scotch, said I was "damned sensitive," half-apologized, and the matter was forgotten—for now.

While working one morning on an outside observation deck, I heard a thud inside. On his bedroom floor, sprawled on his back, lay the Georgia Peach. He was unconscious, his eyes rolled back, breathing shallowly. I thought he was dying.

There was no telephone. "Eavesdroppers on the line," Cobb had told me; "I had it cut off." I ran down the road to a neighboring home and phoned a Carson City doctor, who promised to come immediately.

Back at the lodge, Ty remained stiff and stark on the floor, little bubbles escaping his lips. His face was bluish white. With much straining, I lifted him halfway to the bed, and by shifting holds finally rolled him onto it and covered him with a blanket. Twenty minutes passed. No doctor.

Ten minutes later, I was at the front door, watching for the doctor's car, when I heard a sound. There stood Ty, swaying on his feet. "You want to do some work on the book?" he said.

His recovery didn't seem possible. "But you were out cold a minute ago," I said.

"Just a dizzy spell. Have 'em all the time. Must have hit my head on the bedpost when I fell."

The doctor, arriving, found Cobb's blood pressure standing at a grim 210/90 on the gauge. His temperature was 101 degrees and, from gross neglect of his diabetes, he was in a state of insulin shock, often fatal if not quickly treated. "I'll have to hospitalize you, Mr. Cobb," said the doctor.

Weaving his way to a chair, Cobb coldly waved him away. "Just send me your bill," he grunted. "I'm going home."

"Home" was the multimillionaire's main residence at Atherton, California, on the San Francisco Peninsula, 250 miles away, and it was there he headed later that night.

With some hot soup and insulin in him, Cobb had recovered with the same unbelievable speed he'd shown in baseball. In his heyday, trainers often sewed up deep spike cuts in his knees, shins, and thighs, on a clubhouse bench, without anesthetic, and he didn't lose an inning. Famed sportswriter Grantland Rice, one 1920 day in New York, sat beside a bedridden, feverish Cobb, whose thighs, from sliding, were a mass of raw flesh. Rice urged him not to play. Sixteen hours later, Cobb beat the Yankees with five hits in six times at bat, plus two steals.

On the ride to Atherton, he yelled insults at several motorists who moved too slowly to suit him. Reaching home, Ty said he felt ready for another drink.

My latest surprise was Cobb's eleven-room, two-story, richly landscaped Spanish-California villa at 48 Spencer Lane, an exclusive neighborhood. You could have held a ball game on the grounds. But the rich mansion had no lights, no heat, no hot water. It was in blackout.

"I'm suing the Pacific Gas and Electric Company," he explained, "for overcharging me on the service. Those rinky-dinks tacked an extra sixteen dollars on my bill. Bunch of crooks. When I wouldn't pay, they cut off my utilities. Okay—I'll see them in court."

For months previously, Ty Cobb had lived in an all but totally dark house. The only illumination was candlelight. The only cooking facility was a portable Coleman camper's stove. Bathing was impossible, unless you could take it cold. The electric stove, refrigerator, deep freeze, radio, and television, of course, didn't work. Cobb had vowed to "hold the fort" until his case against PG&E was settled. Simultaneously, he had filed a sixty-thousand-dollar suit in San Francisco Superior Court against the State of California to recover state income taxes already collected—on the argument that he wasn't a permanent resident of California, but of Nevada, Georgia, Arizona, and other waypoints. State's attorneys claimed he spent at least six months per year in Atherton, and thus had no case. "I'm gone so much from here," Cobb claimed, "that I'll win hands down." All legal opinion, I later learned, held just the opposite view, but Cobb ignored the lawyers' advice.

Next morning, I arranged with Ty's gardener, Hank, to turn on the lawn sprinklers. In the outdoor sunshine, a cold-water shower was easier to take. From then on, the backyard became my regular washroom.

The problem of lighting a desk, enabling us to work on the book, was solved by stringing two hundred feet of cord, plugged into an outlet of a neighboring house, through hedges and flower gardens and into the window of Cobb's study, where a single naked bulb hung over the chandelier provided illumination. The flickering shadows cast by the single light made the vast old house seem haunted. No "ghost" writer ever had more ironical surroundings.

At various points around the premises, Ty showed me where he'd once installed high-voltage wires to stop trespassers. "Curiosity seekers?" I asked. "Hell, no," he said. "Detectives broke in here looking for evidence against me in a divorce suit. After a couple of them got burned, they stopped coming."

To reach our bedrooms, my host and I groped our way down long, black corridors. Twice he fell in the dark, and finally he collapsed completely. He was so ill that he was forced to check in to Stanford Hospital in nearby Palo Alto. Here another shock was in store.

One of the physicians treating Ty, a Dr. E. R. Brown, said, "Do you mean to say that this man has traveled seven hundred miles in the last month without medical care?"

"Doctor," I said, "I've hauled him in and out of saloons, motels, gambling joints, steambaths, and snowbanks. There's no holding him."

"It's a miracle he's alive. He has most of the major ailments I know about."

Dr. Brown didn't reveal Ty's main ailment to me. Cobb himself broke the news one night from his hospital bed. "It's cancer," he said bluntly. "About a year ago I had most of my prostate gland removed when they found it was malignant. Now it's spread up into the back bones. These pill-peddlers here won't admit it, but I haven't got a chance." Cobb made me swear I'd never divulge his secret before he died. "If it gets in the papers, the sob sisters will have a field day. I don't want sympathy from anybody."

At Stanford, where he absorbed seven massive doses of cobalt radiation, the ultimate cancer treatment, he didn't act like a man on his last legs. Even before his strength returned, he was in the usual form. "They won't let me have a drink," he said indignantly. "I want you to get me a bottle of sixteen-year-old. Smuggle it in your tape-recorder case."

I tried, telling myself that no man with terminal cancer deserves to be dried out, but sharp-eyed nurses and orderlies were watching. They searched Ty's closet, found the bottle, and over his hollers of protest appropriated it.

"We'll have to slip them the oskafagus," said Ty.

Thereafter, a drink of scotch and water sat in plain view in his room, on his bedside table, under the very noses of his physicians—and nobody suspected a thing. The whiskey was in an ordinary water glass, and in the liquid reposed Ty's false teeth. Nobody thought to frisk the dental fluid.

There were no dull moments while Cobb was at Stanford, one of the largest and highest-rated medical centers in the United States. He was critical of everything. He told one specialist that he was not even qualified to be an intern, and advised the hospital dietitian—loudly—that she and the kitchen workers were in a conspiracy to poison him with their "foul" dishes. To a nurse he snapped, "If Florence Nightingale knew about you, she'd spin in her grave."

Between blasts he did manage to buckle down to work on the book, dictating long into the night into a microphone suspended over his bed. Slowly the stormy details of his professional life came out. He spoke often of having "forgiven" his many baseball enemies, and then lashed out at them with such passionate phrases that it was clear he'd done no such thing. High on his hate list were John McGraw of the Giants; New York sportswriters; Hub Leonard, a pitcher who in 1926 accused Cobb and Tris Speaker of fixing a Detroit-Cleveland game, which led to Cobb's retirement as Tiger manager; American League president Ban Johnson; one-time Detroit owner Frank Navin; former baseball commissioner Kenesaw Mountain Landis; and all those who intimated that Cobb ever used his spikes on another player without having been attacked first.

After a night when he slipped out of the hospital, against all orders, and drove with me to a San Francisco Giants–Cincinnati Reds game at Candlestick Park, thirty miles away, Stanford Hospital decided it couldn't keep Tyrus R. Cobb, and he was discharged. For his extensive treatment, his bill ran to more than twelve hundred dollars.

"That's a nice racket you boys have here," he told the discharging doctors. "You clip the customers, charge them for the use of everything from bedpans to the steam heat."

"Good-bye, Mr. Cobb," snapped the medical men.

Soon after this Ty caught a plane to Georgia and I went along. "I want to see some of the old places again before I die," he declared.

It now was Christmas Eve of 1960 and I'd been with him for a lot of months and completed only four chapters. The project had begun to look hopeless. In Royston, his birthplace, a town of twenty-five hundred, Cobb wanted to head for the local cemetery. I drove him there and helped him climb a windswept hill through the growing dusk. Light snow fell. Faintly, Yule chimes could be heard.

Amongst the many headstones, Ty looked for the plot he'd reserved for himself while in California; he couldn't find it. His temper began to boil: "Dammit, I ordered the biggest mausoleum in the grave-yard! I know it's around here somewhere." On the next hill, we found it: a large marble walk-in-size structure with COBB engraved over the entrance.

"You want to pray with me?" he said, gruffly. We knelt and tears came to his eyes.

Within the tomb, he pointed to crypts occupied by the bodies of his father, Professor William Herschel Cobb, his mother, Amanda Chitwood Cobb, and his sister, Florence, whom he'd had disinterred and placed there. "My father," he said reverently, "was the greatest man I ever knew. He was a scholar, state senator, editor, and philosopher— a saintly man. I worshiped him. So did all the people around here. He was the only man who ever made me do his bidding."

Rising painfully, Ty braced himself against the marble crypt that soon would hold his body. There was an eerie silence in the tomb. He said deliberately, "My father had his head blown off with a shotgun when I was eighteen years old—*by a member of my own family.* I didn't get over that. I've never gotten over it."

We went back down the hill to the car. I asked no questions that day. Later, from family sources and old Georgian friends of the dia-mond idol, I learned details of the killing. News of it reached Ty in Augusta, where he was playing minor-league ball, on August 9, 1905. A few days later he was told that he'd been purchased by the Detroit Tigers and was to report immediately. "In my grief," Cobb later said, "going up didn't matter much . . . it felt like the end of me."

CAME MARCH of 1961 and I remained stuck to the Georgia Peach like court plaster. He'd decided we were born pals, meant for each other, that we'd complete a baseball book that would beat everything ever published. He had astonished doctors by rallying from the spreading cancer, and between bouts of transmitting his life and times to a tape recorder, he was raising more whoopee than he had at Lake Tahoe and Reno.

Spring-training time for the big leagues had arrived, and we were ensconced in a deluxe suite at the Ramada Inn at Scottsdale, Arizona, close by the practice parks of the Red Sox, Indians, Giants, and Cubs. Here, each year, Cobb held court. He didn't go to see anybody. Ford Frick, Joe Cronin, Ted Williams, and other diamond notables came to him. While explaining to sportswriters why modern stars couldn't compare to the Wagners, Lajoies, Speakers, Jacksons, Johnsons, Mathewsons, and Planks of his day, Ty did other things.

For one, he commissioned a well-known Arizona artist to paint him in oils. He was emaciated, having dropped from 208 pounds to 176. The preliminary sketches showed up his sagging cheeks and thin neck. "I wouldn't let you kalsomine my toilet," ripped out Ty as he fired the artist.

But he was anything but eccentric when analyzing the Dow-Jones averages and playing the stock market. Twice a week he phoned experts around the country, determined good buys, and bought in blocks of five hundred to fifteen hundred shares. He made money consistently, even when bedridden, with a mind that read behind the fluctuations of a dozen different issues. "The State of Georgia," Ty remarked, "will realize about one million dollars from inheritance taxes when I'm dead. But there isn't a man alive who knows what I'm worth." According to the *Sporting News*, there was evidence upon Cobb's death that his worth approximated $12 million. Whatever the true figure, he did not confide the precise amount to me—or, most probably, to anyone except the attorneys who drafted his last will and testament. And Cobb fought off making his will until the last moment.

His fortune began accumulating in 1909, when he bought cotton futures and United (later General) Motors stock and did well in copper-mining investments. As of 1961 he was also "Mr. Coca-Cola," holding more than twenty thousand shares of that stock, valued at eighty-five dollars per share. Wherever he traveled, he carried with him, stuffed into an old brown leather bag, more than $1 million in stock certificates and negotiable government bonds. The bag was never locked up. Cobb assumed nobody would dare rob him. He tossed the bag into any handy corner of a room, inviting theft. Finally, in Scottsdale, it turned up missing.

Playing Sherlock, he narrowed the suspects to a room maid and a man he'd hired to cook meals. When questioned, the maid broke into tears and the cook quit—fired, said Cobb. Hours later, I discovered the bag under a pile of dirty laundry.

Major-league owners and league officials hated to see Cobb coming, for he thought their product was putrid and said so, incessantly. "Today they hit for ridiculous averages, can't bunt, can't steal, can't hit-and-run, can't place-hit to the opposite field, and you can't call them ballplayers." He told sportswriters, "I blame Ford Frick, Joe Cronin, Bill Harridge, Horace Stoneham, Dan Topping, and others for trading in crazy style and wrecking baseball's traditional league lines. These days, any tax-dodging mugwump with a bankroll can buy a franchise, field some semipros, and get away with it. Where's our integrity? Where's *baseball*?"

No one could quiet Cobb. Who else had a record lifetime batting average of .367, made 4,191 hits, scored 2,244 runs, won 12 batting titles, stole 892 bases, repeatedly beat whole teams by his own efforts alone? Who was first into the Hall of Fame? Not Babe Ruth—but Cobb, by a landslide vote. And whose records still mostly stood, more than thirty years later? Say it again—*thirty years*.

By early April, he could barely make it up the ramp of the Scottsdale stadium, even with my help. He had to stop, gulping for breath, because of his failing ticker. But he kept coming to games, loving the indelible sounds of a ballpark. His courage was tremendous. "Always be ready to catch me if I start to fall," he said. "I'd hate to go down in front of the fans."

People of all ages were overcome with emotion upon meeting him; no sports celebrity I've known produced such an effect upon the public. At a 1959 stop in Las Vegas, Clark Gable himself had stood in a line to shake the gnarly Cobb hand.

We went to buy a cane. At a surgical supply house, Cobb inspected a dozen twenty-five-dollar malacca sticks, then bought the cheapest white-ash cane they had—four dollars. "I'm a plain man," he informed the clerk, the ten-thousand-dollar diamond ring on his finger glittering.

But pride kept the old tiger from ever using the cane, any more than he'd wear the six-hundred-dollar hearing aid built into the bow of his glasses other than away from the crowd.

One day a Mexican taxi driver aggravated Cobb with his driving. Throwing the fare on the ground, Cobb waited until the cabbie had bent to retrieve it, then tried to punt him like a football.

"What's your sideline," he inquired, "selling opium?"

It was all I could do to keep the driver from swinging at him. Later, a lawyer called on Cobb, threatening a damage suit. "Get in line, there's five hundred ahead of you," said Tyrus, waving him away.

Every day was a new adventure. He was fighting back against the pain that engulfed him—cobalt treatments no longer helped—and anywhere we went I could count on trouble. He threw a salt shaker at a Phoenix waiter, narrowly missing. One of his most treasured friendships—with Ted Williams, peerless batsman of the 1930s to 1950s—came to an end.

From the early 1940s, Williams had sat at Ty Cobb's feet. They met often, and exchanged long letters on the science of batting. At Scottsdale one day, Williams dropped by Ty's rooms. He hugged Ty, fondly rumpled his hair, and accepted a drink. Presently the two fell into an argument over which players should make up the all-time, all-star team. Williams declared, "I want DiMaggio and Hornsby over anybody you can mention."

Cobb's face grew dark. "Don't give me that! Hornsby couldn't go back for a pop fly and he lacked smartness. DiMaggio couldn't hit with Tris Speaker or Joe Jackson."

"The hell you say!" came back Williams jauntily. "Hornsby out-hit *you* a couple of years."

Almost leaping from his chair, Cobb shook a fist. He'd been given the insult supreme—for Cobb always resented, and finally hated, Rogers Hornsby. Not until Cobb was in his sixteenth season did the ten-years-younger Hornsby top him in the batting averages. "Get——
—away from me!" choked Cobb. "Don't come back!"

Williams left with a quizzical expression, not sure how much Cobb meant it. The old man meant it all the way. He never invited Williams back, or talked to him, or spoke his name again. "I cross him off," he told me.

We left Arizona shortly thereafter for my home in Santa Barbara,

California. Now failing fast, Ty had accepted an invitation to be my guest. Two doctors inspected him at the beach house by the Pacific and gave their opinions: he had a few months of life left, no more. The cancer had invaded the tissue and bones of his skull. His pain was unrelenting—requiring steady sedation—yet with teeth bared, sweat streaking his face, he fought off medical science. "They'll never get me on their f—— hypnotics," he swore. "I'll never die an addict . . . an idiot . . ."

He shouted, "Where's anybody who cares about me? Where are they? The world's lousy . . . no good."

One night later, on May 1, the Georgian sat propped up in bed, overlooking a starlit ocean. He had a habit, each night, of rolling up his trousers and placing them under his pillow—an early-century ballplayer's trick, dating from the time when Ty slept in strange places and might be robbed. I knew that his ever-present Luger was tucked into that pants roll.

I'd never seen him so sunk in despair. At last the fire was going out. "Do we die a little at a time, or all at once?" he wondered aloud. "I think Max had the right idea."

The reference was to his one-time friend, multimillionaire Max Fleischmann, who'd cheated lingering death by cancer some years earlier by putting a bullet through his brain. Ty spoke of Babe Ruth and Rogers Hornsby, other carcinoma victims. "If Babe had been told what he had in time, he could've got it over with."

Cobb was well read in poetry. One night he quoted a passage he'd always liked by Don Marquis: "There I stood at the gate of God, drunk but unafraid."

Had I left Ty alone that night, I believe he would have pulled the trigger. His three living children—two sons were dead—had withdrawn from him. In the wide world that had sung his fame, he had not one intimate friend remaining.

But we talked, and prayed, until dawn, and slight sleep came. In the morning, aided by friends, we put him into a car and drove him home, to the big, gloomy house up north in Atherton. Ty spoke only twice during the six-hour drive.

"Have you got enough to finish the book?" he asked.

"More than enough."

"Give 'em the word then. I had to fight all my life to survive. They all were against me . . . tried every dirty trick to cut me down. But I beat the bastards and left them in the ditch. Make sure the book says that . . ."

I was leaving him now, permanently, and had to ask one question I'd never put to him before.

"Why did you fight so hard in baseball, Ty?"

He'd never looked fiercer than then, when he answered. "I did it for my father, who was an exalted man. They killed him when he was still young. They blew his head off the same week I became a major-leaguer. He never got to see me play. Not one game, not an inning. But I knew he was watching me . . . and I never let him down. *Never.*"

You can make what you want of that. Keep in mind that Casey Stengel said, later: "I never saw anyone like Cobb. No one even close to him as the greatest ballplayer. Ruth was sensational. Cobb went beyond that. When he wiggled those wild eyes at a pitcher, you knew you were looking at the one bird no one could beat. It was like he was superhuman."

To me it seems that the violent death of a dominating father whom a sensitive, highly talented boy loved and feared deeply, engendered, through some strangely supreme desire to vindicate that "saintly" father, the most violent, successful, thoroughly maladjusted personality ever to pass across American sports. The shock ticked the eighteen-year-old's mind, making him capable of incredible feats.

Off the field and on, he remained at war with the world. To reinforce the pattern, he was viciously hazed by Detroit Tiger veterans when he was a rookie. He was bullied, ostracized, and beaten up — in one instance, a 210-pound catcher named Charlie Schmidt broke the 165-pound Ty Cobb's nose and closed both of his eyes. It was persecution, immediately heaped upon one of the deepest desolations a young man can experience.

There can be no doubt about it: Ty Cobb was a badly disturbed personality. It is not hard to understand why he spent his entire adult life in deep conflict. Nor why a member of his family, in the winter of 1960, told me, "I've spent a lot of time terrified of him . . . and I think he was psychotic from the time that he left Georgia to play in the big league."

I believe that he was far more than the fiercest of all competitors. He was a vindicator, a man who believed that "father was watching" and who could not put that father's terrible death out of his mind. The memory of it menaced his sanity.

The fact that he recognized and feared mental illness is revealed in a tape recording he made, in which he describes his own view of himself: "I was like a steel spring with a growing and dangerous flaw in it. If it is wound too tight or has the slightest weak point, the spring will fly apart and then it is done for . . ."

The last time I saw him, he was sitting in his armchair in the Atherton mansion. The place was still without lights or heat. I shook his hand in farewell—a degree of closeness had developed between us, if short of friendship—and he held it a moment longer.

"What about it? Do you think they'll remember me?" He tried to say it as if it weren't important.

"They'll always remember you," I replied.

On July 8, I received in the mail a photograph of Ty's mausoleum on the hillside in the Royston cemetery with the words scribbled on the back: "Any time now." Nine days later, at age seventy-four, he died in an Atlanta hospital. Before going, he opened the brown bag, piled $1 million in negotiable securities beside his bed, and placed the Luger atop them.

From all of major-league baseball, three men, and three men only, attended his funeral.

SO ENDED the battle. "He was the greatest and most amazing ballplayer I ever saw," attested Hall of Famer George Sisler, himself a candidate for best-ever honors. "There will never be another like him, he was a genius," said baseball sage Connie Mack in his old age. To Babe Ruth he was "the hardest to beat SOB of them all." So ended the struggle of the most feared, castigated, and acclaimed figure ever to plant his spikes in a batter's box. It was final innings on a personal tragedy. Ty Cobb had himself entombed in a chamber directly across from that of his father, Professor William Herschel Cobb, in dusty little Royston-town where it had all begun.

"FIRE IN MY BELLY"

Hagenback's Hippodrome and Wild Beast Show was camped near the town, with a calliope's caterwauling and the smell of tanbark setting the kids of the place to kicking up their heels. Royston, Georgia, needed a spell of fun.

An upland cotton, corn, and hog-raising dot on the map in the state's northeast outback, Royston (population eight hundred) and surrounding Franklin County had survived a ruinous Civil War. Thirty-five years after the shooting stopped, the region remained at hazard. As of 1899, with hard times persisting in the Reconstruction South, pecans and peaches had been introduced as supplementary cash crops, a boost to the economy. "We try to let no neighbor go hungry," stated the weekly, upbeat Royston *Record*.

Strung across the main street by Hagenback's circus was an acrobat's high wire. Twice a day a daring, bespangled performer walked the twenty-foot-high tightrope, with no net below to save him from splattering over the brick-clay roadway if he fell. It was an eye-popping act to the town's youngsters. To one of them it was a challenge.

"I can do that," said Tyrus Cobb, thirteen-year-old son of the local schoolmaster.

"You'd get killed," jeered his mates.

"No, I wouldn't," insisted Tyrus.

"Then do it!"

Long afterward in Royston it was retold by old-timers how Professor William Herschel Cobb's boy mounted to a dry-goods store's second story and climbed out onto the wire. Wearing a homespun shirt and farm boots, he imitated the acrobat by using a long pole for balance. The walk went well for a dozen or so feet—then Tyrus swayed. To cries of alarm he quickly recovered and moved along with catty little steps. Nearly across he stopped and lifted one hand off the pole to wave at onlookers. They cheered his cockiness. He finished the passage and became known around the settlement as a "good 'un."

The *Record* mentioned his stunt—the first time the name of Tyrus Cobb appeared in print. Enjoying the attention, at fourteen he jumped into a pond to help save a companion from drowning, although he was not much good at swimming. In 1901, at fifteen, he was back in the news, this time embarrassed by shooting himself. While butchering hogs on his father's farm, he left his loaded .22 Winchester leaning against a fence. A tree branch sprung and a shot knocked him kicking. Tyrus was hit near the heart in the lower left shoulder. He was moved by slow train eighty miles to Atlanta, where doctors were unable to locate the bullet. The probes they used had him yelling down the hospital, so he was put to sleep. When he awakened the bullet was still in him. The technology of the period was insufficient to find it, and he was sent home stitched and bandaged. Tyrus carried the metal in his body for the rest of his life, complaining of a burning sensation on cold days.

The young Cobb was slight, small for his age, notably pigeon-toed, and hyperactive. He was a devilish prankster, addicted to schoolyard fights and fast on his feet. He liked taking risks; jumping off barn roofs was a specialty. Asa Conroy, the local dry-goodsman, once said, "He was well raised. Polite to the ladies. His father was a big man, very strong and strict." Conroy recalled that, like almost everybody in Royston, the boy disliked Yankees and detested the North for having ravaged the South while defeating it. Although Franklin County had escaped the havoc wrought by Sherman's army as it looted and pillaged its way from Atlanta to the sea, in much of Georgia the destruction of barely three decades earlier had left wounds that would be generations healing. Reading books selected by his scholarly father, Tyrus gloried in accounts of various Confederate battle victories. As far as he was concerned, the South had not been beaten, only worn down by superior numbers and supplies. Among his prized keepsakes was an old Confederate garrison cap.

HE WAS born December 18, 1886, in a three-room pine-and-clay cabin. Baseball's future giant—in the vernacular of Ring Lardner, "a bozo so great that he makes the toughest of games look like a tea party"—was not a Royston native, but from an even more backwater Georgia valley called the Narrows, adjacent to Franklin County in Banks County. The Narrows was the most broodingly silent of places—a shout from one thick-forested spot across the Tugaloo River might be heard by nobody. Some ten dozen scattered farm families lived in an outpost where no railway reached, where no town hall or sheriff's office stood.

In the 1870s a handful of busted-out Civil War veterans and natives of a land shadowed by the Great Smoky Mountains loosely joined to chop out a living from the staples of corn, cotton, vetch, other hays, and peanuts. The Narrows, omitted from most maps, was a butt of jokes, as in: "Count to seventy-five and you've got about all of the humans in that country . . . Nobody can count all the coons, possum, skunks, and whiskey stills."

Tyrus Raymond Cobb's own account of his earliest days, told years later to this writer, in part went: "I was born the hard way. It was a close call. Some people around the Narrows didn't think I'd make it." It was a tight squeeze. Amanda Chitwood Cobb, his mother, had been a child bride of only twelve years of age in 1883 when she married his father. A postwedding photo of the pair showed a giant beside a midget. Three years later, when she bore Tyrus, Amanda was a thin, slightly breasted fifteen-year-old. The first of her three children, he was a good-sized seven-pounder. "She had a tough time getting me delivered," Cobb related. "There was no hacksaw [doctor] around there. They only had a midwife. Mother bled a lot . . . suffered."

No evidence indicates that anyone in the Narrows was especially shocked when the twenty-year-old resident schoolteacher, William Herschel Cobb, wedded a girl of twelve. That had happened before, and not infrequently. It remained ordinary practice in the 1880s for a bachelor farmer with five or ten stake-claimed acres and a few sharecroppers under him to pick, through expediency and loneliness, a hard worker from among the females nearing puberty and make himself a household. Gossip had it that Amanda still played with toys when she married, and read grammar books upon becoming a mother. "She was a damned good cook," reported Ty Cobb.

In 1960, as a curious researcher, I queried Banks County pioneers about the three-year lapse between Amanda's marriage and her production of Ty. "Who knows?" replied one Royston old-timer. "Her father, Caleb Chitwood, was the biggest landowner around here, and word got out that he didn't at all like his kid's getting spliced so young. He was supposed to have raised the roof. Don't forget that Chitwood also was the main support of the Narrows' only school back then. And Ty's father was the teacher at that school." Maybe, it was intimated, W. H. Cobb agreed to refrain from sex until Caleb's daughter was a little older. Since in the end she proved fertile, what else could explain it?

Another curiosity: why was W. H. Cobb, a mustached six-footer with a no-nonsense air, a graduate of North Carolina Agricultural College, such a roamer? Apparently he had better academic credentials than the average backcountry educator of his day. Yet, steadily on the horse-and-buggy trot, "Professor" Cobb moved around through two local counties, teaching classes in the towns of Commerce, Lavonia, Harmony Grove, Homer, Carnesville, and eventually in Royston. He was a pedagogical version of a traveling salesman. One of Ty's first memories was of sitting barefoot at age four—"maybe five"—on the tailgate of a horse-hack bucketing along a rough clay trail to one more village, where W. H. Cobb had landed an instructor's job. By then Tyrus had a younger brother, Paul. "We used to wrestle in the wagon all the way to whatever burg came next," he chuckled. "When little old Paul got sore, he'd bite me."

In naming the first son, the senior Cobb dipped into his interest in war and warriors. Tyrus was not named for Tyr, a Norse god of arms-bearing, as would later be claimed by members of the sports press. In 332 B.C., sweeping across Asia Minor, Alexander the Great was halted by defenders of the ancient Phoenician city of Tyre. Through seven months of carnage, the Tyrians kept Alexander's army at bay. Thence came the newborn's name. The child's middle name of Raymond, which he much disliked, came from a distant relative, a gambler by profession, but friendly with the Professor.

So much traveling, living in rented, poorly heated roadside board-inghouses and drafty tent camps, seemed to harm Tyrus's health. From birth to almost age six, he suffered from "the pip" and undiagnosed fevers. Yet he never doubted his roving father. From the beginning he loved, revered, and was dominated by the austere Professor Cobb. His sire was one of those authoritative men who also are sympathetic to a boy's needs—tough but fair.

The second-strongest character in the boy-child's life was tough, gingery, tobacco-spitting John "Squire" Cobb, his woods-wise grand-father. After the Professor and family finally became permanently set-tled in Royston in 1895, Tyrus often visited the home of his grandpa in the summertime. With close to one square mile in holdings across the state line near Murphy, North Carolina, the Squire was a fairly pros-perous farmer, set apart by owning trotting horses and eating steak for breakfast. Although a limping and semicrippled veteran of the Civil War, Squire Cobb led nine-year-old Ty into the hills to hunt rabbits, squirrels, and wildfowl, meanwhile spinning skin-prickling tales. Some, Cobb recalled, went like this:

Squire Cobb: Do you own a knife, boy?"

Tyrus: "No, but I got a slingshot."

Squire: "Well, I've been thinking that before this day is out, I'd meet a boy who needed a knife. And here's one for you I can spare."

Tyrus (accepting a brand-new pearl-handled pig-sticker with a shiny silver shield embedded in it, a knife he would keep for all of his life): "Golly, can I take it with me on a hunt?"

Squire: "By all means. But be careful with it. It's sharper than a bobcat's paws."

It was all the greater gift because, as Squire Cobb explained, from a knife Tyrus would graduate to a long rifle, like the gun that had saved Grandpa's life when he tangled with a huge bear. "A slavering monster twelve feet tall, teeth as long as a corncob . . . and me with just a rifle," he told him. Ty couldn't wait to hear the outcome.

After a chilling delay, the lighting of his pipe, the Squire would drawl, "If I'd missed with that rifle, Tyrus—*you wouldn't be here today.*" A bearskin rug carpeted the plank floor. "That's not *him,*" the Squire would continue. "The one I fought was even bigger."

ONE SCORCHING-HOT summer day, in or around 1897, word reached
Squire Cobb that he was needed in Asheville, North Carolina, seventy-
five miles away. His wisdom and stature in the area had led to his election as foreman of the county grand jury. The jury adjudicated
everything from boundary disputes to pig thefts before they became a
shooting matter. Tyrus was allowed to ride along to Asheville. At a
meeting hall there, the Squire handed down the verdict. In rage, the
loser grabbed the Squire's shirt and yelled threats. "Get behind my
desk," said the Squire to Tyrus.

At eleven Tyrus had never seen grown men in a serious fight.
Instead of hiding, as he remembered it, he jumped in to kick the
attacker's knee. A slap from the man knocked him dizzy. Someone
then punched the disturber of the peace. Tyrus got off the deck to see
his grandfather whip out a pocket pistol. "Get on your way," he coldly
ordered. Backing down, the man left. The Squire, on his way home by
buggy, told Tyrus that he'd done something foolish, but the kicks had
been appreciated.

Things could get thrilling in North Carolina—at least the way a
latter-day Cobb liked to tell it.

In the next few years he hit the schoolbooks harder in Royston, so
as to qualify for visits to the Squire's homestead. He owned a bench-
legged squirrel dog, Old Bob. The well-trained hound accompanied his
master on train trips to Murphy. In his ballplaying heyday, one of the
swift-striking Georgian's greatest talents was tricking opponents.
Doubtless some of this cunning had its roots planted when he rode the
rails from Royston to Murphy, reading his hometown *Record,* the *Police
Gazette,* and other newspapers. Dogs were not allowed in the coaches
of the Southern Railway. Concealed on the floor of Tyrus's seat under
a jumble of newsprint rode the smuggled Old Bob. The camouflaging
worked almost all of the time.

TYRUS RAYMOND Cobb was part of the South's postwar crop of youngsters who were replacing the approximately 258,000 Confederate soldiers killed in the war. By the last part of the century, Georgia's
population had slowly made a comeback to 1.7 million. A newly
designed state flag had been adopted. Blacks were unable to vote or be
elected to office, and without many exceptions were unable to hold
better than straw-boss positions in agriculture.

Automatically, Tyrus didn't play with black children, although by order of his father he worked alongside them in seeding and crop harvesting. Professor Cobb, the respected school supervisor of Franklin County and part-time land investor, had acquired leases on one-hundred-odd acres of tillable soil. He needed all the help his family could provide. Connected with farming was the need felt by W. H. Cobb to knock a rising arrogance out of his son. It did not become a Cobb to strut, break rules, and boast. One way to bring Tyrus into line was to sweat him behind a plow or hay reaper. There was plenty of that work doled out.

The first signs of Ty's uncontrollable temper appeared during his school days; it was a condition that would dangerously worsen. In North Carolina, Squire Cobb handed out none of the rebukes and penalties regularly issued by Ty's father. The old gent was forgiving of all sins except "hard cussing." He only shook his head when he heard that ten-year-old Tyrus was suspended from Royston District School for a few days after hitting and kicking a classmate friend for missing a word in a spelling contest between boy and girl teams. When the girls' team won, Tyrus was so burned that he beat up the teammate. His punishment for that was mucking out cowsheds. Many years later he said of the school incident, "I never could stand losing. Second place didn't interest me. I had a fire in my belly."

When he paid boyhood visits to the North Carolina farm of the Squire, a series of letters reached Tyrus. In many of them a worried Professor Cobb sharply warned his offspring to "stop your unsuitable acts," to overcome his fierce temper, and "defeat the demon who lurks in all human nature." Tyrus took it hard. "Father doesn't like me," he grieved.

"No," counseled the Squire, "Your pa wants you to go on to a university, to be liked, and be a success." In this matter the eldest Cobb could point to his own six children, most of whom he had sent to a church college. He suggested that Ty might return to his parent's good graces by writing something original on man's relation to the natural world, and sending it to the weekly Royston newspaper, owned and edited by Professor Cobb. It might be printed.

Tyrus titled his article "Possums and Myself." After praising possums for their finer points, he continued to tell how past midnight Old Bob had been "bellering in the woods," how he'd dragged himself from sleep, how they'd treed "Brother Possum," and how he'd shot, killed, gutted, and skinned him "who felt no pain and made a fine cap for wearing."

Ladies of the Royston sewing circles may have found the story too stark, but editor Cobb was pleased and showed it in a following letter: "You are making good progress in aligning yourself with the grand outdoors, yet always remember to remain in control of yourself, to be dutiful, to be proud but courteously proud." He enclosed a clipping of Tyrus's article, with the author's byline above it.

In the 1910s and 1920s, when Cobb was cutting down infielders with sharpened steel spikes and throwing punches and vitriol at those who crossed him, the Georgia Peach would show business associates some of the "be good, be decent" letters of W. H. Cobb that he had retained. The associates would either wince or go somewhere to laugh.

Long on animal spirits, the young Cobb generally was humorless, with growing antisocial tendencies. "Get off your high horse," he was often told. Bud Bryant, a boyhood chum, once was asked by a press correspondent to sum up Cobb at ages ten to fifteen. Bryant said, "Oh, we had some fights, toe-to-toe stuff. He'd win one, next time I'd get the best of it. You couldn't make the little bastard stay down. Born to win. Touchy and stubborn about the smallest things. There were times he'd disappear or climb a tree and stay there for hours because his mother made him wash some kitchen pots or sing in church. Could never laugh it off when the joke was on him. Ty was damned serious. Concentrated on whatever he did. He had a stammer he couldn't overcome."

I also consulted Bryant. "My God, how he loved himself—and his father," added Bryant. "But there was a way about him that made us think he'd go far. Would become a big man at something. He had these piercing pale eyes, for one thing."

Bryant and others were asked about Cobb's mother. By their recollection, Ty seldom mentioned Amanda, the ex–"baby" bride. She was overshadowed by her erudite, ambitious, classics-quoting husband. Amanda was small and pretty, with Ty's pinkish skin and fair hair, said witnesses. She was a homebody who didn't go to dances and such things very often.

Schoolmates dared to call Tyrus "Squeaky," for his high-pitched voice. Not for long, however. "Squeaky" almost assured another fistfight. Ty drew pleasure from putting down any challenge. A Royston sporting figure of the day, Bob McCreary, remembered him: "He could throw a rock out of sight at twelve or so and outwrestle any of us at catch-as-catch-can not long later. He was always thinking of new things to try. Once, down at the pond, Ty said he could hold his breath underwater longer than any of us. We lasted maybe a minute, while he was still down there. Someone, probably Ty, invented the crazy trick of laying on a railroad track and being last to roll off before the locomotive got there. He didn't lose that one often."

Would-be athlete Tyrus, at a skinny thirteen, sent away to Atlanta for a book, *How to Sprint*, by champion American dashman Dan Kelly. On a regular basis, for he was disciplined even if lacking in obedience, he practiced snap starts and running with his knees pumping high. He won at least one recorded event—a fifty-yard race at a Franklin County fair—and wore the blue ribbon on his shirt for months.

Next to contesting, he was most interested in his lengthy roster of prominent ancestors. Previous Cobbs had been fighters of the Cherokee, pro- and antislavery exponents, academicians, statesmen, and generals. The tribe dated back to Joseph Cobb, an emigré from England in 1611 who eventually became a tobacco tycoon, owning Cobbham, a Virginia estate. There also had been Thomas Willis Cobb, a Revolutionary War colonel who was said to have counseled George Washington and reportedly reached 111 years of age. Another, Thomas Reade Rootes Cobb—Ty's favorite on the family tree—had been *facile princeps* at the University of Georgia, codifier of Georgia law, organizer of the state's first law school, and a brigadier general killed by a shellburst at Fredericksburg. Long afterward, Ty informed interviewers that this same Thomas R. R. Cobb wrote a large part of the Confederate Constitution. "Which would have worked," he insisted, "if we'd had more troops and cannon. At this Cobb's burial, General Robert E. Lee said, 'Know ye not that a prince and great man is fallen this day?'"

From studying the Cobb genealogy, Ty was equally familiar with Thomas Cobb, an 1824 U.S. senator from Georgia, after whom Cobb County was named. And he was much aware of Howell Cobb, Georgia's governor in 1851 as well as a general who gamely held out with three thousand ragged militiamen until overwhelmed by the Federals at Macon in 1865. One historical note on General Cobb quoted President Andrew Johnson as saying at war's end that he most wanted to capture and hang by the neck until dead three particular Secessionist leaders, one of them Howell Cobb.

The Professor's well-stocked library was open to Ty; he boned up on so many battles and their strategy as to cause concern by W. H. and Amanda Cobb that his eyesight might be harmed. In his early teens he came to interpret the war and his forebears' roles in it in terms of defiance by an oppressed, underdog society. He *knew* that northern historians gave a false picture. "We won at Norfolk, Chicamauga, Antietam, Yorktown, both times at Bull Run, and a hell of a lot of other places, didn't we?" he reminded schoolboy friends.

A concerned, impatient W. H. Cobb felt that his offspring was smart enough to qualify one day for a career in the law, as a physician, or perhaps in engineering. Yet Tyrus showed no sign of real interest in any of these professions. To encourage the fourteen-year-old, W. H. asked an attorney friend, Colonel W. R. Little, to advise the youngster. Little, who resembled Buffalo Bill with his bulky body and long, shaggy hair, invited Tyrus to visit his office. To be sure that Ty didn't duck out, his father went along. Little mentioned Blackstone. "Sir William Blackstone," he said, "was an English judge who did much to create our common law. You can start with his dictionary, learn some terms lawyers use."

"How long will that take?" asked Tyrus.

"All the spare time you can find," said the Colonel.

For days a conscripted Tyrus struggled with Blackstone, finding him as boring as watching a hen peck corn. To W. H.'s considerable disappointment he gave it up and never returned.

Medicine was a possibility—either that or an appointment to West Point. Professor Cobb, thirty-seven years old, had been elected Royston's mayor and by 1900 was the proprietor of the Royston *Record*. His eye was trained on election to the Georgia senate, a goal he would soon reach. He was seen by politicians beyond his town and county as smart and well known—maybe even a future governor. Through his contribution to establishing a public, tax-financed educational system in northern Georgia, W. H. was acquainted with influential people in Virginia, the Carolinas, and beyond. He might well be able to secure an appointment to West Point for his footloose offspring.

Tyrus foresaw that regimentation would be his fate at a military academy, and he was too free-swinging for that. Doctoring, he guessed, might work for him. An area physician, Dr. Sam Moss, encouraged the idea. Moss had first noticed Tyrus when the Doc's services had been needed at Grandfather Squire Cobb's farm. While out ridge-running for wild pigs, Ty drove a tree prong through his big toe. Grannie Cobb, with a reputation for her use of roots, barks, and herbs as healing potions, fed him a foul-tasting brew. He came through without infection. But then his bowels went on a spree. "It'd hit me so fast that I'd barely have time to run for the Chic Sale in the back orchard," he wrote in a 1961 memoir. "And I'd spend the rest of the day there." In came Doc Moss to apply a cure.

Not long after, a white boy of Royston shot a black boy in the belly. Moss and another doctor invited Tyrus to observe the surgery. By flickering oil lamp on a kitchen table, they went to work. Moss told Ty, "You're the anesthetist," and handed him a dousing mask and a bottle of chloroform. Cobb's account of the surgery went like this: "I put the boy under without much trouble and the docs opened him up. After failing to locate the bullet, they began searching for a perforation of the intestine. Both being elderly men, their eyes grew tired under the oil lamp. 'You look, Tyrus,' said Moss. 'Blasted if I can find any puncture.'

"I went over the intestine until I found a bruise, but no hole. 'Aha,' said Moss, 'the bullet slanted off somewhere into his side. He's lucky.'"

Sewed up, the patient survived. Tyrus discovered that bloody tissue and exposed intestines did not make him faint. The experience had been exciting. Yet he felt no call to become a country healer.

Professor Cobb maintained the pressure. By now, he insisted, Tyrus should have discovered some upper-class ambition, scored better in school, and left off drifting. Once more the Professor brought up the idea of a West Point education. Tyrus remained uninterested. Nevertheless, W. H. put out feelers in political circles.

Fifty years later, in a 1950 interview with the baseball legend, *Los Angeles Times* columnist Braven Dyer asked about Cobb's refusal of an appointment to West Point.

Dyer remarked, "If you'd gone to the Point, the U.S. would have had two General MacArthurs."

Cobb: "No—it would have had two George Pattons."

Feeling guilty at letting down his father, Ty nonetheless continued to mosey through the days. Some nights, unable to sleep, Tyrus would go hiking in the hills with his dog, Old Bob. Why was it that a way of life he didn't want was expected of him? Why were adults so damned serious? What next?

Enter still heavier farm labor. From the time he had left short pants, he'd decided that it was out of the question that he would become a farmer of clay-belt cotton and corn. That didn't require brains, only endurance. To be a farmer meant to do stoopwork and cultivating in ninety-degree heat, side by side with black croppers. That left blacks his virtual equal. W. H. Cobb, short of hands on his acres, also used his son to plant and harrow. To make sure Tyrus kept the furrows straight he was under supervision of a black foreman, Uncle Ezra.

Tyrus didn't care to be seen by girls while working in the fields. When a special girl from school passed along a road bordering the fields, he would hand Ezra the horse's reins and hide from sight in a ditch. He considered himself a Cobb of standing, a "townie." He didn't belong out here, breathing clay dust. Manual labor was the lot of Negroes and poor whites.

W. H. Cobb's temporary answer to the career question was to find his son a summertime job in nearby Carnesville, apprenticed to a cotton factor. In the commission agent's sheds he learned about the maturing of bolls, ginning, grading, and the product's shipment to market. His effort there somewhat pacified his father, but the 120-pound junior Cobb saw no future in weighing and hoisting bales for a livelihood.

By 1901, at fifteen, losing his freckles, growing rapidly, with fuzz sprouting on his chest, Tyrus considered running away to Atlanta, where a friend of his clerked in a Wells Fargo office and made a good eight dollars per week. Tyrus hesitated, and in the end he wasn't up to the move. The Professor's dominant shadow over him, parental loyalty, and home ties were too deeply implanted for him to turn runaway. Had he skipped to Atlanta then, he believed years later, baseball never would have known him. "Might have become a pool-hall hustler," he guessed in retrospect. "Or gone out west to homestead."

Atlanta and Augusta newspapers reached Royston by slow mail. On sports pages he read that the 1904 Olympic Games were to be staged in St. Louis. He daydreamed about competing—fast runner that he was—in the Olympics. Meantime, he began to read about other happenings some one thousand miles to the north. Until then, with the southern U.S. not represented in the game, he had paid slight attention to major-league baseball. A Royston merchant raved to him about Honus Wagner, the famed "Flying Dutchman" shortstop of the Pittsburgh Pirates. "Who?" replied Tyrus. Kidded about his ignorance, he looked into the big-time game. He became aware of such heroes as Rube Waddell, on his way to setting strikeout records at Philadelphia, Wee Willie Keeler, the tiny but wonderful Brooklyn outfielder, Napoleon Lajoie, big hitter of Philadelphia, and Denton "Cy" Young, a pitching marvel at St. Louis and Boston whose nickname derived from "cyclone." Another whose pugnacious style Tyrus liked was war-like John "Muggsy" McGraw, an enemy of umpires and attacker of opponents in Baltimore and New York.

Star ballplayers, he noticed, moved around a lot from team to team. That appealed to Cobb—he was naturally a wanderer. Which team beat another didn't matter to him. What attracted him were the headlined celebrities, such as Christy "Big Six" Mathewson in New York, who sported high-collar shirts and earned an astounding five thousand to eight thousand dollars and more per season. Someone lent him a copy of *Spalding's Official Base Ball Guide*. He read that northern metropolises were "going wild in an unprecedented way about the sport" and that "there are five seasons—spring, summer, autumn, winter—and baseball season." Tyrus hadn't been aware that the game he and local lads played with a flat board and homemade twine ball could be such a big thing. That you might be able to play for good money hadn't crossed his mind.

CHAPTER THREE

WALKING THE TIGHTROPE

A s the big battalions marched in the War Between the States, traveling with them went shaved-down farm rails, ax handles, and wagon tongues—makeshift bats —along with horsehide-covered yarn balls. During time-outs from battle, both Confederate and Union troops chose up sides for the growing sport of town ball. On open spaces, the sound of base hits rang out. Sheet music was named the "Union Ball Club March," the "Home-Run Quickstep."

These Americans were looking for a good game to play. In even earlier form, a ball-bat-base type of contest could be traced to 1778 and Valley Forge in the Revolution, probably the first organized, reliably recorded such match staged in the country.

The adolescent Tyrus Cobb, just short years after the Civil War, knew little about town ball. All he had seen of it had come while he acted as batboy for the "first nine" of his hometown of Royston, the hard-drinking, semipro Royston Reds. You could hear the rambunctious Reds coming. They toured northeast Georgia, playing any opponent available. Wearing crimson uniforms jolting to the eye, the Nosebleed Reds had an average age of twenty or twenty-one. Below them stood the Royston Rompers, a ragtag group of boys aged twelve to about sixteen. Late in his life Cobb recorded: "As a kid, I didn't see a chance to ever reach the Reds. Maybe the Rompers. I was undersized . . . still had a runny nose . . . didn't know what a hard-on was. Didn't expect much."

Originally he did not even own a bat. Using a flat-sided board, Tyrus got along on sandlots. To ask his father for the money to buy one of the advertised models from a mail-order house was out of the question. To the Professor, unathletic and a bookworm, ball games were a waste of time.

Help finally came in the spring of 1899 from Elmer Cunningham, the town's supplier of waterwheels and coffins. Orders for burial boxes of pine were stacked up at Cunningham's shop after a Franklin County influenza epidemic killed dozens, and he told his son Joe and Tyrus that if they would haul in raw lumber from the woods, he would give them the leftover pieces. When the two were through whittling, they had semiround billets of wood intended for burial boxes. They were clumsy but gave off an impressive *crack!* in action. Tyrus called his best stick, one with prominent knots in it, "Big Yellow." He would take it to bed with him.

Along with his bats, Cobb always credited his Aunt Norah Chitwood for his start as a ballplayer. "Wonderful woman," he said of her. Auntie was on his side. Well aware of Professor Cobb's lack of sympathy with anything that didn't improve the mind, she drove Tyrus by buggy from Squire Cobb's farm to the down-mountain settlements of Murphy and Andrews to play baseball. There Tyrus found the early going too tough for him. One of the rules held over from the game's pioneer forms was "soaking." In "soaking," base runners could be put out not only by throws to a bag and by hand, but by throwing to hit them anywhere on the body. Conking the skull was preferable, because it might take a star opponent out of the lineup until his senses returned. In one game, Tyrus hit a shallow single. Taking off with a "yaaaaah!" scream to unnerve the fielder, he headed for second base. Came a blackout. He had been hit hard by a soaker to the ear. The next thing he knew, Aunt Norah was helping carry him off the lot with an expression of my-god-what-have-I-done? She cried, "Oh, you're bleeding!"

Ty mumbled that he felt fine. But the buggy rolled homeward and that was all for him that day.

He wasn't accepted by the Murphy gang at country ball, but he kept showing up for more. Norah and Squire Cobb suspected that he was in over his head against older boys; Tyrus knew it for a fact. To be put out between bases was among the worst of "boneheaders." You were supposed to be an elusive target, ducking, dodging, and generally maneuvering to avoid fast throws. The Cobb conceptualization of base-running tactics began here. In the big league he was to define this as "watching the fielders' eyes, their jump on the ball, body lean, throwing and release habits—every little damned thing about them . . . keeping one jump ahead of the defense." Diagnosis and counteraction would be Cobb's quintessential stamp for years to come.

His weak batwork on sandlots improved when he took to standing as far back from the plate as possible. His new, self-contrived deep stance gave him an extra split second in which to time pitches and react. One day, in a tattered jersey of the Murphy Maulers, playing before some fifty fans, Ty slugged a fastball two hundred feet to a rail fence, a triple. Two runs scored. Murphy won. He never forgot that three-bagger, because after that teammates showed him a degree of respect.

Back in Royston, Tyrus baled hay to earn $1.25, enough to purchase a "professional" glove, a flimsy, laceless pad that soon fell apart, forcing him for a while to play bare-handed. At the home dinner table, Tyrus attributed his torn fingernails to horseplay with neighborhood kids.

Someone with the Royston Rompers team for juniors lent him a catcher's mitt. Backstopping was risky. Face masks were hard to come by. As was virtually guaranteed, a foul tip whacked and closed Tyrus's eye. That night the roof was raised on the two-story Cobb home on Central Street as never before over ballplaying. Tyrus never had seen his father so steamed up.

"Stop it!" ordered the Professor. "There's nothing so useless on earth as knocking a string ball around a pasture with ruffians!"

Tyrus's homemade pine bats were confiscated. Not until months later was Bob McCreary, a good semipro player and a Masonic Order brother of the Professor, able to persuade W. H. to relent. McCreary argued that Royston boys of thirteen and up derived muscle-building benefits from town and lesser varieties of ball. Discipline, too, was enforced. McCreary promised to keep an eye on Ty, and pledged that the boy would not take a drink of corn liquor or chew tobacco. "He's doing better than most at school," argued McCreary. "Let him feel like a man."

Tyrus returned to the game, on a short leash. Against Harmony Grove he hit three line-drive singles for the Rompers while making an acrobatic game-saving grab at shortstop. His performance was noticed by schoolmates. But the Professor remained adamant that the fun and games must end soon. Tyrus had to stop wasting time and find a field of endeavor where he could follow his father as a community leader. To the schoolman, Cobbs attained distinction in life through superior intelligence in mathematics, law, politics, history, business management, or teaching. Education was everything. His son had other ideas.

IN 1902, a sinewy sixteen-year-old of five feet, seven inches and 140 pounds, a left-handed hitter and right-handed thrower, was given a tryout by the "big team," the Royston Reds.

When he moved up for tryouts, the Reds had greeted him sourly. They saw no asset in someone who had to use a hands-apart split grip to compensate for his lack of batting power. He was unimpressive in looks, with his sharp nose, large ears, pale skin, pigeon-toed walk, and high-pitched voice. An infielder, Crawfish Cummings, suggested that he bow out: "We've got too many left-handers already."

"I can hit right side, too," said Ty. This was untrue in the accepted definition of switch-hitting; he could only bunt right-handed.

"How about throwing? Can you do that both ways, too?"

"Well, I've done that," said Ty. "But mostly I'm right and I plan to play ball here."

Surprisingly, he passed all tests. Of the fourteen roster players, pitchers not included, nine were in their twenties; the others were thirty or more.

It was an important honor in upper Georgia to be a Red. A whole two-hundred pound hog now brought only four dollars, exports of cotton and tree fruit to market had slumped, and jobs were as scarce as—went the wisecrack—a virgin in McGafferty's saloon. Against that, fans sometimes threw money onto the field at the unpaid town team when it badly beat an opponent. In his diary, Ty wrote: "Collected ninety-two cents today . . . others got more."

No uniform on hand was small enough to fit Ty's wiry frame.

Again Aunt Norah came to his aid. She cut flannel pieces to his size, dyed them a screeching red, and the rookie was ready to go.

He was no threat to anyone at first, either as a shortstop or in the outfield, but he ran the bases well enough during preseason practice to please McCreary and the hard-nosed Reds, champions of Banks County. They hit line drives at him, screaming liners and grounders that could knock out teeth. He had never handled anything so difficult. Ty couldn't jerk his head away from grass-cutters without dishonor, so he stayed down and scooped up a high percentage of the drives. For weeks he had mostly sat on the bench, in charge of cleaning bats after muddy games and collecting foul balls.

A pair of matches was scheduled with hot-rival Elberton, two counties away in Broad River country. A gatekeeper stopped the small Cobb at the park entrance to ask. "You the ratshit Reds' equipment boy?" Cobb replied, "No, I play." The gateman laughed. Ty was not admitted until Bob McCreary came along to claim him.

Getting even, he had a busy day against Elberton. He figured out their base-stealing signals, stole a base himself, and started two double plays. Noting that Royston's new boy batted left-handed and might pull to the right side, the Elbertons shaded their outfield in that direction. Seeing their deployment, Ty shifted his plate stance from square to open and placed both of his singles down the third-base line to the opposite open space in left field. The Reds won, 7–5, and his mates bought their rookie a bacon sandwich in appreciation.

It was partly in physiological and partly in spiritual terms that Cobb, in later years, replayed those turning-point innings at Elberton. In 1953 he told Grantland Rice, of the syndicated "Sportlight" column: "That day the bat actually tingled in my hands . . . it gave off an electrical impulse that shot through my body . . . a great feeling . . . it told me I'd found something I could do extremely well." Rice's subsequent analysis in his autobiographical *The Tumult and the Shouting* went: "From that start, Cobb never missed an opportunity to refine his craft. A man apart. The shrewdest athlete and perhaps the shrewdest man I ever met."

After hitting sprees in other towns, the newcomer was taken aside by McCreary. "You may look like a horsefly out there and you waste too much motion," said McCreary, "but, by God, you show a lot of ability. You might be a natch."

"What's a natch?" asked Cobb.

"A natural—one in a million."

Royston's players were country miles below the professional level, yet McCreary's words made the youngster feel special. His bats *did* tingle. The man he most admired in the major leagues was Napoleon "Big Frenchy" Lajoie of the Philadelphia Phillies. Had not Lajoie begun in the tank town of Fall River up in New England and made it big as a hitter?

A sensational fielding play by Ty pulled against Harmony Grove was talked about around town. In the eighth inning Harmony loaded the bases with two out. A high drive was poled to farthest left field. Ty, in center field, intuited that the Reds' fielder in left couldn't run fast enough to make the catch. Sprinting behind him, diving as the ball went off his teammate's fingers, he made a one-handed grab. Almost simultaneously he crashed into the fence. But he held on to the ball, a game-winning effort. Royston "cranks"—as fans were then called—cheered him for a catch they wouldn't forget.

He continued to dive and scramble, and crowds threw coins his way—he once picked up eleven dollars as his share. Side opportunities developed in late season. Villages not scheduled against the Reds wanted to see the little Franklin County streak doing his act. Cobb's territory expanded. He was offered and accepted two and a half dollars per game from Anderson, South Carolina, for moonlighting against Hartwell, Georgia's, town team. Keeping the secret from his father, he used the alias "Jack Jones." Anderson was far enough from Royston that Professor Cobb almost surely would not hear of the deception. By taking pay he had professionalized himself. If his path led to a college campus, as W. H. Cobb insisted it would, he might be ineligible for amateur sport. Playing pro games under an alias was a common dodge of the day, but a risky one for anyone contemplating college. He played well for Anderson, learned a few things, and the five dollars jingling in his pocket felt good.

"Don't ever do that again," warned McCreary. "I've given your old man my promise to keep you straight. If he gets wind that you're selling yourself, I'll never be his friend again."

His desire to move ahead seemed feverish to others. Within two months, Ty—"Tyrus" had been dropped except at home—had spent the five dollars, along with occasional cash contributions from fans, and was broke. With high hopes, he entered a turkey shoot offering money prizes. His game-hunter's eyes let him down—he won nothing. With nowhere to borrow funds, he resorted to theft in broad daylight, a move Ty professed to regret all his life. His purpose was to raise enough to buy a new outfielder's glove. To a sixteen-year-old, it wasn't a real crime. His father's library contained everything from McGuffey's *Eclectic Reader* to the *Odyssey* to mathematics treatises, and the disappearance of a few books would not be noticed. Someday he would reclaim and replace them. Down at the dry-goods store was displayed a new style of glove, one with a good pocket. Ty's glove was tattered. He pinched two volumes to buy the glove.

For the Professor's son to walk around town with schoolbooks in hand was commonplace. His mistake was trying to sell to the wrong man. Professor Cobb heard about it. Shocked, he called Ty into his study. "I thought I was raising a straight shooter, not a thief!" he exploded. "Now you see why I consider baseball a bad business! Your associates are ruining you!" Ty wept. He asked for forgiveness. His punishment was to be indefinitely banned from the Reds team and given extra farm duties. What hurt most was the contempt his father showed.

"I hated to be backed into a corner," Cobb said of this time. He rationalized that it was much better to work the fields for long hours than to be banned for keeps from ballplaying. Field work built muscle, and the calluses he grew on his hands would help when he returned to making tough stops of hard line drives.

He never forgot that hot, seesaw summer of 1902. No reprieve was in sight. The senior Cobb was out of town much of the time, forming political connections and lobbying for better countywide educational facilities. Mother Amanda was busy caring for Tyrus's ten-year-old sister, Florence, and fourteen-year-old brother, Paul. From across the cornfields Tyrus could almost hear bats smacking balls at the Reds' practice grounds.

In September, W. H. Cobb returned. He inspected the land his boy had worked and passed out compliments. Corncribs were filled. Land was plowed. Decades later, Ty had clear recall of a new warmth between the Professor and himself. Within months, Ty had changed. So had W. H., who wanted peace between them, a strong rapprochement. Tyrus, said W. H., looked "manly." A growth spurt put him at five

feet, nine inches tall and 150 pounds—slope-shouldered and muscular, especially in the chest, arms, and thighs.

THE TWO Cobbs went by rail to Athens, one of the first sizable town-
ships Ty had seen, to buy livestock. Instead of having his opinion dismissed, Ty was consulted. He knew a sound animal when he saw one.
He remembered touting W. H. off a saddle horse in which he showed
interest. "He's too long in the barrel and lacks strength," pointed out
Tyrus.

"You might be right," replied W. H.

Tyrus took another tour around the horse. "And his hock action
looks draggy."

"I agree," said W. H. "We won't buy him."

A meeting of minds occurred in other ways, such as when buying
a suit of clothes. Ty habitually went around in any old outfit; W. H. said
he needed something proper for social events. Together they picked
out a dark outfit of good broadcloth. In many other matters, one Cobb
reached out—the other responded. "It was the sweetest thing in the
world to be accepted by my father . . . until then he'd held me down
. . . I couldn't reach him," Ty was to record. "I was still hoping he
would recognize me as a man."

Next spring Tyrus quietly unpacked his uniform and rejoined the
Reds ball club. His schoolwork had improved. No longer was there talk
of hiring a tutor. Tyrus had won a school oratorical contest. Perhaps
resignedly, knowing he was bound to lose, the Professor let him go.

Absence had not cost the rookie his touch. He rattled off so many
base hits, among them his first home run, that crowds of up to six
hundred turned out to watch. His added strength enabled Cobb,
crouched low and far back in the box, to handle speed, curveball
drops, and assorted other pitching with almost equal ability. He was
learning how to protect the plate. Statistics weren't kept, but by his
own estimate (really a wild guess) he was averaging around .450.

He was also handy in field fights. Rural games were often interrupted by fist-slinging by players and spectators. Against the Cleveland, Georgia, nine, a ball was planted in a base-running Reds player's
mouth with enough force to bring blood. The first man out of the Reds'
dugout was Cobb. Sprinting to second base, he hit the offending opponent with a football-style tackle and beat his head on the ground. Both

squads went at it with pleasure. Under a pileup, Cobb sprained a thumb and suffered a cut ear. But he finished the game and afterward tried to renew the fight. "He's a wild little tiger," it was said. When a brawl started, it was often instigated by Cobb. His motto was "Hit them first—and last—at all times."

At sixteen, Tyrus had yet to see a big-league team in action. Reading in the press that the Cleveland Blues (later Indians) of the American League were spring-training in Atlanta, less than a hundred miles away, he and friend Joe Cunningham hopped a wheat wagon to the capital city. At Piedmont Park, banners and bunting welcomed the Clevelanders. Sitting close to the dugout, Cobb was all eyes for the most famous of second basemen, Napoleon Lajoie. The great Lajoie didn't speak to Ty, but winked at him. Another player, Bill Bradley, chatted with the kids, letting them take his photo in a batting pose. "Think you could hit this kind of pitching?" joked Bradley.

"Someday, maybe," said Ty seriously. He meant he might be ready in six or eight years.

"Sure, someday," chuckled Bradley. "If you can hit the slopper [spitball]."

Lajoie connected for several long hits in an intersquad game that day. Cobb recorded his impressions in a notebook: "Nap is a big fellow, over six feet, 190 lbs . . . righthanded . . . likes the fastball high . . . plays 2b like a deer. Hit .422 average last season, one of best ever."

While in the big city, Ty bought two books, *Scientific Baseball*, by Fred Pfeffer, and *A Ballplayer's Career*, by the legendary Adrian "Cap" Anson. He marked the most important information with checks in the margins. Long afterward, in 1960, when I was paging through his notebooks of that period, along one edge I found this notation: "Don't wiggle bat . . . keep straight on shoulder to save time . . . Never take eye off pitcher . . . time his windup for chance of steal."

Nowhere in his note-taking did the new star of the Reds speculate about ever reaching a high professional level. Such a leap was so improbable that Ty kept all such thoughts to himself. He knew that lower-category pro leagues existed in such cities as Indianapolis, Jersey City, Baltimore, St. Paul and Columbus, but in the southern United States, soon after the twentieth century dawned, a teenage semipro's chances of moving up to the big league were minuscule. The Southern League, with such affiliates as Nashville, Memphis, New Orleans,

Atlanta, and Birmingham, was rated Class A. At this level major-league talent was germinated, but only occasionally.

In late 1903, Cobb read a *Police Gazette* notice that a new Class C circuit had been organized that winter, named the South Atlantic, or "Sally" League—"two bits for a ticket, a scrappy presentation guaranteed to please all." He visited a hometown sawmill where Billy Clarke and Van Bagwell were employed. Both of these ex–Royston Reds players had gone through tryouts with minor pro clubs, had failed to be signed, and had returned home to hang up their spikes. "Do you think I might make it in the low minors?" Cobb asked. Clarke thought that it was possible in a few years, not now. Bagwell said, "I think you might do it if you play outfield where your speed will count. But who knows?"

Bucked up even by a split vote, Cobb talked to the Reverend John Yarborough, a minister who knew something about baseball beyond Royston. Yarborough was doubtful—"Those boys down south play rough, maybe you should wait to grow up." But he didn't rule out the possibility—if the senior Cobb approved.

On writing paper supplied by the minister, who didn't suspect that the Professor would be kept uninformed of the plan, Cobb sent job applications to not one but all six Sally League teams. In his best handwriting, the letters went to club managers. His inquiries read something like this, he remembered and related to me:

> Sir:
>
> I play the infield and outfield for a good team here. I lead the Royston first team in batting, second in fielding. Knowing you have many fine players, I feel I could do much better with your coaching. Please consider my application to try out with (name of club) for the 1904 season.
>
> Yrs. truly,
> Tyrus Cobb

No mention was made of his age. He gave Van Bagwell's address for a reply.

Time passed, with no answer from any source. Cobb hung around the mailbox. He was about to lose hope when a letter arrived from the Augusta Tourists' manager and part-owner, Cornelius "Con" Strouthers. It was terse:

Tyrus Cobb:

This will notify you that you are free to join our spring
training practice with the understanding that you pay
your own expenses. Reply promptly.

Dynamite stuff! As fast as he could pick up the Reverend Yarborough's pen, he answered. Days later a contract arrived, stipulating pay
of fifty dollars a month if the Tourists found him up to their speed.
Con Strouthers added that he would not be issued a Tourists' uniform
for the tryout, so he should bring his present suit. Fifty dollars per
month, Cobb knew, was about all that "yannigans" (rookies) received
in the Sally League.

After signing the document he faced his main problem. For three
days he kept the deal he had negotiated a secret, fearing the showdown
that would come when he broke the news. Earlier, Cobb senior had
run for and won a Georgia senate seat, and to have a son playing that
ruffianly game of baseball for a living would not sit well with Georgia
conservatives and church people.

Continuing to stall, Ty confided what he had done to his mother.
Amanda, a quiet, unassertive type, shook her head. Wishing to stay out
of it, she offered no opinion. To perform for the local Reds was one
thing; to leave home for the same purpose meant a bitter clash with the
Professor.

Cobb waited until the day before he was to catch a train to Augusta
to confess. The showdown, when it came, lasted until three o'clock in
the morning. Fully expecting W. H. to roar and maybe disown him, Ty
was instead faced with solemnity and logic. The Professor was shocked
that the boy had entered into a legal agreement without consulting the
head of the family. He felt sorrow that such a promising student was
putting university training behind him. Pacing the floor, hands clasped
behind him, he gravely said, "This is a fool's act. I ask you to reconsider. You are only seventeen and at a crucial point. One path leads to
a rewarding future, the other will leave you shiftless, a mere muscle-
worker. I ask you again—reconsider."

"I know it hurts you, but I just have to go," Ty kept interrupting.

"You're deceiving yourself. You'll be surrounded by illiterates and
no-goods. Believe me, it's not for you. These men avoid work for play.

Some have been known to commit murder and suicide. Fifty dollars a month is nothing to what would come otherwise."

Ty argued that he couldn't help himself: "I signed that contract because I want to find out what I can do. I'm almost sure I can make good. I'll stay out of trouble."

(Frank "Lefty" O'Doul, a slugger for the Philadelphia Phillies and Brooklyn Dodgers in the 1920s and 1930s and confidant of Cobb in the 1960s, used to say, "Ty never could tell this story without crying. For someone who played ball like it was the goddamn Civil War all over again, he was a very sensitive guy.")

Cobb left Royston for the test with considerable backing. The Professor, ending a useless dispute, sat at his rolltop desk to write out six checks worth fifteen dollars each. These were easily cashable at Augusta banks, due to his prominence, and should carry Ty until he saw a paycheck from the Augusta Tourists—if ever he did. W. H. added two ten-dollar bills for traveling money. "To be used sparingly," said the Professor. "I don't want to hear you've been drinking or around bad women." Evidently he had spies who would be keeping an eye out. So Ty suspected.

Tyrus promised to behave. He had been in a few poolrooms that W. H. didn't know about, had tried beer and craps shooting, but that was the extent of his sinning. Anything more sophisticated—gambling dens, prostitutes—was out of the question. He was a virgin.

He left next day on the Georgia Southern Line on the ninety-mile trip to Augusta, carrying a telescope grip containing his flaming red Royston uniform in a roll, his "tip" (glove), and a single pair of infielder shoes. If he was sent to the outfield, the shoes would have to do double duty. His luggage had been packed for several days; he had no intention of not reporting to spring camp, however the conflict with his father ended. He was definitely leaving home.

In retirement years, whenever he thought back on this time Cobb saw it as critical. He left home scared. "The odds were no damned good and I knew it," he told this writer. He was still far from fully grown, and was going up against mature men. He was headed into the unknown against competitors of whose caliber Cobb had no firsthand information. He had no knowledge of the pitching he would be facing. Professional skills had yet to be learned—using the bunt, executing the hit-and-run, the double play. The eyes of Royston would be upon him. What if he broke an arm or leg against an outfield fence? What would be his value then? A crippling injury would mean finding work in strange country. For he would not go back to working on a farm. He owed a great deal to the man who, against his own wishes, had made it possible for him to satisfy a need. That was fatherly love. One way or another, it would be repaid.

CHAPTER FOUR

Low Comedy
in the Bushes

A rising fun-and-games climate was gradually replacing America's puritan tradition of hard, long hours of work by the time Cobb entered pro baseball. It was becoming more and more acceptable for some at least of the 86 million American citizens to relax at ballparks and horse-racing tracks; to enjoy prizefights, archery, and rifle shooting; and to race bicycles, play golf and tennis, and row boats for money and trophies. One of the early evangelists of variable athletic competition, as practiced by the ancient Greeks, was Grantland Rice. A 1900 Phi Beta Kappa graduate of Vanderbilt University, Rice became a popular sports columnist for the *Atlanta Journal,* on his way to national fame.

Late one afternoon, while the *Journal's* presses rolled on the day's edition, Rice sat playing dime-ante poker in a back room at the paper. He was interrupted by a messenger with a telegram from Anniston, Alabama. Rice wasn't sure where Anniston was located, nor did he recognize the wire's sender, who identified himself as "James Jackson, news-tipster." The communique read: "Tyrus Raymond Cobb, the dashing young star from Royston, has just started playing ball with Anniston. He is a terrific hitter and faster than a deer. At the age of 17 he is undoubtedly a phenom."

Rice, laughing, returned to his poker. Tearing up the telegram, he later took time to inform the unknown tipster through Western Union, "After this the mails are good enough for Cobb."

Anniston, a mill town in Alabama's northeast iron-ore region, fielded a team in something called the Tennessee-Alabama-Southeast League, composed of semipros and small-college horsehiders. An organization that was so far down the competitive ladder held no interest for metropolitan Atlanta sport-page readers. As for the highly recommended Cobb, no file existed on him in Rice's growing collection of biographies of southern U.S. professional ballplayers.

But then there followed to the *Journal* a steady flow of applause: "Keep your eye on Ty Cobb . . . he is one of the finest hitters I've seen." "Watch Cobb of Anniston, he is sure to be a sensation." "Have you seen Ty Cobb play ball yet? He is the fastest mover in the game." "Cobb had three hits yesterday, made two great catches." "A sure big leaguer in the making." Rice could count on a dozen or so such letters, postcards, and wires arriving monthly, sent by "interested fans" and "faithful readers" who signed themselves as Jackson, Brown, Kelly, Jones, Smith, and Stewart, among other interested parties.

Routinely discarding such mail, Grant Rice did not suspect perpetration of a fraud, mainly because the bulletins were signed in multiform longhand styles, from slanting, scrawled, Spencerian, and Palmer methods to roundhand and wide-looped. Pencils and inks also varied. Finally, in self-defense, Rice wrote a "blind" column about someone he had never seen, hailing the arrival of a "new wonder boy named Cobb" who was "the darling of the fans" and a "hot number" with a ball club across the border from Georgia. Rice hoped that the acknowledgment would end the plague of Cobb plugs. No such luck; drumbeating notices continued to arrive from points in Tennessee, Alabama, and Georgia.

Not until 1951, at a General Electric Company banquet honoring the sixty-five-year-old Cobb, did the seventy-one-year-old Granny Rice learn that he had been flimflammed by penman Ty, who was the secret author of the notices. Cobb now confessed that he had acted as his own press agent, and he alone had pumped out the praise. He also admitted to having played only twenty-two games at Anniston, with far from the spectacular results he had described via the post. In other words, he had lied like hell.

In the 1950s, Rice was the acknowledged dean of American sport commentators. Learning he had been suckered by a mere babe of seventeen surprised and irritated him. "That was a damned sneaky thing to do, Cobb," snapped Rice. "What made you do it to me?"

"I was in a hurry, Granny," answered Cobb.

Rice forgave him, and the two men resumed a long-standing friendship.

The desperate rush to be noticed came after Cobb had reported to Augusta on schedule, played in two games, and on April 24 had been handed his release. Abruptly Cobb found himself an unemployed free agent. Five days after his release he was in the outfield of the Anniston Steelers, a club he had never heard of until then, and one at the professional game's lowest possible level. It was from there that he began his letter barrage to the press.

From early April, when he had first reached the Augusta Tourists' training camp, very little had gone right. He had checked into a cheap hotel— "a bedbug joint" in his words to me—and hurried out to Warren Park, the Tourists' four-thousand-capacity home field. To him, the bandbox park seemed huge. He had come supplied with letters of introduction to a few Augusta businessmen from his Royston boosters, who had not however included the name of the Tourists' manager, Con Strouthers. The brusque manager barely glanced at the rookie, telling him, "Get suited up, go shag some flies." Some thirty-five candidates were competing for sixteen to eighteen jobs. Utilityman Cobb's first assignment was to run down and return foul balls sprayed off the bats of other prospects. While batting practice went on he did outfield wind sprints and knee bends.

Otherwise, Ty merely stood around in his gaudy Royston uniform, trying to strike some rhythm with the tough-looking Tourists. "In that monkey-suit," said first baseman Harry Bussey, "you should join the fire-department volunteers." Ty moved himself to the infield during six-man defensive drills and worsened his situation by preempting grounders hit to others and yelling it up—"Woweeee!"—when he made a good stop. He would gladly have shed his red outfit, but a set of Tourist flannels was not offered.

Approaching the plate for some swings, he was jostled aside.

"Get the hell away," growled Mike McMillan, a large outfielder, glaring at him.

Cobb bristled, as usual, when challenged. "It's my ups," he pointed out.

"Beat it," repeated McMillan, shouldering him into the backstop netting that served as a batting cage.

Cobb came back with fists raised, and suddenly he was surrounded by players who knocked off his cap and scuffed his new shoes. The boss, Strouthers, looked on unconcernedly. Cobb's gripe that he was tired of sitting around was wasted. "You make your own place here," explained Strouthers.

While half a dozen preseason contests were being played, the novice pro did not leave the dugout, a flimsy lean-to that leaked when it rained. During pregame practice, uninvited to take part, he moved to center field and sat on the grass watching, waiting for something to happen. "I couldn't figure it out at first, then I got mad," Cobb related years afterward. "It was humiliating to be taken for a pissant. I wondered why Augusta had bothered to call me up in the first place." The fact was that Ty had originally approached Augusta; the roughing-up he took was standard maliciousness in a day when young contenders for veterans' jobs found their suits cut to shreds, their shoes nailed to the floor. Cobb's welcome was to have his pants and shirt "juiced"— sprayed with tobacco leavings.

Strouthers—who had never risen above the bottom minor leagues as a player—made no move to use Cobb in his lineup when the Detroit Tigers, touring the region in exhibitions, played the Tourists at Warren Park. Cobb stayed anchored to the bench. That did not stop him from closely watching Detroit's rangy center fielder, a left-hander like himself—Wahoo Sam Crawford. The Tigers, who had finished a bad fifth in the American League in 1903 with 65 wins and 71 losses, tore into the Tourists as if it were midseason in the majors. Cobb saw Crawford, a .332 batting star in the previous season, leisurely trot to first base after drawing a base on balls, then suddenly switch into high gear and race for second. The Tourists were caught napping. While they scrambled to nail Crawford at second, where he threw up a broad cloud of dust, a Tiger runner who had seconds earlier wandered down the line from third base sped home to score by inches. Cobb stored away that delayed, closely timed play for future use.

He noted, too, that while at bat Crawford seemed to be sneaking peeks at the mitt of the Augusta catcher. Was he stealing the catcher's finger signs to the pitcher? It looked that way to Cobb, although he had never seen this trick. In the outfield, on a wallop heading for the fence, Crawford drifted under the ball, leaped at the exact right moment, and picked the chance off the boards, making the play look easy.

After the Tourists were beaten, Cobb hesitantly walked up to the future Hall of Famer Crawford to say, "That was a great catch, Mr. Crawford. What's the best way to judge long fly balls?" Crawford didn't mind talking about his specialty. While giving the rawboned boy his first big-league coaching, he also offered the first friendly words that Cobb had heard recently. Wahoo (from Wahoo, Nebraska) was a town barber in the off-season and had a wheat-belt twang, and Cobb's speech was filled with "cain't" for "can't," "ah" for "I," and "yuh" for "you." Still, they understood each other. Crawford said, "You go [on flies] by the sound of the bat. A sound like a gun going off means the ball's hit hard . . . you start back in a big hurry. Use the crossover step, left or right, on the getaway. Run on the balls of your feet . . . Look over your shoulder to tell where the ball's headed, so's you run under it . . . Don't do any backpedaling, that gets you nowhere." He went on, "Use both hands whenever you can . . . If you get a real good jump on a ball hit to your front, be moving forward on the catch so as to make a stronger throw." Liking Cobb's concentrated interest, the loquacious Wahoo passed on other tips: "Make up your mind in advance to what base you'll throw . . . Throw on one hop to the bag, not on the fly . . . Before a road game bounce a ball off the fence in different places, testing for force and direction of the rebound."

Cobb wanted to hear more. "Hell, I can't gab all day," said Wahoo. "Break in a backup glove or two in case your number-one leather is ripped." Cobb didn't admit that he could barely afford one old glove.

Cobb was encouraged to show Wahoo his own particular glove. As an experiment, he had cut the leather out of the palm to expose raw flesh, so that any catch essentially was a bare-handeder. Crawford grinned, saying, "I did that as a kid—to keep balls from sliding off the leather. No more, though."

"It works for me," said Cobb.

"Then keep it until you can't stand the blood it'll draw," said Wahoo. And then he admonished, "Don't drink on game days."

Trying not to stammer—one of the holdover curses of his boyhood—Cobb thanked Crawford before going off to contemplate what he had learned. Some of it was basic. But at least half of what he had heard was new to him. He would always remember Crawford's kindness.

On opening day of the Tourists' regular Sally League season, Con Strouthers was short of a middle fielder. First baseman Harry Bussey, a salary holdout, was ineligible to play, meaning that center fielder McMillan moved to first base. Who would replace McMillan? On the lineup card Strouthers wrote: "Cobb, cf," listing him seventh in the batting order.

This was a reluctant decision, Cobb had reason to believe. Strouthers wanted to see his tryout ended and have the noisy rookie gone down the road, enabling Augusta to sign a replacement. Coming to bat, Cobb received no instructions beyond, "Don't swing at anything in the dirt." He took the field steamed up beyond normal.

In the season's opener, the opponent was a strong Columbia, South Carolina, team, featuring a fastballing pitcher, George Engel. It was a damp, grayish day with fifteen hundred or so fans on hand when Ty Cobb bowed in as a professional baseball player. Using his Roystonized grip—left fist gripping his stick six to seven inches above his right—he grounded out on his first time up. Next time he dug Engel's pitch up and over third base into the left-field corner, against the fence. As Columbia's fielder chased a ricocheting ball, Cobb hustled around the bases. The throw-in to the plate was close, but a head-first slide beat the relay by an arm's length for an inside-the-park home run. That drew cheers—but not in Augusta's dugout. It was quiet there. In the sixth inning, doubling up the middle, Cobb met the same indifference. Columbia won, 8–7, and Augusta fans went home for dinner, talking about the slender, big-eared newcomer with speed and a sting in his light bat.

A husband and wife from Cornelia, Georgia, near Royston, who were visiting Augusta, made the gesture of inviting Ty to join them for dinner on the night of his home run. Otherwise, he would have dined alone.

Strouthers said nothing hopeful. He griped that Cobb broke too many bats in practice. Bats of willow, ash, or spruce cost seventy-five cents apiece. "I only broke two," said Cobb. "You don't let me do much swinging." Two, said Strouthers, were too many.

Momentarily Cobb thought of mailing a news clipping of his break-in game to his father. The *Augusta Chronicle,* Georgia's oldest newspaper—"we never missed a single daily edition during the War Between the States," the *Chronicle* could boast—didn't miss Cobb's feat, either. In a side note to the main game report it mentioned that "Outfielder T. Cobb was auspicious in his first local showing . . . Four-base and two-base pry-ups are a better act than anyone could expect from a beginner."

On second thought, Cobb didn't send the news item home. Nothing was settled. He might strike out four straight times in his next start. He had been cold-shouldered and "hey-rube'd."

In a second game with Columbia, Cobb told me, he doubled, fielded well, and stole a base. This may be inaccurate—Fred Lieb in his authoritative 1946 book, *The Detroit Tigers,* reported him as going hitless. Faded old box scores do not settle the matter. His stolen base, however, was Cobb's first in organized ball.

Leaving the park, Cobb was called into Strouther's office. It took about fifteen minutes for the ax to fall. The contract Cobb wanted so badly, placing him on the payroll and picking up some of his room-and-board expenses, was not forthcoming. In his blunt way, Strouthers said, "Our outfield problem is settled. Bussey just got word from the league office taking him off suspension. He's going to first base and McMillan back to center. That makes you low man out, Cobb. You're a free agent . . . you can sign with any team that wants you."

"But I'm hitting for you," choked out Cobb.

"You've had a few knocks, that's all, and your throwing isn't up to snuff," retorted Strouthers, who then pointed out that since Cobb had not earned a place on the Tourist roster, the club owed him nothing. He had to gain a permanent berth to collect any pay. "But, tell you what . . ." Strouthers offered him five dollars cash.

"I wouldn't play for you if you asked me!" shouted Cobb. "You didn't give me a fair chance, only eighteen innings!" He refused the five dollars.

To Augusta's regular players, the scene was all too predictable and laughable. A gag about fresh bushers was retold:

Manager: "You're gone, pack your duds."

Rookie: "But won't you give me a recommendation?"

Manager (writing it out): "This fellow played one game for me and I'm satisfied."

Not many fans noticed Cobb's disappearance, and few questions were asked. Back at his hotel, Cobb sat alone in his room. Augusta was a place where he would have been happy to live. The growing port of forty-five thousand on the Savannah River had charm, with its blooming flowers, paved streets, healthy climate, and feeling of busyness. He hated to leave before he had shown he belonged.

Nap Rucker, a member of the Tourists at the time, was a witness to how hard Cobb took his discharge. According to Rucker and others, Cobb's drive to make good was so strong that he became physically ill. As Rucker related it, "the kid" shed tears, raved, and threatened to get a gun and shoot Strouthers. In later years Cobb denied that he had any violent intentions at the time. He called Rucker "full of bullshit" and brushed off the stories with: "I was hurt and damned mad for a while, but I wasn't stupid at seventeen. When that Strouthers and his gang made it miserable for me from the start, I halfway expected I wouldn't last long. It was something you could feel in the air."

Muddy Ruel, a major-league catcher who was close to Cobb, put it this way: "Long years after it happened, Cobb was still burned up by the way Augusta dumped him. And proud of how he finally got even with Strouthers. More than even—he got revenge."

Grantland Rice's opinion of his condition then was: "I don't know how much the Augusta affair affected Cobb. Severely, I'm sure. During those early years I found him to be an extremely peculiar soul, brooding and bubbling with violence, devious, suspicious and combative all the way. This twisted attitude he never lost."

Whatever his resentment, after April 28 Cobb did not waste time. He contacted several other Sally League franchises, asked for a tryout, and was told that the clubs were set for the season. He wrote as far away as Memphis in the Southern League, but got no reply. Dreading to return home a failure in his father's eyes, he applied for a cotton warehouse clerking job. Nothing was open. As April ended he had spent part of the funds supplied by Professor Cobb, and the basic need to support himself had him trapped and in no emotional shape to find a solution.

Thad "Mobile Kid" Hayes, a rookie pitcher who had also been cut by the Tourists, joined Cobb on a trolley ride into the countryside.

They sat on a fence and talked it over. Hayes remarked that he could always find work back in Mobile, where his family owned property, and he might be able to find employment for friend Ty as well. Neither liked the prospect of giving up his effort to play professionally. Bitten by the ball bug, why should they quit so soon? Hayes had a suggestion. They could try Anniston, in Alabama, where a wildcat semipro town team scheduled three to four games weekly against opponents from southern Tennessee and upper Alabama. Anniston fans were a hot group, and Hayes knew the club owner.

"How fast a team is Anniston?" asked Cobb.

"Not as good as Augusta," answered Hayes, "but some of the college boys they have are so good that Class A scouts come to watch them. But they're an outlaw outfit not recognized in New York or Chicago."

Cobb was teetering on the edge of walking away from the game to pick up his schooling as a college freshman. He had a feeling that this might be a career turning point—the maxim "Yield not to misfortunes, press forward more boldly in their face" came to mind from his schoolboy study of the Romans. And he asked more questions. What was the pay like in Anniston? Hayes thought the Anniston Steelers paid fifty to sixty dollars a month, and he had heard they needed another pitcher and an outfielder. Cobb told how his father was set on his attending the University of Georgia for a medical degree. "I guess I should try it," he said, "but I'll phone him first. He'll raise hell, probably call me home."

Their conversation was the opposite of what he expected. The Professor did not react with his usual polemic against baseball. Ty explained that he had been dropped by Augusta without the chance to follow up a promising start. W. H. Cobb skipped the sympathy and asked, "What will you do now?"

His son responded with the Anniston possibility.

"If you get hired there," said Professor Cobb, "you will be leaving the state. Getting farther from home. However, I don't like the idea of you giving up. To quit is the easy way out. Is playing ball still important to you?"

"Yes, it is," said Ty.

"Then go on to this Alabama place. Stay away from drink. Do your best to succeed. You have my blessing. I don't like quitters . . . *don't come home a failure.*"

In one way the Professor was shutting the door to his son's return until results were obtained. In another way he was inspiring his gad-fly heir to go get 'em with everything he had. It was more a demand than a request as Cobb remembered it. Never before had the Professor spoken a positive word about the game. Now he had reversed himself, even if only conditionally. The call took a load off Ty's mind. Father wanted him to keep trying. That was enough.

Thad Hayes, who had gone ahead to Anniston, called Cobb with word that the Steelers could use him in the outfield. A contract was forwarded. Taking a leaf from major-league player signings of the day, protecting the employer from anything including spotted fever contracted by the employee, the Anniston Base Ball Association stipulated:

> Party of the first part agrees to pay the traveling expenses, board and lodging, of said party of the second part . . . and when not so traveling the party of the second part will pay all of his own expenses.
>
> Should the party of the said second part, at any time or times, or in any manner fail to comply with the covenants and agreements herein contained, or should the said party at any time be intemperate, immoral, careless, indifferent or conduct himself in such a manner, whether on or off the field, as to endanger the interest of said party of the first part, or should the second party become ill or otherwise unfit from any cause whatever or prove incompetent in the judgment of the first party, then the party of the first part hereunto shall have the right to discipline, suspend, fine or discharge the party of the second part as it shall deem fit and proper, and the said party of the first part shall be the sole judge as to the sufficiency of the reason for such discipline, suspension, fine or discharge.

Anniston's document rambled on to say that any fine imposed on Cobb would be paid by him or withheld from his salary "as for liquidated damages." Dated April 29, 1904, the contract called for fifty dollars, or exactly what Cobb would have earned at Augusta if that attempt had not been a washout.

He signed the paper "Tyrus R. Cobb," omitting his disliked middle name. One worry was that he would be paying his own living costs when the Steelers were not on the road, a considerable item at the going rate of ten dollars weekly for food and housing. Anniston, far from baseball's mainstream, pulled so little at the gate that bare essentials only were provided. In the Southeastern League to which "Annietown" belonged, players shared one bathtub, one or two baseballs served for entire games no matter how lopsided and black a blur they became, outfields grew weeds, and infields went unrolled. As Cobb figured it, even if he found a cheap boardinghouse, he would be close to broke at season's end.

In his earlier phone talk with Professor Cobb, no mention had been made of further financial help from home should he repeat his failure to stick in a lineup. Anniston was make or break.

After Thad Hayes shuttled back to Augusta to settle his affairs, the two crammed into a single upper berth for the train ride to Anniston, an overnight hop. Doubling up saved money but left them stiff and sore upon reporting on May 2. Cobb carried with him the telescope grip he had brought from Royston, his yellow bats, spare shirts, and a new straw hat, worn at a jaunty tilt. He lacked a decent glove. A replacement glove, costing two dollars, would be stiff and need plenty of rubbing with tobacco juice to become useful.

Anniston, a steel-mill town, was located not far from the iron and steel processing center of Birmingham. From his first few days in northeast Alabama, the smoky haze set Cobb to coughing. Travel was rough. His new team bounced around by horse and buggy to small towns in all weather. Lunch consisted of a bowl of bean soup, with hog jowls and grits often the dinner fare.

The Steelers had several promising collegians, along with a pair of workhorse pitchers who split mound duty from game to game. Cobb soon found he was well up to this caliber of play. He could outrun everybody, had a rifle arm in center field, and hit sizzling one- and two-baggers to all fields. No longer, as a left-handed batsman, was he regularly pulling pitches to his "natural" direction of right field; more and more, when outfields and infields shifted to counter his strength, Cobb opened his stance at the last split second to chop bleeders through third-base gaps and into an unguarded left field. The Cobb-style bunt, destined to become one of the most deadly weapons since Willie Keeler developed the "Baltimore chop" high-bounding infield hit with the 1890s Orioles, took shape when he retracted his bat and punched the ball to a selected spot between the third baseman and pitcher, dead on the baseline and just out of reach.

Another trick he picked up was to bunt for a hit, not as a sacrifice for a teammate on base. In this move he stroked the pitch harder, aiming it to bounce behind a right-handed moundsman's left-sided fall-away on delivery and taking him out of the play, while forcing the second baseman or shortstop to rush in for the throw to first. Making baseball geometry and tactical methods a field of study, Cobb drew upon the advice given him by Wahoo Sam Crawford of Detroit on outfield maneuvers. He often referred to the notebook he kept, filled with Wahoo's tips.

Anniston, after all, was not such a bad training ground. Within weeks Cobb was among the league's top batters with a .350 average and a small clique of fans; the "Cobbies" cheered him from the bleachers. More good fortune came when he met local steel-mill executive and rabid rooter J. B. Darden, who invited the Steelers' lively newcomer to board at his home. Darden would not accept rent, charged nothing for the excellent meals his cook prepared, and even wrangled from the Steelers' owners a pay raise for Cobb to sixty-five dollars a month. Darden's generosity enabled the boy to add five or so pounds to his still spare frame. "You are going a long, long way in baseball," predicted Darden. The thought gave Cobb his biggest lift in months.

At this stage, seeking to regain confidence, he was less impressed with himself than he had been back home with the Royston Reds. Now he took a more balanced view. Maybe he was making so favorable an impression because competition in the semipro Southeastern League was not up to that played in the official minor leagues. At the same time he was smartening up, beginning to see the game calculatingly, comparatively, and more technically.

Publicity was scarce in the deep bushes. Against the Gadsden, Alabama, club, Cobb slid into second base twice for steals, rapped a triple, and drove in the winning runs. For this he drew only a few buried column inches in the Anniston weekly. His performance improved, but his notices did not. In one instance his name was misspelled in an area paper as "Cyrus Cobb."

"I worried about that," he said in a later interview. "I decided that something calling more attention to me was needed." He became busy.

Against Oxford, Alabama, one afternoon he hit for the rare

"cycle"—single, double, triple, and home run in one contest—and was robbed of a second homer. Oxford's left fielder, feigning a catch of a high drive that cleared the fence, jogged in to show the plate umpire—the only umpire on hand—a ball nestled in his glove. The fielder had carried a ball in his hip pocket for just such an occasion. Cobb was not fooled. When the call went against him, he punched the Oxford man, setting off a brawl among players. Trouble spread to the crowd, which piled onto the field. After things cooled, the umpire threw Cobb out.

Cobb went into an act—at least that was how he explained it in later years. He grew profane, shoved the umpire, and spit on the ump's uniform shirt and shoes. With that the Oxford fans renewed the war, attacking Cobb. Police had to be called. While delaying play for nearly an hour, he managed to keep attention focused upon himself. He was fined one day's pay by the league office, made headlines and also history. It was Ty Cobb's first ejection from a game played under organized rules—"one of the best fights I was ever in. People got to know me."

In the Southeastern circuit, three days sometimes went by without a game, offering free time for him to use the Anniston public library to check out Georgia's metropolitan newspapers for any mention of his name. He found nothing. The Associated Press did not carry Anniston results beyond Alabama borders; word of his doings was not reaching anyone who counted in his native state. It was then that, turning volunteer correspondent, he thought up a way to advertise himself with nothing more than pen, paper, and gall. His first target was the *Atlanta Journal*. On a postcard directed to sports editor Grantland Rice, he raved about the abilities of one Ty Cobb, a terrific hitter with the Steelers and a coming star. More colorful accounts went to newspapers in Memphis, New Orleans, and Augusta—especially Augusta, scene of his recent failure. Rice and several other well-read sportswriters fell for the trick and wrote up Cobb in glowing terms.

Luckily for him the Augusta Tourists were playing poor baseball at the time. Their fans were complaining, and the favorable columns and feature stories on Cobb of Anniston were noticed. Augustans remembered the noisy rookie of the past spring who raced around in a flaming-red suit and looked like he might be a hitter. They asked for his recall.

Eventually, Cobb's play decided it. He went on a batting spree, raising his average to .370, best in the Southeastern circuit. He also stole a bunch of bases. On August 5, just short of spending one hundred days in Anniston, he received a telegram from the Augusta Tourists: "WE HAVE ARRANGED YOUR RELEASE STOP REPORT AUGUSTA SOONEST POSSIBLE." The Tourists wanted him back. It was a big break for Cobb, a development for which he had hoped and, indeed, had helped bring about with his fake correspondence—yet he waited to start cheering. The summons was not signed by his nemesis, Con Strouthers, but by Andy Roth. He had not yet formally met Roth, the Tourists' catcher. Augusta's telegram made no mention of Strouthers, a man Cobb despised and had sworn never to play under again. If Roth had moved in as field chief, was Strouthers lurking somewhere in the picture, perhaps in the front office? What would Professor Cobb say if Tyrus was fired for a second time in the same city?

Checking with sources in Augusta, he told them, "I don't want to be burned anymore by that damned Strouthers. I want to be sure he isn't in charge of anything." Informants assured him that Strouthers had resigned and the likable Roth was now in charge.

On August 8 Cobb caught a train back to where he had started, reporting to Warren Park as an exile returned. Little time was left in the season in which to show up well at Class C level, and he had a few reservations about Andy Roth being "his kind" of handler. Taking orders on when to hit away, when to bunt and steal, and where to position himself in the outfield came hard for a naturally spontaneous, hardheaded type who wanted to go by "Don't tell me, I'll tell myself."

His attitude didn't work with the veteran Roth. Stationed in center, right, and left fields from day to day, "second-chance" Cobb mostly played it his way—his inventive way. His hitting against the better pitching in the Sally League was light, and he clashed with the conservative Roth over ways to advance a runner. Roth required base runners to be under control of the first-base coach, via Roth's signals from the dugout, on how big a lead to take off first base, when to play it safe, and when to attempt stealing a base. The same applied at third base, where a coach's hold-or-go order was to be violated only in rare circumstances. This was book baseball, supported by the best thinking in the major leagues.

Cobb was of an opposite opinion—he wanted no beer-bellied traffic cop directing him. Eyesight, timing, and intuition were what counted. Whether he was aware of it or not, he was constructing a foundation for detecting openings and instantly exploiting them, confusing infields. Even if he was thrown out by a yard on a base-advance attempt, he had established the threat that he might go at any moment, especially when the odds were longest against him. Cobb did not mind getting trapped between bases in rundowns. With his reversible speed he was hard to catch. Moreover, solo theatrics singled him out to the crowd.

Customers enjoyed his unpredictable stunting, while Andy Roth burned. After a game in Charleston, South Carolina, in which Cobb twice was thrown out on plays after he overrode Roth's signs, he was publicly bawled out. The manager ran onto the field to cry, "You're fined and benched! This is the last grandstanding you'll do here!"

"We're winning the game on my run, aren't we?" yelled Cobb.

"Be careful, junior, or you'll be catching another train out of town!" threatened Roth.

Rebel Cobb did not play for two days, and when he returned he repeated his ad-lib stealing. Again Roth fined him. This time there was a near fistfight. Intervention was needed from William J. Croke, an Augusta businessman who was in process of buying into the Tourists and assuming the team presidency, to prevent Roth from firing or trading Cobb.

Long after he left Augusta—in quite a different way than by release, trade, or outright discharge—Cobb continued to believe that he had been in the right. Not nearly as experienced as Roth, he saw the catcher even so as a dimwit on strategy and himself as the victim of both ignorance and prejudice. Roth was a redneck, biased against anyone from a "better class" family. Not then or ever did Cobb doubt his intellectual and social superiority over teammates, front office managers, and most club owners.

The 1904 season concluded on an unpromising note. In the short time after he returned from Anniston to Augusta, he had only 32 hits in 37 games, for a .237 average, thirty-third best in the Sally League. Twenty-five of his 32 base blows had been singles; he had been caught stealing almost half of the time, an outcome Andy Roth had foreseen. His fielding had received no significant test. Cobb's guess was that Augusta would not want him back for 1905.

Before the season drew to a close, he proposed to Croke that he be converted into a pitcher—he had always wanted to fill the most commanding position on the field. Teammates, nervous about the wild fastballs that brushed them in practice, suggested that he forget it— with his arm, he would maim or kill somebody. As an outfielder, he had a naturally good distance arm—rubbery and injury resistant.

It was improvement of his batwork that would decide Cobb's future. Left-handers and spitballers tied him in knots. He could not hold back on change-of-speed pitches, pulling himself off-balance with his body ahead of a too-early bat. Lacking coaching to match his talents, the Georgian retreated into a wait-them-out mode at bat, looking for a base on balls or hit-by-pitch, a tactic entirely against his nature. On the favorable side, the few big-time scouts who bothered to look at him ranked him as the fastest runner in the South, and a strange sort of bunter who needed refining. His stealing methods were a laugh.

Bill "Hummingbird" Byron, the funny "singing umpire" of the Sally League, like to recite self-written poems to batters who stood around waiting for a walk. Byron did this even while a batter was in the box. He embarrassed Cobb with:

You'll never hit the bowler
With the bat on your shoulder.

And:

Only hope for runt
Is take one and bunt.

Cobb told Byron to go to hell. The ditty he hated most went:

Stick the bat up your ass
If you can't show us class.

Cobb didn't need Byron or anyone else to tell him he had rushed things by several years, that a kid with his bones and muscles still forming lacked the strength to stand out against matured men. Whatever he accomplished would be a while in coming. It was possible that Cobb at seventeen was the youngest regular player in organized baseball in the southern United States, and maybe beyond that.

In the event that he could not improve in ability, and to please Professor Cobb, as well as with the intent of broadening himself, he corresponded that winter with Oglethorpe College, the University of Georgia, and Middle Georgia Military, among nearby schools. "Only one I missed was Decatur Female Seminary," he later joked, in one of his rare light moments. "I saw that the game I was in paid damned little . . . and management owned you one hundred percent, could fire you at any moment . . . that the smart people on top had all the power. Getting an education was the only way I could be independent, have some real value, like a surgeon or scientist or lawyer."

He was back in Royston by September, with something else on his mind. He had taken a fancy to a Royston girl during his playing days with the Royston Reds. They had corresponded after he left town and the affair seemed serious. She was from a family as prominent as the Cobbs. He had taken her "walking out" to indicate his intentions. She had written that her parents were far from sold on the idea of her marrying a professional ballplayer.

It was one more reason to leave the ballparks, to enroll at a university. His secondary-school grades in the serious subjects had been only fair, but his father, as a county supervisor of education, had many friends in the academic community. The idea of trying for West Point came up again. This time Cobb listened seriously.

CHAPTER FIVE

FOR SALE,
ONE REBEL KID,
$25

He grew whiskers and began shaving on a daily basis for the first time in 1904. His lasting impression of the season was that Andy Roth stood as an unmovable obstacle who hoped that firebrand Cobb would quit. A further discouragement was club ownership—Augustans who counted their profits and did nothing to end dissension in the ranks.

That winter, Professor Cobb had a gift that helped raise Ty's spirits—a gaited black saddle horse. His grandfather, Squire Cobb, had given him his first game-skinning knife and rifle, and it was another happy day when his father presented him with his first mount. He called the horse "Blackie." Cobb explained the name with "He was as dark as an Alabama nigger in a coal mine."

The use of the ritual scurrility of "nigger" or "nigra" was employed in public by Cobb throughout his life. In his later years, even when black stars Jackie Robinson, Satchel Paige, and Larry Doby finally were admitted to the hitherto segregated major leagues after World War II, his attitude did not change; blacks did not belong on pro ball fields any more than in the white man's parlor. Speaking to friends in private, he regularly dropped "coon," "smoke," "Sambo," and "shine" into his discourse. By inheritance, communality, and disposition, Cobb was a fixed racial bigot.

Andy Roth, a tough customer in a fight, was much on Cobb's mind that winter. A showdown with the manager was coming if Augusta renewed his contract, and if he did not pass it all up to become a doctor or an Army officer. Asked in Royston about his plans, Cobb made no allowance that Roth might have reason to object to his wildcatting on the bases. "Just wait," he confided to his former hometown coach, Bob McCreary, "I'll put Roth in the ditch." McCreary, in a scrapbook he kept over the years on "my boy," entered, "There will be no changing of his mind on this." When you made an enemy of Ty Cobb, McCreary knew, he did not forget.

Whichever way the career decision might go, Cobb stayed in shape. Two years earlier he had been so spindly that his hip pockets ran together; now his hindquarters were athletically rounded, his chest stuck out, and his neck was thickening. He had grown to middleweight size so quickly that his clothes needed refitting. Almost every day, in any weather, he ran along Royston roads at jogging speed for a few dozen strides, sprinted for a time, returned to a jog, and resumed sprinting, continuing the pattern for five to six miles. Local admirers, doing roadwork with him, were told, "If it turns out to be college for me, I want to give football a try."

Friends argued against it. That October several regional sportswriters quoted a scout from the New York Highlanders (later Yankees): "I kind of like this country boy. He's all flying arms and legs . . . but worth watching if he calms down." The scout was not talking about the major leagues, but only of possible promotion to a higher minor organization.

Working against Cobb's chances were his cockiness, bullheadedness, and utter lack of humility. Professor Cobb again put him to mucking out stables and sowing winter wheat on the farm. W. H. was surprised to hear that Ty had saved $150 from his small earnings at Anniston and with the Tourists; he congratulated Ty for not misbehaving in the city. But the elder Cobb still wanted his son out of baseball. Much underpaid, traded around like cattle, given no security, ballplayers were not respectable people. A Cincinnati newspaper headlined one report, evidently because it concerned a team doing something unique, "BALLPLAYERS GO TO CHURCH, LISTEN TO SERMON." In West

Virginia, one Jim Carrigan was called out sliding into home plate; he went home, got a shotgun, returned, and killed the umpire. According to Cobb in later years, his father read the report's postscript to Ty: "*A new umpire was substituted and the game went on, Carrigan taking part in it.*" Only a few seasons earlier in Lowndesboro, Alabama, umpire Sam White's skull had been fatally crushed by a bat-wielding player.

This was not sport, but work of the devil, said W. H. Ty had been hearing of sin since he was a child, and he had to admit that in Augusta things got rough. He had watched men go directly from the park to bars, returning next day in no shape to play. No curfew existed on Roth's loosely controlled "joy club." Some Tourists secretly laid bets on their games. Most of the boys spit tobacco, went unshaven—looking tough was the ideal. Warren Park was not a place to bring a lady. It was an Augusta joke that the Tourists could outdo a mink for screwing, Cobb said in later years.

He could only put up the defense that a good many of the Tourists, himself included, could regularly be found at church on Sunday. Some did not drink at all.

In a place like Royston, it was perhaps to be expected that the girl he had been courting broke off their marriage plans. Her father, for reasons close to W. H.'s objections to Ty's would-be career, told Cobb not to come around his home anymore. Ty Cobb's instructions in dictating his autobiography to me in 1960 were to omit any mention of the girl, "Kate," and this was done. "She quit me," he wrote in his notes. He reminisced sourly on this failure. "It was her hard luck," he said. "Kate could have lived high on the hog as my wife. I never saw her again . . . after a while I didn't give a cow turd." Cobb would not marry until four years later, in 1908, by which time he was American League batting champion.

For the next several years, many of the women he met were the ready pickups who hung around ballparks. Or so he claimed. "They were pushovers after a few beers," Cobb put it. Visiting odd bedrooms, he indicated, was not below him. His sex drive now became a steady goad.

On December 18 he celebrated his eighteenth birthday, then made what would later prove to be a wise move. For several months he went to work in the sheds of a cotton factor at Carnesville, Georgia, the same agent who had formerly employed him as a fifteen-year-old bale sorter. This time Cobb was inside the industry to learn more. Within seven years of that date, while playing for Detroit, he would spend time at the local cotton-trading exchange, using his knowledge to buy premium-grade shares in small, then gradually larger amounts. With World War I approaching, he figured correctly that huge amounts of the fiber would be consumed for uniforms. After the war, with cotton short, he would clean up roughly $150,000 on the investment, the first really important money he had seen to that point.

COBB HOPED to hear from the Augusta Tourists that spring, but he did not. He traveled to Augusta, visited Warren Park, and found the place empty. No one was there to update him on what was happening with the club. A month or so later he was relieved to receive a letter from Andy Roth. Roth sounded as if they remained friendly. Was Ty returning for the 1905 season? asked Roth.

Cobb was much relieved to hear from the Tourists' management but did not let on. Instead, he replied that a raise to $125 monthly from the previous $65 would suit him. Roth was shocked—$125 was out of the question for someone who had played in but thirty-seven pro games. Top pay for Augusta's veterans was $250 a month. Cobb answered that he might do better by staying out for a year and then asking for a sale or trade elsewhere. Or he might go to college, as his family wished. He interpreted it as a good sign that Roth had opened the negotiation, not the reverse.

As a bargainer Cobb still had much to learn, but he felt he was smartening up on how to "work" a front office. The key component was to appear to be unconcerned.

Roth stood firm on $65, maybe $75. Ty replied that he wanted to talk to President Bill Croke of the Tourists. Cobb repeated to Roth's boss that southern colleges would be pleased to enroll him. His extreme youth probably influenced Croke's decision; the school threat might not have been believed from a twenty-five-year-old. Croke, thinking of Cobb's age, foot speed, crowd-pleasing steals, room to develop, and the casual interest already shown in him by higher-league scouts, which might lead to a sale or trade upward, settled for between $90 and $125 (Cobb always insisted that he got $125 from Croke; other sources placed it lower). It wasn't bad income, in the day of the dollar steak dinner and seventeen-dollar suit of clothes. The settlement also put Roth in his place.

On a later spring day in Augusta Ty was pedaling his bicycle down the city's Broad Street when a rogue horse knocked him down. The wrist of his right, throwing arm was sprained. In a fury, Ty kicked the horse. The buggy driver jumped down to exchange words and a cop broke up their scuffle. No arrests were made, but word got around that the Tourists' hot-tempered left fielder had kicked an animal, and the story reached Roth. "About what you'd expect from Cobb," Roth reportedly said. "He's trouble and a yard wide."

ON MARCH 30, 1905, with his wrist still bandaged, Ty reported to camp for what would become seven months of humiliation, retaliation, improvement, and, finally, tragedy that would rock him to his depths. Hardened as he was becoming, 1905 was almost more than the former rookie could bear.

The season started normally. Detroit's Tigers were again training in Augusta, hoping to live down their seventh-place American League finish of the past pennant race. Somehow the big-leaguers did not seem as big and intimidating to Cobb this time around. On hand with Detroit—everyone seemed to have a nickname—were Twilight Ed Killian, Germany Schaefer, Wild Bill Donovan, Frosty Thomas, Nig Clarke, Sir Richard Cooley, Link Lowe, Pinky Lindsay, and Wahoo Sam Crawford, the dazzling outfielder who had instructed Ty on outfield play the previous spring.

Some of the Tigers recalled seeing "that little monkey in the red suit" who was trying out with Augusta in 1904, who had caused horse-laughs with his headlong dives after foul balls and swings and misses at easy practice pitching. Frank J. Navin, the former bookkeeper and financial consultant of the Tigers who had acquired part ownership of the Detroit franchise, was advised by his second baseman, Germany Schaefer, "Wait until you see this baby. He's a scream. Acts like his pants are on fire even in workouts. Wants to steal every base. He can't hit Molly Poop." (Molly Poop being a mythical figure symbolizing terrible batting ability.)

Navin, taking a look, did not laugh. The first thing he noticed was Cobb dashing onto the field at game time when others walked, and making outfield grabs by cutting across other fielders' private territory.

"He's raw," said Navin, "but one of the fastest out of the box I've seen outside the majors."

In a pair of exhibitions between the Tigers and Tourists, racehorse Cobb partially refuted Schaefer with a single off Detroit's ace, Bill Donovan, and by stealing two bases. Class C performers were not supposed to do that. He followed with a one-bagger off Jesse Stovall's fastball and was effective against a classy flutterball pitching prospect, Eddie "Knuckles" Cicotte, who would go on to win 90 games over four consecutive seasons with the Chicago White Sox and in 1920 become one of eight "Black Sox" who were banned for life for fixing the World Series. Against Cicotte's stuff, Ty delivered a triple and single. He tipped his hat to the Detroit bench. The Tigers held their noses in reply.

When the season opened, Andy Roth mostly played him in left field, although Cobb preferred center field for its wider range of chances. He complained about it. Roth said, "Well, you can always sit on the bench." Ty let it pass and bore down harder at the plate. Improvement was tediously slow. With a batting average of under .260 in the early weeks, he stranded too many base runners. Roth constantly rode him. Expert observers, however, could see signs here and there that the Rooster—his latest nickname—would not remain what he still appeared to be: a below-standard run producer.

As a base runner Cobb used psychology that startled. In one case, with two Tourists out in the ninth inning and a 1–0 game to Macon seemingly lost, Cobb was the runner on first base. He took off for second with no chance of making it safely. The second baseman stood waiting with the catcher's throw in hand for a sure putout. Ty stopped ten feet short of the base, dropped his head, and called to the second baseman, "Ah, the hell with it . . . it's too hot today to keep running. You got me—I'm out." He slowly limped back toward first base as if conceding a game-ending putout and heading for the dugout. Macon's fielder went for it. Since Cobb had quit on the play and it was so hot, why bother going after him for the formal tag?

With the fielder lulled, Ty suddenly burst into a sprint, forcing the baseman to hastily snap-throw to first base, a throw that sailed wildly to the boards. While the Macons chased the ball, Ty raced to third base, from where he later scored to make it 1–1. In extra innings, Augusta won, 2–1.

Planting disinformation, faking out the defense with inventive moves, was something he did well. One of his giddiest stunts was to arrange for the baseball to disappear from sight in broad daylight. It began, he recalled, with an Augusta fan who ran a barbershop where Ty had his hair trimmed. Cobb explained to me how the trick worked: "This barber sat down close to the rail at our games, yelling a lot. You could hear his big mouth on the field. I invited him to help out. Told him that if he ever saw me sliding back into first base on a pickoff play he was to wait a few seconds, then yell that the ball went into our bullpen. He asked why should he do that and I told him never mind, just damned well do it."

On the day when the barber let out his prearranged yell, Cobb had taken a normal lead off first base. On a pickoff attempt he dived back. He and the throw arrived at the same time, Cobb having timed it so that the ball hit his hip. In a cloud of dirt he rolled atop the ball. Spinning around, the first baseman couldn't locate the ball—Cobb had tucked it into his baggy shirt like a magician with a canary. Right on cue, the barber roared, "IT'S GONE THROUGH—INTO THE BULLPEN!" While two basemen and the right fielder frantically ran in that direction, Ty raced to second base. While the search went on, he continued to third, where, partly concealed by more flying dirt, he slipped the ball out of sight under the loosely fitted canvas bag. Then he completed the circuit from first to home plate to score. As he had figured it, all eyes were on the desperate hunt for a lost ball. "The umpire, after a long argument involving everybody, ruled me safe," a grinning Cobb ended the story. "Wrong call, of course. No ball was in play, they couldn't find it anywhere. I'd told our batboy before the game to be ready . . . He sneaked out during the big fuss at the plate, bent to tie his shoe, and removed the ball from under third base and made off with it."

Of a variety of maneuvers whereby he duped opponents through some villainy or other, the Case of the Vanished Horsehide was his favorite. It was only small-town byplay, but an artist later diagramed it in the nationally circulated *Sporting Life*. It was an example of how Cobb, just learning his trade, thought ahead, created unusual predicaments, and, with the barber's help, invoked the power of suggestion.

With the Tourists he also experimented with turning his back on the pitcher as he wound up, addressing the catcher—"Hey, blubber belly!"—and now and then disconcerting the catcher into a passed ball. Or he would limp around when on base with a faked injury, call for the trainer, and after the defense was relaxed streak to the next sack. With umpires, he used the tactic of complimenting them on their keen eyesight and good work, until on a close strike-or-ball decision they would unconsciously favor Cobb. When catchers screamed "Robbery!" Cobb would back up the ump with: "You should run this mug out of here. You're calling a good game." In his mature years the Georgia Peach made a broad analogy: "If you're in a saloon and somebody punches the bartender, who gets free drinks for the next month? Why, the guy who flattens the guy who hit the bartender."

Craftiness was useful, but it was not until he began to hit regularly that his Augusta fans grew in number. By late June of the season he had climbed to a .315 average, then to .320, second best among the Tourists. He had not curtailed his unauthorized base stealing, however, despite Andy Roth's complaints, and Roth gave him clubhouse blasts he would never forgive. Their differences came to the flash point over an incident featuring a cat and a bag of popcorn. Bored with a dull game, Cobb let loose on the field an "unlucky" black cat, who dug a hole back of third base and relieved himself. Time-out had to be called until the cat had finished covering up his stool.

"What SOB did that?" cried Roth.

"Cobb paid a groundskeeper to do it," said several voices at once.

Cobb didn't lie. He just shrugged.

"Five-buck fine!" ruled Roth. "Do anything like that again and you're out of the lineup."

Within days, before a game with Savannah, the boy misbehaved again. He bought a nickel bag of popcorn, carried it into the outfield, and was munching away when a tall fly ball was lifted to his left. Struggling not to spill the popcorn while making the putout, he failed both ways: the ball hit the bag, sprayed popcorn, and he missed the catch.

The unprecedented error caused one run to score on pitcher Eddie Cicotte, who had a shutout game going (Cicotte had been loaned to Augusta for the season, and would move up to join the Tigers before season's end). Some twenty-five hundred fans saw it as funny. Cobb had to kick white kernels out of his way while finishing the inning. At the bench, Cicotte swung a punch at him. Cobb went down, got up, and they banged each other around. Nobody broke up the fight, which ended in a draw. Blood was spilled.

Roth, who had been waiting for such an opening, responded by summoning Cobb to his office to say, "You're gone. We've sold your contract to Charleston." Roth was in the process of being replaced as manager, so technically was exceeding his rights in so announcing.

"I'm hitting third highest in the league!" Cobb came back. "How can you do that?"

"Because Cicotte won't play with you in the lineup. Others feel the same way," Roth said. That made it twice that he had been rejected in Augusta.

Cobb told off the manager. The next day several Tourists' officials, led by President Bill Croke, met with the demoralized outfielder at his hotel as a peacemaking delegation. As Cobb told the story years afterward, Croke said, "Roth had no right to deal for you. Let's talk it over."

"Why sell me to Charleston?" Cobb asked. "That's a bad club."

"It's worse than that," admitted Croke. "Roth was offered twenty-five dollars for you and he took it."

The "Peanut-sale" story, which Cobb always vouched was true, became part of the lore surrounding his early years.

Cobb blew his top. Only six hitters in the Sally League surpassed his overall statistics after fifty-odd season games. He was among the leading base stealers in the South and was helping to sell tickets. Croke calmed him down and Cobb returned, uneasily, to the outfield. Augustans never knew of the twenty-five-dollar price tag. Had the Charleston transfer gone through, evaluating Cobb at the price of a mule, he would have quit and gone home. "My bags were all but packed," he remembered.

That incident, and the unconcealed hostility toward him by other Tourists, caused the youngster to go at his job in withdrawn silence, avoiding off-field contact with teammates. Away from the park he hung out in nickelodeons, and filled time by taking long walks along the Savannah River's banks, fishing the stream, and by reading biographies of Stonewall Jackson, Alexander the Great, and Napoleon. His keenest interest was in Bonaparte, the tactician with an outstanding ability to survive. He read some philosophers. "On a team that played around plenty," observed George Napoleon "Nap" Rucker, his roommate for a brief period, "Cobb was a loner by his own choice."

Rucker broke off their association after a clash over use of a bathtub. In the early low minor leagues it was the standard thing for players to dress in uniforms at their boardinghouse or hotel quarters, rather than at the park, and undress back home after games. The facilities at the Tourists' park offered only sponges and cold water. When on the road it was Cobb's routine to beat Rucker to their room in order to take the first hot bath. One evening that schedule was reversed, and when Cobb hurried home he found Rucker pleasurably soaking in their hotel tub. Cobb cried, "What are you doing there?" Replied Rucker, "What do you think?" Grabbing the pitcher by his shoulders, Cobb tried to wrestle his slippery body from the tub. Rucker resisted. Water and soapsuds spilled. "You gone crazy?" yelled Rucker. Cobb stared at him—"with the wildest eyes I ever saw in a human," claimed Rucker later—and wound up as if to strike him. Rucker faced a man trembling with rage.

"You don't understand!" Cobb gritted. *"I've got to be first at everything—all the time!"*

The amiable left-handed pitcher from Crabapple, Georgia, who would reach the big leagues with Brooklyn in 1907 and win 134 games in his time, found himself another roommate.

Cobb always denied the tub story, but Rucker had a witness who had walked in toward the end of the encounter. It was one more signal to the Tourists that Cobb wasn't "normal" and could be dangerous if provoked, even in a small way. "He was a strange bird, the whole ball club knew it," said Rucker. "Say something to him and he was likely to give you a dirty look."

At Warren Park Cobb hung his clothes on a clubhouse peg apart from the others, replied curtly to questions, and was not a catalyst for team rallies. Given the hit-and-run sign while on first base, he might or might not accept it. When signaled by Roth to move left, right, or deeper in the outfield, he would shake off the order to stay in the place he preferred. His season's error total crept up until it reached 13, for a low .927 fielding average. Yet Cobb was Augusta's best clutch hitter. Without his ability to place balls through infield holes for singles and doubles, the Tourists would stand worse than fourth place in the league.

According to Rucker's recollection, Cobb easily led the league in bench-jockeying. Most such jeering was done merely to annoy and distract. Cobb pushed it to the point of field fights. Calling a bald opponent "skinhead" was a warm-up for him. If someone had an arrest record, he would hear "jailbird!" or "leg-irons." An ugly man was "pig-face" or "ratface." The Royston Rooster learned in advance of a player's weakness, and in a high screech made sure the crowd knew of it.

Jacksonville, Florida, had a pitcher, Lefty Betts, who was proud of his control and sinkerball. With Cobb at bat, Betts was set to deliver when he heard the yell, "Give me your Lady Godiva!" It came from Cobb.

"My what?" asked Betts.

"Your Lady Godiva!" barked Cobb. "A sinker that's got nothing on it!"

Betts let go his best beanball. Cobb ducked. On the next pitch—a sinkerball that he knew positively would follow—he drilled a double into center field to beat Jacksonville, 3–1.

On the field he was a questionable asset, off it a loner; how could anyone figure such an odd character? On road trips where rail service was undependable, the Tourists sometimes resorted to horse-and-buggy transport. Horsepower was needed after they played league games as visitors in a Sally League park, then moved on to nonleague "hick-towner" games against rural teams miles away from a train line. In such traveling, ballplayers grew hungry and raided orchards of fruit and gardens of vegetables. When it rained, the Tourists put up crude gunnysacking and canvas until things cleared and they could resume their jolting ride along dirt roads to communities spread about Georgia, Tennessee, South Carolina, and Florida. Cobb's shelter was always pitched well away from those of his teammates. Arriving at their destination, he would find a boardinghouse not being used by other Tourists.

Across the Southeast the breach between Cobb and his teammates became a topic of conversation among baseball men. One day in midseason, a businessman named Charles D. Carr, who was about to join Bill Croke as a major stockholder of the Tourists franchise, called Cobb aside, put a friendly hand on his shoulder, and asked, "What's the real problem, Ty, behind all this dissension?"

Cobb stared at Carr and replied, "Nothing, except that most of your boys and Roth are sons of bitches." He walked away.

SHOTGUN BLASTS

S o it went for him, a rebel in the ranks, through his first full season. Heavy June rains hit the Sally League. Cobb caught a cold he couldn't shake and played mechanically, without zip. Then, in midsummer, George Leidy came into the picture. "He made all the difference in the world to me," remembered Cobb.

Nearing forty, Leidy, a good-natured, softspoken veteran of the southern-southwestern U.S. minor leagues, played in the Augusta outfield next door to Cobb, and believed that the fractious rookie was a fine talent in the making. In midseason Leidy was named manager of the Tourists, replacing Andy Roth. With Roth gone, Ty was open to suggestions, and Leidy began a course of instruction. Initially it amounted to a suggestion here and there; since Cobb was listening, Leidy broadened the lessons. He was equipped to do an expert job; he was a former Class AA star and had done some big-league scouting. Articulate, perceptive, Dad Leidy was known to have a touch for identifying raw prospects who might move up the ladder.

Stationed next to him on the field, Leidy noted Cobb's weaknesses, including a growing taste for hard drink. Branching out socially, he had joined a group of college-age sports from well-off Augusta families who hit the bottle, bet on horse races, and dallied with girls from Broad Street bars. Leidy saw him reporting to work hung over from partying. When I acted as Cobb's collaborator in the early 1960s, he often thought back to that time: "I was losing my ambition to go higher and knew it. Well, hell, I didn't know what I was doing." And: "Just a half-smart kid against that bastard Roth and his team."

Soon after taking charge of the Tourists, Leidy invited Ty to take a trolley ride with him to a nearby amusement park. He had noticed that Cobb's mind worked faster than others', that he thought ahead of the inning at hand. He had been held back by Con Strouthers, Roth, and his own ungoverned temper. The two sat on a park bench for the first of what would become a series of talks. Realizing that it would be useless to criticize him, Leidy worked on his imagination. Cobb always afterward credited his new boss as "changing my life one hundred percent."

The older man did all the talking. Ty listened, and remembered Leidy saying, "Augusta is nothing. In New York, Boston, Chicago, Detroit, and other cities they have ballparks that would swallow several the size of the one we play in. They wouldn't open the gates for our kind of draw. You've heard of the Polo Grounds and the huge new one they're planning in Chicago, Comiskey Park? Will seat fifty thousand. Up there the big-time arenas are like the ones the Romans used for sports shows. You sure should see them." Leidy told how teams rode in private railway cars with special food, stayed at the best hotels. As for being well known, U.S. presidents shook the hands of the top players. Newspapers played them up in bannerlines and photo spreads.

The old-timer caught Ty's full attention when he mentioned that baseball was verging on becoming big business, that six- and seven-thousand-dollar salaries for stars were around the corner. Ty's annual contract was for just over six hundred dollars.

Nobody reached the majors, said Leidy, without long, hard preparation. The National League's marvelous Honus Wagner of Pittsburgh had been an ordinary infielder until he built himself a trench around shortstop, dug in, practiced endlessly on bad-hop grounders in bare feet, and became the very best at his position. Christy "Big Six" Mathewson had gone, through discipline and application, from a poor-control pitcher to a strikeout king, winner of 33 games in 1904 for the

New York Giants. Other cases were related, such as that of the New York Highlanders' Willie Keeler, a small man who worked at hitting until his hands bled.

In successive weeks Leidy built incentive. He came to the point with: "You don't know what you've got. It's my belief that in a year or two, no more, you can be up there making ten times the money you're getting now. For one thing, you have faster reactions and more break-away speed than almost anyone I've seen and I've seen the best of them. I'm sure you can become a better hitter than ninety-nine percent of the big boys. But it won't happen if you don't straighten up. Stop breaking training. Stay sober. Apply yourself every minute. You're not playing ball, you're playing *at* it."

So Cobb always told the Leidy story, his favorite piece of autobiography. As dime-novelish as it sounded, he insisted that every word of it was true. Cobb became sold on growing up and becoming a success when Dad Leidy had put a hand on his shoulder and "with tears in his eyes" promised him, "You can go down in the history books, have every lad in America idolizing you." And maybe the story was mainly true, at that. When he spoke of meetings between himself and Leidy in future years—"emotional, a wonderful shared feeling between us"—Cobb was being truthful.

Persuasion led to extra batting practice by the hour. When the Tourists were idle, Leidy pitched Ty curves, knucklers, balls in on the fists and low and away, change-ups, chin-grazers, and "lightning" (a term then used for fastballs). He broke down Cobb's erratic batting form, restructuring his cut at the ball. The veteran preached against overstriding, a Cobb habit, and converted him to a controlled, six-inch strider from all three stances: open, straightaway, and closed. Leidy gave him a "quiet head," with no more bobbing of the skull, shoulders, and hips, which translated into a smooth, level arc of the bat. They worked on grip. As a youth Ty had experimented with the hands-apart choke hold, but then switched to a big, free swing, providing power but inevitably a string of strikeouts. "Forget home runs," Leidy advised. "Move your hands up and spread them a few inches." (Cobb habitually choked the bat for most of the rest of his days.) A nervous hand-hitch between the time the pitch was released and reached the plate was corrected.

Leidy was destiny in a dirty sweatshirt—cussing, berating,

demanding improvement. He made Ty feel foolish by tying a rope around his waist and having an assistant coach jerk him onto his rump when he lunged at a pitch outside the strike zone. Cobb hated to be dumped, but he took it. Leidy drove a tall stake in the ground, put a ball atop it, and had his pupil cleanly slice it off, a forerunner of modern batting-tee practice. Since nobody had corrected it, Cobb was a guesser at what kind of pitch was coming. "Guess hitters don't get out of Cowturd, Iowa," lectured Leidy. "Get deep in the box, take a longer look at the spin, be ready for anything."

The ambidextrous Leidy pitched to him only left-handed, since lefties were Cobb's most pronounced weakness. Patiently, Leidy went on to show how, with the front shoulder pointed at the pitcher, it should remain there until the last split second, a delayed action enabling Ty to connect with late-breaking curves and outside pitches. Cobb had big paws—hands and wrists. The coach acted out in slow motion how to employ another source of power, the sharp snapping of the wrists upon contact with the ball.

Daily, until the Augusta field was dark, Leidy tutored him on the quick hip pivot, on following through on his swing, on hit-and-run technique, on how to duck a beanball by collapsing straight down instead of falling back or forward. Some of the classes were held in the early mornings. Too tired after long sessions to join his downtown college gang, Ty began sleeping organized hours. He had no idea of diet. George Leidy did. Alcohol was out "ninety-nine percent of the time" by Cobb's estimate.

In San Francisco some thirty years later a noted teacher named Frank "Lefty" O'Doul would employ much the same methods on a rookie named Joe DiMaggio. "Did O'Doul use the rope trick on you, too?" Cobb once asked DiMag. "And twice on Sunday," said Joe.

Up to now Ty had been mostly a one-way slider into bases—headfirst. "Unless you like eating dirt, give it up," ordered Leidy. "Basemen coming down on your neck with spikes ain't good. And you could dislocate a shoulder." They borrowed an old base bag from the groundskeeper, spaded up the soil in a corner of Warren Park, and set the bag at one end of a runway. On early mornings Ty practiced all the known slides: hook left, hook right, bent leg, rolling, sitting-standing, sliding past the bag and reaching back to tag it, sliding to break up the double play, plus a few he invented—such as sticking sharpened spikes into legs, arms, and bellies at twenty miles an hour when basemen obstructed him. After games, he slid fifty or more times, or until his hips were raw. Sometimes Cobb came into the clubhouse with blood staining his pants.

In July, still attending Leidy's free clinic, he wrote home to Professor Cobb, "Had two doubles and singles vs. star Alabama team. Stole two. Making good progress." Friends had tipped him that his father, no longer quite obsessed with the idea that his son should come to his senses and find honest employment, had been showing newspaper clippings about the youngster's feats to friends.

W. H. Cobb now understood what "AB," "DP," "H," and "R" meant in a box score, according to what Ty now heard. After 130-odd pro games over parts of two seasons in a dozen southern towns and cities where his roaming heir had appeared, the Professor had yet to attend a single contest. But he seemed to be softening. W. H. remained a strong political presence in Georgia legislative and educational circles. To have the Cobb name published in columns of the *Atlanta Journal* or *Augusta Chronicle,* even when Ty went 0 for 5 or the teams brawled on the field, was not the public shame that W. H. had feared. To the contrary, an Augusta victory brought slaps on W. H.'s back in conference rooms. Baseball was becoming very popular in Georgia. In a notebook Ty kept, he pensively wrote, "I hope Father comes out to see me play some day."

Dad Leidy was inspired to rebuild Ty both because it was his nature and because he felt sure that he had lucked into an important find, requiring only two or three more seasons of training on fundamentals and one or two of polishing. All that was needed was time. In the outfield, where Cobb too often was apt to turn a fly ball into a three-base error, Leidy hit him fifty balls almost daily. In an attempt at humor, a local sport journal wrote, "By the million they knock flies to his left, his right and short of him. And—hooray!—he catches many of them. The hardest of all is the fly hit directly at him and sinking. Oh, what trouble! But Ty Cobb—whoops!—falls on his face without the pill in his trap less often than before. In 10 years he might become expert."

In a lasting way, Leidy built within Ty the confidence that comes with fine timing at bat. A repertoire of slides came second in importance. The teacher did not work on Cobb's violent temper, however;

form and mechanics were all that any one man could deal with where a player as combative as Cobb was concerned.

Andy Roth, deposed as manager but still a team member, one day joked about Ty's efforts to improve. "Are you Leidy's trained monkey?" asked Roth. "He whistles and you run."

"Go to hell," said Cobb.

"Put your mitts where your mouth is," challenged the husky catcher.

How about right now?" said Cobb. He was a forty-pound underdog in weight, he remembered, but had been spoiling to even matters with Roth.

Their fight was anything goes. Feelings had festered so long that the Tourist players saw no reason to break it up. Cobb went berserk, punching anywhere he could reach Roth, from jaw to crotch. Roth applied a choke hold and was cutting off his wind until Ty bit Roth's ear and wrenched on it like a bulldog. Blood was lost by both. Roth tore loose to batter Cobb's eye, closing it. He head-butted Cobb to the ground. Cobb kicked Roth while he was down and a moment later had Roth on his back. It went on to a no-decision when some of the Tourists finally intervened.

Each was helped away, exhausted and needing bandaging. Cobb ranked this one as among the dozen or so dirtiest brawls he ever engaged in. It effectively eliminated Roth as a leading team factor—he was laid up for several days—while reinforcing Leidy's influence. Cobb, after all, hadn't been the favorite.

On the buggy ride home, Leidy said, "You made a dumb move. Roth had all the pull in size."

"Didn't bother me," said Cobb flatly. "If it had gone against me, I'd have gotten him with a bat."

Although the Tourists lost fifteen of the next twenty games in July, an improved Cobb stood out afield and at the plate. For some reason he had stopped using the bunt. On an off day, Leidy took him to Atlanta to watch a new pitching "marvel" named Happy Harry Hale. A six-foot, six-inch stringbean from Happy Hollow, Tennessee, Hale threw shutout balls for four innings. "Now watch what happens," predicted Leidy. What the other side then did was to bunt, bunt, bunt. Happy Harry looked silly trying to field the well-placed taps. He spiked his own hand, fell down twice, had to be removed.

Cobb only had to be shown once. Beginning then, he practiced bunting to an old sweater laid down forty feet away. When he could accurately stop a straight bunt on or near the sweater, he moved to other types—the squeeze, drag, sacrifice, the backspin bunt. Before very long Cobb and that bastardized base hit, the bunt, would be as synonymous as Lewis and Clark, Pat and Mike.

UP NORTH the Detroit Tigers had heard gossip about what Leidy was accomplishing with his speedy pupil, and they sent scout Heinie Youngman to take a look. It was highly improbable that a Class C new-comer could be of any use to the Tigers. Yet something moved Detroit manager Bill Armour to learn more. Youngman found "bird dogs" from the fast American Association and International League already present in Augusta. Youngman saw an ideally shaped ballplayer, long in the leg, lean, heavily muscled in places where it counted—the thighs, arms, and shoulder girdle—with pale, glittering eyes that met your gaze head-on. His southland drawl was prominent. Heinie Youngman said, "I'd like to ask you some personal questions." Perversely, Cobb answered, "Yuh cain if yoh don't mind that ah might not answer 'em."

According to Youngman, he informed Bill Armour in Detroit, "That was strike one on him. Here I was giving a kid down in the sticks a chance to be noticed and he's telling me that maybe, or maybe not, he'll talk." Youngman was not the first to encounter Cobb's exasperating temperament, but he was first to testify to it for the history books.

Cobb gave brief answers to inquiries, implying that he did not discuss his private life with strangers. About all that he would say was that he was a native Georgian who didn't drink whiskey, would be nineteen in December, farmed in the winter, was unmarried, and had a high school education, with college a strong possibility. Asked about his father, he opened up a bit to brag, "He teaches and preaches and helps make laws. Ah would say he's the best-known man in Franklin County, Georgia." Ty was noncommittal about his mother. "She cooks," he said shortly.

Youngman gave up and watched him beat Columbia's Spartans with a diving, tumbling catch and a pair of clutch hits, and came away impressed despite himself. He told the Tigers that just maybe, in a pinch, Cobb might be useful.

By early August, hundred-degree heat blanketed Augusta. Players dunked their heads in buckets of shaved ice. Many slumped. Cobb seemed immune. In midmonth, against Macon, Georgia, he hit a single. Macon's first baseman grinned at him. "I hear you're going up."

"Up where?" asked Ty, not understanding.

"To the big time—Cleveland or Detroit."

"Don't fun me," said Cobb, thinking it a joke.

"No joke," said the baseman. "It's supposed to be true."

Years later, at a Hall of Fame affair, Cobb confirmed the story: "It hadn't crossed my mind that any club that high up was interested in me. The Augusta owners hadn't said anything about it. Just before I talked to Youngman and some other scouts, I'd jammed my thumb sliding . . . it was swollen up, and hurt like hell. So it went right past me when the rumor started."

Although he lacked the sophistication and perception to understand what was going on around him, he stayed in the news. He ran his base steals to a league-leading 40 and was hitting at a .320 figure, also near the Sally League top. Leidy's weeks of schooling had made a difference in most departments.

ON THE night of August 8, Cobb attended a barn dance until a late hour, and slept in next day. About 10:00 A.M. the following morning a messenger boy handed Ty a telegram—from Royston. It was signed by longtime friend Joe Cunningham, the schoolmate he once had made bats with out of leftover lumber. Joe's words leaped out, leaving him stunned:

COME AT ONCE STOP VERY SORRY STOP YOUR FATHER DEAD IN SHOOTING ACCIDENT STOP HURRY.

To Cobb's best recall, everything after that was a blur. He was dazed, speechless. When he could speak he phoned Cunningham. Everything in his hometown was in confusion. Cunningham cried, "The Professor's been shot! . . . We don't know how it happened . . . looks like someone got him with a shotgun . . . God, Ty, he's dead!"

Others came on the phone. In the babble Cobb thought he heard it said that somehow his mother was involved in the shooting. Ty's younger brother, Paul, came on the line to sob, confirm the death, and add a few details.

Hurrying home by train, Cobb had to face the circumstance that his father, the man he most admired and honored, who had opposed baseball and thought it a great mistake for his son, yet had bowed to Ty's wishes and made it possible for him to test himself, never would see him in a game. Now he could not repay the trust shown in him. The man he looked up to as wise and saintly was dead. And not by accident, some in Royston were saying.

When his train reached Royston, friends among a crowd at the station told Cobb that this was no ordinary gunplay. He quickly learned the facts of an affair that was rocking northeastern Georgia. For—no doubt whatever about it—it was Ty Cobb's mother, Amanda, who had pulled the triggers of the double-barreled shotgun that had blown off his father's head.

CHAPTER SEVEN

BITTER TIMES

abe Ruth's father, George Herman Ruth, Sr., died of a skull fracture suffered during a brawl outside his Baltimore saloon in 1918. By then the Babe was twenty-three, established as a combined 24-game-winning pitcher and .325-hitting long-ball slugger of the Boston Red Sox, paid seven thousand dollars per season. By contrast, when his father was gunned down in 1905, Ty Cobb was eighteen, a novice outfielder with not an inning of more than Class C experience, and seasonal earnings of six hundred to seven hundred dollars. By all reports, Ruth was not close to his male parent. He considered a reform school for boys, to which he had been confined for years, to be his home. Cobb, since childhood, had all but idolized Professor W. H. Cobb.

The sudden, gruesome death of his forty-four-year-old father struck Ty a blow from which he admittedly never recovered. During the close to one year I spent writing Cobb's autobiography with him, he sometimes broke away from baseball to speak emotionally. "I have loved only two men in my life—Jesus Christ and my father," Cobb would say, with tears in his eyes.

On August 9, 1905, in Royston, he walked into a scene of grief and confusion. Sheriffs, doctors, news reporters, and stunned townfolk overran the family home and the street outside. William Herschel Cobb, the deceased, had been an educator, sometime state official, and prominent Democrat mentioned as a potential Georgia governor. One of the first explanations Ty heard of events of the prior day and night came from neighbor lad Joe Cunningham and another boyhood friend, Clifford Ginn: "He was shot about midnight . . . He'd climbed onto the porch of his house . . . it happened up there . . . They're trying to find out how he was killed."

Neither of them was willing to tell him that his mother, Amanda, had pulled the trigger.

Inside the two-story brick home with its heirloom furnishings, Ty found a hysterical Amanda Cobb sobbing, "I thought it was a burglar . . . I didn't know!" Ty's sixteen-year-old brother, Paul, and thirteen-year-old sister, Florence, were in as bad shape as their mother. When he could break away, Ty asked Dr. H. F. McCreary, the family physician, for a straight answer: who did it? McCreary said, "Amanda says someone was trying to force his way in and in the dark she used a shotgun on him. It's a terrible accident." When Ty asked to see the remains, he was told they were too mangled for viewing. At the forty-foot distance, Amanda had used a heavy-gauge shotgun—and had fired twice.

"Incredible" was the word used around Royston to describe the sequence of occurrences that had cut down the former state senator and Franklin County school commissioner in his prime of life. Why, in the first place, had W. H. Cobb climbed to his home's second story to a position outside his wife's bedroom in the middle of the night? Was it really a case of mistaken identity, as claimed by Amanda Cobb?

There was only one eyewitness—the new widow. As she related it, W. H., on the evening of August 8, had dined with the family, after which their children, Paul and Florence, had left to stay overnight with friends. Unexpectedly, W. H. announced that he was leaving on out-of-town business "for a few days." Hitching up his buggy he departed at about 6:00 P.M. But did he leave Royston? Witnesses were to come forward to attest that he had been seen walking a Royston street at about 11:00 P.M.

At 10:30 P.M. or so of what had been a ninety-degree day, Amanda retired to her bedroom. Just after midnight Mrs. Cobb said she was jolted from sleep by a scratching noise at a window; then the sound increased so loudly that she was sure it was a break-in attempt. Investigating, Amanda could see by moonlight only a large, ominous figure wrenching at the window frame and lock. The effort grew still noisier. For moments she hesitated, but then, being alone in the home, she grabbed up a twin-barreled shotgun from a corner rack of the room and in fright fired one load.

She testified that panic overcame her, that she screamed and triggered a second blast. When she crept to the demolished window Amanda dimly saw a bloody figure sprawled over the porch roof. She could barely identify the body of her husband. From the neck up not much was left.

Nearby neighbors, hearing the gun's roar and rushing to the scene, were sickened by the sight. Professor Cobb had taken one blast in the stomach, from which his intestines spewed, another to the head, tearing off his upper skull. Doc McCreary arrived, pronounced W. H. dead as of 1:30 A.M., and secured for a coroner's jury a six-shot revolver stuck in the victim's side pocket.

The significance of the gun was immediately linked to gossip around town. For some months in Royston, back-of-the-hand rumor had it that thirty-four-year-old Amanda, a shapely woman, was unfaithful. Gossip grew that she had a lover who joined her when W. H. was out of town, which was frequently. Supposedly, the Professor heard the allegations and suspicion festered within him. And so he had faked leaving town, parked his buggy out of sight, doubled back by foot, and climbed his porch to catch Amanda in the act. The common law held that a man had the right to protect the sanctity of his home and, so went grapevine talk, Cobb doubtless intended to use a gun on Amanda's paramour—maybe on both of them.

Royston's social set and others branded this story as wholly untrue; Amanda was a dedicated wife, an admirable mother, now the victim of gross slander. Given her character, the slaying of W. H. Cobb was obviously purely accidental. She was entertaining no one when he came porch climbing.

Yet why had he made that moonlight climb? A strange act for a man, unless he had a powerful motive . . .

When a coroner's jury convened the next day, August 10, it voted for Amanda's arrest on the count of voluntary manslaughter. Ty Cobb sat beside his mother at the courthouse and she broke down at the finding. Amanda was charged with the unlawful killing of a human being by design or intention. The result of that charge remained to be decided by formal jury trial.

"We will withhold serving the warrant for her arrest until after the funeral," announced the jury foreman. Ty thanked the jury, then all but collapsed himself.

On August 11, at the Cobb home—now the center of a scandal that was bound to spread luridly to Augusta, where Ty was well known as a ballplayer—the funeral was held. Ty had to borrow a dark suit— his small wardrobe was in Augusta. With two black horses on parade, he and his father's fellow Masons lowered the casket into the grave. Next day Amanda was arrested by the county sheriff, posted a stiff seven-thousand-dollar bail to avoid jail time, and within two weeks was indicted by a grand jury. Her trial would not come for many months, due to a crowded court docket.

Riding his horse Blackie, Cobb vanished into the hills. When old companion Joe Cunningham caught up with him, he was pale and still shaking. He told Cunningham, "I'll never get over this." At the grave he had said, "There goes the best man I ever knew." Fifty-five years afterward, Cunningham remembered, "I know for a fact that he never got over it. It was like he took an oath in W. H.'s name. A lot of what he'd done until then in playing ball was to win his father's respect . . . his admiration. Their differences over baseball were coming around to that point. It was always on his mind that his father never would see him in action, crowds cheering him, all that. Ty was just too self-centered and proud to accept W. H.'s death as a very tough break. He was all tied into the man and the thing his family had about winning medals in wars, government, and such. After the shooting, I figure that much of what he did on the diamond was for W. H. Seemed he was out to pay tribute to him in death." Cunningham added, "I can't be sure of it, but Ty made plays after that which nobody else could make. Not anybody in the game. The thing is, W. H. opposed his playing ball. But he cared enough to let Ty go and prove he was a man. Ty owed him for that and he never stopped paying back."

A New York sportswriting contemporary of Cobb's in the 1920s, sports editor Paul Gallico of the New York *Daily News*, agreed with Cunningham's evaluation. In his 1965 memoir, *The Golden People*, Gallico wrote, "The roughnecks of baseball put steel into him . . . but also there was the traumatic experience of his father's terrible death. Cobb brought a strange fury, cruelty and viciousness to the game."

Gallico saw him as "a mass of paradoxes," "a rogue elephant," and "such a tortured being that what we were observing then was in all likelihood a highly neurotic individual." Gallico added, "Cobb's admission that he never got over his father's death is all any modern psychiatrist would ask for in plumbing the cause of illness."

In the same blunt appraisal, Gallico saw Cobb as the greatest player who ever lived, "greater even than Babe Ruth or Honus Wagner, a unique, compelling character . . . an astonishing man who infused such drama, flesh and blood into the chill records he set that his like has not been seen since."

Cobb's closest friends found no evidence that he hated his mother for the killing. At Amanda's trial for voluntary manslaughter, he would stand by her. Ty's younger brother, Paul, who became a fairly good hitter in semipro ball and climbed high enough to be drafted by the St. Louis Browns in 1908, confirmed that Cobb, when he owned a home of his own, invited Amanda to stay with him. "But," said Paul Cobb, "he never allowed any mention of the shooting, it was all closed tight within him." Amanda, living to age sixty-five, was buried by Ty next to his father's grave in Royston. The sanctity of the Cobb family image was preserved.

Throughout the ordeal of sheriffs, juries, and speculation, Cobb, for the most part, was stoic. Four days after the funeral, on August 15, he rode to the grave, placed flowers upon it, packed up, and rejoined the Tourists in Augusta. Had anyone on the club wisecracked about reports in the Augusta press of the "mystery killing," Cobb, no doubt, would have gone after him with a bat. By his own description he was "sick at heart" upon returning. But the players remained silent.

Clubhouse chatter in his absence had it that the Royston Rooster was about to achieve what most of the members of Augusta's team could only fantasize might happen to a member—a call-up to the high minors, or to Mount Olympus, the majors. Cobb's matchless ability to concentrate, even at a time like this, was shown when he hit a double and single against the Charleston Sea Gulls in his first start after reporting back, during which he blindsided an infielder with a hard slide for a stolen base. He continued not to socialize with his teammates.

On the morning of August 19, 1905, his employer, William J. Croke, called him in. "They want you in Detroit right away," began Croke. A beaming George Leidy was standing by.

Cobb was amazed. "They want me *now*, with the season almost over?" he asked.

"Don't get any big ideas," warned Croke. "The Tigers are hurting for outfielders. They're down to three men there—injuries. You'll probably just be a fill-in for Duff Cooley in left field or center."

Cooley? Ty had kept track of the Tigers for the fun of it and the fourteen-year veteran, thirty-two-year-old Duff "Sir Richard" Cooley, was a greyhound at outrunning fly balls, although showing signs of slowing. To step into Cooley's shoes without ever having so much as seen a major-league ballpark was mind-bending.

"Don't worry, Ty," broke in Leidy. "Even if it doesn't work out right away you'll be getting great experience."

In an ideal world, Cobb, at this moment, would have been rushing to tell his father of his miraculous jump to the Big Show. Now there would be no one at the other end of the phone.

THE THRILL and chill of going up without warning would have been tempered had Cobb known the whole fact: Frank Navin, secretary–general manager of the Tigers, did not want to plug his outfield gap with a low-level teenager with no experience above the bushes, and particularly not one with a reputation as a "stunt-crazy" infielder and sometimes reckless base runner. To quote a leading Detroit Tigers historian, Harry Salsinger of the *Detroit News*, "They [the Tigers] had quite forgotten about Cobb. Faintly, they recalled the 'nut' on the Augusta team . . . he'd had a good season, seemed to have promise. Nothing more."

Luck played a large role in Cobb's candidacy. Navin had run out of options. After declining to act for several days, he changed his mind. Back in the spring, with the Bengals training at Augusta, Navin, in lieu of paying rent to his hosts, had loaned young pitcher Eddie Cicotte to the Tourists for the season. In return, Bill Croke had guaranteed Navin his pick for 1906 of anyone on the Tourist roster for the sum of $750. Came August and the season's near end, and Navin, in exercising his option and slightly moving it up, preferred a versatile twenty-one-year-old Tourist outfielder-infielder named Clyde Engle over Cobb. He would have selected Engle but for the intervention of two men. Singing Bill Byron, a Sally League umpire and respected judge of quality, had harangued Detroit's manager, Bill Armour, arguing, "This one is a born hitter—he'll surprise you with all the things he can do. Runs like a scalded dog. Has good instincts. Take him, not Engle."

Armour was skeptical. "I'm told he's got some screws loose, that the team doesn't like Cobb."

Byron admitted this was true, saying, "It's not all his fault. Jealousy is involved. Sure, Cobb's got to be controlled. But as he stands right now he's a hell of a prospect, even this far down in the minors."

While the decision hung fire, George Leidy worked on Heinie Youngman, the Detroit scout who had earlier interviewed the Rooster. Youngman, too, had serious reservations: "He would hardly talk to me," said Youngman. "The Tourist players think he's got a screw loose."

"He'll work out, I promise you," argued Leidy, crossing his fingers. "When he does you're going to see the best young player between Maine and California."

Even with such strong recommendations, the Tigers still favored Engle. "What saved me," recorded Cobb in time, "was that Engle tailed off in the August heat and I hung on and was leading the Sally with a .326 average. Otherwise I wouldn't have been chosen." Croke feared that Cobb would be drafted by a higher club at the current draft price of $350. Three-fifty would not much help Croke's pressing financial bind at Augusta, so he took the $750, and did so in the nick of time. One week after a relieved Croke sold his problem-maker—for $500 plus $250 "adjustment money" for losing Cobb's services for the rest of the season—four teams from higher leagues claimed him in organized baseball's draft. Other eyes had been watching Cobb all along.

As had happened a season earlier when Cobb had been sloughed off to lowly Anniston, Alabama, a band of his special fans had formed in town. The "Cobbies" cheered every time he ticked a foul ball. Ty played his final game with the Tourists on August 25 against Macon. Of the fifteen hundred in the crowd, about 90 percent seemed to be there to celebrate his advancement to the American League. "Give 'em hell in Detroit!" went the cry.

As he stood in the on-deck area, preparing for his first at-bat, a delegation of citizens approached. Augusta's mayor led the parade. Cobbies had taken up a collection and now presented Cobb with flowers and a fifty-dollar gold watch. Embarrassed, he muttered his thanks, then turned to face Macon's pitcher.

He swung for strike one. He unbuttoned his shirt, swinging and missing for strike two. "On the next pitch," Cobb described it, "I couldn't have connected with a six-by-eight plank if the pitcher had tossed the ball underhanded up to the plate."

"Stuuuuhhhrike three!"

His fans sat in silence, except for one group that boomed, "Let Detroit have him!"

Characteristic for Cobb after a failure, he singled twice, stole a bag, and made a circus outfield catch before the game ended.

On the season, his numbers were good here, bad there, and far from portentous. He'd hit safely about one-third of the time—134 base hits in 411 at-bats—and scored 60 runs. He'd stolen a high 41 bases in 104 games. His assists on putouts came to a modest 15. If Detroit hadn't needed roster help in a hurry, Navin might have vetoed the deal, for Cobb's fielding average of .927 was the lowest in the league among regular outfielders. Some of this, however, was explained by his encroaching on chances belonging to other fielders. Over and above spotty defensive work, he had been in several intramural knock-down-drag-out fights.

Across the United States were minor-league baseball players with higher overall statistics. Out in the Pacific Coast League, for instance, Harry Lumley of Los Angeles had batted at a .387 figure. But the Tigers couldn't afford the sales price of Lumley and others like him, and went for Cobb in considerable part because he came so cheap. Thanks to George Leidy's hard schooling, he was given a rare chance. The key point was that he had made the grade, temporarily at least, while still a postadolescent, aged eighteen.

Clyde Engle, the player who had almost beaten Ty to the big time at Detroit, became a historical footnote. Engle reached the majors at New York in 1909 and in eight years there never once hit .300.

Prior to packing his bags and leaving on August 26, Cobb sounded off, again typically, in what boss Bill Croke considered to be the height of ingratitude. An item appeared in the *Augusta Chronicle* in which Cobb complained that he should have received a percentage of his $750 purchase price. Ten percent, he thought, would be fair. "Imagine that," Croke was quoted. "The Rooster's been here for only 104 games and wants a money-cut. He wants it from the club that made his big jump to the majors possible and which is paying his travel expenses to Detroit when we didn't have to do any such thing."

Cobb replied that he had been much underpaid through the season, as his promotion to Detroit proved. But what could you expect from an outfit that fined you for breaking bats?

DETROIT WAS 730 miles away. Cobb was worn out when he caught a train on the night of August 26. Only a few Tourists saw him off. The odds were long against an immature player who had not been allowed to serve a normal apprenticeship in the most difficult of team sports. Through extraordinary circumstances, Detroit had acquired a beginner who was unlikely to finish the season. He was not fully grown, had never set foot in a big-league stadium, and he was in alien country. The Civil War was still a touchy matter. The first time some Yankee in Detroit, Washington, or New York heard his Dixie accent and made a remark derogatory to the South's military effort, there would very likely be a fight.

Beyond that, Cobb had shown little inclination to take orders. If he defied his new manager, he would be on his way home. In that case, with his father gone and a family to support, what would he do? The now-oldest male Cobb of Royston, Georgia, appeared to have burned his bridges behind him.

CHAPTER EIGHT

PILGRIM WITH A PANCAKE GLOVE

At the century's outset, the seasonal payrolls for many major-league clubs, covering twenty to thirty players, stood as low as seventy to eighty thousand dollars. To refer to "poorly paid ballplayers" was a tautology. Good hitters and pitchers died broke, pensions did not exist, salary arbitration had not been invented. Boys off a hay-farm wagon with a sketchy education were far outmatched when bargaining against avaricious franchise holders controlling one of the more shameless monopolies in the history of American commerce. Ultimately the gap between the "Johnny Grab" operators and cheap skilled labor would change, but not for another seventy years.

While his father was alive, Cobb had not needed to worry about money. Suddenly, it was a concern. On the trip north he considered his assets and came up short. Years after that, relying on memory, he estimated, "I had about two hundred dollars in an Augusta bank and seventy-five dollars cash in my pocket and that was it until I saw something from Detroit. It was so late in the season when I went up that I couldn't expect much from the club."

He did not understand banking procedure, such as interest and transfers of credit. When his seventy-five dollars ran out, he was not sure what would happen; "I didn't know what the hell was going on."

At the time, the game of baseball was reshaping itself. In 1901 the foul-strike rule had been adopted by the National League, whereby the first and second foul balls off the bat counted as strikes. The American League followed suit two years later. For a batter such as pesky Cobb, who could repeatedly foul off deliveries until he drew a pitch he liked, that was bad news.

A far more momentous shake-up had also occurred. Byron Bancroft "Ban" Johnson, of Cincinnati, saw no reason why the National League should maintain a stranglehold on big-league franchises. Johnson geared up and went to war with the National League monopoly by changing the name of his strong minor Western League to the American League and claiming parity with the existing cartel. Johnson and his partners controlled franchise bases in Detroit, Philadelphia, St. Louis, Boston, Chicago, Cleveland, Washington, and Baltimore, and for the 1901 season enticed away from the Nationals such headliners as Nap Lajoie, Clark Griffith, Fielder Jones, Jimmy Collins, John McGraw, Cy Young, Jesse Burkett, Rube Waddell, Jack Chesbro, and Wee Willie Keeler. Soon enough the Nationals tired of a costly trade struggle, and in 1903 signed a peace treaty according equal status to Johnson's group. By this act, bifurcated baseball and the modern World Series were born. In that first Series, in 1903, the American League's Boston Pilgrims (soon to be called Red Sox) rubbed it in with a victory over the Honus Wagner–led Pittsburgh Pirates of the National League.

For Cobb, who knew little of such inside maneuvering, the timing of that event was fortunate. He reached the game's top level only two years after the baseball war ended, amidst a beginning boom time. Combined attendance at major-league games soon would jump from a reported 3.6 million in 1900 to 5.8 million in 1905, and to more than 7.2 million by 1910.

Detroit prospered doubly. The city could boast not only of a money-making team, but of jobs being made available from another birth—that of a foul-smelling contraption on wheels. In 1903–04, James W. Packard helped found the Packard Motor Company in Detroit, and David D. Buick and Henry Ford tooled up to do business. The Motor City, as the river center soon would be called, was at a pioneer stage when Cobb arrived there on the night of August 29, 1905.

HE WALKED the streets, a stranger in America's thirteenth-largest metropolis, wholly on his own in a place he had never expected to see. Having effectively cut all ties with Augusta's team management through a series of clashes, he had nowhere to go in baseball if his hastily arranged tryout with the Tigers failed. In betting terms it was perhaps 100–1 that he would not last long here. Cobb would not be out of his teens for another sixteen months.

The events of recent weeks left him feeling rootless. Reconstructing the situation of that late summer, he told me, "I wasn't so much scared as nervous and anxious. Nothing was familiar. I didn't know anyone between the train depot and the boondocks. Hell, I didn't even know where the Tigers' ballpark was located." He had never seen a big-league park or an official game between two big-league teams.

In the past nineteen days, Cobb had buried a beloved one, feuded with Augusta players and executives, led the Sally League in batting, been astonished to learn that a major organization wanted his services, and been bounced around on a lengthy railroad trip to where he now stood: on busy, downtown Woodward Avenue, looking for a cab to land him at a hotel. He arrived in town at 11:00 P.M., but the place still hummed with bike traffic, market vendors, and theater-goers. Trolleys clanged, cab whistles shrilled, ice wagons clattered past.

En route to the city of 400,000, the one-time frontier fur-trading post of Antoine Cadillac and then home of Calvinist settlers, Cobb had stopped off at Royston. His mother remained bedridden, almost incommunicado after her unbelievable, possibly criminal shooting of Professor Cobb. It had been Ty's task to dispose of his father's personal belongings. In conversations with me fifty-five years later, he never mentioned how he reacted to this, other than to allude to it as the most painful thing he had ever imagined and that he closed it off inside himself.

For his invasion of the North he carried only his dish-shaped Spalding glove, three well-boned hickory and ash bats, and one clothing bag, along with the fifty-dollar gold watch presented to Ty in his final Augusta appearance. No representative of the Tiger club was at the Detroit train depot to greet him.

Directing a horse-cabby to drive him to an inexpensive hotel near the Tigers' home field, he was asked, "Bennett Park or Burns Park?" Cobb did not know that the Tigers, because of a civic no-Sunday-ball prohibition, performed weekdays at Bennett and on the Sabbath at

Burns, in neighboring Springswell Township. He settled for a room near Bennett in a wooden-sided inn called Ryan's—"$8 Weekly Bed & Board, Cash Only." As Cobb recalled, Ryan, the proprietor and a Tiger fan, said, "I saw your picture in the paper . . . about how you're joining the team." This came as a surprise. Nobody had informed him that three days earlier the *Detroit Free Press* had printed his photo, a blurred image taken earlier in Augusta, showing rookie Ty in street suit and polka-dot bow tie. A notice had also appeared under the byline of the *Free Press*'s baseball correspondent, Joe Jackson. Hotelman Ryan had kept a copy of the one-column piece by Jackson, and Ty read his first big-city write-up.

Jackson's column rated him as reportedly having exceptional speed out of the batter's box, but was lukewarm about his chances to stick with the Tigers once their personnel emergency ended. Forty-one games remained on their schedule, not enough dates for a new hand to make much of an impression. It was by forfeit—injuries to two Tigers —that the raw "nubbin" had gained a trial. He was one more in a line of recruits brought up by teams in a late-season pinch. Almost none of them lasted.

Manager Bill Armour's collection of inconsistent hitters—with only one man, reliable outfielder Sam Crawford, averaging close to .300— would end the season in considerably less than glorious fashion:

Dick Cooley, of, .247
Bill Coughlin, 3b, .252
Sam Crawford, of, .297
Lew Drill, c, .261
Pinky Lindsay, 1b, .267
Bobby Lowe, of-inf, .193
Matty McIntyre, of, .263
Charlie O'Leary, ss, .213
Germany Schaefer, 2b, .244

No Tiger other than Wahoo Crawford (.433) owned a slugging average above .333. Pitching almost alone had carried the club to third place, behind the Philadelphia Athletics and Chicago White Sox, who were locked in a photo finish for the pennant. One freshly incubated outfielder would have as much impact on Detroit's hope of improving its record as a marshmallow hurled against the Majestic Building, a fourteen-story Detroit skyscraper.

As he read on, Cobb saw that columnist Joe Jackson wrote off his .326 average, tops in the Sally League, as meaningless. What he had accomplished in the Georgia backwater had no application to major-league baseball. Jackson foresaw a .275 batting mark as about the best that could be expected from Cobb—which would be "satisfactory."

In so saying, the *Free Press*'s forecaster was putting a newcomer on the spot. A .275 average was no easy attainment. In the 1905 season, pitching utterly dominated the American League. In the entire circuit, ridiculously, only four first-string players finished the campaign at .300 or above, and the pennant-winning Philadelphia Athletics showed an embarrassing team batting average of .255. During a year of wholesale slump by veterans, Ty would be expected to hit against well-seasoned pitchers he had never seen in person, among them New York's Jack Chesbro, a spectacular recent 41-game winner, sinkerballing Addie Joss of Cleveland, and the curious strikeout specialist, Rube Waddell of Philadelphia. All in all, it wasn't too much of an exaggeration to compare the matchup to sending a new, unranked prizefighter up against the ruling heavyweight champion, Jim Jeffries.

Due to report the next day, August 30, Ty needed sleep. He picked the wrong place. The legend began here that he was so much of a rube that he mistakenly checked into a whorehouse on his first night in the city. Actually Ryan's Bed and Board had no loose ladies, but it did contain a burlesque joint on the first floor. Rooming above it, he got little rest while the din went on.

Early the next day, in rumpled street clothes and a straw boater, carrying his equipment, he caught another horse-cab to Bennett Park, where the Tigers were scheduled that afternoon against the New York Highlanders. Bennett, at Trumbull and Michigan avenues, was on the edge of Corktown, an enclave of hard-boozing, hard-rooting Irish-American fans. Once Bennett had been a hay-and-grain market; now it was boxed in by a high wooden fence to block gate-crashers and held eighty-five hundred at capacity, with adjoining "wildcat" bleachers for three hundred at fifteen cents per seat. Inside the park, prices ranged from one dollar for boxes to fifty cents in the grandstand. Bennett Park did not have a real dugout; even the game's foremost stars sat on rough benches. There was no smaller-seating park in the American League.

Partly because of that, Detroit had been threatened with loss of its franchise by autocratic American League president Ban Johnson. Civic leaders struck back at Johnson, saying that he belonged in Detroit's Eden Musee, a museum featuring a chamber of horrors. Fans of a city growing toward 500,000 in the nascent age of the automobile prized their ball team highly, win or lose. The Tigers, also called the "Bengals," "Striped Cats," and "Felines," had been around since 1887.

Cobb, ill at ease, met manager Bill Armour in his office. Armour seemed to be a man in pain, what with a spotty-hitting lineup also known on defense for turning singles into stand-up doubles. At thirty-seven, Armour wore a bushy mustache and disguised his small stature by wearing a padded vest and suit coat. "Little Bill" was in his first season as field chief, and already being criticized. Cobb noticed his nervous habit of twisting his hands. Armour said, "Glad to see you. We've got some disabled men. I'm starting you today in center field. You should get together with Jimmy Barrett on our signals." Barrett, a good slap-hitter, was the injured outfielder to be replaced by Cobb that afternoon. It came without warning. Cobb: "I hadn't expected to start a game for a while . . . it was a jolt. I didn't know New York's pitchers except that they were fast."

Before the action began, a presence appeared. He was Frank J. Navin, former pro gambler and insurance salesman who had won the confidence of the Tigers' millionaire playboy owner, William H. "Good Times" Yawkey, and had taken over the running of the team. Secretary Navin, big, chubby, and poker-faced, was said to bet as high as a thousand dollars on a horse race; when in his cups he bet more. Not bothering to shake hands, Navin looked over the Georgia import—a lean, muscular type of five feet, ten inches and 160 pounds, with fair to reddish hair neatly combed back over a side part and with steady eyes.

At first meeting, Ty felt intimidated by the man. Navin was cold of manner. He barely nodded, and made no response when Cobb stated that he appreciated the chance that the Tigers were giving him. The youthful Cobb had a feeling that Navin would be a tough boss to get along with. He was not too inexperienced to see that if he played a few bad games in a row, Navin would have him headed home in no time— bats, glove, the Augusta fans' gold watch, and all.

Upon leaving Augusta, he had hoped to be paid from $400 to $500 by Detroit in his role as final-month replacement—if he cracked the lineup. Navin handed him a contract worth $1,500 over the full season, breaking down to $250 for the one month's work at hand. Lacking recourse, he signed. He was outfitted with a uniform that did not fit particularly well: gray-white flannels (laundry service was slow with the Tigers) with an Old English *D* across the shirt, black stockings, and white-and-black cap. A pair of steel-cleated shoes was found to fit his size-ten feet.

Injured Jimmy Barrett coached him on the Tigers' hit-and-run, take-or-swing, steal-or-stay signals, Cobb remembered, adding, "We've got a way of swiping New York's signs. See that advertisement on the center-field fence? Well, I'll be sitting next to it in the stands with a spyglass strong enough to pick up warts on their catcher's hands. I can read his signals to Jack Chesbro—he's pitching for them today—on almost every throw. That's where the fence sign—'*The Detroit News*, Best Newspaper in the West'—comes in."

Barrett went on. "When you're batting, keep your eyes on the letter *B* in the sign. You'll notice the slots in it open and close. If the slot's open in the upper half of the *B*, it means I've read their signals from the catcher. It's a fastball coming. If the bottom slot closes you can expect a curve or some kind of drop. One of our boys is working the slots after I give him the word."

"I'm not used to this," Cobb protested. "Can't I get up there and hit my regular way?" It was not the cheating that bothered him; he was feeling a severe case of nerves, and adding another element could hurt his concentration.

Barrett shrugged. "Your decision, kid, you're the hitter. But against Chesbro you can use the extra help." Barrett's reference was to Jack Chesbro's spitball, a pitch disguised as a straight fastball, which when well wetted dived to ankle height. Since 1900, Happy Jack Chesbro had pitched his way to what by season's end would be 126 wins against but 56 losses. In 1904 he had piled up a record of 41 victories to 12 losses. This was who the unlucky Cobb would face in his first major-league game.

Bill Armour's reaction to Cobb's refusal of scoreboard help was unfavorable. The general feeling was that Cobb had better show something and do it in a hurry.

When Cobb came to bat for the first time in the majors—it was August 30, 1905—he came with a refinement of his own. Waiting for his turn against Chesbro, he had carried not one, not two, but three bats. Swinging them vigorously around in warm-up, he discarded two and stepped into the box. Down home Ty had found that warming up this way made the remaining bat, through weight contrast, feel lighter and springier. It was one of the small advantages he forever sought. This, though, was hardly the time for displaying so much lumber. Catcher Red Kleinow asked, "You up here to hit or kill chickens?" Detroit fans rarely if ever had seen a triple-bat stunt before, but even though it looked like grandstanding they refrained from booing for the moment. A midweek turnout of twelve hundred customers could not even find Cobb's name on their scorecards, for the reason that it was not listed.

His debut went like this:

Chesbro faced outfielder Matty McIntyre leading off the first inning. McIntyre doubled. First baseman Pinky Lindsay singled McIntyre home. Next, infielder Germany Schaefer bunt-sacrificed Lindsay to second base. Sam Crawford bounced out to the mound, Lindsay advanced to third. The angry Chesbro bore down on Cobb, hitting fifth.

"Up came a fairly tall, gaunt, almost gawky-looking boy who seemed jittery," reported the *Detroit News* next day. "Chesbro fired a high fastball and Cobb swung and missed. A fastball high is the one pitch that the majority of minor leaguers can't resist. While Cobb had seen many such pitches in the Sally League, he'd never seen one so sizzling fast as the one he missed.

"Chesbro followed with a waist-high curve that Silk O'Loughlin, the plate umpire, called 'st-r-r-r-ike tuh.' Chesbro figured that Cobb would expect another high, fast spitter, but waist-high instead of letters-high. Cobb stepped into the pitch and blasted it deep past New York's center fielder, Eddie Hahn. Streaking to first, Cobb turned sharply without lessening his speed and easily slid safely into second."

Pinky Lindsay trotted home to score and the Tigers led 2–0. It had been a clean, two-out, run-manufacturing base hit by the new boy, against prohibitive odds.

A very wary Chesbro walked the kid on his next time up.

In a close game, Cobb made no more hits that day, but prevented New York from scoring with a pair of catches in center field. On a double-steal attempt, Cobb was thrown out, through no fault of his. His legs sore from so much recent traveling, he limped to the bench when it ended with a 5–3 Detroit victory. "You did well," said Bill Armour, "especially working Chesbro for a walk."

Nobody offered him a congratulatory dinner, so he dined alone that night, and moved out of Ryan's Bed and Board with its burlesque annex and sound effects into cheap housing closer to Bennett Park.

To reach the park by foot meant dodging a sputtering, smoke-belching variety of fifteen-mile-an-hour vehicles—Marvels, Reos, Hupmobiles, Aerocars, Buicks, Packards, and Model N Fords (the famous Model T type Ford, at $850, would not appear until 1908). As of 1905, Detroit had more than seventy firms producing 22,800 gas cars annually. Cobb envied the begoggled, duster-coated drivers. If ever he could afford to own one . . .

FOLLOWING HIS first appearance, he read in Detroit's *Free Press*: "Cobb, the juvenile outfielder, got away well. Tyrus was well-received and may consider a two-base pry-up as a much better career opener than usually comes a young fellow's way." Sportswriters also liked his stance at bat, marked by a slight crouch with feet close together, his rather heavy 38-ounce club (about 2.4 pounds) held steady at shoulder height and set to whip around in coordination with a short forward stride. His swing was a contained, economical one, not from the heels.

In a rematch with the New Yorkers the next day, August 31, the opinion of the press was split. Some observers cheered his two singles in four times up off right-handed change-up specialist Jack Powell, a 23-game winner in 1904. His base hits were a useful contribution to a 5–0 Tiger shutout of the Highlanders. But offsetting this was a first-inning headfirst steal attempt in which the catcher's throw easily beat him. That allowed baseman Kid Elberfeld time to slam his knee into the back of Cobb's neck and grind his face into the dirt. "The professional teach," it was called—a naked attack on apprentice ballplayers to discourage stealing. Cobb's nose was skinned and he bled a bit. Bill Armour said, "I wanted to see what you could do against Red Kleinow's arm. It was damned dumb to go in leading with your head." Down in Augusta, months earlier, George Leidy had warned him of the same error. After Elberfeld's roughing-up, Cobb rarely went into a base other than feet first, with neck muscles bunched. He filed away the name of Norman Arthur "Kid" Elberfeld for purposes of evening the score at another time—if there was another time.

Another bush-league exhibition came in the seventh inning of his second start. He violated the basic rule of never running through a stop signal given by a coach. Base runner Cobb tried to score from second base on a single to medium-deep center field. Ignoring Bill Coughlin's hold-up sign at third base, he was tagged out by a near body length and roundly booed. "Archie Hahn, the Olympic sprint champ," wrote a critic, "couldn't have made that work."

Evaluating afterward those break-in days, Cobb recorded, "I was riding high one moment, in the dumps the next. The worse thing was not knowing if I belonged there or not. It was all maybe. Maybe I did, maybe not. That put me into too much of a hurry to look good."

His main handicap was that he felt inferior alongside mature big-leaguers: "I'd never dreamed that men could field and hit so wonderfully. Such speed, class, style, and lightning thinking. It was common then for games to be low scoring and close scoring—1–0, 2–1, 3–2—decided by gaining the last inch of advantage. Scientific ball at its best. It hasn't been matched since."

In a Labor Day game came plays that he felt decided whether he would leave town or stay. Chicago's scrappy White Sox, bidding for the pennant in the late season, visited Bennett Park for a doubleheader. A turnout of seventy-six hundred rambunctious fans packed along baselines and outfield restraining ropes. Hazers yelled at Cobb in center field, "Hey, sprout, does your ma know you're out?" This was touching on sensitive ground. Cobb glared back. After that someone threw a cheap child's toy at him. He kicked it all the way to the ropes. Detroit's agitators were now aware of something—the new boy could not stand to be razzed.

Amidst an uproar, Chicago's Jiggs Donahue drove a ball deep to left center. It resembled a two-base hit until Cobb, racing under it at the last moment, speared the ball one-handedly, almost blindly, over his shoulder. He shot it back to the infield, saving two runs. A few innings later he again showed off his throwing arm. Donahue was at first base when Ty chased a long grounder, pocketed it, and fired two-hundred-odd feet on a line to third base. Donahue, out to stretch the hit into a two-base advance, was out sliding. Detroit beat the White Sox. Back on the bench, Germany Schaefer nudged Ty, saying, "Can't you hear the folks? Go out and take a bow."

Cobb was unsure how a rookie should respond to cheers and just sat there. Schaefer pushed him to his feet. For the next moments he heard his first big-time crowd salute.

Twenty-four hours later, he was in trouble. Against the White Sox, he took a bead on a fly ball and with no forethought went after it. The chance clearly was in left fielder Matty McIntyre's territory, of which McIntyre was highly possessive. A bad man to cross, McIntyre had batted a weak .254 and .265 in the past two seasons; his job was in danger. Cobb infuriated McIntyre by cutting in front of him, in what one sportswriter called "a high, senile prance, for one so young," and causing him to drop the ball.

He was capable of worse gaucheries. At Washington he let three fly balls pop out of his glove for errors in two games, and missed a steal sign. His teammates gave Cobb a razzing. Armour replaced him in center field with McIntyre, sending the rookie to left field.

A few games later, Adrian "Addie" Joss was on the mound for Cleveland, mowing down Tigers with a curveball that gave him one of the lowest lifetime earned-run averages in history (1.88). After reaching Joss earlier for a single, Cobb came to bat in the ninth inning of a deadlocked game. He worked Joss to a full count before singling again.

In the press section, as Cobb later learned, Harry Salsinger of the *News* said, "Look at that idiotic lead Cobb's taking off first. Joss will pick him off easily."

Instead, a sacrifice moved him to second base, where he once more took a lead bordering on the foolhardy. Joss whirled and threw to the bag. Cobb beat the tag by the smallest of margins. He darted back and forth, yipping at Joss. Batter Matty McIntyre hit a slow-bounding ball that took a last high hop and was barely knocked down by Cleveland's second baseman. Now Detroit had its first look at the advertised speed of the Georgian. Advancing to third base and beyond in a flash, while in full stride he glanced back at the second-base situation. The fielder momentarily did not have the spinning ball under control. Cobb saw him juggling it. Without a pause Cobb raced on. The play at home plate was tight, but he beat a hurried high throw to Cleveland's catcher, Nig Clarke, to win the game. The crowd yelled his name this time.

Bill Armour was impressed by the sight of a beginner successfully moving from second to home on a ball hit to the shallow infield.

"That's one of the best running jobs I've ever seen," he told the press. "He must have traveled that last ninety feet in three seconds."

By that impetuous final-inning dash, Cobb put the Tigers at the .500 mark for the first time since early season. They finished in third place with a 79–74 (.516) record, the best any Detroit team had done since 1901. By improving to third place, Armour had probably saved his job. Numerous managers had come and gone—George Stallings, Frank Dwyer, Ed Barrow, Bobby Lowe—since the century's turn. The authoritative *Reach Guide* of 1905 said, "Armour did an admirable job of managing and his colorful new second-base combination of Charley O'Leary and Germany Schaefer . . . and a young outfielder named Cobb . . . added new strength to the team."

As the season's end neared, Ty was considered worth keeping on the roster, although seen as a hot-and-cold performer who could make teammates and fans tear their hair. He was notably deficient at fielding hard-bounding grounders, and weak against some forms of left-handed pitching. Guy "Doc" White of Chicago broke up laughing after striking out the youth four times in one afternoon. "I thought I'd be released after that game," Cobb remembered. "By September I kept waiting for the ax to fall . . . why it didn't I still don't know."

One answer to that might have been the home run he hit that late season against Washington. His first big-league home run was a three-run, inside-the-park job. The ball, pulled into the right-field corner, bounced away from the fielder and Cobb simply outran its return. "He went so fast," commented the *Detroit News,* "that he almost ran over the two Tigers scoring ahead of him, Sam Crawford and Germany Schaefer. This kid can outleg the No. 1 horse hitch at the Central Fire Department."

A strikeout victim too much of the time, he compensated to a degree by going on batting spurts. When Detroit finished its season at Cleveland on October 7, Tiger regulars urged Armour to bench the kid and let Jimmy Barrett, slowed by a knee injury, end the campaign at his former outfield position. Cobb had replaced Barrett back on August 30. "Can't do it," replied Armour. "Frank Navin wants to see more of him. We're not sure what to do about him next season. He's got plenty of fight."

Armour noticed how Cobb had handled the matter of Bill "Jap" Barbeau, Cleveland's second baseman. Barbeau one day had tried to block Cobb's slide into the bag. A hurtling body, spikes extended, had hit Barbeau at the knees, sending him backward, stunned. Torn from his grip, the ball had rolled into the outfield. Cobb was safe, Barbeau's leg had been cut, and the game-winning run had scored.

To take a man out of a play by charging him at full force was a football tactic seldom used in this game. But an attitude was growing in Cobb that argued that while it was standard practice to impede a runner's access to a base by any means, fair or foul, there was a limit beyond which the defense should not go. Within baseline boundaries, access should be equal for offense and defense. The rulebook was vague on the subject. Cobb's interpretation was becoming one of *Give me room or get hurt.*

Not until he grew to more than six feet and 185 to 190 pounds and was proficient in the use of momentum was he fully able to enforce his belief. As it stood now, he was making a start at confronting those who shut him off—at times by slamming balls into his face. "I have some loose teeth to prove it," he pointed out that winter. Bloodying his spikes on basemen would in time involve him in more field fights and off-field brawls and inflame the national audience and press more than any other aspect of his play.

Along with handling Barbeau, he had two base hits against Cleveland on October 7. That concluded his tryout with the Tigers. He had appeared in all 41 games left on the schedule after he reported. Batting down the lineup in fifth place most of the time, he had produced 36 hits in 150 times at bat for a .240 average. Included were 6 doubles, no triples, and 1 home run. His runs scored came to 19, not a bad showing for so few games. Armour did not let him try for steals, and his bases stolen came to only 2. He had won at least 4 games with his bat and feet.

In the field, against the wind that whirled in Bennett Park, he had made 85 putouts and 6 assists with just 4 errors, for a .958 average— not bad at all. Through all of his years Cobb insisted that, at the outset, he was a poor fielder. His total of errors does not support that description. His reason for playing down his defensive work had to do with the Georgian's claim that he was in no way a natural ballplayer. He wanted it certified and understood that he succeeded only by detailed observation, application, and perseverance. "Not until 1907," he said, "could I be considered sound in the field and beginning to understand hitting. I earned everything I did by damned hard effort."

His .240 average for a minor part of the season just ended would represent the only time in twenty-four big-league years that Cobb averaged under .300—a tremendous feat. No major-league batter from Honus Wagner, Shoeless Joe Jackson, Nap Lajoie, Rogers Hornsby, Tris Speaker, George Sisler, Paul Waner, Harry Heilmann, Jimmie Foxx, Charlie Gehringer, Al Simmons, Babe Ruth, and Lou Gehrig to Joe DiMaggio, Stan Musial, Ted Williams, Mickey Mantle, Willie Mays, and Hank Aaron—has ever maintained over an extended career an unbroken .300-and-up record. All failed at least once to hit .300. Cobb missed hitting .300 or better only in part of one season; thereafter he did it for *twenty-three consecutive years.* His sustained excellence remains the all-time record, with the probability that no hitter will ever tie or equal it.

BASEBALL WRITERS, puzzled by the upstart Cobb that autumn, pictured him as a question mark followed by an exclamation point. The *News's* Harry Salsinger saw him as "a ghost in advancing when he manages a hit" and "good at ducking beanballs" and "one who might develop into an offensive threat." Paul Brusky of the *Times* went overboard with "here is an infant prodigy." Brusky had been intrigued enough to check out Cobb's recent past, and was aware of the killing of Professor Cobb of sixty days earlier. He let his readers know that the youngster had played with a heavy burden of grief. In *Sporting Life,* Brusky admired his "wonderful ability" to resume play so soon after his father's funeral. The phrase "small miracle" was tossed around.

Other Tigers had not surpassed Cobb's .240 mark by much. As previously noted, aside from Sam Crawford's near-.300 performance—best on the club—infielders Schaefer and Pinky Lindsay and outfielders Charley Hickman, Bobby Lowe, and Matty McIntyre had batted at from .193 to .267. Armour's need for power ran right down the lineup.

Although major-league baseball attendance in general was climbing, the Tigers, despite finishing third, were at the bottom in 1905 in American League home draw, with 193,384, or an average of only 1,264 patrons per game. So poor was the showing that it was predicted that the franchise would be moved from the low-income Corktown district of Detroit to a larger eastern metropolis.

WHILE COBB prepared for a return to a mother facing criminal proceedings in the case of her dead husband, club secretary Frank Navin remained silent on the question of whether Cobb had shown enough ability to be retained for 1906. Armour was not talking, either. Gossip had it that economy measures would be imposed next year. Cobb failed to see how, under management's existing policy, more money could be saved. On long, hot road trips, game suits went unlaundered; players washed them in sinks on trains and hung them out windows, where the uniforms were peppered by flying cinders. Bathing facilities at parks and at second-rate hotels were few and primitive; men often dried in their own sweat upon leaving a city. Lacking a trainer, players with cuts or abrasions were bandaged by teammates. Only the best pitchers and a few veterans were provided with sleeping berths on trains. Most of the Tigers, Cobb included, slept sitting up. Road meals came cold and unappetizing.

Boss Navin, however, riding up front in a private compartment, dined and slept in comfort. "Navin kept us badly housed and fed through my early years with Detroit," Cobb attested. "That went for a lot of clubs in those days. But we were about the worst at getting pissed upon by the ownership."

Other trouble was shaping up. Cobb was unpopular with a majority of the Tigers. Matty McIntyre and pitching mainstay Ed "Twilight" Killian set the tone by ignoring him on and off the field. The team's main men had little in common with an eighteen-year-old from a distant part of the country. Most of the members were northerners and midwesterners. Cobb's pronounced southernness—with his slurry drawl and a stiff, formal way of addressing people—was not "regular." He did not drink or joke around. Moreover, Cobbs had fought against the Union in the Civil War.

During the first days after his arrival he was not seen as a threat to take someone's job. But once his occasional flashy play indicated that he might turn out to be more than a short-term replacement, resentment built among the established outfield corps of Charley Hickman, Matty McIntyre, Jimmy Barrett, and Duff Cooley. Only fun-loving infielder Germany Schaefer and utilityman Bobby Lowe hospitably invited him to sit with them at dinner. There was no room for him at postgame gab sessions in hotel lobbies, at floating poker games, at barbershop-quartet singing. It was ostracism, by men who were old pros at it. The team's attitude had not yet hardened into outright hazing—that was coming—but Cobb, reviewing his 1905 experience, wrote, "It was a them-against-me setup . . . it wasn't about to get better." It was not much comfort to know that rookies everywhere were treated like plague carriers, a baseball practice as old as the day when umpires wore top hats and derbies and four strikes composed an out.

At the last moment, early in October, Cobb changed his mind about leaving immediately for home. Word from Royston concerning his father's estate was troubling. Cobb had always thought that the Professor was well fixed. Now letters from his family showed that much of W. H.'s property was mortgaged, and the cost of lawyers to defend his mother in her forthcoming trial for voluntary manslaughter had mounted. The cash problem was serious.

Cobb stayed on in Detroit for a few days to pick up ninety dollars for a pair of postseason games matching the Tigers with a local all-star semipro team. While on the field, he was approached by a reporter from a Lansing, Michigan, newspaper. The man brought up the subject of Amanda Cobb and her shotgunning of W. H. "What are her chances for acquittal?" asked the reporter.

"Get away from me," Cobb warned.

When the reporter persisted in his questioning, he was grabbed by the shirt and britches and sent staggering. It drew a reprimand from Frank Navin as the postseason ran out.

Cobb's final act of an incredible month was to try pinning down Armour on what he could expect next spring. "It's all up in the air," said Armour, who liked Cracker Cobb for his hustle. "I haven't been offered a contract, myself. Maybe neither of us will be here next time."

"If I come back," pressed Cobb, "do you think I can get twelve hundred dollars for the season?"

Replied Armour, "Navin has to pay some of the boys more than twice that. He thinks you might be a comer. So don't be bashful about getting all you can."

Uncertainty remained. Cobb would say in later years that he was not even sure at this point that he could afford to stay on as a ballplayer.

CHAPTER NINE

"A HANDFUL OF HELL"

"Temperamental, humorless, egocentric, Cobb proved an inviting target for the hardboiled primitives on the team . . . with Detroit he had no friends, whatever . . . they hated his guts."

Historian Harold Seymour, in *Baseball: The Golden Age*

In December, midway through the 1905–06 off-season, Cobb reached his nineteenth birthday without receiving a Detroit contract. Weeks of silence by the front office passed. In November two events had seemed to signal his return to a minor league, and to a team not even based in the United States. Toronto of the Eastern League needed an outfielder, and the low eighteen-hundred-dollar asking price on Detroit's rookie fill-in attracted the Canadians. In addition, Frank Navin had recently signed Davy "Kangaroo" Jones, formerly a stout outfielder with the Chicago Cubs. With Jones on hand and a Toronto deal percolating, Navin delayed resigning a marginal player.

Tired of waiting, Cobb did not help his shaky situation when he violated a Navin rule concerning outside employment. Near Atlanta, the University of Georgia operated a prep-school training camp for baseball and track athletes it was recruiting, and who needed coaching. Local boy Cobb was offered $250 and travel expenses to coach the kids. Navin and Armour, as a matter of policy, refused to allow it. Cobb defied the rule, signed with Georgia, and left for camp.

Years later, reviewing the dispute, he held a thumb and finger an inch apart, saying, "I came this close to giving up playing ball for a living—for good. I would not drop down to Toronto, which was out there in moose and snow country. Working for a university was a good deal for me . . . though I probably was the youngest college coach in the country." The arrangement was an odd one: some of Cobb's pupils were as old as their teacher.

In January a contract for fifteen hundred dollars—some three hundred dollars more than he had expected—arrived from the Tigers. He signed for his first full big-league season as a backup behind out-field starters Sam Crawford, Matty McIntyre, and Davy Jones and reserves Jimmy Barrett and Sam Thompson. He was, to borrow a current expression, "low dog in the meat yard"—the lowest-paid carry-over member of the twenty-four-man squad. If a favorable trade or sales proposal came along, he figured to be dealt away by Navin. "His teammates," said the *Sporting Journal*, "wanted no part of someone who might one day take somebody's job. They banded to run him off the club with some of the hardest hazing ever seen."

THE DETROIT Baseball and Amusement Company opened spring train-ing in Augusta at Warren Park with low pennant hopes. The Tigers' dump-Cobb faction wasted no time. It became busy—"in midseason form," as Cobb described it—during batting practice. There was no room in the box for him. Big Matty McIntyre and others blocked his way; as soon as one hitter finished his ten workout swings, another crowded in ahead of next-man-up Cobb. He was dismissed with, "Go knock some flies to the yannigans [rookies]." Handed a long, thin stick known as a fungo bat, he drew the job of exercising fielders. It was insulting—fungoing was usually relegated to a coach or some retired player. Stuck with this duty, his chance to sharpen his eye against spring pitching was slipping away.

Practice games had barely started when he found his only good glove unexplainably ripped in the stitching, and a pair of his favorite bats gone from the rack. On a tip from a groundskeeper he looked behind a fence and in the weeds found the bats—both shattered at the handles. Cobb never found out for sure who did it.

Augusta's antiquated Albion Hotel was the Tigers' headquarters, an inn offering a single toilet with bathtub on each floor. Ringleaders Matty McIntyre and Ed Siever, with others, dawdled in the water while Cobb hung around a chilly hallway draped in a towel. After a hot, dirty game, he would find himself locked out of an empty washroom. At other times the hot water supply deliberately was exhausted. In the Albion dining room a pea flicked off someone's knife would splat off Cobb's head. Or he would find a piece of rotten fruit squishing in his coat pocket. His hat was impaled on a rack. In the clubhouse his shoes were nailed to the floor.

Cobb's instinctive reaction was to punch someone. In his words, "I told that damned little Bill Armour I was about to settle this man to man if he didn't move in. Instead of coming down on the gang he went on playing poker with them. Oh, he'd make a half-assed remark now and then that things were going too far. But he let me know it was my problem—and there could be no brawling on the team."

Cobb asked a few uninvolved Tigers what he should do. They were unhelpful. In a slugout against a half-dozen players, he stood no chance. But to let them walk on him was something he could not tolerate.

Job protection, money, and pride—strong elements—kept the feud going. Matty McIntyre, with his swiftness and good arm, soon appeared to have won a starting outfield position. At twenty-six he was a club leader. Davy Jones was all but sure to handle another outfield spot. Steadily effective Sam Crawford was a star, and entrenched as an outfield regular in his eighth major-league season. There was Jimmy Barrett, formerly a .300 hitter but now declining, and coming off an unhealed leg injury. There was Freddie Payne, a utility type. And there was Cobb. Three of the six would not see much action, possibly be traded or sold. Survival was especially important to McIntyre, who was having trouble maintaining a .260 plate average as the spring tour meandered through the South.

Someone tacked a note on Cobb's hotel door: "LEAVE HERE WHILE YOU CAN." Suspects were plentiful, but he didn't bother to ask around the Albion for any witnesses. He went out and for twenty-five dollars bought a gun. "I was catching hell by the handful," he said later. "That gun was forced on me."

COBB'S WEAPON was a snub-nosed Frontier Colt pistol, provided by a former teammate with his old hometown team, the Royston Reds. Ty saw the Colt as making all the difference in the event he was jumped some night by a group. He wore the gun, he told me, in a holster near his armpit. Practicing his draw, he became fast. He kept the pistol a secret for weeks. When Bill Armour heard rumors that Cobb was armed, he moved to confiscate the weapon. Cobb denied its existence. "I stood still for a search," he remembered, "and they didn't find a fucking thing."

ON MARCH 30 Cobb left camp to attend his mother's trial for voluntary manslaughter. More than seven months had passed since Amanda Cobb had pulled the triggers of the shotgun that had killed Professor Cobb. During the hiatus the trial's outcome had hung as a miserable dead weight over her son. Amanda Cobb had run up medical bills while she slowly "recovered from shock." She now needed a nurse, and had retained a battery of defense lawyers. Of the approximately $215 per month the Tigers were paying him, Ty was sending home $100 or more for family support and to apply to the debt against the Royston farm, a legacy of the late Professor.

The site of Amanda's trial was Lavonia, Georgia, where a sizable crowd gathered to look on. Already Ty Cobb was a regional celebrity—no other local product had ever reached the major leagues—and people from across the territory slapped his back and shook his hand, when all he wanted was to see the ordeal ended. The thought of a Cobb going to prison was chilling.

Amanda had been free from custody on seven thousand dollars bond. At the opening of her trial the small, pale-faced woman was near collapse. Her son sat stonily by as the examination proceeded. For some seven hours of testimony and deliberation the widow awaited her fate. The state's prosecutor focused his questioning on why there had been a five- to ten-second interval between the two shots she had fired through her bedroom window. On the morning after the killing Amanda had described such a time span to a sheriff. In court she explained that panic had overwhelmed her. In firing twice, she had reacted in ongoing terror.

The rumor of a lover some Royston neighbors insisted Amanda had taken—supposedly inciting her husband's domestic break-in—was not mentioned during the proceeding. No "lover" was named or produced, although in Royston a name was whispered about. Supposedly the man was young, a well-to-do Royston planter, known to Ty Cobb only as a family friend and an occasional visitor to Professor Cobb's farm and to his political gatherings.

Amanda was acquitted by an all-male jury. Cobb left the building in silence. Gossip would persist in his hometown; it would be one reason why in the future he would not live in Royston, a place where his mother was seen by many as a murderer.

Bill Armour and Frank Navin objected to Cobb's continuing absence from camp after the trial concluded. Why was it necessary for him to return to Royston with his mother for several days? Why, following that, did he go jaunting with his younger brother, Paul, to Atlanta? His answer was that business concerning the endangered Cobb acreage in Royston required him to speak with bankers. As for Paul, he had problems as a freshman student at Georgia Tech. Family came first. "Poor damned way to make my ball club," Navin warned him.

As it worked out, Cobb did not catch up to the barnstorming Tigers by train, buggy, and trolley until they reached Birmingham, Alabama, on April 7, where he had three straight base hits. He continued to look sharp. Navin, for once, was quiet. The boy had recovered from an ordeal with remarkable speed.

ALWAYS ADAPTIVE, he now was "seeing" a pitched ball with more acuteness. His even shorter stride, with little forward movement of head and body, aided his balance and balance enabled him to focus with steady vision. He was fully committed to a choke grip, which allowed him to spread hits to all fields. He also went to a new "knuckles-on-down" grip, where he held the bat with knuckles of both hands tensed in a straight line. That way he got a sharper wrist snap at contact. He claimed that on some pitches, such as a slow curve, he could actually see the stitches on the spinning ball. Few since have claimed this.

En route to Detroit for the season opening, he awoke in the Boody House hotel in Toledo with a 102-degree temperature and in racking pain. Before then it had been noticed by infielder Herman "Germany" Schaefer—not one of Ty's enemies—that he had been gripping his chair tightly while eating. Schaefer asked why. "Because it hurts like fury to swallow," admitted Cobb. Even drinking soup was painful. He consulted the Boody House physician, who told him he had tonsillitis.

Tonsillectomies in the early 1900s were sometimes a risky procedure. This one turned into butchery. "Putting a stranglehold on my neck, without anesthetic, this doc cut me seven times before he was finished," Cobb told of his agony. "Each time a piece [of tissue] came out, blood spouted and choked me. Between some of the seven cuts I'd collapse on a sofa. He didn't seem to know what he was doing. Germany had to half-carry me back to my room, bleeding and gagging. This went on for two days."

A year later Cobb checked out the "surgeon." He learned that over the winter the man had been sent to an asylum for the insane. According to Cobb, "the son of a bitch had some sort of brain disease."

Twenty-four hours after the operation—Ty never forgave the Tiger management for this—he was sent in to play in an exhibition game against Columbus of the American Association. He was shaky, still weak, and in pain, yet Armour used him for seven innings. On sheer guts he made a two-base hit, then said, "I'm leaving," and walked out and collapsed in bed.

By late spring his dislike of Armour had turned to contempt. Some Tiger fans liked Armour for his colorful ways; others felt that he had poor control of his personnel. Certainly he did little to help his promising rookie from Georgia. When his men were not misplaying fly balls and reacting late to double plays on the field, they broke curfew, hung out at bars, and gambled on the ponies. Struggling to win a job, Cobb limited his drinking to an occasional glass of ale.

Armour was critical when he messed up a play, and sparing with praise when it was deserved. To Cobb and his small Detroit following, no excuse existed for the manager's inability to see what was under his nose—an extraordinary talent awaiting fulfillment. How Armour could fail to recognize someone so promising was mystifying. "I looked around and saw nobody who could do things that I couldn't," Cobb wrote in his diary. And: "I am as good a baserunner as the best of them." (After the season ended Armour would be fired, and his replacement, Hughie Jennings, would hold office for only a few days before predicting around town, "Hear me! This boy has it. He has the makings to become the greatest player who ever lived.")

More bad fortune—and a few good things—came along. A "slider," an abrasion of the hipbone caused by hitting hard dirt in base-stealing tries, became infected and filled with pus. Cobb was hospitalized in serious condition. No teammate took the time to visit him at Detroit's Fort Street hospital. Invalided for several days, Ty did see Frank Navin—once. Navin did not offer to pay any part of his man's medical bill. Cobb recalled this with: "Although we had no injury insurance then and I was bad off, Navin kept his hands in his pockets."

Cobb had about four hundred dollars to his name and owed considerably more than that on farm debts in Royston when the American League kicked off the campaign in mid-April. His weight had dropped to 168 pounds after the pair of illnesses. But he was cheered by the arrival of some fine new bats, custom-lathed to his liking by the Louisville Slugger plant in Kentucky and replacing those destroyed in spring camp by secret hands. Cobb felt hopeful of hitting .280 or so if he could gain weight and get into one hundred or more games on the season.

Bennett Field on opening day rattled to the rafters with the sounds of an overflow crowd of fifteen thousand, many of whom wanted to see Cobb play center field in his breakneck style. They were disappointed. Armour kept him benched, putting Davy Jones, Matty McIntyre, and Sam Crawford in the outfield.

After sitting idle for a week, Cobb got a break when Sam Crawford strained a leg muscle. Sent to right field, Cobb showed nothing special, went hitless at St. Louis, and made a costly error on a fly ball against Cleveland. Elsewhere he overslid a base for an out. Several times he was replaced for a pinch hitter.

With his hitting judged only fair and while drawing more complaints from Armour, he resorted to the bunt—both the sacrifice variety and bunting for the hit. He began to tap pitches down third- and first-base lines, scoring runners from third, and with his instant acceleration often beating out throws to first. It was a way to moderate a slump, and it worked, temporarily at least. (One day that summer Cobb was timed with a stopwatch at one hundred yards. His 10-flat sprint in uniform pants and baseball shoes compared well with world-record-holder Dan Kelly's 9.6 seconds in underwear, track shoes, and with specialized training.)

Sniping continued from the McIntyre-Siever faction, inventors of new nasty tricks on road trips. A wet wad of newsprint would come flying down the train aisle to smack Cobb on the neck. When he came back with fists raised, no one would admit that he had done the throwing. Another device was to deprive him of a roommate. Only one player, Edgar "Eddie" Willett, a rookie pitcher, was willing to share lodging with T.C., and their teaming-up lasted but briefly. A southerner, Virginia-born, pleasant and good-looking, the twenty-two-year-old Willett bunked with the Georgian at home and away until one day he announced that he was moving out. Willett admitted that he had been warned by certain Tigers to find other housing or "get hurt bad." Cobb reportedly told Willett, "You are at the crossroads, Edgar. Those men just want to get at me through you. And they'll make a whiskey-head out of you, like them. If I was in your place I'd tell them to go to hell." But Willett, further unnerved by the gun Cobb carried with him on team travels, moved out of their small quarters in Detroit's Brunswick Hotel.

Cobb never forgave him for that surrender. In his 1961 autobiography, *My Life*, Cobb wrote, "The sporty life caught up with Willett. In six seasons he was finished." This was a Cobb fabrication; Willett pitched eight years for Detroit, winning 95 games between 1908 and 1913.

But then Matty McIntyre and his clique went too far. In Chicago a line drive split the left-center-field spacing between Cobb and McIntyre. The latter waved off the chance and pointed a finger at Cobb—who did not go for the ball, either. Skidding on the grass between them, the ball bounded to the fence for a three-base hit. When this occurred a second time, Armour blew his straw hat. The story goes that he asked McIntyre, "How is it that you don't make plays that are yours and never bear down when Cobb's on base? You do nothing to advance him."

"Why should I help that no-good son of a bitch?" shouted McIntyre, making his motive clear. Even if it cost Detroit ball games, McIntyre was not cooperating.

To the bench—suspended—went the veteran, and into the outfield on a steady basis went Cobb. His hitting improved; within weeks, with a .317 mark, he was leading the team both in hitting in the clutch and for average, while on defense he was making outstanding catches of difficult flies. By July he had stolen a dozen bases. In Boston one of his spectacular catches and his double won a game; against New York he walloped pitching, mixed in bunts, and scored from second on an infield roller, forcing errors at two bases. Around the league there was speculation about this prospect, not yet twenty years old, who played baseball with his head and not just his body. Connie Mack, leader of the defending champion Philadelphia A's, remarked, "I wouldn't mind having him on my side."

Mid-1906 was always identified by Cobb as the beginning of his counterattack against his enemies on the Tigers. But it was no more than a start, an indication only of what he could do on the field if not impeded.

As the season rolled along, Joe Jackson of the *Detroit Free Press* began calling Cobb "a peach of a player," then the "Georgia Peach." The tag caught on. Descriptive nicknames were common as salutes to the famous, and Jackson thought Detroit's youthful pepperpot deserved one, too. The trouble was that the honoree liked his own moniker too much to suit the other Tigers. He took to referring to himself as "the Peach." To Detroit writers, and those of Cleveland, Boston, Chicago, and elsewhere, he would offhandedly mention, "The Peach went three for four yesterday and the buzzers [booers] were happy." He posed for pictures eating a Georgia peach. How did he feel? "Peachy!" After he became a lineup regular he cultivated executives of the sporting press and tabloid publishers with wide circulation, among them Alfred Spink of the *Sporting News* and Richard Fox of the *Police Gazette*. When he began drawing as many inches of space as some of the game's most admired players, his reputation as a grandstander (a "hot dog" today) was fixed. In the early twentieth century, ballplayers called a personal write-up "getting a splash." Before long Cobb would be up to his haircut in publicity such as only a few other Tigers received.

His style of dress also irked some of his teammates. Off-duty, the Tigers dressed roughly. By contrast, Peachy "cut a dash" in vested, check-patterned suits (once he could afford them), bright bow ties, and beribboned Panama hats. He became something of a dandy. His street shoes were always well shined. "You can see the Reb coming a block away," said teammates. He did not hang out in the Fort Street saloons of lower Detroit, patronize whores, gamble at the nearby Grosse Point pioneer auto races, or bet on horses. Filthy talk, the lingua franca of baseball, was then used by him only sparingly. He was a practicing Baptist. On a bench of hard cases, in various ways he was miscast.

His practice of carrying three bats to the plate and twirling them like dumbbells aggravated men of far greater experience. "He's ding-toed," the Tigers said, referring to his slightly pigeon-toed walk as if it were an affliction. Cobb's habit of retiring after dinner to his room to read books, make notes, and replay games looked like still more stuck-uppity behavior. In his free time he visited museums, galleries, dance halls, and nickelodeon houses—alone. A barber at Gogenriders's Tonsorial Parlor (haircuts fifteen cents; shave ten) gave Ty opera tickets, and by 1907 he became a buff. He even took ballroom dancing lessons.

More to the point, he did not fit in because he refused to swallow the abuse that was as inventive as the McIntyres, Sievers, Schmidts, and Killians could make it. He was willing to fight, anywhere, if the odds were not loaded against him. Now close to 180 pounds, he was as big as the next man. Backing him up—and nobody could forget it—was the Frontier Colt pistol he carried, concealed in his jacket or mackinaw.

IN LATE June, with the Tigers battling to stay within hailing distance of Fielder Jones's Chicago White Sox, Clark Griffith's New York Highlanders, and Nap Lajoie's Clevelanders, Cobb climbed to a .348 batting mark, up among the league leaders.

Then—plop! In a matter of weeks he fell to .318. What had been a smooth swing turned jerky. He swung at balls outside the strike zone. His hands were seen to quiver and his legs seemed unsteady. He seemed confused about ball-and-strike counts. His running speed was reduced. Between June 20 and July 15 he became a much different and less potent offensive threat.

Armour asked, "What's wrong?" Cobb, keeping his own counsel, replied that he was "off his feed." Armour reported to Frank Navin, "The boy's gone all wrong and I can't see why."

Navin—not that he was much of a judge of form in a ballplayer—took a look and was puzzled. The Tiger president called in Billy "Kid" Gleason, a one-time Detroit strategist now near the end of his career. "He doesn't look healthy," said Gleason. "He looks tired, like he doesn't give a damn."

Cobb knew why he had slumped. He was ill and dangerously so. By his way of describing it, he had "caught a handful of hell."

MISSING PERSON

On July 17, during a series at Boston, Cobb disappeared. He was nowhere to be found—not at his team's hotel or clubhouse or at any Boston spot where ballplayers hung out between games.

Bill Armour initially offered no explanation for the vanishing act, but then he said that Cobb had been ordered back to Detroit for treatment of "stomach trouble." That story appeared to be true. Then, on July 21, Cobb disappeared once more, and could not be located by members of the press corps.

Armour asked the writers not to play it up—the matter was private club business. Not until later did the press learn that Cobb's illness was so serious that he could no longer function on the field, and had been sent to a sanatorium, suffering from a nervous breakdown. That was the only fact released by management.

In the early 1900s, psychological study and treatment of mentally disturbed players was a little-understood science. Those in trouble were treated as sports-page comic characters, and called "bugs," "loonies," "nutters," and "bad actors." All too often the emotionally distressed, given no help at all, destroyed themselves. From 1900 to World War I, sixteen suicides by active or recently active big-leaguers were reported—among them Detroit pitcher Win Mercer (poison), Boston Nationals pitcher Dan McGann (gunshot), Chick Stahl, Red Sox outfielder (carbolic acid), and Christy Mathewson's brother Nick (gunshot). A man's torment, under the circumstance of a short career and fast living, went unrelieved. "They come up farm-sober, go bad in the big-time, and drink themselves out of the business," observed the *Police Gazette.*

Reporters on Detroit's four newspapers covering the Tigers were aware that Cobb was unwanted and ostracized by the team and was fighting back, but either nobody seemed to realize what this was costing him, or else they were indifferent to it. None of the observers, for instance, had noticed his behavior before games. Adjacent to Bennett Field's left-field stands was a wooden shack in which the grounds-keeper stored old base bags, lime sacks, grass cutters, and the like. During warm-ups before games, Cobb used the shack as a retreat, a place where he could find temporary peace. He had reached the point where facing steady insults and rejection was more than he could bear.

Decades later, in a letter to me, he wrote, "That shack was my hideout . . . when I came onto the field, to take practice, the gang would hit me with bad plays I'd made. If I went for the water bucket, somebody would kick it over. They cut nicks in my bats, put horse turds in my spare shoes. They were waiting for me every time I turned around."

"My nerves were shot to hell," he wrote of that summer. "I was like a steel spring with a dangerous flaw in it . . . if wound too tight the spring will fly apart and then it is done for."

By his own testimony, we see Cobb at this point of his life: In the groundskeeper's shack he paces the floor. Warming up ninety feet away are men who have excluded him and caused him to fear for his safety, to carry a gun. Batting practice is under way and the Tigers wait for him to appear, so that pitcher Siever, Killian, or Mullin can throw at his ankles and feet and pretend that the ball "got away."

He emerges into the sunlight. Backs are turned to him. He goes to the outfield to shag flies. As he expects, few balls are hit his way. He leans against an outfield wall, marking time. A few fans in the stands, out early for the game, call to him, as fans do when a player is slumping: "Hey, Cobb, get off your tail, show us something."

For three baseball seasons little has gone right for him, other than his vault to the major leagues straight from the low minors. Now yet another team is aligned against him.

Under that pressure, his mental and physical health have reached the cracking point.

HIS CASE was treated in a sanatorium over a period of forty-four days; not until September was he judged fit enough to rejoin the club, even on a curtailed schedule. Armour and Navin continued to put out the fictional tale that he was suffering from stomach trouble and, since he was not around to be questioned, the Detroit papers went along with "Cobb's bellyache" as the reason for his long absence.

The sanatorium where he was confined by the team doctor was located on the Detroit outskirts. He received medication that kept him sleeping for long periods. No visitors were allowed while the patient was recovering. As Cobb related years later, the rest home was in a heavily wooded area, and he took long walks in the forest, fished in a lake, and received no news of the Tigers. Detroit newspapers were not made available to him. Doctors urged him to forget about baseball and the worries connected with the game.

For a brief time, his breakdown caused a worn-out Ty Cobb to consider quitting for the rest of the season. "I thought of it awhile," he said in his memoirs. "But I felt like I was getting close to making a real reputation for myself. And I never quit on anything in my life, even when it looked like the smart play. Matter of honor. I rested up . . . pulled out of it.

"When I got back I was going to show them some ballplaying like the fans hadn't seen in some time." To increase the chance of that, he left the sanatorium toward the end of his convalescence to play in semipro games outside of Detroit. Cobb found that, although with lessened power, he could once again swing a bat without shaking.

UPON HIS return to the lineup in September, nothing much had changed. Cobb's enemies knew where he had been, if not the details of his illness, and made the expected comments. Pitcher Ed Siever wondered, "Did you have a dose of the clap?" Cobb ignored the hazers; his power of concentration was extraordinary. Underweight, he soon regained his speed and batting eye and then the pounds. Within ten days, he stole six bases and doubled and singled against Chicago's pennant-headed White Sox. Cleveland's Bob "Dusty" Rhoades threw a beanball that grazed him. Getting up from the dirt, Cobb shook his bat at Rhoads in warning. Then he hit a pitch deep into the right-center-field stands for a home run.

At Washington he took off from first base on Germany Schaefer's weak bunt and advanced to third, chased by throws just too late to catch him.

Harum-scarum stealing again became his habit. At New York he pulled one of his most outrageous pieces of base-running. New York catcher Fred Mitchell later reconstructed it in *Sporting News*:

> Cobb was the runner at third base. I was catching, Frank LaPorte was our third baseman. Cobb made a sudden move to the plate. I shot the ball to LaPorte, but Cobb got back safely.
>
> LaPorte took a few steps toward the pitcher. The pitcher walked toward LaPorte. Cobb slightly sauntered off the bag. As players often do, LaPorte tossed the ball a foot or two in the air and caught it while talking to the pitcher. Cobb apparently was paying no attention. He was looking toward his own dugout.
>
> LaPorte again tossed the ball into the air and did it twice more. With the fourth toss, at that instant, Cobb made a break for the plate. I never in my life saw a man spring into action so fast. Bear in mind that LaPorte was about 55 feet from the home plate. Cobb was at least 85.
>
> There was yelling and confusion. LaPorte didn't see Cobb, didn't realize what was happening. By the time LaPorte awoke and threw home, Cobb had slid across the plate and scored standing up, brushing off his uniform!

For a recent invalid to be able to play like that seemed to discourage Matty McIntyre, who was swinging hard but ineffectively. He asked to be traded away from Detroit, but was turned down. McIntyre's sidekick, Siever, co-leader of the Cobb-hating faction, appeared in the clubhouse drunk, was fined by Armour and suspended. After wrecking a few tin lockers with a bat, Siever left Bennett Park in a rage.

The discontent spread. Old pro Sam Crawford complained about his twenty-five-hundred-dollar salary. Catcher Jack Warner, turning clubhouse lawyer, criticized Armour's field methods and was dropped from the roster.

Cobb's natural batting form gradually returned. His nerves under control, he built back his average to .315, then a few points higher. Improbably, in September, despite his bout at the sanatorium he still had a chance to finish near the top in the league batting race, even while dissension left the Tigers far out of the running for the pennant. He played with grim concentration. In Chicago the poor-hitting— .230—but defensively artistic White Sox had stood in fourth place in early August. But then a major-league record of 19 consecutive victories carried the Sox, known as the Hitless Wonders, to the top with a final 93–58 mark, enough to nose out the runner-up New York Highlanders' 90–61 for the league championship.

Cobb doubted Detroit's ability to win the pennant. "I saw no hope of reaching the Series, not when I was carrying the team more than anyone right after being sick," he remembered.

OSTRACIZED BY almost all of the team regulars, Cobb had a limited social life. On free days late that season he would walk down Detroit's bustling Automobile Row on Woodward Avenue and stop at the fashionable Pontchartrain Hotel bar. Detroit fans were plentiful at "the Pontch." The Peach's loudest fan was millionaire John Kelsey, an exuberant Irishman whose charitable deeds had made him legendary in Detroit. Good John Kelsey was a master of malapropisms. He referred to field laborers of Ireland as "pheasants." To Kelsey, the French national anthem was "'The Mayonnaise.'" Even pronouncing Cobb's name was difficult.

"Here's that grand boyo, Cy Tobb! Up from fair Dublin down in Georgia," announced Kelsey to the saloon crowd. "A cheer, gentlemen, for Cy Tobb!"

No one bothered to correct Kelsey on the "Cy," the "Tobb," or "Dublin," and Tyrus, enjoying the first hard drinks of his life in stylish social circles, met get-rich-quick automobile men and listened to their advice on investing in horseless carriages.

He enjoyed a reunion with young Louis Chevrolet, champion race-car driver of France, who was in the United States to race the famous Barney Oldfield on midwestern tracks. Earlier Chevrolet and Cobb had met at a speedway.

"Could I learn to drive a racer?" asked Ty.

"Probably," replied the bilingual Chevrolet. "But you might get killed, *mon ami.*"

Chevrolet knew nothing about baseball, but he remarked that if the Tigers paid as little as Cobb said, then why didn't Ty take a job in the expanding new auto industry? Several companies were turning out ten to fifteen passenger models per month, priced at $650 or, with the addition of fancy canvas tops and windshields, costing $1,000 and more. Two Oldsmobiles had crossed from New York to Oregon in an eye-opening fifty-five days. With Chevrolet's help, Cobb might find a good position in the sales field or as a demonstration driver.

Cobb replied, "I think I'll stay on. Breaks are coming my way."

A SHOWDOWN with his teammates erupted in the late season at St. Louis. The Browns' big hitter, George Stone, drove a ball between Cobb in center field and McIntyre in left. It was a familiar story. Both started for the ball, but stopped dead to exchange glares and shouted accusations. The base hit rolled all the way to the fence for an inside-park two-run homer. Ed Siever was pitching. Siever cursed Cobb so loudly that the crowd could hear.

Back on the bench, Siever offered profane descriptions of Ty's ancestry. Cobb challenged, "Get up! Get on your feet!" Siever stayed seated, muttering that he had a game to pitch.

At the Planter's Hotel in St. Louis that night, Cobb was buying a cigar when Siever walked by and was heard by Cobb to say, "You're still a Dixie prick whose folks live off nigger slaves." When Ty grabbed Siever, pitcher Bill Donovan got between them. "No fighting here!" Donovan ordered. "Step outside for that."

Cobb's reply, he would say next day, was, "I want no trouble—I didn't start this."

A "war party" of Tigers, as Cobb saw it, gathered in the hotel lobby. Concealed behind a pillar, Cobb tried to overhear their conversation. Then, suddenly, around the pillar came big Siever. "He threw a left at me that would have taken off my head if it'd landed," went Cobb's blow-by-blow description. Ducking and moving inside the punch, he swung a right to the jaw that started Siever to the floor, followed by solid punches that put him down, bleeding and dazed.

All the pent-up enmity boiled over. Other Tigers started for Cobb, who was now furiously kicking the helpless Siever. A mass attack on him was about to start. Cries from hotel customers of "Call the police!" prevented a brawl. Siever, jaw swollen and one eye closed, was carried out. Cobb's left hand was swollen.

Navin placed most of the blame on his youngest player, and fined him fifty dollars—big money for the time. Cobb replied that where he came from, men had been killed for using Siever's language. To end the feuding, Navin considered sending Cobb down to a minor league. Scheduled to pitch in Chicago, Siever was incapacitated.

Later that night of October 6 the Tigers were scheduled to travel from St. Louis to Chicago. For hours they would be confined within a train. Navin promised that if any more violence occurred, he would trade all those involved. "By god, I'll send you all to Washington!" he threatened. The Capitals were the second-worst team in the American League.

Cobb's version of what transpired en route to Chicago was unilateral, prejudiced testimony, but most of it could be confirmed through other sources. Witnesses to the scene told interviewers, "Murder was in the air that night . . . There was a good chance that somebody would be shot . . . Cobb had a terrible temper—the world's worst . . . He had plenty of reason to think he'd be attacked sometime during the night . . . It was all out of control."

In 1961, collecting his thoughts for the memoir he was writing, Cobb declared that on this night he was ready to shoot somebody. He told how Bill Donovan, in an aside on the depot platform before leaving St. Louis, reminded him, "These guys *hate* you. They'll do anything to hurt you." Cobb said his reaction was, "I figure they're expecting me not to make this trip and avoid them . . . well, they're wrong. I'm going."

With his bat bag, uniform roll, and luggage he boarded the night express. Team trainer Tom McMahon reprimanded him for kicking Siever when he was down. Cobb denied any kicking, saying, "I didn't have to kick him, he was well licked when he went down." McMahon insisted he had seen half a dozen hard kicks strike Siever's head and ribs, kicks that could be deadly. After mounting the train, Cobb looked up Siever. The pitcher had a large beefsteak applied to his battered face. Cobb offered a conditional apology. *If* he had been so carried away that he had kicked Siever when he was down, he was sorry. Otherwise he had no regrets. "Make what you want of it," he finished.

The Georgian wrote in his personal remarks, "Siever kept mumbling, 'I'll get you.' Stretched out in my train berth. But didn't sleep. Ready—all night." Several times he heard whispers outside his berth curtains. Expecting an attack, he stayed awake most of the way to Chicago. "I would have shot the first man who came into that berth after me," he wrote afterward to Bob McCreary, his team manager in Royston, Georgia, days. His gun remained ready.

At Chicago he did not stop at Detroit's team hotel, but checked into an undisclosed address. That set a pattern for the future—the other Tigers housed in one place, Cobb off somewhere by himself. In the majors, teams stuck together. An observer, George Cutshaw, once said, "That was when it began—Ty going it alone. He was a loner from 1906 on."

As the season neared an end, he looked for job opportunities in other cities, and pressed Detroit for a trade. He thought that his strong batting mark might attract a bidder, such as Jimmy McAleer's depressed St. Louis entry or Jake Stahl's seventh-place Washington Nationals. Another hope was Boston—the Beantowners had just finished in last place after a bad year in 1905. But the Georgian was too new a quantity, had not been around long enough to form front-office connections, and no team bid for him.

From the time when he had heard that the Tigers were bringing him up from Augusta and the Sally League, he had held the idea of building a career in a lively sports city. Months later he stood disillusioned and discouraged. Armour and the veteran players had given him no coaching, had not even made him feel welcome. In a 1961 interview with a national magazine he said, "They almost ran me out of town. But I stuck it out. If my father had been there I know what he would have recommended—and I went by that. Which was to give as much as I took—and something more." He quoted a Shakespearean passage from *Hamlet* recommended to him as a boy by Professor W. H. Cobb: "Beware of entrance into a quarrel; but being in, bear't that the oppos'd may beware of thee." That was explicit enough as a warning. Cobb called it the best guide for a ballplayer ever written.

Detroit was a bad team, badly handled. It finished sixth at 71–78 —.477. Experts had no reason whatever to foresee that the Tigers of a season later, in a complete reversal of form, would finish atop the American League and reach the World Series.

Cobb's accomplishments of that first full major-league season of 1906 have been underrated by baseball historians. By any measure they were impressive. Baseball fan Bob Hope one day introduced Cobb to an audience, and compared the team owners of 1906 to the United States Congress. "Ty's rejection was like the Congress turning down Thomas A. Edison when he brought his first electrical invention to the government in 1868," cracked Hope. "Both Ty and Tom later did fairly well."

Considering the team hostility toward him, the emotional trauma and loss of forty-four days of play, the throat and hip surgery, and his manager's failure to provide help, it was remarkable that a player of so limited experience was able to appear in 97 games. As it was, the Peach's .320 for the season, best among the Tigers, enabled him to out-hit some outstanding batsmen — Socks Seybold of the Athletics, Elmer Flick of Cleveland, Kid Elberfeld and Willie Keeler of New York, Fielder Jones of Chicago, Jake Stahl of Washington, and more.

George "Socker" Stone of St. Louis led the league with a .358 mark, followed by Nap Lajoie at .355 and Hal Chase at .323. Then came the fledgling Cobb, tied for fourth best with Bunk Congalton of Cleveland. The versatile Cobb scored 45 runs in 98 games. His power rating was good — 13 doubles and 7 triples in 358 at-bats. His base steals came to 23. The Tigers as a team averaged a poor .242. Cobb overshadowed even Sam Crawford, outhitting the team's main man by 25 points.

He enjoyed his revenge, and the newspapers picked it up. Every-one in the batting order was outperformed by the player that the Tigers had sworn in March to run out of town. He had no sympathy for the likes of Twilight Ed Killian, the star pitcher who had helped lead the vituperation against Cobb, and who fell to a 9–6 win-loss record this time around. It was Killian who had joined in smashing Cobb's bats in Augusta seven months earlier; Cobb was sure that Killian was one of the guilty parties because he had tracked down a boast to a saloon where Twilight Ed had remarked, "We fixed his wagon good."

Before leaving Detroit for home in October, Ty talked with owner William H. "Good Times" Yawkey. As a contract-negotiating move, Tyrus mentioned that Honus Wagner had led the National League with a .339 average; in fact, only four National Leaguers had beaten or equalled Cobb's .320 figure. Inclusive of both leagues, with current averages only considered, one could argue that Cobb already was at least ninth-best batsman among the several hundred presently active players. Was that not impressive?

Yawkey's reaction was, "When you can cover half the ground that the Dutchman does, and draw half as many people to my ballpark as Wagner does at Pittsburgh, come and see me again."

Cobb guessed that the Detroit management was not sold on him as a property who was likely to increase in value, following his mid-season emotional breakdown. That could and probably would be taken for a sign of weakness and the word would go out to other teams, too. Also, there was the cost of living to consider. His income did not cover big-city overhead. "It costs like hell to live here," he wrote to his old Royston schoolmate Joe Cunningham. "Runs $3 to $4 a day no matter how close I cut it." There was no hope of buying the automobile he wanted.

Yawkey handed him a hundred-dollar bonus. That made it sixteen hundred dollars' pay for the best part of a year's work. He counseled Cobb to try to make peace with his fellow players: "I don't like what has happened." His new man's constant differences with the team were intolerable. Still, it was implied that Good Times Yawkey would not trade away Cobb for the 1907 season.

HOME FOLK in the winter of 1906–07 found him changed from a year ago. He was broody, short-tempered, and unsociable. Joe Cunningham, as close to a friend as Cobb permitted himself to have, recalled in later years that Ty no longer wanted anyone with him on wild-turkey and pig hunts, but now went out alone into the upper Georgia foothills of the Great Smoky Mountains. He did not speak of the Detroit situation at home, nor mention his father's name. Playing in off-season semipro games in Atlanta and Athens he was savage against far inferior opponents. Cunningham told of instances where Cobb ran right over basemen with his honed spikes and cut them. Cunningham noted that he did not need to do this to impress people with his big-league ability. "It was more than that," said Cunningham. "Tyrus was always angry."

Those who knew how badly he had been hurt in the foreign territory of Detroit made allowances. He was a home boy come home, a hero, and people took him for that.

THERE WAS one way to get more money out of Detroit and get it soon. During the season, walking past a jewelry store on a Detroit night with infielder Bobby Lowe, Cobb had noticed a gold watch on display. A sign read: "TO BE AWARDED THE BATTING CHAMPION OF THE AMERICAN LEAGUE, 1907."

"If hard work will do it," Cobb told Lowe, "I'm going to win that watch."

Link Lowe was amused. The Pennsylvanian had been in the majors for eighteen years, had hit above .300 five times, and not once had come close to earning a championship watch. "You've only been around for a few games," said Lowe. "Don't you think that's hurrying it?"

"No," answered Cobb coldly, "I don't."

CHAPTER ELEVEN

INTIMIDATOR

"Before a fight we had in 1921, I asked Cobb if he was carrying a knife . . . He said if he had a knife, he'd cut my throat . . . then he knocked me down and tried to kick my head in . . . He came close."

Billy Evans, Hall of Fame umpire, 1953

"He forced a lot of his trouble, but a hell of a lot of it was dumped on him."

Tris Speaker, Hall of Fame outfielder, 1956

It always struck Ernest Hemingway as the strangest twist to Cobb's nature that without warning he could switch from equanimity to militancy. The two men, for a time in the 1930s, had been big-game hunting partners out west. During a 1954 "Sport Night" at the San Francisco Press Club, Hemingway was asked, "How would you describe him? What was Cobb like?"

Hemingway grimaced, replying, "He had a screw loose. I never knew anyone like him. It was like his brain was miswired so that the least damned thing would set him off." On a bighorn-sheep hunt in the Wyoming back country, said the Nobel prize–winning author, their guide led them down a wrong trail into a swamp: "It was easy enough to climb back out, but Cobb went wacko, grabbed his rifle like a bat, and decked the guide. I jumped in too late to stop it. He was raving over nothing. That was it for me—I packed out next day and after that avoided him."

In the 1910s, growing up in Oak Park, Illinois, and Kansas City, Hemingway was as devout a fan as Cobb ever had—much like another worshiper, young Army officer Douglas MacArthur—and the novelist followed Cobb's successes and malefic adventures for decades. Later, seeing no change in his rages and indigestible actions off the field,

Hemingway changed his mind. Roughhouse as he was himself, Papa wrote a letter in July of 1948 to Lillian Ross of the *New Yorker.* Published later, the letter expressed his opinion that Tyrus Cobb was the supreme player of all time—but an "absolute shit."

LESS THAN ten months had passed since his emotional breakdown and recovery when the Georgian began a 1907 season in which Detroit was not considered a factor in the pennant race, and Chicago and Philadelphia seemed to hold the winning American League cards. He was depressed. His financial position was shakier than ever. The fearsome boll weevil plague had invaded the cotton crop of his inherited acres and done heavy damage. Detroit could not be blamed for his low pay, which was up from $1,500 to $2,400; Yawkey and Navin were coming off a year when attendance at Bennett Park had dropped by nearly 30,000 to 135,000 paid admissions, with receipts of under $80,000. The experiment of declaring Detroit a big-league city appeared to be foundering, after consecutive finishes of third, seventh, fifth, seventh, third, and sixth.

By now Bill Armour had been fired, replaced as manager by Hughie Jennings, a jaunty, redheaded Irishman of thirteen major-league campaigns once known for his lively hitting with the Baltimore Orioles and Brooklyn Superbas, and a disciple of the brawling John McGraw school of baseball. Jennings made news copy with a series of misadventures—near death in an auto crash, being hit by pitches forty-nine times in one season, and diving into an empty swimming pool at the cost of a fractured skull. "Nothing can kill Jennings," went the crack, "except a new ball team."

Over the winter, Cobb had written to Detroit, "I have no money for buying spring cotton and wheat seed. Have forty acres going fallow." He disliked asking for a pay advance of five hundred dollars, but did so. Bill Yawkey, from his bank-owner's office, grumbled that Tyrus could have earned the five hundred playing winter-league semipro ball in Dixie. Cobb answered that he had done that, performing as pitcher-outfielder for the Augusta Sockers and other teams—at ten to fifteen dollars per game. It seemed not to have occurred to his superiors that it was a sorry note for their number-one hitter to be back scrambling for small change with Georgia bush-leaguers. However, the Tigers advanced him three hundred dollars at interest on a six-month note.

At age twenty, built now like a running back in today's pro football, Cobb first met the new leader, Jennings, in spring camp at Augusta. As Cobb told the story years later, Jennings, for openers, gave him news of Matty McIntyre and Ed Siever. The two were more determined than ever to have Cobb gone from the club. From Florida, where McIntyre was located, had come word that they wanted a disruptive influence on the team eliminated, or else they would not sign contracts. "They're asking to be traded if we keep you," said Jennings. "They say they won't play with you anymore."

Cobb said he felt the same way. "Can you deal for me in this league?" he asked. "I want to stay in the American."

Jennings was dubious. "We don't see a trade to our liking available," he said. "What I want you to do is stop all this fighting. Get smart. And I want you to play the hit-and-run more and use the double steal with Claude Rossman." A rangy first baseman lately obtained from Cleveland, Rossman had hit .308 for the Naps.

"I hit .320," Cobb reminded Jennings. He felt he could work with Rossman, if Rossman could remember the Tigers' complicated signals.

Rossman was intelligent, assured Jennings. And no doubt Cobb had heard that Jennings was known as the "Eeee-yahhhh Man" for yelling that penetrating cry from the coaching box. There was a reason for this. "My yell is to keep you boys awake," Jennings went on. "When I change it and pause for a few seconds between the 'Eeee' and the 'yahhhh,' that's the sign for Rossman to bunt you over from first to second."

Retaining doubts about the workability of screaming signals, the Peach came to bat for the first time in 1907. He lined a triple off the fence, stole a base, and scored three runs on the day. It was a forewarning. It would be a hell of a season—and, despite all the marplots and interruptions, one of the finest times of Cobb's life. Jennings, a gambler, would give him the green light on bases, and he would run so wildly and productively that special "Cobb defenses" would fail to stop him from leading the American League in base-stealing. There would be serious injuries—doctors would treat raw, infected sores acquired from sliding, and stitch a gashed hand—yet he'd execute such characteristic Cobb devices as scoring from first base on a single, scoring from second on a bunt, and stealing a guarded home plate from third. Backed by almost the same cast of Tigers that had flopped in 1906, Cobb would lead Detroit in a tight race for the pennant against the Athletics and White Sox. When the season ended, twenty-five thousand fans in the Motor City would be staging torchlit parades through the streets.

SOMEHOW—JENNINGS couldn't understand it—the team's distaste for lone-wolf Cobb appeared transferable to the lowliest people on the Tiger staff. During spring training in the south, Cobb found one of his four-fingered gloves missing some fingers. He assumed that the groundskeeper was behind the dirty deed. The groundsman, a black man named Bungy Davis, denied it. But then one morning Bungy tried to shake Cobb's hand and clap him on the shoulder. Cobb slapped Bungy to the ground and kicked him in the head. Bungy ran for a shack adjoining the clubhouse, with Cobb in pursuit. Bungy hid himself, but his wife faced a raving Cobb with, "Leave Bungy alone!" Several players heard Mrs. Davis yell, "If you hurt my man I'll have the law on you!"

When Cobb slammed the woman to her knees and began choking her insanely, the Tigers came running. Charlie "Boss" Schmidt, a powerfully built catcher from Coal Hill, Arkansas, and quondam heavyweight prizefighter, jumped on Cobb and tore him away.

Schmidt was reputed to have fought exhibitions against world-title-contender Sam Langford and coming champion Jack Johnson. He could bend steel rods in half, was all hairy brute, and had no use for bullies. He called Cobb a "rotten skunk" and let go a punch that sent him reeling.

Hughie Jennings and others broke it up, formed a circle around a struggling, incoherent Cobb, and marched him to the boss's office. Jennings blistered him, ending with, "You're gone from Detroit." Cobb protested that Bungy had been drunk and had overstepped bounds in a South where blacks didn't get familiar with whites.

The shameful "Bungy affair" occurred on March 16, and on March 17 Jennings and Navin were on the telegraph in an effort to send their woman-beater elsewhere. Cleveland manager Nap Lajoie was offered a straight trade of his former league batting champ, Elmer Flick, for Cobb. Flick had been a stubborn salary holdout, but had just signed. Lajoie openly stated that he saw nothing much more in Cobb than a clubhouse problem player, surely not equal to Flick in ability. Connie

Mack of the Athletics showed a brief interest. But Mack had solid-hitting Socks Seybold, Topsy Hartsell, and Rube Oldring in his outfield, and he also passed.

New York's Clark Griffith offered sore-armed Frank Delahanty, even-up. Despite Delahanty's "average player" status, Jennings was tempted, but finally backed away. Stalemate. Afterward, for years the press would wonder what might have happened had Cobb become a Highlander and then, after the team's name switch, a Yankee. In New York, Cobb would have had all that great press coverage and been teamed with Babe Ruth. Cobb's contradictory reply: "Ruth came along seven years too late to be of any good to me. And look at the rotten Yankee record." Between 1907 and 1918 the New York American League entry finished better than fourth only once; under seven managerial changes, they did not win a pennant until 1921.

Not one franchise in either major league would commit itself to taking on a man who carried a loaded gun, played the loner, had throttled a woman, and remained unproved as a run producer. The hardest knock came from Pongo Joe Cantillon, manager of lowly Washington, who was quoted, "At this rate the kid won't last until opening day."

In the March 18 edition of the *Detroit News* a story appeared:

WHY COBB MUST
BE SACRIFICED

—

'Harmony In Any Case'
Is Manager Jennings'
Final Decision

—

—

Cobb Knows He Has No
Friends On Team: Is
Proportionately Aggressive

Under the byline of *News* correspondent Malcolm W. Bingay came a denunciation: "The situation is this—Cobb did have some who stuck by him when the training season opened. They turned against him when he got into trouble with Charlie Schmidt, the most even-tempered man on the team. Cobb admits himself now that he has not a friend on the club, and even if he should come out and admit he was in the wrong it would help matters little. No matter what action he should take there would be fifteen more players against him."

Not changing his behavior, Cobb a day later got into an argument with Matty McIntyre that almost became one more fistfight. Jennings stopped it just in time.

JENNINGS "REGRETTED" having to give up on a player he had planned to use regularly, but when the Tigers' tour reached the Carolinas he still did not have a buyer in sight. So he could not oblige Cobb, who fully agreed he should be dealt away.

With no solution in sight, unrepentant and defiant, Cobb walked out of camp for Royston and home. He was on strike until the stalemate was resolved.

Cobb's state of mind was not helped by the knowledge that his mother's name was still being bandied about in Augusta and Atlanta, in the matter of the fatal shooting of twenty months earlier.

Cobb never learned who started the rumor, a new version of the killing, but it appeared that women in Royston had it as "God's truth" that Amanda Cobb had deliberately shot her husband. Her acquittal had been a miscarriage of justice. The women's tale went that Amanda had not fired at an "intruding burglar" from her bedroom window at midnight; far from it. Their story was that Amanda was two-timing the Professor, and that he heard of it when he asked a neighbor to close a house of ill repute the neighbor was running in Royston. The neighbor told him to look at his own home first. When Cobb asked him what he meant by that, the man tipped him that Amanda had a secret lover. Checking up, Cobb found clues suggesting his wife was guilty.

An infuriated Amanda, so went the account, warned her mate that if she found him sneaking around the house, she'd shoot him—which she did when he came prowling. There had been some suspicious gaps in Amanda's testimony at her trial. New rumor fed on it.

Such a scandal was nothing the Georgia press dared publish, but the love-triangle story spread by word of mouth to southern ballparks. Such gossip was to haunt Cobb for years. Long after he stopped swinging a bat, the *Detroit News Magazine* and other journals would run the "love-nest" yarn in some detail. For now, early in 1907, it was something Cobb had to endure.

When he quit the Tiger road trip that spring, what passed between mother and son in the several days he was gone to Royston remains unknown. But any fair estimate of Cobb must take into account that in 1907 he was still reliving a death that anguished him and undoubtedly was causing an extreme emotional reaction.

THOSE WHO thought Cobb a mental case were vindicated by what happened next. Returning to training on March 23, Cobb had a rematch fight with Boss Schmidt. Of all things to do, taking on Schmidt was the most unwise. With a forty-pound weight advantage, the ex–pro boxer could handle Cobb easily. Their second battle came because of Schmidt's previous disgust with the way Tyrus had abused groundskeeper Bungy and wife, and because Cobb foolishly taunted Schmidt about his clumsiness at the backstop position. Schmidt called Cobb "a yellow dog." They went at it on the clay infield of the park at Meridian, Mississippi, before an exhibition game.

Cobb always claimed that Schmidt sneak-punched him and he never had a chance. "I had just laced my shoes and was walking toward the outfield," he described it, "when I heard a voice growl, 'Cobb.' I turned and Schmidt's punch caught me with both hands at my side . . . a wallop that knocked me down and broke my nose . . . From then on a terrible anger was on me."

A dozen or so Tigers gathered around to cheer while Schmidt handed Cobb the most one-sided licking of his career. In a nothing-barred fight, Schmidt hammered away until the smaller man's mouth was gashed, his eyes nearly closed, and he was spattered with blood. Schmidt ended it only when Cobb went down for the fourth time, able only to rise to his knees. But it was noticed by players that at no point did he quit. The loser kept getting off the ground. "You did better than I thought you could," consoled Wild Bill Donovan, the pitcher who had partially sided with Cobb during his 1906 clashes with his teammates.

The damage was extensive enough to leave Cobb unable to play at Meridian that day. At Vicksburg, still limping, Cobb remained out of action. A doctor who stitched his mouth and chin asked, "What ran over you—a horse?"

Everything about Cobb—the Colt pistol he packed was only part of it—left his teammates and even Jennings feeling uneasy. Sam Crawford, the club's best run producer until now, once told how Cobb suspected him of not bearing down at bat when the Peach was on base and positioned to score. Cobb already had a beef with Crawford, believing he had been one of those who earlier had smashed his bats.

"He walked up to me red in the face and wanted to fight," Wahoo Sam said. "I didn't know what he might pull on me—a knife, brass knucks, or a gun. I waited until some other players came along and said, 'Let's go.' He changed his mind pretty fast then."

ONCE MORE Jennings tried for a trade—Cobb for Billy Hogg of New York. A curveballer, Hogg in two seasons had won 23, lost 26. President Yawkey, intervening, killed the deal. As the season started, fans saw small hope for more than another sixth-place finish. Adding up the past three years, it came to 242 losses to 212 wins for Detroit. Most of the same talent was returning: Pinky Lindsay, Charlie O'Leary, Bill Coughlin, and Dutch Schaefer in the infield, Matty McIntyre, Davy Jones, Sam Crawford, and Cobb in the outfield. Just one pitcher, George Mullin, could show 20 or more wins for the prior year.

With McIntyre refusing to play alongside Cobb, his enemy, Jennings experimentally shifted Crawford to center field, thereby splitting McIntyre in left and Cobb in right, far away from each other. Jennings theorized that there would be no more wrangling over who should handle a fly ball or a drive up the alleys. That is what Jennings hoped for. But his problems had only begun.

From opening day on, when his two hits, a key stolen base, and two runs scored helped beat Cleveland 2–0, Cobb lived in a four-second world. Stealing became his chosen instrument for putting runs on the board. Sprinting from first base to second was only the preliminary to traveling another 180 feet to home—sequential thievery based on getting the jump on pitchers by reaching full speed in three steps, and one way or another avoiding tags. At upward of twenty miles an hour, Ty Cobb on the bases was a big blur to fielders.

He began keeping book on opposing batteries, noting their weaknesses and tip-offs. "Boston had a left-hander, Jesse Tannehill," he named as an example, "who had a habit of squeezing and resqueezing the ball before he threw to the plate. I stole three times on him in nine innings. Long Tom Hughes of Washington stiffened his right leg just before he spun and threw to first. There were others around you could beat with mental speed."

By "mental speed" Cobb meant that he obtained a full picture of the pitcher who stood there deciding which way to go—whether to pitch or try for a pickoff. He took extremely long leads, often forcing as many as fifteen throw-overs as he dove back headfirst. "In the rain," he said, "I looked like a mud pie." But he wore out the pitchers. Through all of this he was memorizing the action of moundsmen's knees, hips, and, in particular, feet and elbows. Cobb told me, "Cy Young [whose 511 total victories of 1890–1911 remain the record as of today] had me stopped for a while. Then I saw something. Other pitchers would throw a decoy ball over to first only fairly hard, then turn as if to pitch and shoot another one to first at full speed. Young's speed never varied, except when he stood with elbows slightly away from his chest. That meant a hard pickoff coming. With his elbows pulled in, it was damn sure he was going to the hitter. Well, you can imagine what that was worth."

Leaving the park one day after double-stealing, he was asked by Young, "What am I doing, bo?" Replied Cobb, "Not a thing—you're the toughest of them all to read." Young walked away, shaking his head.

Detroit started 1907 unimpressively, as did their right fielder. Not until the arrival of June and warm weather—Cobb thrived on the heat he'd grown up with in balmy Georgia—did he get going. Then his bat-work climbed from .250 to above .350. He was fisting off-plate pitches for singles and doubles and running recklessly. Against Chicago, with Cobb on second base, on a ball hit deep into the hole at shortstop, Cobb ignored an urgent stop sign from third-base coach Jennings. Rounding third he sideswiped Jennings, sent him sprawling, and continued toward the plate. As Cobb analyzed it in a split second, the shortstop had to knock down a spinning ball, regain his balance, turn toward the plate, and plant himself for a longish throw home. Cobb beat the throw by inches. Umpire Frank "Silk" O'Loughlin hesitated, then yelled, "Yerrrrr—safe!" And muttered, "Damned if I see how."

Unlikely plays of this type were constructed in part by Cobb spotting small advantages as he ran, and by forcing fielders, caught by surprise, to throw before they were ready or could get ready. Even experienced men would commit fielding errors when jolted by a totally unexpected tactic. Success depended upon two factors: gall and foot speed.

Fastballing George Mullin was on the mound for Detroit when

Cobb, whom Mullin disliked, won a game for him. It began with a single that Cobb stretched into a double. In moving to second, Cobb flashed his spikes at Cleveland's Rabbit Nill, and the unnerved shortstop, ducking away, failed to make the tag. Moments later Cobb riskily moved to third, beating catcher Nig Clarke's hurried, off-line throw. Then, after another Naps' misplay on a pickoff attempt, he came home to score.

A proposition, not well recognized until then, was stated by Cobb: a defensive play was at least five times as difficult to make as an offensive play. The potential was there for an unassisted fielder's error, a bad throw, a misplay from a bad hop of the ball, the shielding of the ball by the runner, and a mixup of responsibility between two infielders or two outfielders. On offense you had fewer ways to fail after putting the ball in play. Therefore: attack, with the confidence that the odds are with you. *Attack, attack—always attack.* Once you put the ball in play, the defense has to retire you. Make them throw it. Let them beat themselves with a mistake.

As the schedule moved into June, the surprising Tigers were in a close race with Chicago and Cleveland for the league lead, and without question the individual whom Detroit's management had repeatedly tried to get rid of was the player making it happen. Sportswriters spoke of his "theory of suggestibility," and even his apparent use of ventriloquism, as in the following: One World Series day in October, as Cobb remembered it, he romped down the line to second base against the Chicago Cubs and seemed a probable out. Second baseman Johnny Evers took a throw-in from shallow center field with his back to the bag and with shortstop Joe Tinker out of his line of vision. Evers heard the cry, "Tag him!"

Hearing that, Evers swept his glove around—and touched only thin air. Evers's first thought, as Cobb had expected, was—*why did Tinker tell me to do that?* His mind was on Tinker's seeming call, not on the runner.

It required a second or more for Evers to realize he had been tricked, that it was Cobb's voice he had heard. It took a bit longer for him to recover from his lunge, wheel into a throwing stance, and fire to third base. Evers was slightly late. Not having paused, and with his broad back blocking Evers's full view of third base, Cobb did a hook-slide and was safe by inches.

Another element entered here, showing how Cobb's mind worked. Crab Evers and Tinker, in company with first baseman Frank Chance, were a heralded (and overrated) double-play combination. But Evers and Tinker did not like each other. Most of the time they did not speak. Aware of this, Cobb, as he remembered it, figured that in the instant before Evers realized that he had been duped by Cobb, he would be all the more upset at Tinker and liable to err on the next play.

Back to the regular season. To prevent or reduce Cobb's multiple base thefts, league catchers began to use the trick of placing their heavy face masks—"birdcages"—squarely on the third-base line when Cobb was headed home. That gave him two choices. He could slide into and through the masks, at the risk of tearing a foot or ankle tendon, or come in over the top. Using the first route would be an act of surrender, so Cobb came in high and hard. In late June, against Cleveland's Harry Bemis, who was an early-day Johnny Bench at blocking home plate, Cobb went for the score with spikes out in front like lances. He knocked Bemis back several feet. The ball rolled free. Cobb was still on the ground when an infuriated Bemis, retrieving the ball, began beating him over the head with it. Dazed and bloodied by repeated blows, Cobb tried to crawl away. Not one Detroit player came to his rescue. Jennings ran from his coach's box, shoved Bemis back, and dragged his man away. Detroit fans threw odds and ends at Bemis, who was ejected by the umpire.

A trainer bandaged Cobb's head. He went on that day to score four runs in one game for the first time in his big-league career. Hurt or not, he never wavered from his doctrine: *attack*.

In July he was better yet. Against Rube Waddell of Philadelphia he stole home, another career first, had a three-steal game versus Washington, and in the outfield was outstanding in doubling runners off base when they tested his arm. In New York, Clark Griffith, who would always deeply regret his failure to trade for Cobb that spring, said, "He does things I've never seen. And he doesn't drink at all, from what I hear."

Whiskey and brandy did not attract him, and would not do so until World War I, when he would develop a taste for hard liquor. He did not chew tobacco or smoke cigars. Baseball men were impressed by his progress at so early an age. He was so damned *young* to be doing all this. "He could pose for Castoria ads for kids," someone said.

THE TIGER management and players fighting for an unexpected league championship were an odd mixture. One Detroit front-office figure, Jimmy Burns, was a wrestler, cockfighter, and saloonkeeper on the side. Secretary–general manager Navin originally had bought into the franchise with five thousand dollars won in an all-night poker game. He was a heavy horse-track gambler. Navin was called "The Chinaman" for his slitted eyes. Number-one boss Yawkey, worth millions in Midwest timber harvesting, feared pickpockets and mugs and went around with Tommy Ryan, light heavyweight champion of the world, as his bodyguard. Straw-haired second baseman Herman "Germany" Schaefer toured the Lyceum vaudeville circuit in the off-season with a soft-shoe and poetry-reciting act.

One day Schaefer was sent in as a pinch hitter. His recent season's averages had been a paltry .238 and .258. The pudgy Herman faced Doc White of Chicago, one of the best of spitballers, but he doffed his cap and bellowed to the crowd, "Ladies and gents, permit me to present to you Herman Schaefer, the world's premier batsman, who will now give a demonstration of his marvelous hitting power. I thank you."

The crowd booed. Schaefer then smashed the longest home run seen in Chicago for years. He slid into first base, hollering, "At the quarter, Schaefer leads by a head!" He slid into second with, "Schaefer leads by a length!" At third it was, "Schaefer leads by a mile!" and at home plate he slid in with, "That concludes the demonstration by the great Schaefer and I thank you one and all!"

The Punchinello of the ballpark once amazed the crowd by stealing second base and then crazily reversing his route, "stealing" his way back to first—just to see if it could be done. On some days, he could upstage even Cobb.

The same was true of Hugh Ambrose Jennings, the thirty-six-year-old dramatist hired to revitalize the club. Jennings's four-part act was to tear up grass on the sideline, let go his "Eeee—yahhhh!" yell, and blow a shrill policeman's whistle. He also did an Indian war dance. Suspended for ten days by American League president Ban Johnson for "objectionable" noisemaking, Jennings moved into the stands, where he clanged a cowbell. Detroit fans loved Jennings—with all the nonsense going on, the Tigers were winning for a change, were they not?

You could not love Cobb, only watch him with awe. He brought about "a miracle a day," according to Jennings, and was "absolutely fearless—why, he's running on legs so gashed and unhealed that he loses a cup of blood in nine innings of sliding." Molded sliding pads were not yet invented. Cobb's pads were of a cheap fabric that bunched around his hips and limited his maneuverability so much that at last he discarded them and ran "naked." On bare flesh, he went on stealing with a high percentage of success.

Amidst pennant fever, there appeared in Washington in his big-league debut a gawky, six-foot, two-inch right-hander who had started in southern California as a catcher and been discovered in the Idaho bushes by a traveling cigar salesman. The cigar drummer had passed the word that the hayseed, now a pitcher, had thrown 72 innings without allowing a run. Walter Perry Johnson was extremely long-armed, and with his slingshot delivery had shocking speed, along with good control. At nineteen he broke in against the Tigers on an August day.

Routinely Cobb inspected all new players, even rookies, before facing them. After watching Johnson warm up, he told Jennings, "Have everybody stand deep in the box today. This farmer throws out of his hip pocket so fast that you can't follow it."

As for Cobb, he bunted, and the rookie misfielded the bunts. Cobb also did the usual on the base paths, and Detroit beat Johnson, 3–2. That night, Cobb said, he urged Navin as follows: "Get this kid even if it costs you twenty-five thousand dollars. That's the best arm I've ever seen. He's so fast it scared me. When he learns a curve, nobody can stop him."

Big Train Johnson never did find an outstanding curve, yet the quiet man became a pistonlike career winner of 416 games, threw 110 shutouts, and once rang up 16 consecutive decisions. "And all he did for the next twenty years was beat Detroit," said Cobb, sarcastically, long afterward. "Jackass Navin did nothing to sign him when Johnson was still available."

The Tigers continued to hover in first place or close to it until September, when Cobb was laid up. At Cleveland he consulted a doctor for his "sliders"—raw sores spread from ankles to thighs—and was advised to use salve and stay off his feet in bed. Otherwise infection was likely. Cobb on that same day went after a fly ball hit into a roped-back crowd bordering right field. Diving for it, he made the catch, but landed on a broken bottle. His right, throwing hand was gashed from thumb to palm. Except perhaps for players who have stayed in the game despite broken bones, nothing much in the records beats what then transpired. With a bandaged hand he remained in the lineup and made several mostly one-handed base hits.

Making two to four base-stealing attempts per day, he gave his wounds no time to heal. In St. Louis the press spoke of him as "a model of bravery," although he was as much disliked and feared in Browns country as in any locality. A bottle thrown by a fan and thought to be aimed at Cobb hit umpire Billy Evans in the head.

Meanwhile, with sulfas and penicillin nonexistent, Cobb's hand became infected. When the Tigers reached Chicago, he was again urged to bench himself. Instead, caught up in a pennant race, he made two hits good for two runs, stole two bases, scored two more runs, and raced from first base to score on another of his "dazzlers." His hand was still swollen, but he removed the bandage, saying it bothered him.

His methods and toughness when injured caused opponents to declare that Cobb was more than an intimidator; he was an outlaw who played dirty, made no excuses, and stood pain with incredible fortitude. The *Philadelphia Bulletin* demanded that the league suspend him indefinitely—this after he spiked Danny Murphy of the Athletics with his "corkscrew" slide, in which he swerved away from the baseman, then slashed back into him to make him drop the ball. Cobb's message was "The slide is legal, get out of my way."

Veteran baseball writers found him uncooperative. *Cleveland News* writer Ed Bang tried to interview the Peach before a game. A "strange glare" drove Bang away. "To him it was war," wrote Bang. "He couldn't stand being interrupted [in his concentration]. He gave me such a look that I walked away." Several New York newspapers, hitherto caught sleeping by Cobb's fast development, now suggested that here was the best ballplayer in the United States, at least for the moment.

Beyond doubt the Tigers would not have made a run at the championship, after so many failures, without the fiery Cobb. His injured hand mostly healed, he was batting at nearly .350 after a series at Washington in which he connected for thirteen hits in eighteen at-bats—a .722 rate. He tripled and doubled in four runs versus St. Louis. Three steals a day were common. Often these gambles were outlandish and doomed from the outset. But Cobb was planting what he called "the threat"—making them worry about when and where and on what pitching count he would strike.

After a New York series where he had again "toured the world" to score on a single, the *New York World* editorialized, "With young Cobb there's never any telling what might happen . . . the fantastic, impossible twist is an easy possibility and we sit there like children wondering what miracle he'll perform next. There is an infectious, diabolical humor about his coups. He seems to derive unholy joy at the havoc he causes. Cobb charging home when expected to stay at third makes it more than a game—we see *drama*. He's the Br'er Fox of baseball, a never-failing source of enchantment."

Yet he frequently failed—he was cut down on wild steal attempts three times in one day—and the Detroit management, with no choice but privately to be much impressed with his work, remained cold to him publicly. Cobb was equally standoffish. "The fans gave me a diamond-studded watch for becoming the first man in the league to get one hundred hits," he remembered. "None of the fat-ass Tiger bosses showed up for the award."

By September his legs were in such bad shape that he needed aid to pull on his uniform pants. No teammate helped; a clubhouse attendant did the pulling. The widening schism between team and star showed again when on a ninety-degree day he stole second against Washington and wrenched a knee, then stole third with a football-type collision with the baseman. He called time-out and limped around.

Cobb described what happened in his memoir. "Up came Rowdy Coughlin for our side and he hit to Billy Shipke at third base for the Nats.

"I was groggy, but saw an opening. I dashed in and then up and down the third-base line with three infielders and the catcher after me. I was in a hotbox . . . finally, Jim Delahanty caught up, slammed the ball into the small of my back. The force of that on top of my [earlier] exertions and the terrific heat all but knocked me out . . . I sprawled forward. After tagging me Delahanty dropped the ball. It rolled loose. I was out, but could see the plate three feet away. They said I looked like a wounded crab as I crawled toward it, using my fingernails . . . the whole park was up yelling."

He was *already out,* but he kept the play going for a purpose. He had almost reached the plate when Delahanty slammed the ball into him again. Cobb collapsed entirely. A trainer and Jennings half-carried him to the bench. None of the Tigers applauded him, although they knew what really had happened. By diverting and sustaining attention to himself, Cobb had ensured that Coughlin was safe at first and another Tiger runner was safe at second. Now a single would win the game, and so it did.

EVENTUALLY THE race for the league championship narrowed to the Philadelphia A's and the Tigers. Some twenty-five thousand fans packed into Columbia Park in Philly, overflowing the stands and perching atop ladders, fences, hay bales, and roofs bordering the outfield. Detroit led the Athletics by 8 percentage points when a three-game series opened on September 27. "I looked out my hotel window," said Cobb, "and it was like the British were invading again." Forty-five thousand people surrounded the park. The *New York Times* headlined: "Reaching an end, this is the greatest struggle in the history of baseball."

Pressed for money, as always, Cobb mainly was thinking of the fifteen-hundred-dollar or so individual shares awaiting the winner of the coming World Series. He carried five lucky coins in his pocket and, half a century later, still had them amongst his glittering collection of diamond and ruby watches, cups, stickpins, plaques, scrolls, and other trophies at his mountain lodge in Nevada.

Detroit won the opener, 5–4, with Bill Donovan outpitching Eddie Plank. Rain washed out the next game. Then came a Sunday holiday. It boiled down to a September 30 decider, with ace Bill Donovan opposing Jimmy Dygert and Rube Waddell.

Going into the ninth inning, the Tigers, trailing by an 8–6 score, were desperate. Cobb came to bat. In the most important at-bat of his life thus far, he faced George Edward "Rube" Waddell, winner of 110 games in the past five seasons. The six-foot, two-inch, 190-pound Waddell threw left-handed and elsewhere was ambidextrous—he could drink with either hand and, when necessary, it was said, flat on his back. The *Sporting News* called him "that amazing sousepaw." To keep Rube sober, A's manager Connie Mack once arranged to have him arrested and jailed on concocted false charges. To obtain liquor when broke, Waddell stole team baseballs to trade in saloons for refreshments. In the off-season he worked as a bartender.

Waddell had owned a mockingbird that could imitate a peanut vendor's shrill whistle until, reportedly, some of the A's strangled him.

Cobb figured that the high-strung Rube could be upset and shouted to him, "Where's your cuckoo bird, bo?" Tapping his bat on the plate, Cobb asked if Waddell had visited any good jails lately. Ossie Schreckengost, the A's catcher—"Schreck" for short—admired Cobb for his ability and warned him, "Now you'll get it."

But no beanball followed. Waddell delivered his fastball for a strike. On the next pitch, Cobb pulled a curveball over the right-field fence for a two-run home run, knotting the score at 8–8. The A's dignified owner, Connie Mack, upset the bat rack when he fell off the bench. "I knew it was gone the second I hit it," glowed Cobb later that night at the Aldine Hotel. "I expected a breaker and got it." His clutch homer, as it developed, saved the pennant for Detroit.

It was a contest to remember—"my most thrilling," said Cobb— that ended only after nearly four hours and seventeen innings of battling and rioting. With the score still tied in the fourteenth, the Tigers survived by what became famous as the "when-a-cop-took-a-stroll play." Harry Davis of the A's hit a long fly to the outfield ropes. Sam Crawford muffed the catch for what seemed a two-base error. The Tigers claimed interference—"a cop got in Crawford's way!" Connie Mack argued that the officer was only trying to move away and give Crawford some room.

Plate umpire Silk O'Loughlin hesitated on the call while players exchanged shoves. Always the opportunist, Cobb told teammate Claude Rossman that Monte Cross of the A's had called him "a Jew bastard." Rossman punched Cross and was arrested and ejected by police. With Rossman banned, the situation became so serious that base umpire Tommy Connolly consulted with O'Loughlin and ruled that it had been interference by the cop. Harry Davis was called out.

No scoring followed, and the game staggered on into one of the longest ever played, called by darkness in the seventeenth with the count 9–9. The A's lacked time in a dwindling season to catch up and the Tigers finished with a rush to take their first title in twenty years, dating back to 1887 in the Old National League. Cobb, the "Big Roar from Michigan," contributed a single, double, key homer, a stolen base, and two runs scored.

A bitter Mack issued a statement: "If there ever was such a thing as crooked baseball, today's game would stand as a good example." Mack knew for a fact that the umpires had conspired against him. Newspapers were shocked, replying that Mack's language could not have been worse—he was charging the umpires with deliberately throwing a game.

After the decisive Philadelphia series, the Tigers moved to Washington, where Cobb attracted U.S. senators, curious to learn if the Peach was real. They came away talking about the four bases he stole in one game and his thirteen hits in eighteen at-bats during a series that Detroit swept, 4–0. As his final act of the season, he homered and tripled off St. Louis pitching.

Bonfire-lit parades in Motor City lasted into the night. Firemen feared that a section of Lafayette Boulevard would be burned down by the twenty-five thousand celebrants. Cobb and Bill Donovan buttons were struck off. The Peach received fifty free meals at Halloran's Diamond Grill. A dog painted with tiger stripes was presented to Cobb, who shipped him home to Augusta, where "Tiger" was featured in a parade down Broad Street. A week's billing at Detroit's Gayety Theater was offered Cobb, doing a "how I did it" monologue. He turned it down.

FINAL STATISTICS gave Cobb the American League batting championship, making him the youngest man ever to accomplish that feat in the major leagues. Not only was his .350 the AL's highest and tied with the National League's best, but he led the circuit in hits, with 212, in runs scored plus runs driven in, with 213, and in steals, with 49. In total bases, 286, he led both leagues. He had accounted for close to one-third of the Tigers' collective 696 runs. Owner Frank Navin could not disclaim the fact that without him a team formerly going nowhere would not have finished close to its mark of 92 wins against 58 losses. Pitchers Donovan, Killian, Mullin, and Siever had a combined 89 victories, in considerable part because of Cobb's base-running, his hitting, and his appearance in 150 games while bandaged for cuts, muscle tears, and infection.

Yet, although the Tigers had reached the World Series, no apology was forthcoming from those who had taunted Cobb and tried to bring off a trade. "Having a bear year didn't seem to matter much," he said in looking back. "But the boys did me a favor. They went their way, I went mine. And I had a lot of time alone to think how I would improve. At midnight and later I'd be up reviewing plays made in the past. Could see where I'd gone wrong, how I would hit pitchers like Joss in Cleveland, Plank and Vickers in Philly, Slow Joe Doyle in New York, Johnson in Washington. I'd picture them in my mind's eye . . ."

The Dixie Demon was the toast of the town, drawing more press space in Detroit than anyone save workhorse Donovan. Navin was forced to recognize a seasonal comparison with two other notables who were earning triple or more Cobb's salary:

	At-Bats	Runs	Hits	Doubles and Triples	RBIs	Batting Average
Nap Lajoie	509	53	153	38	63	.301
Honus Wagner	515	98	180	52	91	.350
Ty Cobb	605	97	212	44	116	.350

In a close-to-the-vest era in which one or two runs regularly decided games, the Georgian had not diluted his efforts by going for home runs. His hitting was contained. Even so he had 5 homers, 3 more than Lajoie and only 1 less than Wagner. His 11 errors and 30 assists placed him high in AL-NL fielding.

Six months earlier he had been trade bait. Now, entering postseason play against the Chicago Cubs, he was a celebrity.

IN THE World Series the Tigers' earnings would have been considerably less if Germany Schaefer and Cobb had not made a bold request. Baseball's National Commission, meeting before the Series, was surprised when the two stood up and asked, "What happens with the players' share of Series receipts if there is a tie game?" No one had sought such clarification until now. Under rules laid down in 1905, players shared in proceeds of the first four contests. No provision was made for a deadlocked game within the first four. Schaefer and Cobb proposed that the hired hands should get a cut if a replay of a tie was required. Since the odds against that happening were long, the commission agreed to a revised division, cutting in teams.

Next day in the Series opener, before a sellout crowd of 24,377 at the West Side Ball Park of the Cubs, the two clubs played to a twelve-inning 3–3 tie called by darkness. A long shot had come in—to the players' profit.

The weather was cold and the hospitable Chicagoans greeted the Tigers by gathering outside their hotel with sticks and stones. Bill Yawkey countered the threat by placing Doc "Six-Gun" Crowe, a giant sheriff from Arizona, on guard duty in the lobby. Reporter Bill Phelon of the *Chicago Daily Journal* explained why elements of the National Guard were called out: "In an onslaught by the bugs, the ballyard-fortress became a garrison . . . Thousands scaled the parapets despite barbed-wire entanglements . . . Major Charles Williams of the armed guard lost his pants."

Manager Frank Chance's Cubs, after devastating the National League with a 107–45 win-loss mark in regular play, were favored to win with ease. The prediction was correct. In a five-game walkover Series, nineteen Cub runs were scored to the Tigers' six. On sore legs, and with a bad cold, Cobb could do little with pitchers Big Ed Reulbach, Jack Pfiester, Orvie Overall, and Mordecai "Three-Finger" Brown. When he wasn't grounding out (eight times in the Series), he was popping up, striking out, or flying out. When he moved up in the box to beat breaking balls, the Cubs knocked him down with dusters. Cobb invited Pfiester to fight. Pfiester declined. Detroit catcher Boss Schmidt made so many throwing errors that he set a record. Not until game number four, in Detroit, did Cobb manage an extra-baser, a triple off Overall. His Series total was four hits in twenty tries for a .200 average. On the bases he was shut out on steals by catcher Johnny Kling.

Only 7,370 at Detroit attended the final game, where the home-towners were shut out, 2–0. Cobb struck out twice, singled and stole one base. Financially, the short Series was a flop. Critics observed that perhaps the Tigers' seasonal showing was illusionary, that they did not belong in the big show. Cobb was overrated, claimed some experts. Cobb's untypically modest response was, "Well, I'm still learning."

Becoming a Series "goat" was a blow. It stung enough that he cut short scheduled appearances in post-Series exhibitions and after a few games left for home. His Series check was for $1,945.96, a reprieve from debt for the part-time farmer. It would have been considerably less if Bill Yawkey had not tossed $15,000 into the players' pool from his losing owner's share. That winter Cobb's observation about Yawkey's generosity was, "He's one of the richest men in Michigan and can afford it. Look at what we drew." With a team payroll of about

$35,000, Detroit pulled close to 300,000 customers, a solid gain over 1906.

In a new suit and derby, Cobb came home to welcoming parades. He now felt and dressed like a star. "But I knew I had it in me to do much better," he said. "I was taking too many third strikes with the bat on my shoulder." His legs were a worry. For risking permanent injury while leading the club to a pennant, he had earned $4,345, minus the repaid $300 loan from Navin in March. Cobb had planned to invest some of his Series check in the Aerocar Company or Detroit Auto Vehicle Company, two up-and-coming manufacturers. But that autumn a crisis hit Wall Street, affecting an overexpanded new auto industry. By October both Aerocar and Detroit Auto were in bankruptcy. Cobb was saved a loss that might have prevented—or at least delayed—his getting married.

She was a sixteen-year-old Augusta schoolgirl, a member of the socially prominent Lombard clan of Georgia, and a beauty.

CHAPTER TWELVE

OUTLAW AND PUBLIC ENEMY

The circumstances of Cobb's marriage in August of the 1908 season were typical of his conduct. A brusque, intolerant way of going about his affairs marked Cobb from the beginning. If someone was scheduled to meet him for a game of pool or for a buggy ride, and was late, he walked out. Even Grantland Rice, his favorite scribe, needed to make an appointment to conduct an interview. "Do you consider baseball a business?" Rice asked him. "If it isn't," said Cobb, "then Standard Oil is a sport."

With only two exceptions, Cobb until then had little serious time for the ladies. "I met a girl named Claire Hodgson," he told me, "and for a while it got interesting." Hodgson was a shapely brunette who danced with Georgia theatrical companies and was talented enough to reach the Ziegfeld Follies of Broadway a few years after her romance with Cobb ended. Later, in one of the most unlikely coincidences in baseball, Hodgson in the early 1920s met Babe Ruth in New York and—with Cobb far behind her—married him. She wrote a book, *The Babe and I,* in which she termed Cobb "the greatest," but listed the Bambino as first in her heart.

Cobb may have struck out in that romance, but he did very well indeed in the late summer of 1908. Cobb's chosen mate was a pretty brunette heiress to a reputed $300,000 fortune, and fourteen years old when he first began courting her. By the summer of 1908, Charlotte "Charlie" Marion Lombard was nearing her seventeenth birthday. She lived at The Oaks, a sprawling estate south of Augusta. Roswell Lombard, father of the lively Charlie, had numerous interests, among them cotton acreage, an iron-and-steel works, blooded horses, and vaudeville theaters. A distinguished, mustached man, Lombard had refused to permit the marriage until his little girl finished her schooling at St. Mary's convent; he was opposed to "cradle-robbing." Cobb once intimated that as a suitor he had not been in accord with the delay insisted upon by Lombard. Cobb's own mother had been twelve when she became a bride. Still, he was forced to wait until Charlie reached seventeen to start building the large family he wanted.

The wedding was a gala affair. "Half of Georgia tried to get in on the hitching," reported the bridegroom's uncle, A. C. Ginn. Gifts arrived by the wagonload—several loads of them.

The timing of the wedding—August 6—was not exactly appreciated by the Detroit management. In the hunt for a second straight league title, Detroit was in first place by one game over the St. Louis Browns by late July, with their most valuable man hitting close to .340. At Boston Cobb had sneaked in from the outfield to trap a runner off second base for an unassisted putout; he had raced from first base to score on an infield hit while the Beantowners threw late or wildly; had gone 3 for 4 in batting against Boston's Cy Young. He had hit Kid Elberfeld's New York club so readily that the Kid was convinced he had been tricked, and cried, "The ball's been treated—it's not legal!" Elberfeld raised so much hell about something being "not right" with the ball that an umpire used a knife to cut it in half. It was legal.

That June, Cobb's built-in prejudice against blacks again had surfaced, this time ending him up in a court of law as the defendant. He was leaving the Pontchartrain Hotel in June when a streetworker who was spreading fresh asphalt shouted at him for walking too close to the gooey stuff. A bit spilled on Cobb's trouser cuff. A discussion over this led to Cobb knocking the black worker, one Fred Collins, on his back. Collins's head was injured. Forty-eight hours later Cobb faced a judge on assault and battery charges. Although handed only a suspended sentence, he was ordered to pay Collins seventy-five dollars to cover court costs or face a damage suit. Cobb's testimony that Collins had been out of line and had spoken insultingly to him was good enough reason for Judge Edward Jeffries—a Tiger fan—to hand down no more than a suspension without fine.

At the same Pontchartrain, as reported by the *Chicago Defender*, an early news organ for blacks, Cobb had kicked a chambermaid in the stomach and knocked her down some stairs because she flared back when he called her "nigger." The hotel's manager protested and ordered Cobb to leave the place. The story was suppressed by the newspapers, but years later Harold Seymour was moved to track down the details for his book, *Baseball: The Golden Age*. Seymour's research showed that the press had finessed the incident, and that because of Cobb's prominence the woman was quietly paid off in exchange for her dropping a ten-thousand-dollar lawsuit.

In his racial prejudice, Cobb, at age twenty-two, was far from alone. Almost all players and executives of the majors, whatever their point of origin, supported the policy of excluding blacks from the big time, even though as far back as 1886 a Southern League of Colored Base Ballists had existed and produced talent of unmistakable class. Cobb, however, stood out in the viciousness of his hatred; repeatedly he turned violent on streets and in other public places.

"I'm sure he would have gone to New York in a big trade," his teammate, Davy Jones, once said, "but New York was too racially mixed to afford him." Jones believed that most blacks of Detroit hated Cobb, but, under the eye of the white community, kept their feelings to themselves.

ON AUGUST 2 a story datelined Washington, D.C., where the Tigers were playing on a road stand, went over the wires. It read in part: "Tyrus Cobb is to desert his teammates to get married. He will return to Detroit accompanied by his wife . . . The couple will spend the greater part of the winter abroad." Mention was made that the absentee had obtained Hughie Jennings's permission to take off.

No such permission had been given, said Sam Crawford when I visited the seventy-seven-year-old Hall of Famer at his Pearblossom, California, home in 1957. "He just walked out and left us flat in mid-season," said Crawford bleakly. With his team fighting for the pennant, Cobb proceeded to absent himself for six days, without even bothering to notify the management of his intentions until shortly before he left. Cobb caught an Augusta-bound train on August 3, and was married on August 6. Down home, Georgia governor Hoke Smith and other notables had arranged to attend the wedding ceremonies. But up north, Frank Navin was making expensive plans to expand Bennett Park by three thousand seats, and he badly needed another championship. To Navin and Detroit co-owner Bill Yawkey, the departure of Cobb was inexcusable. In a subsequent dispute with Cobb, Navin spoke of his 1908 defection as the most arrogant act he had ever heard of in baseball.

Cobb's leaving the team was one of the earliest of a series of acts by Cobb establishing him as a special case, exempt from the usual organization rules, and presaging his eventual status as a law unto himself. Moreover, he was showing his employers that without him the Tigers were not the same ball club, a point that would be raised time and again in coming salary battles. At his wedding he confided to Georgia friends, "Navin's a skinflint. He isn't paying me enough [four thousand dollars] to put missing a few games ahead of a personal matter."

The bride, in a New York–styled gown, and Cobb, in formal attire, took their oaths before the Reverend Thomas Walker in the ballroom of the Lombard estate. For the wedding-cake-cutting ceremony, the groom brought along the black thirty-five-ounce bat that had been serving him so well.

(The bat was one more of his superstitions. It was lucky for him to encounter a wagonload of hay, or find a dime on the street, or to rub a black child's head before a game. Seeing a black cat or a snake was bad news. In 1914, writing for a national publication, Cobb stressed, "When I'm going good, not slumping, I try to do everything just the same way as I did when on a hitting streak. I always go to the ballpark by the same route, put on my uniform the same way. I try to recall which sock I'd donned first. If it was my left I will not give the right one precedence for a raise in pay." And, "I hang my towel on the same peg." Cobb had a furious row in 1909 with a clubhouse boy after he had made four hits in five ups. His towel was improperly pegged. "That next afternoon I did not get a hit and blamed it on the misplaced towel. My run of luck had been broken by it. After my bath that day the towel was placed on the old, lucky peg and I busted 'em for fair the next afternoon.")

Ladies attending the wedding may have seen the baseball bat as symbolically inappropriate at this gathering, but Cobb kept his Louisville Slugger beside him during the reception at the local Hotel Genesta. Late that night the newlyweds took a train back to Detroit. Returning to the game on August 9, almost a week after departing, the Peach had a good day—a triple, single, and stolen base in a 5–2 win over Washington's Nationals. He blew no kisses to his bride in the stands, as Babe Ruth would do with Claire Hodgson Ruth when on the day after their wedding he walloped a home run at Yankee Stadium. But the Tiger star did doff his hat to the crowd, an uncommon act for Cobb.

During his absence the Tigers had about stayed even in the standings. Fans and civic leaders forgave his walkout and the *Detroit News* headlined: "MONEY COMES IN FOR COBB'S WEDDING GIFT." Ten thousand blank pledges were distributed at the ballpark, with donations to be made with the donor's name or initials at the box office. "There is no limit to the amount given," stated the *News,* leading off with a fifty-dollar contribution. "Anything from five cents up will be gratefully taken. The idea is to let every lover of the game, man, woman or child, reward work well done." Called the Cobb Appreciation Fund, it brought him fine silverware and a cut-glass set for the home he and Charlie planned to build one day.

It also brought chagrin. Very soon he fell into one of his worst slumps. Strikeouts and groundouts greatly outnumbered base hits as he and the team floundered for a while, before rallying in September to rejoin the title chase. Several writers expressed the opinion that the Peach looked tired. A few hints were cast that honeymooning—he had his wife traveling with him on the road—did not mix with connecting off the likes of Walter Johnson, Addie Joss, Rube Waddell, and, especially, Edward Augustin "Big Ed" Walsh of the Chicago White Sox. A handsome ex–coal miner turned "dipsy-doodling" spitballer, Walsh was on his way in 1908 to winning 40 games against 15 losses, while hurling an immense, record 465 innings. Walsh's astonishing ironman work had kept the Sox in the running.

Coming down to the wire, Walsh beat the Tigers, 6–1, on October 5, his salivator breaking sharply for his fortieth victory. Cleveland lost to St. Louis, giving Detroit only a half-game lead over the White Sox and the Naps, with one game to go. Detroiters jammed the streets around scoreboards mounted on newspaper balconies and flashing results.

At Chicago, before an unruly crowd of nearly thirty thousand, the White Sox sent Doc White to the mound in an attempt to overtake the Tigers and win the American League championship. White, who had won 18 games that season, got absolutely nowhere. In the first inning Cobb tripled in two runs. Later, Ed Walsh, who had worked only the day before, came in; he was followed in turn by Frank Smith. The Tigers took a 7–0 lead, and behind Bill Donovan's shutout pitching went on to clinch their second straight pennant. At one point there was a near fight when Cobb, who was feuding with Walsh, spit on the ground near Walsh's feet as a commentary on Big Ed's spitball pitch. Ty also tripled in his second time at bat, in what he always considered the two best back-to-back hits he ever made. He added two singles, and feinted so successfully when on first that he caused Walsh to throw the ball away on a pickoff attempt.

Detroit fans stayed up through the night to watch the victory flag being raised at dawn over City Hall—the same banner that had flown over the USS *Detroit* in the Spanish-American War. Wisecracks about the debilitating effect of Cobb's marriage were dropped.

He could hardly wait for the World Series to begin. To relax tense muscles, he took long steambaths at the Detroit Athletic Club. In part he was out to vindicate what they had said of him after his .200 average of the previous year's Series. New York's *American* called Cobb "a strutter from a South which hasn't won a war lately" and who was "insolently" sure of himself. The "advertised snarl" on his face when at bat was really a "sneer." But the *American* could not overlook the just-concluded season's numbers, wherein "Speed Boy" had won his second straight batting title at .324, led the AL in hits (188), RBIs (101), doubles (36), triples (20), and total bases reached (248). His base steals dropped from 49 to 39, partly the product of pulled tendons and of catchers bearing down on him even harder. In the field his assists (23) led everyone.

His statistical showing at the plate was the more impressive because in 1908 the American League was thick with pitchers with 2.50 or below earned-run averages. One hundred and ten shutouts were thrown leaguewide, and only four batters had averaged .300 or above. It was becoming so difficult to get on base against pitchers with controlled speed, a variety of change-ups and spitters, shine and emery balls, that some owners wondered whether fielders' gloves should be barred, in a return to bare-handed days.

To boost attendance, something would have to be done to pump up dwindling batting averages. "I'll play without a glove," said Cobb deliberately, "on the day they rule out the beanball."

BOTHERED BY a cold, and sneezing his way into another World Series against the Chicago Cubs, a rematch of the 1907 finalists, Cobb predicted a Tiger victory this time around. From what Cobb said later on, he was sure enough of this to bet on the outcome, a common sub rosa practice by players in those days. How would he do? "I'll hit Chicago, don't worry," he promised.

This time Detroit had no excuse for what happened. Finishing in a tie with the New York Giants in the National League, Frank Chance's Cubs had been forced to a playoff only two days before the Series opened. To break an identical 98–55 season's deadlock the Cubs had needed to come from behind to win a close clincher from John McGraw's Giants. They were even more weary than the Tigers.

In the first two Series matchups, Cobb produced only three singles, and Detroit lost 10–6 and 6–1. In game number three he got hot and drove out four hits in five appearances, one double included. Mixed in was a display of baserunning that left Cubs rooters crying in their beer. From first base he began a campaign of brash, noisy intimidation.

"Kling!" he bawled to Cubs' catcher John "Noisy" Kling, "I'm going on the next one!" Kling's arm was accurate—in game number five of the 1907 Series he had cut down Cobb trying to steal third. He waved the ball in warning.

"Speedy Tyrus went into second base as he'd boldly promised so hard," wrote Grantland Rice in the Nashville *Tennessean,* "that he knocked the bag from its moorings and was safe as he sent baseman Joe Tinker flying." Acting as if irritated by a defective base bag, Cobb kicked it a few times. His real purpose, soon revealed, was to move the bag a few inches closer to third base. With that, he again shouted to Kling and pitcher Ed Reulbach loudly enough for people in the close seats to hear: "I'm going on the next one!"

Kling was unnerved. His throw to Harry Steinfeldt at third base was too late to catch Cobb, whose fall-away slide gave Steinfeldt only a toe to tag. He had called his shots twice and made good on both. With George Mullin pitching well, Detroit won, 8–3.

Was not announcing his intentions in advance a foolish act? Would it not make Kling all the more alert and determined? "No," said Cobb at age seventy-three, with a clear memory of the plays. "I knew Kling's mind, how he'd be shook up by it and would have to collect himself before throwing. All I needed was inches."

After that, however, the Cubs closed it out, winning a five-game Series with no trouble. Three-Finger Brown and Orvie Overall threw consecutive 3–0 shutouts. In the two closing games Cobb made no hits, striking out, grounding out, or flying out five times. He also misfielded Chance's fly ball. "Series-jinxed" was the term applied to him by some writers. Yet his overall Series batting average of .368 could not be dismissed—only two Cubs had bettered it. No Tiger had come close to him.

Like so many modern standout players who have refused press interviews after a defeat, Cobb left Bennett Park in haste.

THE 1908 season represented a turning point of Cobb's life. Finally, after three years of indecision, he reached the conclusion that he belonged permanently in the game. Cobb wrote in his diary, "I now made up my mind that the gang couldn't keep me down . . . Anytime a man can last more than 400 games and put his team into two Series, his path is chosen for him." Charlie Cobb may not have agreed with that decision. Just seventeen years old, she disliked living for months far away from her Georgia family. She faced the fact, however, that her husband gave her no say in the matter.

Poor attendance at the last two Series games—turnouts of 12,900 and 6,200—held each Tiger to loser's shares of $871 apiece from the box-office division. Cobb was diligent in rooting out every other odd dime. He picked up $1,200 in postseason exhibitions and a $250 purse for entering an around-the-bases sprinting contest.

How fast was he really? At Chicago he beat some of the top runners by going from home base to first in 3.5 seconds and touring four bases in 13.5 seconds, doing it in cut-down uniform pants and baseball shoes. If alive today, given starting blocks, technique training, and the springy shoes of Carl Lewis, he might well be an Olympic Games prospect.

That winter, always restless, he spread himself across the South and East. In Louisiana he played against semipros for cash guarantees. Bush ballparks doubled their attendance by his presence. He drove a Thomas Flyer in the New York to North Carolina Good Roads Tour, a promotional event of the auto industry. Between 1900 and 1918, U.S. motor-vehicle production rose from 4,000 units to 187,000, and driver registration from 8,000 to 469,000. Cobb, who was fortunate to have arrived at the outset of automania, owed much of his future financial affluence to endorsing cars, tires, batteries, owning dealerships, and buying early General Motors stock.

Coach Dan McGugin of Vanderbilt University invited him to attend football practice. Cobb watched the boys bang heads for a while and asked if he could try running the ball. McGugin was hesitant. After taking part in a few "dummy" plays (no tackling), Cobb insisted on donning pads and helmet and engaging in a real scrimmage. McGugin was astonished when he cut off-tackle and ran eighty-five yards for a touchdown the first time he handled the ball. "That convinced me," McGugin told a reporter, "that here is the greatest athlete in the country."

A FEW weeks of quiet living at home was enough, after which Cobb needed action. He seemed to require the sounds and sight of a crowd roaring. A New Orleans fight promoter signed him to referee a card of club matches. Before the first fight ended, the audience was howling protests; instead of stopping a bout in which one pug was being battered around the ring, bleeding and nearly unconscious, Cobb let it keep going. With the crowd out of hand, policemen forcibly evicted Cobb from the ring, and the promoter had him removed from the building. After that, the one-night-stand referee left for Georgia to hunt quail and to give Charlie some of his time.

DURING THE off-season the couple lived at The Oaks, the home of Charlie's father, Roswell Lombard. A wing of Lombard's large house was provided for them, along with a household maid. Cobb couldn't afford his own place as yet. He got along well with a father-in-law who was prominent in his own right.

DOMESTIC PEACE and quiet may have been Cobb's lot that winter, but in seven American League cities there were those who wanted him drummed from the game, either through a long-term suspension or permanent barring. From 1908 until the World War I years and beyond, his lawless ways, coupled with his ability to beat teams single-handedly, whether by accepted means or otherwise, would embroil Cobb in almost endless run-ins with opponents, fans, the press, policemen, law courts, his owner, and the American League office. Byron Bancroft Johnson, American League president and advocate of less rowdyism on field and the sanitizing of baseball so that women would be attracted to games, was quoted as saying, "Every time I look up I hear about Mr. Cobb making trouble. He seems unable to conform to the accepted rules of baseball or society."

In Philadelphia, Boston, and Cleveland, fans were more direct. They threatened bodily harm, and some of the threats to shoot down Cobb appeared less like the ordinary recriminations aimed at a controversial figure than genuine warnings of deadly intent.

High on the list of those who wanted him ruled off the diamond was Cornelius McGillicuddy Mack, the "Tall Tactician" and manager of the Philadelphia Athletics. Mack was dignified, soft-spoken, and conservative. He would rule the A's for fifty years. After Cobb spiked Home Run Baker in a celebrated incident in late August, Mack called Cobb, his *bête noire,* such names as "back-alley artist," "a no-good ruffian," and "a malefactor no league can afford."

"I wouldn't let Cobb play for me if he did it for nothing," Mack stated.

Conflicting accounts of one Baker-Cobb incident back in August had been widely published. John Franklin Baker, a five-foot, eleven-inch, 170-pound former butcher from Trappe, Maryland, was on his way to fame as the deadball era's leading power hitter. In 1911–13 he would knock 33 balls out of parks and be nicknamed Home Run Baker; the beetle-browed ex–meat man was a symbol of power at the plate.

It had not been proved, either way, that their collision had been a case of Cobb deliberately going for Baker's body on a steal, or the third baseman's awkwardness in trying for a tag. Cobb had drawn a walk, stolen second, and soon after tried to take third. Baker, taking a strong throw from A's catcher Paddy Livingston, had his man out by two feet.

At full momentum Cobb faked a hookslide to his left while whipping his right leg across to the bag. Baker, stabbing at the runner bare-handed, went down in pain. Blood ran down his hand and forearm. The runner was safe; Baker was cut an undetermined amount. The A's quickly bandaged him and he stayed in the game.

It was an impossible play to call. Harry Salsinger of the *Detroit News* saw it this way: "Cobb was blocked . . . and came in spikes flying high and glittering in the sunlight. A photograph taken of the play proved nothing. It could have been an accident."

Baker replied, "It was on purpose. After I put the ball on his left leg and had him out, he did a scissors-like motion of his right leg. One-eighth of an inch deeper and he'd have ended my career. I wouldn't have been able to throw." Baker added that while he lay on his back, injured, Cobb invited him to settle the matter with fists back of the stands. A crazy thing to do, thought Baker.

Cobb denied intent, and pointed out that Baker needed only a small sticking plaster on the cut. He maintained, "Mack's big favorite is Eddie Collins, who slides into base the way I do—he's hurt more men than I have." Mack called that a lie.

A majority of American League teams took the side of Baker and Mack; they believed that Cobb intended to rule the base paths, come what may.

Another incentive for Mack's reaction was that after slicing Baker, Cobb had gone on a batting binge such as comes to few men, averaging .640 in one stretch as the Tigers swept sixteen of twenty games. His presence in the lineup meant a probable pennant for Detroit.

Mack's enrollment in the Cobb-haters had begun in 1909 at spring training at San Antonio, Texas. A third straight pennant was in prospect for the Tigers. They badly beat New York, 16–5, in their home opener on May 11 before a crowd of about twelve thousand, with their ace running the bases with abandon and doubling twice. In another New York match Cobb singled three times and tripled while accounting for five runs. A half-century later he told *San Francisco Examiner* sports columnist Prescott Sullivan, "In those two games, I arrived as a big-leaguer."

For twenty-four years Cobb's life was one of unrelieved, preter-natural conflict, a bannerline writer's joy. In the summer of 1909 the Georgian set some kind of record by becoming the only famous baseball player to be jumped and mugged by a group in his own home city on his way to a game. In Detroit, he was attacked by several men, who knifed him and set off a brawl in which Cobb finally drove off a mob and later claimed to have killed one of the attackers with a pistol butt.

The matter, however, soon took second place to another ugly development. Early in September, Cobb made spectacular news. It happened when the Tigers were in Cleveland against the Naps. Years later Cobb gave his version of what supposedly happened. "With the idea of entering show business one day as an actor, I dined with George M. Cohan, thirty-one-year-old songwriter-actor who had composed such hits as 'Yankee Doodle Dandy' and 'Give My Regards to Broadway,' and Vaughn Glaser, a playwright. Our dining and drinking ended about one-thirty A.M." At that time Cobb was driven to the Tigers' hotel, the Euclid. He was not drunk, Cobb was to testify in court. He *was* angered by the night elevator operator, a black man, who allegedly said, "We got no elevators after midnight . . . you can walk up to your room."

"Get going up," ordered Cobb, waving a fist. They arose, but to the wrong floor. Cobb berated the lift man, slapped him, and they returned to the lobby. There the guest was approached in an "insolent" way by the hotel's black night watchman–house detective, one George Stansfield. He reproached Cobb for being so noisy at a late hour. A shouting match followed between them. As they say in box scores, error by Cobb, assist to Stansfield. Stansfield pulled his nightstick, and upon moving in on Cobb found himself in a fight for his life. They struggled. Both fell down, and while on the floor the husky Stansfield struck Cobb several times with his truncheon. At that Cobb produced a pocketknife and began cutting Stansfield—in the ear, shoulder, and hands. Stansfield didn't quit, as evidence showed. He hit Cobb a few more solid blows to the body and head with the stick, then pulled a gun. As Stansfield went down again, Cobb kicked the gun across the lobby and kept up the knife slashing. People from lower-floor rooms came down to witness him kicking Stansfield in the head.

Homicide wasn't far away when a desk clerk and janitors jumped in to pin a flailing Cobb to the floor. Bleeding, he staggered to his room to bandage head wounds. Many years later, Cobb showed me old skull scars, saying, "I didn't want to draw the Tigers into it. But I got in touch with Georgie Cohan at his hotel and had him notify Navin in

Detroit." Such was how Cobb remembered it, in any event. (In point of fact, it is dubious whether Cohan was involved.)

With a police investigation pending, Cobb appeared at League Park the following afternoon, bandaged from ear to chin. Teammates, not knowing the score, watched in amazement as Cobb played all eighteen innings of a doubleheader. In the first game he had three hits off Cy Falkenberg. Hughie Jennings urged him to sit out the second match. He played and made a pair of good outfield catches. By now his bandages were stained red. Of all sights of Ty Cobb on a ballfield, this one may have been the most bizarre.

Navin already was in receipt of some dozen "Black Hand" death-threat letters mailed from Philadelphia as a result of the Baker episode. The unsigned notes asserted that when the Tigers reached that city for crucial meetings beginning September 15, a ballpark sniper, or several, would gun down Cobb in reprisal for the spiking of Baker. In addition, junk and threats had been thrown at him in the Boston park, and he had thumbed his nose at Beantown crowds. One of these exchanges had come during a ten-inning Detroit victory in which the Peach tripled, twice singled, poled a home run, and roughly upended short-stop Charles "Heinie" Wagner on a steal attempt. ("That sort of shitty treatment of me at Boston mostly came from Harvard students," brooded Cobb with unconscious humor in later life. "It's why I sent my son to Yale when he grew up.")

Navin needed to deal with the Cleveland situation, and quickly. From a hospital bed, watchman Stansfield had sworn out an arrest warrant charging aggravated criminal assault with intent to kill. To lose Cobb's bat and his hustle to drawn-out court procedures or a prison sentence in all probability would end Detroit's championship hopes. The second-place Athletics were pressing close.

Before he went on the Euclid Hotel rampage, Cobb had been nothing less than phenomenal. Against New York he had doubled for two RBIs, and at Washington hit two home runs in a game for the first time. Again against the Highlanders (they would not become the "Yankees" until 1913) he had driven in or personally scored all five runs in a 5–3 Detroit cliffhanger win. So dependable had he become in the pinch that—the story goes—one day the *Detroit News* published an extra edition before a sixteen-inning struggle with Washington had ended. While the teams played on, newsboys ran the streets, telling readers that heroic Tyrus had beaten the Nationals with a last-moment base hit. It wasn't true. Faith in local journalism fell. The story has it that William "Billy" Durant, founder of General Motors, bawled out a *News* editor in public.

"How could you print that?" demanded Durant. "Why, dammit, the game ended with Cobb striking out with the bases full—and we lost."

"How often does the Peach do that?" replied the crestfallen editor.

Interest was so high in the battle of the Euclid Hotel that *Cleveland News* writer Ed Bang said he filed twenty thousand words on it cross-country. Luckily for Navin, detectives sent to Cleveland's League Park following the event arrived too late to detain Cobb for questioning; by then the Tigers were en route to St. Louis. Stansfield added a five-thousand-dollar civil damage suit to his criminal complaint. His lawyers claimed that their client was suffering severe pain. "He was trying to kill me," Stansfield deposed.

No information was released on what it cost the partnership of Bill Yawkey and Frank Navin in the next days to persuade Stansfield to drop his suit—a settlement figure of ten thousand dollars was rumored—but to Cleveland officials a payoff was not the main issue: Cobb had shown murderous intent. Police were keeping the case open. By leaving town he had committed another crime. The accused man remained subject to apprehension.

Cleveland detective Jake Mintz was reported to have advised Navin that with Cobb's record of violence, he was sure to be convicted in court. Police would watch future Detroit team travel and the next time a train carrying the Tigers entered Ohio, that train would be entered and the offender seized and brought to trial.

If and when the Tigers hung on in the late season and qualified for the World Series, they probably would open the playoff against the Pittsburgh Pirates at Pittsburgh on October 8. Passing through Ohio on the Lake Shore Line was the regular route for the Tigers when going east. Cobb got out a map and made plans to avoid jail and to not miss the Series.

"Ohio is blocked to me," he wrote a Georgia friend. "But I can get to Pittsburgh another way . . . although it means going into Canada and then a lot of train-hopping."

BEFORE DETROIT could clinch a third straight World Series appearance, the matter of defeating the Athletics at hostile Philadelphia had to be faced. The Tigers led the A's by four games when the teams squared off at Philly on September 16 for four decisive contests. A clean sweep by the A's would mean a tie for first place. Connie Mack's campaign to punish Cobb for spiking Frank Baker had led to group frenzy. Placards carried by "Philly Phanatics" outside Shibe Park, the A's new concrete-and-steel arena seating twenty-five thousand, showed a knife sticking out of Cobb's chest.

Hughie Jennings, given the public temper at the rematch, was reluctant to use Cobb. Syndicated columnist Bugs Baer wrote that Cobb was well advised to sit out these games. Dire warnings came from Horace Vogel of the *Philadelphia Bulletin,* a longtime Cobb hater, who sounded like he wanted a hanging. A frightened Charlie Cobb urged her husband not to appear. His fans in Augusta and Atlanta wired and phoned to the same purpose. They wanted revenge.

Ban Johnson did little to cool feelings. Earlier, the league chief, a former sportswriter, had stated, "One more attempt at spiking a fellow player will put a sudden quietus on this man's career . . . Cobb will stop it or quit the game." Johnson was talking about outright banishment. A few days later, however, he waffled, saying, "Cobb has learned his lesson and will behave." Philadelphians did not care if he came onto the field waving a white surrender flag.

The Peach and Jennings sat in a suite at Philadelphia's Aldine Hotel on the night before game number one. On a table before them were thirteen anonymous letters. Each promised Cobb's termination. Some were specific: "If you're not too cowardly to show up, you'll be dead. Our guns are ready." And: "I'll be on a roof across from the park with a rifle and in the third inning I'll put a bullet through your heart." Other notices, preserved by Cobb in the event of a lawsuit, named the killing as happening by knife during a field melee bound to follow the first game.

Jennings was on the spot. He had been forced to revamp his slumping infield. Several Tigers were hurt. Meanwhile, Mack had his four pitching aces, left-handers Eddie Plank and Harry Krause and right-handers Chief Bender and Cy Morgan, in their best form. The four had produced 20 shutouts on the season. (Detroit's top four throwers had 12 shutouts.) The A's fast-rising Eddie Collins at second base and Home Run Baker at third were hitting at more than .300. So Cobb, at close to a .370 figure, was very much needed.

His conference with Jennings, as Cobb remembered it many years later, went like this:

Jennings: "These home fans mean business. With you standing in right field a good rifleman couldn't miss."

Cobb: "It's all bluff. We'll have an overflow crowd no doubt, and I'll need some protection. Get me some cops. I just hope the A's hit one out past me where I'll have to make a catch falling into the crowd . . . Let's find out how tough they'll get."

Jennings (wincing): "Sit out the first game, at least."

Cobb: "I'm playing."

At a late hour, people by the hundreds milled about the Aldine Hotel, yelling threats. Tiger trainer Harry Tuthill and several hired guards were positioned outside Cobb's hotel room. Tuthill had brought along bottled Detroit water for Cobb's use and personally cooked his food; he trusted nobody.

Connie Mack, alarmed at the town's choler and beginning to wonder if the major leagues' first public execution-murder would occur, arranged for some three hundred policemen to mix with the audience at Shibe Park, which would range from twenty-five thousand to a league record of thirty thousand. A cordon of fifty armed cops would stand behind Cobb, ringing his position in right field.

Cobb was moved from the Aldine Hotel to Shibe Park in a taxicab with a twelve-man police motorcycle escort. "I never heard such noise as when we reached Shibe," he said. During warm-up, other Tigers stood as far away from him as possible.

He wasn't shot at, but at one point there was a loud explosion, causing Cobb to leap upward. A cop explained that it was an auto backfire from nearby Lehigh Avenue.

If the furor slowed Cobb, it was not noticeable in this first game of the Series. He charged into shortstop Jack Barry and gashed his knee. The whole park arose in a roar, but stopped at that, deterred by the heavy security force all around.

"Another strange thing happened," related Cobb in his memoirs. "On a long fly ball I had to dive into the crowd [roped off behind the outfield] to make a one-handed catch. There was a tangle of bodies . . . In diving I fell on a fan's hat and crushed it. So [next inning] I got a $5 bill from my purse and found the fan and said I was reimbursing him. He stood with his mouth open."

President Benjamin Shibe of the Athletics had guards touring the stands with megaphones, asking people to remain peaceful. If Cobb's five dollars for the hat helped along that line, it wasn't noticeable when the game concluded with a 2–0 Philadelphia win. Fans trampled the ropes and Cobb found himself surrounded by mean faces. Just then, according to Cobb in later years, a dozen or so men quickly shoved forward, boxing him in, and saying, "Ty, we know you're a Mason and we're fellow Masons. If you want to run for the dugout, we'll be right with you."

"I never ran off a field in my life," replied Cobb. With Masonic help, Cobb claimed, he reached safety as the crowd overran the field. (In actuality Cobb didn't join the Masonic Order until 1912, three years later.)

At around 10:00 P.M. that night, after dining at the Aldine, Cobb did what Jennings had implored him not to do. He went for a solitary walk amongst a large crowd ominously gathered in the street outside. Cobb stood, a challenging figure, on the hotel steps and called out, "Now I'm going for a walk. And I just want to say that the first rotten, cowardly hound who tries to stop me is going to drop dead, right where he stands. Now get out of my way."

New York reporter Westbrook Pegler estimated the turnout at about three hundred. Cobb kept one hand in his pocket, where he was known to carry a gun. A path opened up, he strolled a few blocks, and returned. "A fool's act," Pegler labeled it. "He did it with no cop close by." Perhaps so, conceded Cobb, but he was armed: "I would have shot the first fee-simple son of a bitch who came at me or showed a weapon. Nobody laid a hand on me."

Pegler and other eastern newspapermen had heard that he was fearless, saw it demonstrated, and complimented Cobb, but did not spare the criticism when he went hitless in one game, had two bunt singles and a sacrifice fly in another, and only two additional singles during the set. Three of the four games went to the Athletics, behind the fine pitching of Eddie Plank and Chief Bender. They threw so tight to Cobb that several times he had to hit the dirt.

"What were you thinking about most during that series?" I once asked Cobb.

"About getting a base hit," he said. "I wasn't doing much."

Rocks were thrown at the Tigers' horse-drawn carriages when they left town, their lead reduced to two games. Jennings let his boys enjoy a "whiskeyfest" on the train to help them relax. They bounced back by beating Boston twice—with Cobb averaging .714 off his five hits in seven times at bat. Meanwhile the Athletics lost two to Chicago. That clinched the title for the Tigers. They finished at 98–54 to the runner-up Athletics' 95–58.

Back in 1904 the Boston Red Sox had set the existing American League record for most season wins at 95. The Tigers' 98 beat that. In an unreal year Detroit stood first. It had two 20-game-winning pitchers, George Mullin (who won 29) and Ed Willett (22). Old reliable Wild Bill Donovan fell to 8–7 on the mound. On offense, besides Cobb, only Sam Crawford at .314 topped the .300 mark. Good defense, and contributions from a few newcomers such as infielder Donie Bush (.273), and from vet Davy Jones (.279) were a help. But it would have been something like a third-place finish for Detroit at best if not for one man, Tyrus Cobb, whose .377 was the highest batting average anywhere in the game.

In numerous ways, Cobb's 1909 season was the most brilliant yet reprehensible any player ever lived through. In that span of time Cobb fixed his reputation both as a very great performer and a deeply flawed human being. At year's end he stood indicted in Cleveland for assault with a deadly weapon, denounced by the black press for flagrant racist behavior, threatened with a life suspension by the league president, targeted by demonstrating Philadelphians, and viewed by tens of thousands as a down-and-dirty ballplayer. He also caught hell from the press in general. The influential *Sporting News* said in September, "Complaints that Cobb uses his spikes to injure and intimidate infielders are so common that his mere denial will not relieve him of the odium that attaches to a player guilty of this infamous practice . . . The list of his victims is too long to attribute the injury of all concerned to accidents. Down with this Cobb!"

Yet his .377 bat mark was 31 points higher than the league's next best, a .346 by Eddie Collins. He was the only player in the league to drive in more than 100 runs—107 to be exact. In total bases, his 296 easily topped everyone in the American League and the National League as well: 242 by Hans Wagner was second best. Cobb accomplished this all while appearing in a full 156 season games, limping through some of them. He became the first man to win the Triple Crown, leading the league in the same season in batting average, home runs, and runs driven in. Through the next seven decades, such Hall of Famers as Ruth, Joe DiMaggio, Stan Musial, Willie Mays, and Hank Aaron would never attain this sweep. If his sweep in 1909 was not the most impressive batting performance of the twentieth century, that would only be because Cobb would have even better seasons in 1911, 1912, 1913, and on up into the 1920s.

Cobb's 1909 title was his third straight batting championship in only his fifth year in the league. Babe Ruth did not lead the league in batting average, in his one and only time as number one in that department, until seven years after he turned from pitching to slugging specialist. The great Rajah—Rogers Hornsby—needed six seasons before he led in average.

BEFORE THE World Series opened against the Pittsburgh Pirates, who had a whopping 110 wins in the National League, Cobb's dilemma was how to reach Pittsburgh, some three hundred miles from Detroit, without being arrested and jailed cn route. In Cleveland a wanted-man warrant in the Stansfield-knifing-gunplay case remained very much active. Ohio authorities held that Cobb had started a near-murderous brawl. He claimed self-defense. His status was that of a fugitive from justice under Ohio felony law. And the way to reach Pittsburgh from the west was via Ohio.

Studying maps, Cobb saw that by zigzagging around on train lines, taking the Michigan-Pennsy Line by way of Canada, passing through Ontario to Buffalo and thence to Erie and Pittsburgh, he could make it to the game. It would require close rail connections and some luck. Cobb's description of it to me went, "In case any cop bastards were on my train, I kept to my compartment and had meals brought in by porters. My best bats were with me all the way."

No other ballplayer had been known to sneak around fugitive-style to reach World Series games. Teammate Del "Sheriff" Gainor later said, "It was a laugh. You should have seen his coattails flying. Ty had to run for trains after games as soon as he'd had a bath. With his bats banging against his legs."

It was comical, and it was tiring. If the Series went the full seven games, it meant that the wanted man would cover close to fourteen hundred extra miles in a nine-day period.

After one rail trip to Detroit and back, he gave up train travel and made the journey in a big touring automobile driven by his uncle, A. C. Ginn. Through much of Ohio, Cobb sat wrapped in a blanket out of sight in the rear seat. "He's mad as hell," Ginn told writer Fred Lieb, who had sworn not to print the story. "But we haven't been caught yet."

His predicament deepened the hard feelings between the team and its star. Losing the Series could cost the Detroiters a bundle of money. They needed their right fielder at his best, not travel-weary. The Tigers felt that Cobb had caused his own troubles. Why had he not walked up the damned hotel stairs on that Friday night in September, instead of pulling a knife on a house detective?

Another danger was extradition. Through the Series, which would last seven games, Cobb feared that Pennsylvania might agree to his release to Ohio.

Interest centered on the first matchup of thirty-five-year-old Honus Wagner, the bowlegged "human vacuum cleaner," holder of four consecutive National League batting titles and seven overall titles (he would win an eighth in 1911), and the young challenger from the West. Cobb was more concerned with studying the Pirates' pitching staff than shaking Wagner's hand for the papers. Pittsburgh was a 3–1 favorite with bookies. The Bucs had easily won the pennant. Could Cobb steal on their ace pitchers Vic Willis, Howie Camnitz, and Lefty Leifield, with their combined 2.07 earned-run average? Cobb thought that he could, if his tired legs held up. Opposing catcher George Gibson had an average throwing arm and was only fair at fielding bunts.

Pregame photographs of Wagner and Cobb emphasized their size, age, and anatomical difference. The Dutchman stood a barrel-like five feet, eleven inches, weighed upward of 200 pounds, and was muscled all over. Except for his heavy thighs and upper legs, his 185-pound rival was slender. The two discussed, among other things, how to treat bats in the off-season. Cobb favored applying the juice of Navy Nerve-Cut tobacco; Wagner had his own prescription. Cobb spoke of hunting in the South, inviting Wagner to join him for a wild-pig shoot. Anything to take a .350 hitter's mind off the game.

Eastern sportswriters were the source of the myth that the Dutchman far outplayed his opponent in a maximum-length Series. Their inaccurate picture of Cobb's performance endures to this day. He didn't shine, but in game number one he scored Detroit's only run in the 4–1 defeat, narrowly missed a triple, and stole a base on Gibson. In game number two, Vic Willis relieved Howie Camnitz on the Pirates' mound. The next few minutes demonstrated Cobb's mental processes and explained why he stole the most impregnable of stations, home base, more often than any of the thirteen-thousand-odd men who have played the game in this century. He remembered analysis of the play:

"Willis came in from the bullpen. We had a two-run rally going. I was the runner at third base. The moment Willis took over I decided to try for a steal. There were four angles to it. My reasoning was that he would have his mind far more on stopping our rally than on me. But first I had to experiment. Willis was a twelve-year veteran and smart. So far I was only guessing he'd be a bit careless in watching me. As soon as he took his pose on the rubber, I walked off third a few times as a test and to disarm Willis, the catcher, and third baseman Bob Byrne. Willis's eyes were fixed on the signal from his catcher. I looked harmless. It was a great moment . . . he'd left an opening. Just as Willis raised his arm to go into his windup, I broke for the plate with everything I had.

"Since a right-handed hitter, George Moriarty, was at bat, I had some protection—the screening effect of his body—for partway down the line. Gibson didn't see me coming at first. Willis did see and reacted like his pants were on fire. He had to check his windup and stance in order to throw home."

Reported one correspondent, "Cobb did it in nothing flat." His home steal, a Series rarity, was done with no rough stuff, but a clean tearing up of dirt for several feet and a toe-hook past Gibson, grabbing for the ball.

Another dividend was that an upset Willis walked Moriarty. Detroit won, 7–2, with Cobb adding a single.

Action switched to Detroit for game three, requiring that Cobb make hurried train connections that bypassed Ohio. He didn't arrive at Bennett Park until batting practice had begun. Feeling "gas pain," he had a run-scoring single and run-scoring double while the Tigers lost, 8–6. Wagner overshadowed him with three base steals to Cobb's none, and three timely hits.

In the next game, Cobb was hit in the stomach by a first-inning pitch, which did not help his nausea. After that he was hot and cold, twice bunting into outs, while also driving in a pair of runs with an opposite-field double. Detroit won this one, 5–0, thanks to George Mullin's shutout pitching. That evened the Series at two games each. The Pirates pulled ahead with an 8–4 victory despite home runs by Sam Crawford and Davy Jones; Cobb came up with just one single in a poor outing. Back in Detroit for number six, Cobb doubled in a run while the Tigers battled back to edge the Bucs, 5–4, and force a seventh-game showdown. In this one, the year's best hitter flied out, bounced out, and in general failed, while Babe Adams, a reserve Pirate pitcher, threw a surprising 8–0 shutout. Cobb kicked his bat halfway to the bench in frustration when for the third straight time the Tigers lost the world championship.

Collectively, the Pirates batted a light .224 in the Series to Detroit's .236. The Tigers totaled fifty-five base hits to the winner's fifty. Because of spotty pitching, failure to bunch hits, and allowing a record-equaling eighteen Pirate base steals, Jennings's men had thrown it away.

Wagner had been a more decisive factor than his opposite number, who was a dozen years younger, but not to the extent that legend has it. The Dutchman averaged .333 overall as compared to Cobb's .231, with eight hits to Cobb's six, and four runs scored to three by Cobb. Each drove in six runs. Wagner stole six bases to Cobb's two. Each had three extra-base hits. Cobb had outhit Wagner over the season by 38 points—.377 to .339, outslugged him by .517 to .489, and outscored him, 116 runs to 92.

Cobb took the Series loss hard; his anger at having been outplayed ran deep. He resented the story that he had tried to spike Wagner in one game. It was told and retold how he had supposedly shouted from first base to Wagner at shortstop, "Key, Krauthead! I'm coming down on the next pitch! Look out, Krauthead!" And when he did come, Wagner supposedly jammed the ball into Cobb's mouth for three stitches (sometimes reported as five) and tagged him out. That anecdote has been repeated by generations of sportswriters; Cobb said that it did not happen, and there is no evidence that it did. Cobb was a busy memorialist, preserving events on paper in the form of memos, annotations, and recorded dialogue, and in his writings he said, "Me insult Wagner, try to spike him? Would have taken a foolhardy man . . . With his powerful body, you were very careful when you slid in his vicinity. I admired Wagner. The story was invented." Wagner also denied the story.

Throughout the playoff the matter of the Cleveland arrest warrant hanging over him worried Cobb. "It bothered my play," he said, "to think of police coming onto the field and handcuffing me."

Cobb's Tiger teammates let him know how they felt about his uninspired work in the Series. If he hadn't been rushing back and forth by rail and car between home base and Pittsburgh to avoid arrest, if he had played at his peak, the Tigers might have collected individual Series winner's shares of $1,825. Instead they drew $1,275 each.

On top of that, his winter plans were delayed. Navin said, "You can't go anywhere until we settle the warrant." Considering the Stansfield legal charges to be very serious, Navin decided that Cobb should face the music. On October 19, Cobb, Navin, and two attorneys were off to see an Ohio judge. One of the lawyers was the former mayor of Cleveland, R. E. McKisson. Well connected in Ohio, McKisson was retained in hope of arranging a milder sentence than a felonious assault charge usually carried. On October 20, the defendant pleaded not guilty. McKisson argued that his client's use of a knife began only after the night watchman of the Euclid Hotel had attacked him with a billyclub. Upon arraignment, the ballplayer posted a five-hundred-dollar bond, with trial set within thirty days. Back at last in Georgia, the Peach was honored with so many banquets that his weight went to nearly two hundred pounds. Charlie Cobb held a reception at The Oaks attended by friends, Augusta and state officials, and her hubby's old Royston Reds teammates—some two hundred admirers in all. Diamond stickpins, a silver bat, and jeweled watch fobs were added to his earlier gift collection.

Attorney McKisson, meantime, had been busy doing, as Cobb was to write, "a helluva job." The case was plea-bargained down so far that when the accused returned to Cleveland on November 22, the judge handled the bloody fight with the black detective not as a criminal matter but as simple assault and battery. The penalty was a hundred-dollar fine and court costs. It was testified that at home Cobb employed blacks as servants and handymen and treated them well. His off-the-record comment at a later time was, "It would have meant jail if I hadn't had so much help—a friendly judge, and with the Detroit ball club's bankroll behind me. We bought this one."

WITH A new Detroit contract worth nine thousand dollars a year for three years in his safety box—the second-highest pay in baseball behind Honus Wagner—Cobb gave thought to buying a car. He knew nothing of mechanics and liked the inexpensive Brush Runabout, but when he heard an expert make a wisecrack about the Brush—"a wooden body, wooden axles, wooden wheels, wooden run"—he changed his mind. When Cobb could afford an automobile it would be an impressive Cadillac Six or Chalmers 30, costing a thousand dollars or up. That time was drawing near.

CHAPTER THIRTEEN

THE GREATEST PLAYER WHO EVER LIVED

Charles Dillon Stengel, soon to be known throughout baseball as "Casey," experienced a thrill early in 1913. The left-handed ex–semipro pitcher was leaving the Brooklyn spring-training camp one day when he encountered "the greatest of them all," and a lifelong friendship resulted:

"This wuz at Augusta an' I never forgot it. I walk out of the park and there is Ty Cobb, himself. And he has the biggest automobile in the world. Big as a boxcar.

"The car wouldn't start. Cobb was kickin' it with both boots and cussin' a blue streak. It was an amazin' sight for a young fella like me to see."

Twenty-three-year-old Stengel, one day to become the most famous of big-league managers, had been drifting around the bushes at Kankakee, Illinois, Maysville, Kentucky, and Montgomery, Alabama, for a few years, idolizing the renowned Cobb from afar. By now he was an outfielder with a pretty fair bat. Stengel had played only seventeen games for the Dodgers, but had hopes of winning steady employment. The Georgia Peach had dropped by the Dodgers' camp for a private workout. He was holding out that April, insisting on more salary and bonuses from a resistant Detroit management. Stengel picked a poor

moment to introduce himself, but he couldn't pass up the opportunity
to meet his hero.

"Brooklyn? You're in a horseshit league!" snapped Cobb. "Know
anything about cars?"

"No, sir," replied Stengel. "You want me to help push it?"

Cobb fumed, "This crate is guaranteed to run for months. I've had
it a few days. Okay, start pushing."

The two shoved for a while and all that resulted was popping
noises and smoke clouds. Stengel made the ritual remark about horses
being more dependable than gas buggies, drawing from Cobb more
invective and kicking of his expensive vehicle. Giving up on it, Cobb
sat on the grass to wait for a trolley car to come along and take him to
the nearest mechanic. Casey sat with him.

During this chance meeting Stengel advanced their acquaintance
by telling how Brooklyn manager Bill Dahlen had only one high-class
outfielder, Zachariah "Zack" Wheat. There was a chance for such a
prospect as himself to win a job. "If you're any good you sure as hell
should," said Cobb. "Those Pigtowners have been sixth or worse for
years. On hitting, Brooklyn's known as the oh-for-four club."

Stengel stated that he was a left-hander; what would Mister Cobb
advise him? One of Cobb's amiable attributes was that he enjoyed
instructing young talent. "Get up in the front of the box against lefties," he said. "Smack it before the ball tails away from you . . . or in on
your fists."

No trolley arrived. Cobb went on talking. "Get yourself hit by
pitches. Before the ump can call you out for doing it on purpose, beat
him to it. Let out a yell. Throw your bat at the pitcher. Limp around,
show that you're hurt. Then steal second base."

Cobb liked the jug-eared rookie enough to act as his counselor
from time to time. Marriage was a risky move, Cobb warned (Stengel
did not marry his Edna until he was thirty-five). And: "Don't ever be
caught with liquor on your breath at game time." More than sixty years
later at his Glendale, California, home, Casey, now an idiosyncratic
character with a Hall of Fame plaque of his own, still enjoyed telling
at length about how momentous it had been for him to meet "the best
bygod ballplayer I ever saw, including some very great ones," and how
a long friendship resulted from his helping Cobb to push his car that
spring day. In 1916, with Brooklyn against the Boston Red Sox in the

World Series, Stengel sought out Cobb, who was on hand as a press-syndicate commentator, to ask, "How would you hit off Ernie Shore?" Shore was slated to start for Boston the next day. They spoke for two hours by Casey's estimate, and because of adjustments made by Cobb against Shore's stuff, Stengel got two hits. Brooklyn lost the Series, but in limited appearances Casey led his club's overall hitting with a .364 mark.

Upon Stengel's being named Brooklyn's manager in 1934, Cobb, at a banquet honoring his unearthly friend, stood and told the cadaver and manhole stories. As a boyhood student at Western Dental College in Kansas City, considering dentistry as an occupation, Casey dissected the mouths and jaws of dead human bodies. "That," said Cobb, "is how he got so gabby—getting right into it."

Stengel was the dental class's clown. "He'd cut off a cadaver's thumb and stick it in somebody's pocket. And put cigars in the bazoos of corpses," declared Cobb, as Casey blushed.

While Casey was a struggling minor-leaguer in Alabama, this later inventor of such managerial maxims as "he executed splendid," "if a fella won't change his nighttime habits, disappear him," and "you could look it up," noticed a manhole cover in the outfield. For the hell of it, Casey climbed in the hole. When a fly ball was hit his way, he wasn't to be seen. "At the last second," chuckled Cobb, "up popped the lid and Mr. Stengel shot from nowhere to catch the ball."

"Bare-handed," interrupted Casey.

THERE HAD not been too much that was humorous about the three-year period of Cobb's career that followed the 1909 World Series defeat. One insurgent act followed another. He made it easy, almost routine, for the press outside of Detroit to demonize him, as when reporting on the day when several cops were needed to wrestle him down after Cobb charged into the bleachers to assault an abusive fan. In a Detroit hotel dining room he slapped the face of one more black, a waiter who served him the wrong order. Meanwhile the Tigers of three straight World Series appearances fell to third place and second, and then to sixth, sixth, fourth, second, third, fourth and seventh—only two runner-up finishes in almost a decade.

Renewed discord among the Tigers was blamed for their falling off in 1910. In Cobb's earlier Detroit experience the bad feelings had been over attempts to maneuver him off the team. Now it was the opposite: how to live with his favored status. Matty McIntyre, Sam Crawford, Davy Jones, and other regulars criticized Hughie Jennings for not lowering the boom on "his pet," who reported for spring-training camp on whatever date he wished, insisted on a set of batter-to-base-runner signs dictated and flashed by Cobb from the plate, and who required, and received, the only private hotel quarters provided team members when on the road.

When his three-year contract at nine thousand dollars per season was about to expire in 1912 he predicted, "They'll be paying me twenty thousand dollars before long or I'll be out of here . . . maybe to New York." As he forecast, within two years Cobb was drawing twenty thousand dollars, when no one else on the club, not even Wahoo Crawford, with a twelve-year .313 average as of 1914, was paid anywhere near that. Navin, hardest of bargainers, weakened on their money differences when he saw the Peach step up with the bases loaded and Detroit trailing by a run or two and deliver one of his pulled-down-the-line singles or fence-reaching doubles. Cobb ran the bases with a high, jaunty step—"*Look at me, folks, and see the best.*"

One day after hitting a stand-up double, Cobb patted second baseman Eddie Collins of the Athletics sympathetically on the back. Collins screamed at him. One more opponent had been jarred out of his composure.

Sportswriters sought to interpret his behavior. As the New York *Daily News*'s Paul Gallico read him, "He is an endless paradox, the most outrageous yet the most inspiring of athletes. No one so aggressive and infuriating has come along. Cobb seems to understand that while Americans profess to be peace-loving people, we actually love violence. With his tendency to undress fielders and catchers with his slashing spikes, there's always the chance that we'll be witness to an accident. On top of that comes his immense conceit."

The brilliant syndicated columnist Ring Lardner was notoriously cynical about baseball's acclaimed importance to America's masses, even its honesty. During the 1919 World Series, which turned out to be fixed by gamblers and eight Chicago White Sox players, Lardner would sit at his typewriter well before the fix was uncovered, whistling to the "I'm Forever Blowing Bubbles" tune, "I'm forever blowing ballgames." Yet with Cobb he was as starstruck as a kid in the bleachers.

'It defies human capability for anyone to *average* almost .400 in the past five seasons," submitted Lardner in 1914. "Is he bribing the pitchers?" The multifaceted Cobb couldn't be diagnosed: "He's simply from a higher league than any we know."

John "Little Napoleon" McGraw (also "Muggsy"), icon of the New York Giants and manager of five National League champions by 1917, rarely was called foolish, but he drew laughs for claiming that "Christy Mathewson is more valuable than Cobb. Christy wins twenty-five to thirty games for us every year; his pitching puts whole teams in slumps." Mathewson, of course, was in action for about 300 innings per season, Cobb for 1,300 or so, while driving in and scoring 200-odd runs in his top seasons. Big Six Mathewson did not steal bases or hit enough to notice.

When he was playing well, Cobb kept his temper under control. When out of his groove, not hitting in high figures, he was all but impossible to team with. "If I went three for four and T.C. was blanked," Sam Crawford once recalled, "he'd turn red and sometimes walk right out of the park with the game still on—same as he did when he left the Tigers to get married." Outfielder Kangaroo Jones verified that.

Jones's troubles with Cobb heated up again during a Chicago White Sox game when Cobb's attention was drawn to an open iron gate in the left-field corner. Chicago had built a new ballpark, and the gate was not fully installed. "Watch me put one through it," said Cobb on the bench. Jones hooted. The opening was about 5 feet wide and 340 feet away.

After a swinging strike thrown by Big Ed Walsh, Cobb placed a fastball over the left fielder's head and through the gate on the bounce for a home run. His astonishingly precise drive won the game for the Tigers, 6–5.

Jones thought that a lot of luck had been involved. He said so, and hard words followed. Back in Detroit, against the Red Sox, Jones was on first base, watching for T.C. to give him the hit-run sign. Jones claimed the signal never was given. With one strike on him, Cobb backed out of the box to yell at Jones, "Don't you know the go sign when you see it?"

Jones took the open insult silently. According to him, Boston's first baseman, Jake Stahl, told Jones, "Anybody who'd holler down here like that is a rotten skunk."

On the next pitch, for strike two, Cobb threw his bat away to shout, "By god, I won't team with anyone who misses the sign twice!" He stomped over to the bench, pulled on a sweater, and refused to continue. Jennings ordered him to finish his hitting turn, Cobb refused, and a substitute hitter was inserted. Shortly afterward Cobb left the park, to the jeers and protests of the crowd.

It was obvious to the Tigers that he had used Jones as a scapegoat. Left-handed Ray Collins, the pitcher at work when Cobb left the scene, always had been a tough fellow for him to hit, so with two strikes on him, Cobb had invented an excuse. In Frank Navin's office a hot exchange ended with Navin's threat to suspend him, but Navin eventually backed off. (Another occasional Cobbian habit, when the hit-and-run or run-and-hit was on, was not to swing at a delivery in the strike zone that looked too difficult to handle, even though this could leave base runners committed and stranded. Almost to a man the Tigers were certain that he was principally out to advance his chance for another league batting title.)

Jones approached Cobb in the clubhouse, declaring, "I won't be your fall guy." Cobb heatedly replied, "Go to hell. I'm not playing until you're out of the lineup." He was serious. Either Jones, a good leadoff man, got the ax, or Cobb was leaving.

Jennings would not hear of trading Kangaroo Jones. Cobb sat in the Bennett Park stands during the following game with Boston in civilian dress. He was "sulking," wrote Ed Spayer in the Detroit News. On the next day he entered the clubhouse just before game time and reached for his flannel uniform. Trainer Harry Tuthill was rubbing down a player.

"Don't bother," said Tuthill. "Jennings said to tell you that you're not in there today. You're benched."

"Does Navin know about this?" asked Cobb.

Tuthill shrugged. "Probably does."

Confronted in his box seat by a seething Cobb, Navin supported Jennings, but, wishing to avoid a major mistake, offered a compromise. Kangaroo Jones would be moved from the number-one or number-two spot in the batting order down to number six. That way Jones would not usually be on base when the Peach came to bat. The arrangement upset Jennings's strategy, but what else was there to do? Cobb had to be appeased. Jones was moved down. Returning to the lineup against

New York, Cobb went on singling, doubling, and stealing when it counted most.

Davy Jones, in 1950, expressed to me what a relief it had been to get out of baseball and into business (he eventually built a chain of profitable drugstores). "Cobb was born without a sense of humor," said Jones. "He was strictly for himself. He spoiled the game for me."

COBB SUSPECTED that Detroit would not win the pennant again, and that the chances that he would take the field in a World Series again anytime soon were poor. "It wasn't hard for me to guess," he said. "Navin and his scouts couldn't make a good trade if it bit them." His own lack of teamsmanship must be counted in. An example of that came during another losing contest at Philadelphia. Fans were walking out after the Athletics ran up a 7–0 lead in the ninth inning. In such almost-hopeless situations the trailing team takes no chances: the percentage move is to play it safe and pray for a miracle. At the game's near ending it is folly to go for a high-risk, no-gain stolen base.

A roar burst from the crowd. Cobb struck a high, slow bounder into the hole between second base and shortstop, which shortstop Jack Barry juggled, then recovered, as the *Detroit News* reported. Cobb kept going, and slid into second base before Barry's throw. Detroit's next batter caromed one off pitcher Jack Coombs's glove that rebounded to Eddie Collins at second. Collins snapped a throw to first to retire the runner, thinking that if Cobb kept going, he would be retired 3–5— first to third. But even before Collins completed his arm action, T.C. was partway to third. Despite the lopsided score, he darted on for the plate, reaching it simultaneously with first baseman Harry Davis's relay—a throw Davis had not expected to make. Cobb was safe in a tangle of bodies. The game ended minutes later with the score 7–1. He had improved his own record with a run scored, but at the risk of being thrown out when his team was behind.

A vaudeville-like name was given Detroit in the years when the club ran out of the money—"Cobb and others." "Tigers" was spelled "Tygers" by some writers. Cobb himself seldom praised his teammates. His snubbing of Sam Crawford, who retired with bitter feelings in 1917, of Jones, of Matty McIntyre, was a way of getting even for the past. Steady-hitting Bobby Veach came to Detroit in 1912 and lasted in the outfield until 1923. Deferential to Cobb, the genial Kentuckian came around in time to saying, "If T.C. didn't like you he could run you off the club. He had that kind of drag with the front office from about 1914 on. He was a sorehead. I hit .355 one year to his .384 and I swear he was jealous of me. What an odd bird." Veach could not forget that in 1914, with postseason exhibition games left on the schedule, their leader dropped out to attend the World Series between the Boston Braves and the Athletics. He was paid a high fee to write a commentary, "Cobb Says." "You can guess what that did for our morale," said Veach.

McIntyre left the Motor City earlier, in 1911, glad to be gone to the Chicago Americans. He, too, could not fathom a Cobb who would prowl the clubhouse before games, darkly muttering to himself, gritting his teeth with game time two hours away. Players who saw a decade or more of him admitted that the teamwide cruel hazing he received when he was a rookie could explain some of his behavior, but not all. The aftershock should have worn off. It had not. Others who knew the facts about his father's death felt that this tragedy relentlessly preyed on his mind. He was still getting even for that loss, in some mentally contorted way. Or so they guessed.

Sam Crawford had said it before and said it again. He felt rather sorry for the one who walked mostly alone, not sharing in team camaraderie. Crawford noted, "That's no way for anyone to live. But I know one thing—he was never sorry for what he did." For as long as he lived Cobb retained a copy of a letter he sent to J. G. Taylor Spink of the *Sporting News*, reading:

> Dear Taylor:
>   Crawford never helped in the outfield by calling to me 'plenty of room' or 'you take it' on a chance. Not only that, when I was on base and tried to steal second to get into scoring position, with Crawford at bat, he would deliberately foul balls off so I'd have to go back to base, so that the first baseman would have to hold me on . . . giving Crawford a bigger hole to hit through. *I ran hundreds of miles having to return to first.*

Crawford, upon learning of the letter in 1946, shook his head. "Cobb dreamed that up," he told several reporters. "He could come in on a ball with the best. He wasn't so good going back for a big lofter in the wind. So he blamed me. As to my fouling them off, it was always my way to pick at pitches until I got one to my strength. Cobb was just the same way."

Far worse than that charge was Cobb's postmortem to Jack Sher, writing for *Reader's Digest*. To Sher he claimed that some teammates actually tipped off opposing pitchers to his batting weak spots. "They were out to get me so much they'd risk losing ball games to see me strike out," he swore. "I never knew of another case where men would do anything so scurvy as that."

In making this charge Cobb neglected to mention what was known as the "pitchers' underground." Cobb, whatever he believed, was not alone in becoming the object of shared intelligence. He was only one of a number of victims of a clandestine union. Moundsmen would pass on information gained from hard experience to others of their kind who were in the employment of opposing teams. If a Red Soxer could be put out with a sinker, or a St. Louis Brownie was susceptible to a change-of-pace, or a new slugger with a weakness entered a league, the "book" would be quietly exchanged by pitchers. Club owners knew it went on but could not stop such fraternizing. The exception was said to be that no tipster ever revealed information on hitters of his own team.

Providing aid to an opponent, in whatever form, bordered on game fixing, which would condemn baseball in the public eye as dishonest. Cobb's supposed detection of plots against him came as early as his third year in the majors. Here and there he saw hands raised to hurt him, he claimed. He named names, "There was Baldy Louden [an infielder]. He and McIntyre failed time and again to score from second on a play where I followed them with a single. Plays were designed to score them, but they didn't make a good enough start off the bat with the pitch. They'd pull up at third, giving the fielder a chance to throw me out going to second. I'd look foolish. They were out to keep me from setting records. When I jumped Louden on it before the whole club he alibied that his legs hurt. When my own legs carried dozens of stitches."

If such double crosses did exist, they failed to hurt his cumulative numbers. From 1910 through 1913 he was all but unstoppable. While the Tigers were sliding to third place in 1911 and then to a 69-wins, 84-losses sixth-place mark in 1912, Cobb himself was slamming all manner of pitching, from screwball to knuckler to spitter, from fast-ball to greaseball. The Peach's averages at ages twenty-four to twenty-seven were so formidable that in the 1980s his statistics were retroactively examined by researchers, to make sure that record-keepers hadn't erred.

Connie Mack, whose Athletics won three pennants in 1910–13, with but one A's hitter, Eddie Collins, coming in above .365, was supposed to have blurted, "If we had Ty Cobb there'd be no point in holding a season."

Ungovernable as he regularly was, often using the black ashwood bat he had kept beside him during his 1908 wedding, Cobb hit .385, .420, .410, and .390 in four successive seasons. Along with that came 261 stolen bases. No one since then has matched that performance. It included 818 hits, 829 runs scored or driven in, 233 extra-base hits, and 1,202 total bases, and brought him his fourth, fifth, sixth, and seventh consecutive AL batting titles. In his 1911 rush Cobb swept every offensive category except home runs, set a record of 248 base hits that would top all major-league hitting for twenty-two years to come. "He hit me hard with runners on or not, in daylight or twilight," said Washington's Walter Johnson, spectacular winner of 118 games during that same 1910–13 stretch. "He would get two or three hits and figure it should have been better. Nobody would wait for the right pitch better than Ty. He just wore you out. The balls we used would get black in the late innings and he'd still hit."

Only one other hitter in history has equalled Cobb's back-to-back .400-plus seasons of 1911–12. Rogers Hornsby, greatest right-handed batsman of all time, hit .424 in 1924 and .403 in 1925. From 1901 onward, to average .400 even once has eluded all but eight hitters—George Sisler, twice; Nap Lajoie; Shoeless Joe Jackson; Harry Heilmann; Bill Terry; and Ted Williams, along with Cobb and Hornsby. No others—not Wagner, Tris Speaker, Al Simmons, Babe Ruth, Jimmie Foxx, Lou Gehrig, Paul Waner, Lefty O'Doul, Joe DiMaggio, Al Kaline, Mickey Mantle, Willie Mays, Hank Aaron—ever reached that exclusive circle. No one since Williams in 1941, more than fifty years ago, has registered that high. Batters have come close, but failed. When Cobb hit .401 in 1922, a full decade after his last previous such performance, he would stand, along with Hornsby, as one of the only players to do it three times.

"Be sure and put in there," T.C. instructed me when we collaborated on the chronicle of his life and times, "that from 1910 through 1914 I outhit both the American and National leagues easily. The Nationals had nobody close to me . . . their best with the bat were at .331, .334, .372, .350, and .329." His memory on this was faultless, his arithmetic exact. At the same time, the Georgian wished to express his contempt for "two-bit, one-gear" hitters of the post–World War II era, who while swinging for the fences—"moneyland"—led entire leagues with "puny" marks of .320, .327, .328, .336, .338, .325, and once even .309. (He did not live to see Carl Yastrzemski win a batting championship in 1968 with .301.)

His .420 and .410 marks of 1911 and 1912 came during seasons in which Cobb spent some days in bed with another dose of bronchial infection, and while hurting from a banged-up knee acquired in chasing an automobile thief. Upon leaving a Cadillac Square restaurant in Detroit, he found a man cranking his car and taking off. Roars from the owner did not stop the thief, and Cobb sprinted after him. *Sporting Life* marveled in its account of how the driver had reached a speed of almost twenty miles an hour when the pursuer caught up, leaped onto the tonneau, grabbed the driver's neck, and knocked him aside. Driverless, the auto swerved around the street, almost hitting a trolley car with people boarding it, in a replay of Keystone Cops comedies then playing in theaters. Cobb gained control of the car and stopped it in time not to kill anyone. The jailed thief, identified as John Miles, nineteen, exclaimed, "If I'd known it was *him*, I'd never have lifted it!" Cobb came out of it with cuts and a knee bruise, but soon recovered.

POWER-DRIVEN conveyances and T.C. did not mix well. There had been a close call with death in 1911 when a taxicab in which he was riding dumped him onto the pavement as it crashed into a Detroit streetcar. Driving in Detroit in 1912, he had been forced to jump for his life before an onrushing car. There was also the day in Augusta when his limousine would not start and a busher named Stengel helped try to push it back to life. Cobb felt jinxed, as did thousands of other investors in embryonic machines ranging from the costly Pope-Toledo, Cadillac, and Stutz Bearcat to the six-hundred-dollar-and-up Chevrolet, Maxwell, and Ford models. The hazards of getting horseless carriages to go and keep going were many. When the U.S. Motor Car

Company and Maxwell went bankrupt, some people cheered. Cart horses did not require cranking, tow trucks, or smelly fuel.

Not long before Cobb began his stay in the .400 bracket, still another affair involving himself and a motor car occurred, this one exposing baseball in the worst possible light. In 1910, the nationally notorious "Chalmers frame-up" began when Hugh Chalmers, president of Chalmers Motor Company, offered gifts of his best models to the batting champions of the American and National leagues. Chalmers, a former star salesman for the National Cash Register Company, saw his giveaways as good promotion in a new field—sports—and he threw in a bonus of free tanks of gasoline, costing seventeen cents a gallon. Chalmers could not foresee that his stunt would become a sickening scandal, one of the first public indicators that baseball was not entirely on the up-and-up.

At midseason, Cobb thought he had little or no chance to win the prize. Napoleon Lajoie, Cleveland's three-time American League bat titleholder, was averaging .399 to Cobb's .372. When the Peach contracted another of the eye ailments that handicapped him from time to time, it appeared to be all over except for the shouting. Fitted with smoked glasses to wear in bright sunlight, he was forced to drop out for ten days in September. He hated to show infirmity, but headlines such as "IS COBB GOING BLIND IN ONE EYE?" had appeared on sport pages. In speaking of what followed, he told me, "I was trying to play down the eyes. A confidential letter I sent to a Cleveland friend became public. I never spoke to that squealer again." A portion of his letter said, ". . . my eyes are not very good now and I have to use one eye to write . . . It throws me out of the running for the auto . . . Lajoie surely will best my present average. Tomorrow I consult a stomach specialist, as this may be the trouble. I can only see well from the left eye . . . the other is smoky. I am very worried."

However, Lajoie did not improve, while Cobb, returning to work with vision remarkably strengthened, collected a double, two triples, and two singles in a doubleheader with New York. At Chicago on October 6 and 7 he went 4 for 7 in two games. In the closing days the race read:

	At-Bats	Hits	Batting Average
Cobb	509	196	.3848 . 385069
Lajoie	591	237	.3841
		227	

The tightest of possible finishes gripped fans across the country, leading to formation of Lajoie and Cobb rooter clubs. A Detroiter named Tim Harrigan, with a big bet down on Cobb to win, dropped dead at the Century Club of Detroit supposedly from overexcitement. Public voting was held on who would win.

On October 6 Cobb's eye trouble reappeared. He sat out two season-ending Chicago engagements. Cleveland's *Plain Dealer* and other Ohio papers scoffed that if he had enough sight to connect at his current rate, then it could only be a case of faint heart—the fear that he would finish poorly and lose points. Moreover, after benching himself in Chicago, he had gone to Philadelphia to appear in an all-star affair. Lajoie, on the other hand, emphasized the *Reach Guide,* "never got cold feet."

Big Frenchy Lajoie's chance to pass his rival at the wire came in an October 9 Cleveland–St. Louis doubleheader. Cobb's season was finished, Lajoie's was not. Eastern gamblers—did they know something?—had Frenchy as a slight favorite to drive away in the deluxe Chalmers. At six feet, one inch and nearly two hundred pounds, Lajoie (pronounced La-zway) was the press's ideal of grace, power, and confidence under pressure. A native of Fall River, Massachusetts, a former livery-stable hack driver, he was lauded by George Trevor of the *New York Sun* as an "eye-filling D'Artagnan of the diamond," along with "living poetry at second base." Lajoie was "a big, swarthy jungle cat whose superiority oozes from him." Back in 1901, for the Philadelphia A's, he had averaged .422 for a full season, although at the time foul balls did not count as strikes.

The colorful Lajoie chewed a plug of tobacco the size of a hockey puck; once he had been suspended for squirting juice into the eye of umpire Frank "Blinky" Dwyer. He had player-managed Cleveland for a while, then quit to gather more player's trophies.

To prevent Cobb, disliked on every American League bench, from edging out Lajoie required the collaboration of St. Louis manager Jack "Peach Pie" O'Connor and his scout, Harry Howell. Their plan was to provide Lajoie with a base hit every time he came up against the Browns on October 9. This could be done in two ways—by feeding him easy pitches, or deploying the Browns' defense to the Frenchman's advantage. The second method was selected as more dependable.

The official scorer of the season-closing doubleheader was a sportswriter, E. V. Parish, who soon realized what was going on but was powerless to prevent it. Supposedly no one informed Lajoie in advance, although some insiders doubted that he was kept ignorant. On his first time at bat he tripled to center field. Fielder Hub Northen fell all over himself misjudging the ball. After that, with third baseman Red Corriden stationed so far back that he was on the outfield grass, Lajoie bunted safely three times. In the second half of the twin bill, with Corriden still playing a ridiculous distance away from him, Lajoie made four more hits, all on bunts that Corriden or shortstop Bobby Wallace were not there to handle. If eight gift base hits didn't let Lajoie surpass Cobb in the race, nothing could.

Parish had visitors at his press-box seat throughout the day. Cleveland and St. Louis reserve players came by to suggest that he score everything by Lajoie a hit. Late in the second game, Parish also was handed a note. American League historians have said that it read: "Mr. Parish: If you can see where Lajoie gets a B.H. instead of a sacrifice I will give you an order for a forty-dollar suit—for sure. Answer by boy, in behalf of——I ask you."

Afterward, Parish would testify that the note was unsigned; but he could smell two large rodents—manager Jack O'Connor and his aide, Harry Howell. Parish envisioned headlines exposing the conspiracy. Bookies who had made Cobb a favorite to win the Chalmers would be more than angry; they would be murderous. Parish ordered the bribe-offerer out of the press box. As for the St. Louis Browns, the inept eighth-place team had nothing to lose. The Browns would be getting even with Cobb for spiking some of them in the past.

When the unsophisticated plot was exposed, it shocked a public conditioned to believe that, regardless of what went on in Wall Street and Washington, D.C., back rooms, the American game of games was honest. There had been only minor doubts about that tradition in recent years. In 1908, umpire Bill Klem had revealed that he had been offered three thousand dollars to arrange a New York Giants win in a National League playoff with the Chicago Cubs. And in 1903 the National Commission had investigated suspected conniving in a Philadelphia-Giants series.

At St. Louis the "gaff," or fix, was all too evident; the *Detroit Free Press* bannered: "ST. LOUIS LAYS DOWN TO LET LAJOIE WIN." The *St. Louis*

Post let go with: "All St. Louis is up in arms over the deplorable spectacle, conceived in stupidity and executed in jealousy. The frame-up to deprive Cobb of the title surely will end the careers of whatever home-team officials ordered this monstrous fraud. This city should subscribe to a fund to buy Ty Cobb a Chalmers auto."

While people awaited the ruling of league president Ban Johnson, unofficial calculations were in disagreement. Chicago's *Tribune* had Lajoie winning the championship by 3 points, .385 to .382. The *Sporting News* called it .38415 to .38411 in favor of Cobb. Other journals had conflicting figures. From Philadelphia, where he was undergoing further eye treatment, Cobb said little, other than to suggest that O'Connor should be fired.

It was widely reported that eight of his Tiger teammates had sent a telegram to Lajoie, prematurely congratulating him on his victory in the Chalmers race. McIntyre, Crawford, Jones, Bush, and Boss Schmidt were said to be among those who signed the message, which they did not deny. Some observers felt that in the unending Cobb-Tigers war the telegram was the most vicious of all acts. Cobb only said, "That was to be expected." He expressed confidence that a just ruling would be made by Johnson, despite their past differences. It was Frank Navin's voice in the matter that he feared more than Ban Johnson's. "That prick, Navin, never has liked me," he told one of the few friendly Tigers, "and his vote will be important."

Enter Hugh Fullerton, New York sportswriter. Fullerton had been a co-scorekeeper of another Detroit game, back in midseason, and at that time had given Cobb credit for a questionable hit. His fellow scorer had changed it to a fielder's error. Digging into his files, Fullerton found the score sheet used that day, restored the hit, and forwarded his amendment to the league office. He urged Johnson to accept his belief that Cobb had been robbed of a single. This complicated things even further for Bob McRoy, the league statistician charged with untangling the issue of who had won.

Other support came from the last place where "runner-up Cobb"—a phrase already being bandied about—expected to find it: Manhattan. In the interest of a square deal, New Yorkers showed sympathy toward their longtime enemy. Heywood Broun of the *New York Morning Telegraph* commanded a large audience as a leading editorialist. A Harvard man and intellectual, Broun's "It Seems to Me" column on world affairs was becoming a staple for sophisticated readers. Of anti-Cobb sentiment Broun wrote:

As the world knows, Tyrus Raymond Cobb is less popular than Napoleon Lajoie. Perhaps Cobb is the least-popular player who ever lived. And why? Whether you like or you dislike this fellow you must concede him one virtue: what he has won he has taken by might of his own play. Pistareen ball players whom he has shown up dislike him, third basemen with bum arms, second basemen with tender skins, catchers who cannot throw out a talented slider—all despise Cobb. And their attitude has infected the stands.

Ahhh—one wonders. Here is the best man in the world at his game, without the shade of a doubt; the best of any time. Yet it seems he is fated to move across the field as did Bobby Burns' gallant scapegoat, who danced beneath the noose— "Sae wantonly, sae dauntingly, sae rantingly gaied he." He played a spring and danced it "round the gallows tree." If Cobb sticks his cap on three hairs, as the Irish say, laughs in the faces of his opponents and steals bases while they stand around with the ball in their hands, is he to be damned by the populace?

With the curious crassity which always leads the mob to rend that hand that feeds and to lick that which whips it, spectators at baseball games do not like this player who gives them more for their hard-earned ticket than any man alive or dead gave them. When humanity put to death its Greatest Servant, all that he could say in condonation was, "Father, forgive them, for they know not what they do!" That was the biggest and truest thing He ever said. Humanity prefers guile and gaud to honesty and worth. Humanity is asinine.

Humanity also paid to see baseball games, however, and the public would not tolerate an attempted fix. One week after the "black day" at St. Louis, Ban Johnson announced the decision. Napoleon Lajoie had compiled a .384084 average—Johnson accepted Frenchy's gift hits from the Browns as legal without batting an eye—but Cobb had hit .384944. That was squeezing decimal points until they screamed, but Cobb was the victor, by the finest of margins. Detroit whooped.

Elsewhere there were boos. Cobb said that he was delighted—and stopped at that. He was in a position to ask how Johnson could credit Lajoie with hits handed to him fraudulently, but passed up the opportunity. He might have to deal with Johnson on another day.

Not until the following spring could a Detroit writer get him to speak on the matter of the eight Tigers who prematurely congratulated Lajoie. "Oh, when I pass some of them on the street," he drawled, "I just honk the horn of my new car at them."

Some analysts of Johnson's decision believed that he ruled as he did in part because Lajoie was thirty-six years old, somewhat slowing up, and would not be a big box-office draw for much longer. By contrast, at twenty-four Ty Cobb would be pulling in crowds for years to come.

Taking his time after the World Series, Johnson forced the St. Louis management to fire Jack O'Connor and Harry Howell, and kept them from being rehired elsewhere. Third baseman Red Corriden and shortstop Bobby Wallace were exonerated. In playing far out of position, they were only following their boss's orders. Wallace replaced O'Connor as manager and St. Louis continued to be the league doormat.

Auto magnate Hugh Chalmers provided the only pleasant note to the affair by generously awarding automobiles to both Cobb and Lajoie. As far as he was concerned, their contest had ended in a tie. Within ten days Cobb was off to Georgia, driving the Chalmers. Over the winter he entered a high speed ten-mile auto race on an Atlanta track where several drivers had been killed. No safety equipment as it is known today was provided. Cobb also rode in exhibitions in tandem with Barney "Fastest Man Alive" Oldfield, who also held the record for most crashes on a speedway. Navin, learning of this in Detroit, threw up his hands. What else could you call Cobb but suicidal?

CURIOUS AS to how deeply Cobb's racial prejudice went, Joe Vila of the *New York Sun* asked him how he felt about recent Tiger trips to Cuba to meet all-star clubs composed solidly of blacks. Cobb's reply, as preserved in his "career" files, was, "A man named Alex Reeves works for me at my Georgia home. Alex is the best darky and houseman I've ever known." Concerning another matter: John McGraw, earlier, had disguised a star black semipro, Charlie Grant, as "Charlie Tokahama, a full-blooded Cherokee." Cobb noted that McGraw didn't get away with smuggling Grant-Tokahama into the New York Giants lineup; the promising young star was exposed and ousted. "There will never be a darky in the majors," T.C. confidently foresaw. "Darkies' place is in the stands or as clubhouse help."

In 1909, a band of Tigers had traveled to Cuba, where they lost eight of twelve exhibitions against a startlingly competent lineup—an ethnic mix of African, Spanish, Yucatec, Jamaican, and other bloodlines—but without Cobb, who declined to join the party. He swore he would never step onto a field against nonwhites.

At a later date Havana promoters offered Detroit a deal to return for a series. Joe Vila prodded Cobb. Still he had no intention of taking part in the coming repeat exhibition—not until Cuba threw in a thousand-dollar bonus and travel expenses so that baseball-happy islanders could see El Supremo perform. "I decided to break my own rule for a few games," he said in an interview. Money was talking.

On the agreed November 1910 date he failed to appear in Havana, angering Cubans and leaving everybody guessing. Cobb leisurely went fishing off south Florida until he felt like boarding a steamer out of Key West. By the time he checked in, the Tigers had won three, lost three, and tied one game against the challengers and needed help in a hurry. Before his debut at a packed Havana park, Cobb was introduced to John "Pop" Lloyd, an infielder rated by U.S. professionals who had seen him as equal to just about anyone in the majors. Lloyd was one of the few shortstops who could go deep into the hole and while sprinting toward the left-field stands throw across his body to first for outs. Meeting Lloyd, Cobb pointedly didn't shake hands. One photo of their meeting survives; Cobb's hands are in his pockets.

In his first game T.C. hit a pair of singles and a home run. "Ten thousand Cubans ran for that homer ball as a souvenir," went the report. Next he went hitless against the bullet fastball of the island's pride, Jose de la Caridad Mendez, known as "the greatest pitcher never allowed in U.S. baseball." On bases, sliding with spikes high, Cobb three times was tagged out by a fearless Lloyd. In a total of five Cuban games Cobb averaged .370. He was outshone by Lloyd, who batted .500. Local reporters asked Cobb when their countrymen would be admitted to top *Yanqui* leagues. He waved away the question. Through a strained series he remained stiff-necked and silent. With his help, the

Detroit Tigers overall won seven of eleven games in Cuba. The results were prototypic proof that skin color had nothing to do with athletic ability, and it pained those white fans who witnessed it.

COBB'S FEATURES were undergoing noticeable changes for so early an age. His jaw was becoming more set. Pouches appeared below his eyes, his nose had sharpened. His somber face was known everywhere. "I could walk into any saloon in the country and be given free drinks," he said. On the street he wore his hat pulled low to avoid unwelcome fans. Before he was twenty-eight he could count forty-odd stitch marks on his thighs, legs, and ankles—purplish, healed-over scars with the appearance of tattoos. When I asked him if the wounds were still painful, he snapped, "What the hell do you think?" At the time he was past seventy.

Playing the game had always been painful for him, and in years to come it would continue to be. Once at Cleveland, with Cobb the runner at first, a ball was safely looped to short left field. He went into second and accidentally collided with baseman Joe Sewell. Wheeler Joe Sewell was one opponent whom Cobb liked, a good guy on his way to the Hall of Fame with a career .312 average. In the collision, Cobb spiked himself. He was carried off the field in agony.

Cleveland's trainer called a doctor, who arrived without an anesthetic. "I can't deaden the pain," he said. The doctor called for volunteers to hold down his patient while he did emergency stitching. Witnesses heard Cobb moan, "I'll take it cold. Just give me a cigar." He was so deeply cut that bone and ligaments could be seen as the doctor stitched away. "How Cobb took it none of us knew," said Sewell. "But he did."

Getting to sleep after ball games was a problem for him. Since boyhood he had suffered from insomnia. He tried sleep potions, exercising on the carpet, and a method known to most ballplayers—sex. He would pick out one of the girls who hung around hotels, looking for a romp with a star player, and who would tire him out. Once, in St. Louis, he invited a girl upstairs. She acted suspiciously. Cobb sensed the old badger game at work. Minutes after the girl walked in, the "husband" would show up, claim she was his wife, and demand a money settlement to prevent publicity alleging rape. Recalled T.C., "I threw this dame out the door just as the badger guy rushed in. They hit with a bang and went down. But that one was easy. Sometimes women would bribe hotel workers to let them in my room. When I came home, I'd find them under my bed."

At times, exhausted after a game, he would fall into bed without eating dinner. For sleepless nights, Cobb kept pencil and paper handy for notemaking, in case he thought of an idea useful on the field: "It seemed that just when I got drowsy something would come to my mind that I didn't want to forget by morning. Couldn't turn off my thinking."

In his "how-to" book, *Busting 'Em,* he told of what an effort it was to arise before 10:00 A.M. Waking up and feeling functional took an hour or more. On the road in extremely hot weather—with no air-conditioning on hundred-degree nights—he would lie naked or fill a bathtub with ice water and soak in it, wishing he were ocean fishing at Sea Island, Georgia, and not a ballplayer.

As noted, one of the assets of being Ty Cobb was the luxury of not having to share hotel space with anyone. Where other Tigers bunked two and even three to a room, he resided alone in all seven American League cities. Hughie Jennings was the victim in an incident that occurred early in 1912 at Chicago's Beach Hotel. Beach management gave Cobb a room adjacent to a noisy Illinois Central Railway switching yard. He complained to the management that he could not sleep amid such a din.

"Sorry, but we have nothing else available at this time of night," said the manager.

The Tigers were to face Manager Nixey Callahan's White Sox the next day. At midnight Cobb hammered on Jennings's door. His temper rising, he warned Jennings, "Get me a room or I'm leaving."

Jennings spoke with the manager, to no avail. The offer was made to transfer Cobb to another hotel. Cobb was willing to go, but only if the entire Detroit team went with him, as a lesson to hotel management.

Nothing was left but for the Peach to move in with Jennings. Again Cobb refused. He could not sleep with anyone else in the room.

Jennings had run out of options. With an important series at hand, it was essential to keep the Tigers' number-one hitter calm and concentrated. He usually hit effectively against White Sox pitching—Ed Walsh, Joe Benz, Eddie Cicotte, Frank Lange. But, standing there at midnight in his nightshirt, Jennings could not very well awaken a whole team to take up new accommodations. Another problem was that Charlie Comiskey, of Chicago's Comiskey Park ownership, had advertised Ty Cobb's name to draw a crowd. If it got around that the Georgian would not appear, thousands of dollars could be lost at the box office.

Cobb's solution was to go to the lobby, suitcase and bat bag packed, and call for a Chicago-to-Detroit railway schedule. At 2:00 A.M. a train was leaving for Detroit and he was aboard it. Detroit's *Free Press* reported: "The unhappy bird flew the coop, his feathers badly flustered."

Jumping a performance contract was a serious matter. Jennings phoned Bill Yawkey in Detroit. "He did *what?*" exclaimed Yawkey. "He didn't like his room," said Jennings. "He just left." For lesser offenses other players had been handed heavy fines and suspensions. Cobb was not even reprimanded.

Yawkey and Navin, at close to $475,000 cost, had built a new park, named Navin Field. It was one of the most modern in the majors, with a capacity of twenty-five thousand. Old Bennett Park had been a disgrace, and the new arena was filled on inaugural day, April 20. Pregame ceremonies featured numbers by the Germanic Harmonie Singing Society. For the Irish of racially diverse Detroit there was a chant: "Oh, the Hogans, Grogans, O'Briens and McGurks, the Clancys, Caseys, Sullivans and Burks!" Pennants flew. Black fans were given extra seating in the colored bleachers. City streetcars were painted yellow-orange, the Tigers' colors. Firecrackers burst.

Before a record-setting turnout, Cobb, now caught up on his sleep, blocked two possible Cleveland home runs with racing catches, singled twice, engineered two double steals with Sam Crawford, and was all over the park in a 6–5 defeat of Cleveland.

His follow-up performance, against St. Louis, was to plant a ball in the right-field bleachers, the first home run hit in Navin Field. The jest went around that maybe he should walk out of more hotels in the middle of the night, if it meant producing like this.

One of the livelier games of the American League in this period came after Detroit's city fathers, but not the clergy, gave their consent to expanded Sunday ball. Although sometimes played, Sabbath games had been discouraged. Detroit was becoming a city of industry and manufacture, however, and factory workers wanted to hear bats crack on their only day off of the week. It was arranged that provided the Sabbath was not profaned by bad behavior in the stands, Sunday might be added to schedules. Churchgoing owner Yawkey was especially anxious for a good, clean game when the Boston Red Sox came in for a Saturday-Sunday series.

Cobb was awaiting his turn at bat when George Moriarty, on third base with the score tied, suddenly set out for the plate. He was called safe with the winning run. Red Sox catcher Bill Carrigan disagreed. Carrigan spit tobacco juice in Moriarty's face. It might have ended there, but Cobb, as sore as if it had happened to him, shouted, "Punch the bastard!"

Moriarty did, and Carrigan swung back. A newspaperman's description went, "Tiger fans did their best to keep it from being a private fight. About 1,000 of them came running." Riot followed. Both teams battled their way to dressing rooms, with citizens in their wake. An hour later the dust had not settled. Catcher Carrigan eventually escaped from the park by borrowing a groundskeeper's overalls. Three cops were injured.

Yawkey himself was seen on a dugout roof, pleading for quiet. This was not the Sunday he had foreseen. Cobb, the instigator of the incident, was nowhere to be found; he had left early.

Two early photos of the Georgia Peach.

Cobb during the early Detroit years.

The Detroit Tiger outfield, 1907-1912. *Left to right:* Davy Jones, Ty Cobb, Wahoo Sam Crawford.

Detroit Manager Hugh (Ee-yah) Jennings on the coaching line.

Napoleon Lajoie, left, and Cobb pictured in the Chalmers automobile that was to go to the winner of the American League batting championship and which touched off the cheating episode in St. Louis.

No doubt the most famous, and oft-reproduced, baseball photo ever taken, but how could it be omitted in a biography of Ty Cobb? He is sliding into third against Jimmy Austin of the St. Louis Browns.

This is the play that touched off the near-riot in Philadelphia in 1909:
Cobb, sliding into third, spikes Home Run Baker.

Cobb at bat in 1915. Note that the grip here is neither with hands spread apart nor choked up.

Christy Mathewson, left, and Cobb in U.S. Army uniform, 1918.

Portrait of the Georgia Peach in the early 1910s.

Cobb and youthful fans.

Cobb, son Herschel, golf champion Bobby Jones, and setter at Field Dog Trials, Waynesboro, Ga.

Cobb at opening game of 1925 World Series, Pittsburgh.

Cobb and sports writer O. B. Keeler at Waynesboro, Ga., ca. 1925.

End of the trail, with Philadelphia Athletics.

The 1928 A's numbered three of the game's greatest hitters of the dead ball era, playing out their string in the age of Ruth, Foxx, Gehrig, and Hornsby. *Left to right:* Eddie Collins, Ty Cobb, Tris Speaker.

Babe Ruth, left, and Cobb deciding which team bats first at a youth baseball contest in the late 1930s.

Ted Williams and Cobb in 1961, the last year of Cobb's life. Note Cobb's inscription: "good shot of 2 lefties."

BATTLE AT HILLTOP PARK

Hilltop Park, at Broadway between 165th and 168th streets in New York, and referred to as the highest elevation on Manhattan Island, was built in 1903 to accommodate the entry of a new team into the American League. The Highlanders, before becoming the Yankees, were bankrolled by Big Bill Devery, former New York police chief, and Frank Farrell, so-called king of the bookie syndicate, controlling a reported 250 poolrooms where gambling on anything that moved, including ball games, was wide open for wagering. Devery reputedly was bag man for operators in illegal enterprises permitted by Tammany Hall. Neither he nor Farrell was what you would term an exemplary citizen; but the American League needed a franchise in the largest of cities, and the pair had the funds to join up. In his later days, when Cobb got around to issuing his exposé of the game, he charged Devery and Farrell with faking their box-office ticket counts as a tax-avoidance method.

At fifteen-thousand-seat Hilltop, the lower seats were only a stone's —or a bottle's—throw from home plate. Park policing was scant. Because of its architecture and its uncontrolled fans, Cobb hated Hilltop more than any league park. Ripe tomatoes were a specialty of the house. He had ducked bottles, marbles, and pieces of chairs. From the time he took his position, the razzing never stopped.

On a breezy day at Hilltop, May 15, 1912, Cobb counterattacked. Among his many career blowups, this one perhaps ranks first. In about ten minutes, he rocked baseball law to its foundation and brought on the first strike in history of a major-class team.

"COBB RUNS AMOK" was headlined after the first game of a Tigers-Highlanders series, when he had collided with Cozy Dolan at third base. Dolan, who in 1924 would be blacklisted from organized ball for offering a five-hundred-dollar bribe to a Philadelphia player to throw a game, gave Cobb a shove. He shoved back. Junk flew from the stands.

Four days later came the capper. "I got out to the park early to take extra hitting practice," Cobb declared later, "and right away a guy sitting near our bench got on me. He yelled things nobody could take. He was hollering, 'Your sister screws niggers' and 'Your mother is a whore.' He kept this up for four innings. I did nothing about it except to yell back that he was a rotten dog. I even went to the Highlanders' bench . . . to warn their manager [Harry Wolverton] to throw this fan out . . . and I asked their president [Farrell] the same during inning breaks. I went right to Farrell's box on this. They did nothing." So went Cobb's version of the affair.

Unknown to Cobb, the spectator, named Claude Lueker, was crippled. Lueker had no fingers on one hand, only two fingers on the other; he had lost them in an industrial accident. He also was connected with a one-time New York County sheriff.

From his manager's seat, Hughie Jennings watched Cobb's face harden—he knew that chilling expression well—and realized what would happen. It did. Leaping a railing, his star hitter trampled fans to get at the tormentor, sitting a dozen rows up in the stands. He battered Lueker's head with at least a full dozen punches, knocked him down, and with his spikes kicked the helpless man in the lower body. Fans scattered with shouts of, "He has no hands!" Witnesses said they heard Cobb retort, "I don't care if he has no legs!" Umpire Silk O'Loughlin ejected Cobb from the game.

League chief Ban Johnson, informed of the incident, issued a ruling: since Cobb was habitually insurgent and prone to violence, he was suspended indefinitely, perhaps permanently. "Any player who is abused by a patron has only to appeal to the umpire for protection," proclaimed Johnson. Johnson was angered, too, by the fact that after his ouster from the game Cobb had remained in place on the bench. Three innings later he was still directing profanity at umpire O'Loughlin. Only then did he obey the order to leave.

Press conferences were called, witnesses summoned, and behind closed doors Cobb testified to Johnson that he had repeatedly urged O'Loughlin and others to have Lueker removed, but without relief. Every member of the Tigers team verified that Lueker, now in a hospital bed, had been the aggressor. All of them had heard the fan call Cobb and his family some intolerable names. What would any man do in such a situation? Johnson decided that the public's protection came first, even though Lueker had initiated the verbal exchange.

Within hours of Lueker's trip to the hospital, Johnson found himself dealing with outraged Tigers. They had stood at Hilltop Park railings with bats raised against the crowd in defense of Cobb while he hammered Lueker and then fought his way back to the field. Some of the players even had gone into the stands to back him up. Jennings was surprised by his men's emotional reaction. At least 80 percent of his club's roster disliked Cobb and resented him. But now 100 percent of the team was lending him support! Sixteen Tigers telegraphed Johnson a promise that they would not play another inning of ball until Cobb was exonerated.

During the fracas, talk arose of the league's players forming a coalition to see to their rights. Until now such a union had failed to become formalized, and since 1910 had been bruited about mostly as an idea. Now the feeling grew that it needed to be enlarged and given muscle. Cobb supported the suggestion. He was heard, and within months, in September, a Base Ball Players Fraternity was incorporated (annual dues eighteen dollars). Within thirty days the BBPF had three hundred members, although such unity among the workforce was opposed by almost every owner and stockholder in the country. "We the men who make baseball must have some rights," Cobb told a roomful of reporters. "Personally, I won't take any more. Let Johnson ban me and the hell with him."

With that, it all became very interesting—and unprecedented. Minor strikes by a single big-leaguer, or by two or three stars in unison, had happened through the years, but never had an entire team refused to take the field. Detroit's collective challenge to the easily irritated Johnson read, "Feeling that Mr. Cobb is being done a grave injustice, we, the undersigned, refuse to play another game until such action is adjusted to our satisfaction. He was fully justified in what he did, as no one could stand such personal abuse. We want him reinstated or there will be no game. We must protect ourselves."

It must have been painful to the Tigers to file that message. Voluntarily they were backing, at considerable risk to themselves, the teammate who had perversely abandoned them during the 1908 pennant race to be married, who had caused internal dissension and anti-Detroit publicity time and again, and who said he wanted to leave them in a trade. The Tigers were thought by some of the press to be behaving not from any love of Cobb, but because they needed his bat and glove in the lineup. More likely, it was a matter of banding together to protest the toleration of extreme abuse by fans; no player should be expected to take such personal insult and invective without retaliating, they felt. Everyone's honor was at stake.

Cobb felt that the revolutionaries would win their case. "That wasn't smart of me," he said at a later time, "since that mugwump Johnson already had no use for me."

Opinion was divided. Most New York papers, as expected, rapped him. The *New York American*, however, was willing to listen. *American* ballot boxes were set up around the city, with citizens asked to vote on how they felt. In the Midwest it was suspected that Cobb would find a way out. The *News* of Motor City wrote, "You can't beat Terrible Ty with a club. If he fell off the Ford Building here he'd land on his feet unhurt. If he fell into the Hudson River he'd come out with baskets full of fish. He's taken more chances of breaking his neck than anyone who ever played this game and the injuries have been received by the other fellow. He kicks himself into more dire situations than any person in public life today . . . and always he comes out the winner with his name on every tongue."

But Johnson held fast. The offender was barred. A National Commission rule stated that a thousand-dollar-per-day fine would be levied on any league member not fielding a team on schedule, except for a train wreck, flood, or other act of God. Navin faced loss of a small fortune. Cobb's length of suspension was unstated.

Detroit's next game, against Philadelphia, saw the Tigers suiting up at Shibe Park and coming out for batting practice, with Cobb among them. "Cobb, get off the field," umpires Bill Dinneen and Bull Perrine ordered. "You're suspended."

He approached the two threateningly, but Jennings persuaded him to leave peaceably. Not so the other Tigers, who departed shouting threats, and returned to their hotel to confer and order a big lunch. Headline: "Tigers Unique In The Annals Of Strikes. First Strikers In The World Who Live At The Expense Of Their Employer While Refusing To Perform." With this went the opinion: "Raving Of Bugs In Stands Must End . . . Bugs Must Be Exterminated."

None of the Tigers was willing to face the Athletics. One day earlier, Connie Mack had called them "quitters with no sense of responsibility." Mack had gone to Jennings with the desperate idea of drafting a team of substitutes from around Philadelphia—semipros, college boys, ex-minor-leaguers. "That way Detroit won't be fined," submitted Mack, "and we'll keep the schedule intact."

On the same day, Cobb quietly pulled the Tigers together at a hotel to say, "Don't do this, boys. I appreciate it but you're only hurting yourselves. I can take it. Go out there and play." Although facing individual fines and possible expulsion, not a man would back down and cancel the strike.

Mack's scheme was adopted. The most farcical lineup the majors ever had known put on Detroit uniforms. Pitching for the subs was Aloysius Travers, a young theology student studying for the priesthood at St. Joseph's College; at second base was a prizefighter, Billy Maharg, alias Graham spelled backward, who could punch people but not hit baseballs; the catcher was Deacon Jim McGuire, a forty-eight-year-old Tiger coach; a forty-one-year-old ex-pro was at first base. Seven sandlotters were drafted. These "park sparrows," experiencing the thrill of becoming big-leaguers for a day, or more, were paid ten to twenty dollars per man and warned, "Don't get killed." The game counted in the AL standings, and about fifteen thousand curious spectators turned out.

Strikebreaking by this hybrid lineup was hilarious to see. Newspaperman Arthur "Bugs" Baer wrote, "These bums in disguise didn't try for a double play, they were lucky to make a putout now and then against the A's great Eddie Collins, Stuffy McInnis and Frank Baker. The sandlotter who replaced Cobb in the outfield wouldn't give his right name. When he came home late and told his wife he'd been playing at Shibe in place of Ty Cobb, she hit him with a skillet."

Defending world champion Philadelphia won by a landslide 24–2. It could have been 30–0, but for the A's taking it easy. Jeering the travesty, the crowd left early, demanding ticket refunds. Seats were torn up, rocks were thrown at ticket windows. Arriving cops were stoned.

Johnson came down harder, canceling next day's game and affirming that every Tiger would join Cobb in indefinite disbarment. Cobb again spoke to the club, asking that members not risk their livelihood. Seeing they were losing the war, the Tigers surrendered. They accepted hundred-dollar fines each upon their decision to meet Washington, but only after Navin agreed to pay their fines.

Mysteriously, Cobb got off with his "indefinite" suspension reduced to but ten days, along with a fifty-dollar fine. "Johnson had no recourse," he claimed. "In a private meeting with him I promised to sue the league for a hundred thousand dollars. And I had big-shot backers."

The most publicized flap in diamond history concluded with the state of Georgia's delegation to the U.S. Congress complimenting their native son for defying "the mailed fist of tyranny," for upholding precepts of southern manhood. Had he acted otherwise regarding the ballpark insults, all Georgia would have felt ashamed of him, etc.

For unknown reasons, Claude Lueker did not sue Cobb. Rumors of retaliation circulated all summer in New York, however, and Cobb said that then and later he received "a few hundred 'Black Hand' letters," many of them mentioning assassination. Meanwhile, Detroit had another series coming up in New York within seven weeks. "Of course I'll play," Cobb informed the press. At Hilltop, in his July return to the scene of turmoil, he acted as if nothing had happened. His nonchalance never was more conspicuous.

It would have been acceptable to Detroit management if he had batted .280 for a while. Instead he delivered six base hits in seven at-bats in a St. Louis doubleheader. Moving to Philadelphia for two doubleheaders he piled up fourteen more hits in nineteen at-bats. He drilled four singles, two doubles and a triple—*seven straight safeties*—and ended a long road trip with a close to .540 average. Under fire by Ban Johnson, exposed to hostile ballpark crowds, Cobb was never hotter. In July he was averaging an "impossible" .521.

IT WAS a time of vindication. At last some strides were being taken by the Base Ball Players Fraternity to combat a situation where superbly skilled athletes had been treated like indentured servants—in many instances not even supplied with a copy of the Uniform Players' Contract upon signing it. "The near-sighted leading the blind" went the expression. With Dave Fultz, a college man and former big-leaguer as BBPF president, the federation shortly collected three hundred members—twelve hundred joined at its peak—and from 1912 on forced through such reforms as a clampdown by owners on spectator abuse of players, a guaranteed hearing for players ejected by umpires and automatically suspended, certification that no man could be traded away at a lesser salary than he had been receiving, and the concession that no one could be farmed out to a lower minor league until clubs in classifications between his old club and the new affiliation were first given a chance to deal for him. Copies of all contracts had to be supplied to the signees. Although falling far short of what unionization in other fields had accomplished, it was a breakthrough. Cobb was particularly proud of the Fraternity's recovery of the $2,348 for Bert Hageman of the Boston Red Sox in a breach-of-contract lawsuit won by the BBPF. "Another thing— until now the cheap owners had made players pay their own travel expenses when traded," said Cobb. "We got rid of that sort of crap." When Fultz invited him to serve as BBPF vice president, Cobb accepted.

As another aftermath of the Hilltop Park imbroglio, the result of the *New York American*'s poll was announced. Was Cobb within his rights, or should fans be allowed to freely express themselves? Surprisingly, the vote was 3,013 for Cobb, 1,167 against the Peach. The sampler vote became useful to the BBPF in its dealings down the road with National Commission autocrats.

IN AUGUST of that 1912 season, Cobb was on another of his heavy-hitting streaks when he drove his Chalmers auto to Detroit's train station. His habit when roadward bound was to have wife Charlie accompany him to the train, then drive herself home to the six-room house he rented near Navin Field. Charlie saw little of him, as it was, and she enjoyed their time together. This time the Tigers were leaving for an exhibition game in Syracuse, New York. It was late on a Sunday with streets deserted, when Cobb found himself never so happy to be armed with a gun.

On Trumbull Avenue, three men stood in the street, waving their arms. As soon as he stopped his car one of the trio demanded his money. To protect his wife, he slid out, to be met by punches from all three. Cobb knocked down one of them, while the others circled. He dropped another. But the third man climbed onto Cobb's back and stuck a knife into him. Cobb pulled out his pistol, which would not fire. He kept on swinging and at one point had two muggers on the ground. When the gang split and ran, he chased them. "I caught up with one and left him in sorry condition," he declared. "I ran down the other. He'd ducked into a dead-end alley between two houses." Using his gun's sight like a blade and the butt end as well, he slashed away until the man's face was faceless, "Left him there, not breathing, in his own rotten blood," he went on with satisfaction. Cobb believed he killed this mugger. A few days later a press report told of an unidentified body found off Trumbull in an alley.

T.C. was bleeding badly, and a hysterical Charlie begged him to go directly to a doctor. The knife used on him had inflicted a six-inch wound in his lower left back. Instead, he drove on to the train station with a kerchief stuck in the cut.

Detroit newspapers had a field day. Extra editions were rushed: "COBB STABBED!" cried the *Free Press*. "Attack On Tyrus Throws Detroit Into Paroxysms." According to the *Free Press*, for a while—until the true facts were ascertained—the city went into mourning at word that the world's foremost ballplayer had been knifed and was dying. One report went: "For an hour or more the business district was practically at a standstill. Men, women and children ceased their work."

By early Monday a correction was out. An error had been made. The wounded Cobb—"amazingly"—had gone on to Syracuse with the team and there rapped out two hits in four times at bat. "Hardly the work of a dead man," observed the *Journal*. Mark Twain's celebrated reply that his reported death was an exaggeration was quoted. The *Journal* noted, caustically, "The report that one of our aldermen had refused a bribe scarcely could have upset the town more."

Upon boarding the train a grim Cobb had told no one of the injury. Teammate Jean Dubuc noticed his blood-soaked coat and a trainer temporarily patched him up. The pair of hits he produced at Syracuse came while wearing a makeshift bandage. Not until after the game did he see a doctor. Stitched up, he didn't miss any start afterward.

Within days he was as frisky as ever. He was all showman, flamboyantly using tactics never before seen. One of his throwaway acts came when, facing an insecure pitcher, he would step back just before the windup, scoop up a handful of dirt, disdainfully toss it toward the mound, and not bother to swing. Or, as a strike whizzed past, he would stand unmoving, gazing at the sky. Pitchers seethed when Cobb turned his back on their throws to converse casually with the Tiger standing on deck. He'd say something like, "This bozo hasn't got a thing" or "Let's do some duck-hunting next winter." Sometimes he wouldn't even bother to swing until the strike count reached 0 and 2. Often enough, this paid off. Cobb in 1911 hit safely in 40 straight games, a record that would stand for twenty-two years and today remains the third-longest of the century for the American League; in 1917, he would put together a 35-game streak, exceeded as of 1993 by only five other major league batters.

Beanballs aimed at or near his head came with repayment. Hub "Dutch" Leonard, a Boston left-hander who struck fear in opponents, ticked Cobb's chin once too often. "So I dragged a bunt which their first baseman was forced to field," he logged in his diary. "Leonard ran to first to take the throw. When he saw I was going for him and not the bag, he kept on running into the coaching box. Damned coward. I ignored the bag, drove right through after him . . . he ran toward the dugout and I missed cutting him by inches . . . He never threw another beaner at me." In years to come Cobb would have more dealings with Leonard.

Several years earlier Cy Morgan, also of Boston, ran and hid on a plate play. As the runner at second base, T.C. raced around third on a wild pitch by Morgan, who was by then covering home. The chance to score was small. "Morgan was at the dish waiting for the throw," Cobb claimed later. "I guess I hadn't taken more than three strides past third when Morgan had the ball in his hands, waiting for me. I thought, *Well, here's where we settle this*. I went straight at him with my steel showing. He turned and ran away, refusing the contact. Later that night he was released by Boston." So Cobb said, anyway.

APPRAISALS THAT the Peach lacked a sense of humor were all too true. He would, however, now and then, find a laugh in the day's routine. But the funny stuff had to be of his own making. When a Detroit team photograph was taken one day, he managed to be in two places at once without ruining or even blurring the film. The Tigers, posed as a group, formed too long a line for the usual camera to capture, so a panoramic camera was used. A press correspondent's story went, "Cobb was standing fourth from the left, with the lens traveling in an arc from one end of the line to the other. Noticing the rate at which it was going, the prank popped into his head that he could beat the machine.

"So the instant the lens passed him he dashed out and around the rear of the camera and dug out for the other end of the line, like he does when stealing home. What a stunt! He arrived in time to take up a position at the side of Manager Jennings—and in the photo he appears beside Jennings, smiling and as composed as he appears in the fourth place from the right." The "impossible" feat was played in papers across the country under such captions as "Peach's Fabled Speed Positively Confirmed by Camera!"

If any cloud showed on his horizon as a player in those prewar years, it was a left-handed, raspy-voiced ex-cowboy from Hubbard City, Texas, six feet of tremendous ballhawking talent: Tris Speaker. Previous contenders for best-in-the-game honors, Wagner and Lajoie, were fading with age. Speaker was slightly younger than Cobb. The best playmaking outfielder ever seen, Speaker played in so close that he was known as a fifth infielder. He was so fast that he could set up far in, yet get back in time for the catch. Speaker also could hit well enough to rival Cobb; his career 793 doubles remain a major-league record to this day. From his early years with the Boston Red Sox, he represented a definite challenge to Cobb's all-around domination. A ditty went:

Said Tristram Speaker to Tyrus Cobb,
"Smoke up, kid, or I'll cop your job."
"October will find you a damned sight meeker,"
Said Tyrus Cobb to Tristram Speaker.

Speaker's abiding frustration was that, while he was shining for Boston and then Cleveland, Cobb always hit a little better than he did. In a season where he averaged .340, Cobb averaged .385; when Speaker did .383, Cobb was at .410; when Speaker posted .352, he was outdone by Cobb's .383. This persisted for almost a decade. The one and only season in which Texas Tris led in their rivalry came in 1916, when his .386 finally topped Cobb, at .371, ending a string of nine consecutive years of American League batting championships for the Georgian. Cobb was slowed by two bouts of influenza that year. His phenomenal nine-year run has never been matched, let alone closely approached, by anyone else who ever swung a bat. And after his one-season lapse the Peach would ring up three more consecutive championship seasons, to run his batting titles to a unique twelve in thirteen years.

Speaker deserves much credit for goading his rival to consistent heights. He once said to me, "We were a lot alike. Our short move into the pitch was much the same. We were both place-hitters. We were lefties." The two entered the Hall of Fame one year apart—Cobb, of course, entering first in 1936. Some historians feel—and Cobb didn't disagree—that Speaker was to him what Lou Gehrig was to Babe Ruth. Speaker's lifetime batting average was .345, seventh best in history.

So unlike each other in most other ways, the easygoing Speaker and the frenetic, rancorous Cobb formed a lasting friendship. They joined in hunting trips from the southern U.S. to Canada. Their only hard words came, said Grey Eagle Speaker, on a hunt for moose in the Canadian Rockies. T.C. raised his gun to fire, Speaker knocked it away. "That's a *lady* moose!" Tris objected. "We don't shoot them." Cobb was angry, but the moment passed.

DURING THIS period of abundance, from 1910 onward, Cobb was approached on a confidential matter by Grantland Rice, his old advisor and critic from Atlanta. Now on the *New York Evening Mail*, in 1913 Granny Rice brought a dire warning to his fellow southerner.

"Hell may break loose soon, Ty," Rice confided. "Frank Chance came into the press box the other day and swore that Hal Chase is throwing games on him. Came right out with it." Chance, the "Peerless Leader," had been named manager of the New York Yankees earlier in the year, inheriting Chase at first base. Normally a fine performer, Chase had recently become erratic.

"Will you print it?" asked Cobb.

"My editors want more proof, so I'm sitting on Chase for the time being," said Rice.

"Well, don't ask me," said Cobb, bristling. "I have no opinion. Where do you get off coming to me?"

Rice was taken aback. "I'm sorry," he apologized, "I shouldn't have brought it up. But you're the biggest name around and the game might need some defending if Chase is working with gamblers."

Months after he reproached Rice for mentioning Chase to him, Cobb acknowledged to another reporter, not for attribution, that he had been well aware that Chase was "dumping" for bookmakers. The suspected Chase was dealt to the Chicago White Sox early in the 1913 season for players worth nowhere near his value. From there he went to the Federal League and after that to Cincinnati, where he was exposed by Cincy manager Christy Mathewson and others as a bribe-taker and passer. Inexplicably, no action whatever was taken against Chase. In 1919 he was signed by the New York Giants, in what was seen as an obvious attempt to whitewash a man valuable at the box office. With the Giants his gambling became so glaring that at long last Prince Hal was banned from the majors forever.

Rice, whenever he retold the story, felt that it showed how little Cobb cared about a potential scandal damaging baseball. The writer felt that he had been indifferent, too busy with his own projects, to help root out an open-and-shut scoundrel. Rice came out of the experience saddened and disillusioned.

ALMOST EVERYWHERE Cobb looked these days, there was money to be made—not in two- or three-figure deals, but in record high numbers. "I was worth two hundred thousand dollars in cash and paper by 1917," he once divulged to his hunting companion, ex-big-league catcher Muddy Ruel. "Now I know the stock market pretty well."

Pioneering California orange growers asked him to endorse their fruit; spas springing up in Florida wanted use of his name. He was offered a starring role in a stage play. Real estate ventures atop his Arizona copper shares paid off. "I had not one loser," he claimed.

With both hands cupped to collect, Cobb was having a wonderful time—off the field. "I was in hog heaven," he put it. "I came into the league with a two-dollar glove, now they're selling fifty thousand gloves a year with my name on them." His patented bat outsold all others. It was said that barbers saved his hair clippings for sale to fans. When he advocated a big breakfast, kids ate hearty.

He had been Woodrow Wilson's guest at the White House in 1913. Comparing their Georgia beginnings, Wilson mentioned that Cobb's populist qualities made him somewhat more a favorite down home than the president of the United States. "Well," said Cobb, "I voted for you against the damned Republicans." He expressed the hope that his country would stay out of the looming world war and found Wilson doubtful. "They'll be sinking our shipping soon," predicted Wilson, according to Cobb.

On trips to New York, Cobb had grown more than somewhat stagestruck. One of his big fans was playwright George Ade, author of such comedies as *Sultan of Sulu* and sketches for *Eddie Foy and the Seven Little Foys*. Through Ade he met young John Barrymore, Will Rogers, and Jack Norworth, the 1907 Tin Pan Alley composer of "Take Me Out to the Ballgame." George M. Cohan, an acquaintance of the Peach since 1909, was a Broadway songwriter-producer so popular that he had turned down ten thousand dollars per week from the Loew's Circuit to hit the boards as a vaudeville headliner. That impressed Cobb.

In 1911, George Ade offered Cobb ten thousand dollars—not per week, but for a three-month run of his play—to perform the co-lead in a touring comedy titled *The College Widow*. Expert coaching would be provided.

"Not interested," said Cobb. "I'd go out there and make a horse's ass of myself."

But ten thousand dollars was hard to reject in a pre–income tax era. (Such a tax was about to be imposed.) And acting wasn't all that much of a crazy venture. Big-league players were earning far more than their team salaries to cavort in off-season burlesque, "vaud," and even the legitimate theater. John McGraw, reported show business journals, was paid $2,500 per week for his Keith Circuit monologue, "Inside Baseball." McGraw could talk all night—about McGraw. Rube Marquard danced the "Marquard Glide" with Blossom Seeley at Hammerstein's Theater in 1911–12. Earlier, two oddballs of the game, Rube Waddell and Bugs Raymond, starred in *Stain of Guilt*. Laughing Larry Doyle, a .300-hitting Giants infielder, played the villain in another melodrama, and so dignified a man as Christy Mathewson had worn greasepaint in 1910 in a number called "Curves." Before them, Turkey Mike Donlin of the Giants, despite serving six months in jail for striking an actress, had drawn raves from *Variety* for his comic hoofing in an act, "Stealing Home."

Cobb reconsidered. In *College Widow* he would be playing a masculine college sport hero, after all, and with proper coaching and the fame of his name, might satisfy the critics. He asked Eddie Foy if he should risk such exposure and Foy said, "Go ahead. You can't be booed more than they boo you on the field in Boston, Cleveland, Philly, and fifty other places."

"What if I forget my lines?" asked T.C.

"Make them up," said Foy. "Ad-lib your way if you forget."

"There's a lot of yelling in this play," said a worried Cobb. "Too much loud stuff."

"Pretend you're addressing an umpire," chuckled Foy. "You're good at that."

In *College Widow*, he was cast as Billy Bolton, an All-American halfback, opposite starlet Sue MacManamy as the distraught college widow. They opened in Newark, New Jersey. Although Cobb blew up in a few lines, he always recalled that the critics were kind. "Not bad for a tyro who stutters a bit," wrote one reviewer. Under hot lights his makeup ran, so that Cobb was wiping his brow while pleading to the widow, "Marry me and we'll live happier than any lovebirds!" Someone in the audience gave out a ballpark-type Bronx cheer. The crowd laughed. Cobb glared.

As the tour traveled south to Georgia and the Carolinas, he found that this was such hard work that swigs of bourbon between acts were needed to get him through a performance. With wife Charlie and his two children in the audience one night, he was left speechless when the kids screamed upon his entrance, "There's our daddy!" Another upsetting moment came when he was required to kiss his costar. He made fumbling, fast passes at Sue MacManamy's lips. The drama critic of the Birmingham, Alabama, *News*, a sportswriter assigned to follow Cobb around, reported that he handled romance and comedy so stiffly that the play was a flop. For that the critic received a stinging Cobb letter, saying, "I make more money than you do . . . I'm a better actor and ballplayer than you—where do inferiors get off criticizing their superiors?"

At most stops in Dixie the opus played to capacity crowds, but it was plain that people came less for laughs than to see the Georgia Peach up close in person. He quarreled with George Ade over the lack of punchlines given his role. *College Widow's* best line came when gridiron hero Billy Bolton has been enrolled by his father in a Baptist college. Upon returning from a trip abroad, Father learns that Billy has switched to a Methodist school. Father is aghast. "Well," he roars, "you're a hell of a Baptist!" Cobb did not like playing straight man, and some rewriting was done to give him more prominence.

Although applauded, he was soon fed up. In New York one day he was driving his open two-seater auto through Central Park when a mounted policeman galloped up and arrested him. He asked why. The cop replied, "Never mind, get out of the car." Grabbing Cobb's coat, the man began dragging him out. Doing what came naturally, T.C. descended and punched the cop so hard that the man's helmet flew off and he staggered away bleeding. *I'll get ninety-nine years for this*, thought Cobb. But then he saw a photographer hiding in the bushes and realized that it was a setup. Press agents for *College Widow* had planted a fake policeman as a means of creating newspaper publicity. Cobb's fists had spoiled the stunt.

Bright stage spotlights, he believed, were hurting his vision, and after six weeks on the road and despite a three-month contract, the Peach quit. He walked out on Ade in Cleveland, leaving the cast without a leading man. Long after the play folded he was quoted, "I looked silly as an actor, but the money was right."

CHAPTER FIFTEEN

A NEW LEAGUE

U nited States Senator Hoke Smith of Georgia, a hard-shelled states-rights Democrat and former secretary of the interior, entertained a visitor in Washington one January day of 1913. The caller was no surprise. Ty Cobb had been corresponding with his home-state congress-man for several months, writing Smith to the effect that ballplayers' contracts were illegal, that his own attorneys felt an investigation was in order, and that Cobb, a prominent victim of monopolistic practice, hoped Smith would look into it.

Smith's reply had been to wire: "SEND ME A COPY OF YOUR CONTRACT INCLUDING RESERVE CLAUSE. ALSO SEND COPY TO GEORGIA FEDERATION OF LABOR."

Cobb not only obliged, but he followed it up with a trip to Washington for a consultation. Smith was delighted to meet Ty Cobb in the flesh. A strong force in the Senate, the lawmaker had played ball on Georgian sandlots as a boy, and now sat with the gallery gods at local Washington Nationals games. He introduced his guest to colleagues as the best ever to wear spikes. Cobb later noted of their meeting, "He studied the reserve clause binding me to Detroit forever . . . and another clause which entitled the club to release players on ten days' notice when he had no equal right to end the agreement . . . and called it highly improper." In the next weeks Hoke Smith laid plans to charge organized baseball's compact with its workforce as "outright peonage." Lining up support from Representative Thomas Hartwick of Georgia and Representative Thomas Gallagher of Illinois, he prepared a resolution stating that ownership of teams as a combine comprised "the most mendacious, audacious and autocratic private monopoly and trust in the world."

By appealing to high federal officials, Cobb paved the way to an interminable legal war, one that would be fought in lesser courts and on up to the U.S. Supreme Court for the next sixty-two years. Not until 1975 would the national game be found in violation of a player's inherent right to work in the vineyard of his choice.

The bedrock of baseball's sixteen-team amalgamation of franchises was a feudal edifice called the "reserve clause." This fiat, instituted in 1879, decreed that a club reserved and retained the services of Player X in perpetuity—until he was washed up, retired, or peddled on the market. Further, owners agreed not to employ anyone reserved by any other American or National League member. The cage was shut tight. In the past a few weak attempts to cite anti-trust codes had proved useless.

Although free agency wasn't achieved in the big leagues until many years later, Ty Cobb stands as the rebel who eighty-one years ago initiated a move toward emancipation. "Nobody gave me much credit for it," he remembered. "But there wasn't another man back then savvy and smart enough to pull the right strings . . . show up the owners for their racket." By agitating in Congress he opened the way to reforms leading to the right of free agency and arbitration of contracts, then progressively to where in 1974 it was possible for a pitcher, Jim "Catfish" Hunter, to force the New York Yankees to pay him $3.5 million in a package deal. Thereafter the figure was regularly exceeded by a long string of beneficiaries who in the 1980s and 1990s grossed multimillions and up per plutocrat.

For the 1913 season Cobb asked for $15,000. That meant a $6,000 raise over what he had drawn in 1910, 1911, and 1912 under an existing extended-service agreement. Navin and Yawkey grudgingly offered $10,500. Cobb declined, saying that he had been the core of a prosperous operation ever since leading Detroit to three World Series appearances. Deficit or near-deficit days were ended. Fans now lined up in the rain to buy tickets, a civic ordinance prohibiting Sunday ball had been overcome in 1911, and Navin Field had been restructured to hold twenty-two thousand—with fire inspectors looking the other way. Profits were way up. Cobb's accountants—he had two of them—estimated the Tigers' franchise value to be $700,000, and Cobb's box-office draw worth $40,000 per season. If a one-man show existed in any American arena or stadium, Cobb the Great was it.

"You know very well they come out to see me," he put it to Yawkey, "and I want $15,000."

Navin, as the press reported, retaliated, "You'll play for me at my price or not at all."

For support, Cobb called upon such fervid admirers as Grantland Rice of the *New York Evening Mail* and Harry Salsinger of the *News*. The columnists publicized his contributions and salary progress:

1906—.320 average (led his team), $1,500 salary
1907—.350 (led league, tied for both leagues' lead), $2,400
        salary
1908—.324 (led his league), $4,500 salary
1909—.377 (led both leagues), $4,500 salary
1910—.385 (led both leagues), $9,000 salary
1911—.420 (led both leagues), $9,000 salary
1912—.410 (led both leagues), $9,000 salary

Beyond doubt there was no performance sheet in the majors to match that. Nevertheless the Tigers flatly rejected his "polite request" (Cobb's words before things became flammable), repeating that $15,000 was unprecedented and outrageous.

Detroit's front office compared the pay of other names of fame to strengthen its stand. Walter "Big Train" Johnson of Washington, with a 32–12 win-loss mark in 1912 and 33 shutouts to date, was a pitching paragon earning $8,000 annually. Hal Chase, leading first baseman of Chicago, drew a supposed $7,000. Christy "Big Six" Mathewson of the New York Giants, a machinelike producer of 138 wins in the past five seasons, was in the $9,000 class. Navin was quoted, "Nobody makes $15,000—Cobb's overimpressed with himself. He'll settle or regret it."

From Augusta, where he was wintering and bagging more wild game, Cobb maintained pressure. Calling a press conference, he made it plain "I am holding out. I will not report to spring training until I receive what I'm worth. That's final." Newsmen inquired how he could afford the suspension he would undoubtedly draw for staying out. He was unconcerned. Until now he had been thought of as mostly one-dimensional, a player who despite his sideline activities was dependent upon Detroit as his main source of steady income. But, Cobb pointed out, "Four years ago I bought shares in Arizona copper mines at three dollars per share. They've hit some good veins and the shares now are worth one thousand dollars each. I'm also partner in sporting goods stores." Also, not long ago, he had sold cotton futures he held for a $7,500 profit. Anything else? "Yes," he said easily, "I've been invited to become a director of the First National Bank of Lavonia, Georgia." Beyond all that, the holdout was opening a Hupmobile agency in Augusta in conjunction with a Detroit manufacturer eager to cash in on his name. Who needed Navin's and Yawkey's money? Not he, suggested Cobb. He now was invested from the South to the Far West.

March 10 arrived and the Tigers assembled for spring workout at Gulfport, Mississippi. An absent Cobb was busy with one more project—the brash organizing of his own team, the All-Georgian All-Stars, with himself as the star turn in the outfield. As promoter-owner of the Stars he took 40 percent off the top of gate receipts. By estimate he would clear $3,500 or so during a three-state tour, with the secondary advantage that he would stay in shape. In some cases the barnstorming All-Stars were moving into towns and villages ahead of Detroit's appearances there, cutting into the Tigers' receipts.

Still Navin and Yawkey did not budge. Spring camp ended in April, the regular season neared, and management faced the fact of its weakening bargaining position. Cobb further strengthened his one-man rebellion by announcing that a Logansport, Indiana, automobile concern had guaranteed him a one-year, fifteen-thousand-dollar deal to act as its sales agent in Chicago. He liked the proposition. Why not a year off from baseball? Tyrus produced a wire he had sent the company: "AM READY TO TALK BUSINESS. AWAIT YOUR ORDERS."

Detroit chose to counterattack. The New York Times printed Navin's strongest riposte yet: "In the past I have put up with a great deal from Mr. Cobb. It has now reached the point of showdown. It is conceded by everybody that he is the best baseball player in the world.

And Mr. Cobb also is the best-paid player in the world. But this is not the issue. The issue is discipline.

"Cobb did not make baseball, baseball made him. A player cannot be bigger than the game which creates him. To give in to Cobb now would be to concede that he is greater than baseball itself, for he has set all its laws at defiance."

Sniffing, Cobb answered that he was busy just now supervising plans for his new three-story Augusta home. The dwelling would feature an ornate spiral staircase, Oriental rugs, and a grand piano. With wife Charlie and their two small children he would move in as of November. While conferring with carpenters and plumbers, he found time to reply, "Navin chooses to drag my name through the mud. His statement that discipline and not money is the important issue is enough to queer his whole vicious attack on me. And I wish to deny that I am the best-paid player in the world."

He did not name his superior, if any, but he seemed to be pointing at John Peter Honus Wagner, the bowlegged, perennial Pittsburgh shortstop who since 1900 had led National League hitting eight times.

Navin retorted in print: "What effect will his I-am-above-the-law theory have on other players? We might as well turn the club over to Cobb and eventually the League."

The holdout returned, "I'm moveable. Let Detroit sell me elsewhere if they can't meet my demand. I think it likely that some other organization can use me."

Bill Yawkey, Navin, and American League panjandrums now fully removed the gloves. They took the public backstage in another *New York Times* interview, stating, "If Cobb does not like a hotel room a clerk gives him, he quits the team for a week. If he doesn't like what a silly man in the grandstand yells at him, he punches his face and is again out of the game [the Lueker suspension episode of 1912]. He quit the game in 1910 when we were fighting for the pennant and publicly stated he would not play in company with a comrade in left field, D. [Davy] Jones, on account of some misunderstanding with him.

"If he doesn't feel like practicing he stays away from the park. He has grown to believe that his greatness has precluded him from being subject to discipline."

On and on it went. Navin said his patience was exhausted and warned that if the boycotter didn't quickly change his mind, the power of the league would crush him. Ban Johnson, speaking for the American League, confirmed that ultimatum. Johnson: "Cobb's an outlaw. He's always been an outlaw. It was his action in mauling a fan at New York that led to a wholesale strike by the Detroit team." Johnson's list of Cobb's crimes "is so long it runs into three pages," commented one baseball writer. An editorialist inquired, "If he's as big an offender against civilization as that, why isn't Ty Cobb in state's prison?"

Always a believer in the timely counterattack, Cobb accepted a vice presidency of the newly formed Base Ball Players Fraternity, which had a list of grievances against the owners longer than Ban Johnson's exhaustive bill of particulars.

On April 17, two weeks after the season had opened, Cobb was summarily suspended by the National Commission and barred from competing in 1913. He took it with suspicious calm. Five days later he left Augusta for Detroit. Word circulated that a "peaceful settlement" was in the works. Checked into the Brunswick Hotel, Cobb had nothing to say to the press about anything, except for an oblique, "I may have a surprise for the fans."

Long afterward Cobb described what he said was the strategy he used. "What happened was that my senator friend, Hoke Smith, had been keeping busy in Washington. I had his telegram to me saying that my contract was antitrust stuff and illegal. Navin knew of the telegram and it scared the hell out of the boys in sixteen cities. Pure dynamite." And there was more up the Georgian's sleeve.

On April 22, Representative Thomas Gallagher filed a bill before Congress with teeth in it. In part it read:

> WHEREAS, the most audacious and autocratic trust in the country is the one which presumes to control the game; that competition is stifled; that territory and games are apportioned; that men are enslaved and forced to accept salaries and terms or forever be barred from playing and of other acts incident to trafficking in a national pastime for pecuniary gain—
>
> THEREFORE be it resolved that the Speaker of the House is hereby directed to appoint a special committee of seven members to investigate the operation of the Baseball Trust . . . to ascertain whether players have been coerced or restrained from the exercise of their just rights . . . to take testimony . . .

that the Attorney General of the United States is hereby directed to use all the powers of his office to summon witnesses and enforce production of all documents, contracts, etc. . . . to punish by criminal prosecution of the Anti-Trust Laws of the United States.

Gallagher's resolution and Hoke Smith's denunciations were quite enough to cause emergency meetings of the National Commission and end months of fireworks. Yawkey and Navin, wanting no close federal inspection, backed down in partial surrender. On April 25, with his lawyer, Cobb drove to Navin Field to sign a one-year contract at $12,000 "plus some unpublicized bonus money" (so Cobb told me). The $15,000 he had demanded "was a bluff from the start," he recorded in a journal he kept and called "my son-of-a-bitch list." What it came down to was an immediate $3,000 pay increase augmented by an off-the-record $2,000 handed him by Yawkey with the words "to be good and take us to another pennant." The final settlement amounted to $14,000.

So vindicated, Cobb was happy to rub baseball's nose in trade unionism and freemen's rights for a long time to come. Thirty-eight years after his Detroit contract battle, he was invited as a "retired authority" to testify before a House subcommittee studying monopoly power, chaired by Emmanuel Celler of New York. As of 1951 Congress continued its off-and-on probes into whether or not the major leagues should be allowed to continue as exempt from antitrust law. The Library of Congress supplies this excerpt from 1951:

CHAIRMAN: *"Would you care to say what happened as a result of your 1913 holdout? Did you go back to Detroit and play and did they give you want you wanted?"*

COBB: *"Yes, sir. Naturally I had this exhibition trip [with the Georgian All-Stars] and made a little out of it. And we finally came to terms."*

CHAIRMAN: *"Do you remember what action, if any, the Georgia Federation of Labor took after Mr. Navin's release of the ultimatum 'you will play with Detroit or you never will play in Organized Baseball'?"*

COBB: *"Yes, sir. Senator Hoke Smith from Georgia . . . and others of Congress . . . asked to see my contract. And then they gave*

out the press statement here in Washington about investigation
of the contract, see. And then Mr. Navin and I got together
pretty quick." [Audience laughter.]

Even with the distraction of earning big money from five directions—seven if you counted the Duplex Razor ads and plugs for Nuxated Iron Pills ["Nuxated Calms My Stomach"] he endorsed at one
thousand dollars each—Cobb had a typical series of seasons from 1913
through 1915. Five hundred and two hits came cracking off his black
and tan Louisville Sluggers during this period, as he gained his seventh, eighth, and ninth consecutive batting crowns with averages of
.390, .368, and .369. That put him one up on Honus Wagner's eight
titles at Pittsburgh. Wagner would amass no more before his retirement at age forty-three. Cobb, at age twenty-eight in 1915, was far from
finished—in fact, he was only getting warmed up for a sweep of the
statistics.

In the same three-year span his base-running became still more
nerve-shattering. He was compared to a phantom, a whirlwind, and a
loose cannon. "I've given it a lot of thought," remarked Branch Rickey,
then managing the St. Louis Browns, "and have concluded that the
only way to slow him is to do what infielders keep trying—grab his
belt as he goes past. And that's illegal." Rickey endlessly raved about a
particular play, one that he found unbelievable for its combination of
improvisation, speed, gambling, swiveling eyeballs, and Cobb's right
foot. Against St. Louis Cobb took extreme twenty-foot leads off first
base on pitcher Carl Weilman. Weilman had a relatively slow pickoff
move. Five times Cobb beat his throws with dives back to the bag.
Then, stealing second when it was 100–1 that he'd try it, he kept
sprinting when a throw to the middle base was slightly fumbled. "The
throw to third to Jimmy Austin to retire him had Cobb beaten by a
good yard." Rickey's bushy eyebrows climbed as he spoke. "In a split
second as the ball headed into Austin's glove, Cobb amazingly kicked
it into our dugout. He did it in such a flash that the umpire refused to
call it interference, which it openly was. The umpire had never seen a
man literally kick a ball out of his way, like you'd swat a gnat, let alone
go on to score the winning run. He said it had to be accidental. Oh, I
was raving mad and screamed at the umpire."

What did Cobb say? Rickey: "Of course he was full of innocence.

The kicking was just luck. I was happy that he didn't spike Austin in the process."

In the 1913–15 span, often on battered legs, the Peach stole 183 bases. His 96 steals of 1915 established a record that would last for fifty-nine years.

NO MATTER what city he was in, Cobb was always in a hurry. In one such instance he came within inches of death. On a Philadelphia evening he hurried from the Franklin Hotel, caught a taxi, and instructed the driver to step on it. From a side street came a bell-clanging trolley car, out of control.

Sitting in the front seat with the cabdriver, Cobb yelled, "Turn! Turn!" The cabbie froze and continued ahead at thirty miles an hour into the trolley's path. Moments before a collision, Cobb grabbed the wheel and spun the cab sideways, but it was too late to avoid the smash-up, which ripped off the taxi's rear wheels and sent Cobb sailing out the door. With the hurtling trolley about to hit him, he rolled away, barely safe. Bruised, his pants torn, he continued to his meeting.

Detroit was caught up in a speed-oriented era, drawn by anything traveling fast. Nothing in Cobb's Tiger contract prohibited him from becoming a begoggled, neck-risking auto race driver. "Whenever I could get away from the ballpark," he wrote, "I enjoyed slamming a big Pope-Toledo, Mercedes, White Streak, or Thomas Flyer around tracks. I'd hit it up on the bricks at 100 m.p.h. in those firespitters." At the Indianapolis Speedway he was timed in forty-five seconds flat for the "flying kilometer," a near record. At a state fair in 1916 he acted as head starter for a five-mile race. After the field of drivers was off, Cobb turned to his "mechanician," a big-league umpire named Brick Owens, and cried, "C'mon, Brick, let's catch them!" Owens was shocked and lost his breakfast when the fence-clipping ride was ended—with a win. Cobb chuckled, "I got even with all umpires that day."

At Savannah, Georgia's, sixteen-mile speedway, he was zooming along, he claimed, at 105 miles an hour with noted race driver Bill McNey at his side. As Cobb told it, McNey reached over and turned off the ignition. "You're too damned reckless for me," said McNey, climbing out. A few days later newspapers carried the story: "RACING STAR MCNEY KILLED IN CRASH." "And me with a family," Cobb ended the story.

"I kept on driving, but that was my last race against time. Couldn't get enough life insurance."

THERE WERE plenty more follies and financial finagling to keep him occupied. In 1913 the Federal League, an independent circuit, declared its plan to expand to major-league status next season. Federal organizers were wealthy speculators, among them Phil de Catesby Ball (St. Louis ice merchant), James Gilmore (coal and paper), Charlie Weeghman (Chicago restaurateur), Robert Ward (bakeries), and Harry Sinclair (Sinclair Oil). They offered salaries well above those of the American League and National League, and they promised to eliminate the detested reserve clause from contracts.

Fed up with a closed shop, several dozen players were lured away from the existing majors. Among those jumping were Joe Tinker and Three-Finger Brown of Cincinnati, Hal Chase of the White Sox, George Mullin of Detroit, aging but valuable pitchers Eddie Plank and Chief Bender of the Philadelphia A's, and the Phillies' double-play tandem of Mickey "Doc" Mullin and Otto Knabe. The exodus grew, until more than eighty current and former major-leaguers kicked over the traces for better deals. Derided in the beginning, the Federal League developed into a definite challenge to the Americans and Nationals. No less a star than Walter Johnson of Washington, ace of hurlers, took six thousand dollars of Federal money, with more to come; within weeks, however, Johnson changed his mind, refunded the six thousand, and returned home.

A main Feds' objective was to sign the best of the best, starting with Cobb. In the press appeared a jingle, showing how one poet saw the trade war:

> Sing a song of dollars
> A pocket full of kale
> See the players jumping
> Hear the magnates rail.

Cobb was "interested." Anything usable against his Detroit employers in what he saw as a nonstop salary struggle was worth considering. As early as 1913 he had met with Federal directors when they put out feelers. Again, early in 1914, he sat down to confer with Harry

Sinclair and Big Jim Gilmore, key officials of the new league. They met, secretly, at the Commodore Hotel in New York.

As Cobb told it, Sinclair, owner or lessee of vast oil-pumping acreage in the western U.S., opened with, "There's nothing we won't provide to have you join us. First we'll write you a three-year contract. Then we'll put the money either in escrow or straight into your bank, at your choice. And you tell us how much you want."

"No, give me your offer," replied Cobb.

"One hundred thousand dollars for each season," shot back Sinclair, "many times more than ever has been paid a ballplayer."

In recreating their conversation for Grantland Rice, Cobb said that he sparred for a while. One hundred thousand dollars was far more than he had expected. Sixty thousand had been his guess. (Fifteen years later, in 1930, the New York Yankees would pay Babe Ruth a record eighty thousand dollars.) Cobb told Sinclair that he doubted the Federals could arrange for suitable big-time parks in the short time available, for teams contemplated in Chicago, Baltimore, Indianapolis, Brooklyn, Kansas City, Pittsburgh, and elsewhere, nor could teams be of the caliber to draw crowds in practical number.

"That's all being taken care of," said Sinclair, confidently. He jolted Cobb more by adding, "If the league should fail, and it won't, I will put in writing that you'll be the highest paid oil-lease man in the history of the Sinclair Company, which as you know is worth one hundred million dollars."

One hundred thousand, against the fourteen thousand he was getting from the Tigers—the temptation was big, he said. But, as Cobb always explained his decision, "I could see fifty thousand and then eighty thousand or more down the line for me where I was. I was sure I could beat the Detroit gang in the end. They maybe I'd buy into a [major] league franchise through a syndicate I was connected with." That way he would never again need to work for anyone. Leaving the Commodore session he spoke with newsmen who had learned of a "mammoth" offer to announce matter-of-factly, "I have declined to move to the Federals. I made my name in the American League and there I'll stay."

Within eighteen months he could congratulate himself on his choice. The Federal—or "outlaw"—League went under in 1915, the victim of expensive litigation and the likelihood of a world war erupting. Some $10 million in losses by both sides in the lengthy bidding war and rivalry were quoted. Cobb could rest content that he had been offered more thousands of dollars for six months or so of work than any other athlete who had ever lived.

THERE WAS a drawback in not defecting to the Federals. Cobb had to continue to coexist with carping, interfering Frank Navin, the man who signed Cobb's paychecks and was said to strut—not walk—down the streets of Detroit. It was bad enough for Cobb's purposes that Detroit between 1913 and 1915 finished in sixth, fourth, and second places; there was also Navin's proved and exposed practice of intercepting and reading Cobb's private mail, he said, to gain an advantage in their negotiations.

"I got wise to this," revealed Cobb in *My Life in Baseball*, "when I noticed that Navin's home telephone number and home address appeared in pencil on the back of my business telegrams. What was it doing there? Navin was convinced that I was on the verge of jumping to the Federal League. To learn more, he had arranged to see my wires, even before Western Union delivered them to me.

"At the time I was writing syndicated stories for Bell Newspaper Syndicate, and set a trap for Navin and sat back and watched the fat man fall into it. Bell was paying me $200 per column for writing 'ghosted' pieces on baseball events, gossip and prediction. I arranged for John N. Wheeler, head of Bell in New York, to wire me: "DO NOTHING UNTIL YOU SEE ME ON NEXT TRIP EAST." When the message was delivered, sure enough, Navin's home address showed up on its reverse side."

A furious Cobb confronted Navin with, "Invasion of certain rights of mine have been made—by you. You've been reading my mail. That's a foul trick and I want it stopped." Otherwise, he threatened, a lawsuit spreading Navin's face over the press would follow.

With other evidence found on messages, Cobb said, Navin could not deny that he had resorted to espionage; "I had him cold." With that, any chance of reaching some degree of accord by the two, let alone forming a friendship, ended forever.

Navin was such a "fee-simple sonofabitch" and "constipated damnfool," wrote Cobb, that he turned down an offer from Clark Griffith, co-owner at Washington, to buy Cobb's contract for $85,000. It would have been a pleasure for the day's leading hitter to join the game's foremost pitcher, Walter Johnson, along with such other Washington standouts as Clyde Milan and Chick Gandil; Johnson and he, Cobb felt, could have won the pennant as a combination.

Now and then Cobb was paid extra to scout promising college and minor-league players. On a visit to the University of Michigan he was impressed by a stocky, twenty-year-old first baseman who could also pitch. He judged the boy to be an all but certain major-leaguer and sent Navin a memo recommending a quick signing. Navin assigned another scout, got back an unfavorable report, and forgot about George Sisler. The St. Louis Browns signed him. He proceeded to hit .371, .407, .420, and the like, finishing with one of the most spectacular career averages in history, a .340, and a place in the Hall of Fame. In the eyes of his original discoverer, to pass up Sisler was no less than team sabotage.

Somehow—to Cobb's disgust—Navin escaped serious blame for Detroit's failure to add a fourth pennant after the straight championships of 1907, 1908, and 1909. Bill Yawkey's designated boss of the Tigers was coasting on his past reputation and, according to Detroit historians Norman Beasley and George W. Stark in their civic biography, *Made in Detroit*, remained popular—"a fine fellow without malice and without an enemy."

Cobb's own expanding reputation was a matter of geography. In Detroit, fans left hams, turkeys, and candies on the porch of a home he rented. In the eastern U.S., from Chicago to Boston, he was detested to the point that at times he wasn't allowed to sleep at night. "Foreign" fans banged tin pans outside his hotel, shouted anti-South slogans ("Isn't Georgia the place you march through?" "Robert E. Lee was a bastard"). They threw junk until fields were littered and time-out had to be called. The *Sporting News*, often a Cobb supporter, was displeased by his steady lone-wolf prowling on the bases, at the sacrifice of coordinated teamwork. Greed "motivated him." Cobb's act in Washington, D.C., of arousing Congress toward antitrust action was not forgotten. "What does Cobb care?" asked the *Sporting News*. "Cobb is for Cobb. He's done more than any individual to give baseball's enemies a chance to attack." Clairvoyantly, the paper saw that "his most glorious days are behind him."

Cobb snapped, "What do twenty-dollar-a-week sportswriters know?" he struck back. "All around the circuit the writers hit me up, wanting an interview. When I give them some of my time, they knife me."

"Oh, yes?" replied Ed Bang in the *Cleveland News*. "Who was it that pulled a knife and cut a hotel detective of this city in the middle of the night?"

His running combat with the press did not take the Peach's mind off another possible objective. At several points during the 1913–15 seasons his batting averages had stood at a blazing .487 and .483. He even had an idea, as outlandish as it sounded, that .500 might be attained in a season. Back in 1887, when a base on balls counted as a base hit and four strikes constituted an out, Tip O'Neill of the pioneer American Association had reached .492 overall, and Pete Browning of the same league had swung at .471. True, the game was different then, not really comparable to today's. Cobb thought about it. What—he conjectured—if he went uninjured for six months, caught league pitchers in an off year, did not draw many bases on balls, and put together one of his phenomenal hitting bursts, such as his 40-game streak of 1911?

No one during his playing years had surpassed Cobb's 248 base hits in 591 plate appearances of 1911, good for that .420 showing. And he had done this while benched for a while with bronchitis. Yes, 300 hits and a .500 mark were possible. So he believed.

EMERGENCE OF A MILLIONAIRE

Before he could shoot for the moon on batting average, Cobb went on a moose-hunting expedition in southern Canada following the 1914 season. He slipped, fell down an embankment, and appeared to have fractured a leg. He was littered out of the woods to a hospital, where it was found to be only a torn ligament. He wrote to an Augusta friend, "Will be home and running in two weeks."

He recovered rapidly, but within months came a scare of far greater concern—his eyesight. He had feared the loss of some clarity back in 1909–10. Once more, pitches that had been clear to him now, on occasion, became slightly blurred. Cloudy vision would appear, disappear, and recur. Before it had been an inflammation; now it was diagnosed at Johns Hopkins in Baltimore as a case of pterygium, or "proud flesh," which very slowly was intruding on the cornea of Cobb's right eye. The ailment was caused, it was believed, by the accumulation of dust and other particles while he was playing more than thirteen hundred games in windy outfields. Soon, the medical warning went, surgery would be needed. For now, fearing the outcome, Cobb postponed it.

When the 1915 season started, nobody could tell he needed an operation from his daily hammering of fastballs, spitters, curves, and change-ups. One day at Philadelphia he drove six bullet balls through or over the infield in six trips. Facing the imperturbable Walter "Big Train" Johnson at Navin Field before a record Detroit turnout of 24,500, Cobb coolly informed catcher Ed Ainsmith, "I'm laying down the next one and a hundred dollars says I'll beat out you two birds." Ainsworth signaled Johnson to throw even harder than he usually fired a ball. Both were helpless when a pitch bunted deep, not as a sacrifice but for a base hit, rolled to Johnson's right side. Lunging for a hopper just beyond his grasp, the Big Train fell down.

Word passed around the league that some managers were levying fifty-dollar fines on any battery allowing Cobb to steal home on them. In St. Louis he doubled, and while prancing and feinting at second base worked on pitcher Grover Cleveland Lowdermilk. "You couldn't get me out in a month!" he taunted. The next batter, Sam Crawford, tapped back to the mound. Lowdermilk was upset enough to fumble the chance and, seeing Cobb streaking to third, stumbled and in his haste to throw did a forward flip. He sprawled on the ground, cursing himself, as Cobb passed third and sped home for another uncanny score.

On the bases he continued to pay for his daring in bruises and blood. In press boxes the rumor circulated that anyone who disabled Cobb would get bonus money. Evidence of this accumulated. Cleveland's first-basing Wheeler "Doc" Johnston caught up with him in a rundown and instead of making a clean tag, slammed a knee into Cobb's lumbar region. It caused spasms. Cobb was out for four games. Heavily taped, he said, "I didn't see anyone coming off our bench to fight for me when they broke my ribs." That had happened at Boston when Rube Foster's intentional duster cracked two ribs, sidelining him for nearly three weeks.

Buck Weaver of the White Sox, six years away from involvement in the "Black Sox" who fixed the 1919 World Series for gamblers' money, stuck a spike into Cobb's knee; not properly cleaned, the wound became infected. Once more he was on the bench. When a sufficient scab formed, he tried his luck playing second base. All out of position, making errors, he returned to a doctor's care.

When not in the lineup, Cobb in 1914–15 saw himself as tenth man on the ball club. He sat off by himself on a reserved chair, as sensitive to the game's pulse as a hawk to shifting wing. He watched for tendencies—did an opponent play the center fielder shallow so as to quickly trap hits down the middle, leaving an area open to line drives? Did the catcher show any telltales in signing for pitches? Did a pitcher pound his glove or hitch up his pants before loosing a fastball? No one minded his silent search for clues, but the Tigers resented his habit of piping to one of them when batting, "Go getcha self a swing!" He was as critical as he was analytical.

Returning to duty, but still notably short of having good legs under him, Tyrus within days touched off another riot. Against the Athletics he seemingly spiked catcher Jack Lapp with intent on a play at the plate. As Lapp lay on the ground, groaning, Cobb spat upon him. Something like twenty fans climbed over railings to try to lay hands on the villain, and cops beat them back. Outside Shibe Park afterward, several dozen Philadelphians gathered to rush the departing Cobb with fists and sticks. Luckily a trolley car came along and he jumped aboard. Down the track rattled the trolley with a small mob in pursuit. Cobb punched and kicked off all he could, but a few climbed onto the car's roof to tear loose the electrical rod. While the conductor struggled to replace the rod, Cobb was glad he'd changed into civilian clothes at Shibe. Ducking away into a sidewalk crowd, he disappeared. "The only cure for Philadelphia is to blow it up," he snarled on a train leaving town.

IN AUGUSTA the situation at home was troubled. Charlotte "Charlie" Cobb, twenty-three, was often ill. Four times during Cobb's annual duels with Joe Jackson and Tris Speaker in defense of his batting championship, she became sick enough to require his breaking off and hurrying home. Three of their five children were born between 1910 and 1916; twice their mother suffered postpartum complications. Cobb always dropped what he was doing and responded to the call, but not always with good grace. "He didn't come home for long—he acted like it was an imposition," said Shirley Cobb Beckwith, his daughter, in a conversation with this author in 1960.

At such times *Baseball Magazine*'s F. C. Lane was one of the very few journalists allowed to visit the spacious Augusta home into which the Cobbs had moved in November of 1913. When missing times at bat to stay at his wife's bedside, Lane's host appeared to be nervous and distracted. Lane found Mrs. Cobb, while sickly, to be "a woman of uncommon judgment and good sense." Their three young children, Ty junior, Shirley, and Herschel, were neatly dressed, respectful.

"It is well that Mrs. Cobb is of this character," wrote Lane, "what with Ty's quick, nervous disposition and scrappy, hotheaded temperament." The reporter added that while Cobb consulted medical specialists about his wife's health, he also spent much time majestically taking bows on Augusta streets, "mitting" admirers. On a side trip to Florida he even took aeroplane flying lessons. Manager Hughie Jennings, hearing of the flying, was said to have hit several roofs.

One more tidbit from Lane concerned five-year-old Ty Junior's backing off from a schoolyard fight with an older kid. His father's instructions were: "This boy insulted you and if you don't go out and lick him, then I will lick you." Lane wrote, "Little Ty lived up to the reputation of his dad in a strenuous manner and since then there has been no doubt whatever of his wish to insist upon his rights."

At home at 2425 William Street, in what a curious Lane called an antebellum southern semimansion with a broad veranda encircling it and shrouded by trees, Cobb spoke of why he was constantly on the warpath up north: "I get into a lot of trouble and have made many enemies. But my philosophy is brief. I think life is too short to be diplomatic. A man's friends shouldn't mind what he does or says—and those who are not his friends, well, the hell with them. They don't count."

That was enough for Lane—the man intended to go on playing outside the rules, challenging baseball to stop him.

Upon his return from one of these forced sojourns in Georgia, you could bet on it that Cobb would rebound in a batting streak. In July of 1913, to cite one instance, he resumed play after a week's absence to find that Shoeless Joe Jackson was slugging at the .412 mark. He trailed Jackson by 11 points. In Cleveland, where Cobb-bashing was akin to a civic duty after a series of brawls with fans and hotel personnel and two near escapes from criminal prosecution, he had one of his all-time best offensive days with two triples and a double—in all, six hits in seven plate appearances. "Six-hitters" were so rare, just as they are nowadays, that Bill Yawkey came down from his owner's box to extend compliments. Cobb shook his hand, but, said witnesses, not warmly. "Money, not compliments, talked with Ty," said author Fred Lieb. "Hey! Hey! The Peach gets ten hits in nine tries!" cried newsboys selling papers outside Dolph's Saloon in central Detroit. People would believe anything about him by now.

Final figures for that 1913 season were .390 for Cobb, .373 for Jackson, who faded before the champion's late comeback, and .363 for Tris Speaker of Boston. In the National League, Jake Daubert's .350 for Brooklyn led. Whatever the complaints, for the seventh consecutive campaign the Georgian had stood foremost.

Some statisticians sought to debunk the result. Because of lost time he had played in only 122 games to Jackson's 148 and Speaker's 141. Cobb retorted that total games and multiplicity of at-bats had nothing to do with it, that he had averaged .390 with a sixth-place team, and that pitching staffs were loaded with 20-game-and-up winners—six of them leaguewide—along with numerous moundsmen with low earned-run averages. Despite injuries he had hit the toughest of them well. As to slumping to 52 base steals in 1913, well below the 75 posted by Clyde "Deerfoot" Milan in Washington, he dismissed that as due to the knee infection, jammed back, turned ankle, and trips back to Augusta. Then, too, he was developing property he owned in Georgia; that had been distracting.

He had become a cigarette addict, complained Cobb, which was bad for his wind. By 1914 the tobacco industry was selling an estimated 2 million pounds of its products in the U.S. In exchange for tobacco stock assigned to Cobb he posed for cigarette testimonials—"and now it's so that I'm smoking a warehouseful a month."

IN 1914, during another late onrush to win an eighth straight batting crown, Cobb gave the national public renewed reason to question his sanity. In still another moment of madness he turned murderous. In this outbreak he twice landed in a Detroit jail and then in criminal court over the ridiculous matter of a twenty-cent piece of fish—perch, as it happened.

His rampage began on a June evening after he had invited Clark Griffith to dinner at his rented Woodland Avenue home. Griffith, manager of the Washington Senators, abetted by Senator Hoke Smith, who by now was an advisor to Cobb, continued to make overtures to Navin to acquire the Tigers' main man by cash or barter. Griffith was coming to dinner to talk it over. Before the meal could be served, a shocked Griffith witnessed his host under arrest and facing a jail term on an evening that confirmed the growing belief in sport circles that he was wrongheaded—twisted by some sort of unpredictable dementia.

Before dinner, Charlie Cobb, having joined her husband in Detroit, complained that a butcher down the street had acted insultingly to her when she returned some fish she felt was spoiled, her cook concurring. Cobb, excusing himself to Griffith, phoned the butcher and called him a series of names. Then he pocketed a revolver he always kept handy and took off for Carpenter's Meat Market. An account of what happened later was summarized in Doc Greene's "Press Box" column in the Detroit *News*:

"The Georgia Peach entered a meat market at 1526 Hamilton Street operated by one William Carpenter. He waved a loaded .32 revolver and declared 'somebody has insulted my wife!' The hassle turned out to be over a purchase of 20 cents worth of perch.

"A meat worker, Howard Harding, who was Carpenter's wife's brother, tried to protect the proprietor and finally the pair went outside. Cobb handed his revolver to one bystander, his hat to another, and proceeded to brutally beat up the youngster."

Doc Green's column didn't detail the whole wretched affair. After a police paddy wagon arrived to handcuff and remove a screaming Cobb to jail, court testimony would establish that he had forced the butcher to phone Mrs. Cobb and apologize and meanwhile smashed glassed-in meat displays and wrecked some furniture. Harding, who was black, had brandished a meat cleaver in defense of the shop. Furthermore, before Cobb and Harding moved outside to the street, Cobb had fought indoors with Harding, hitting him over the head at least three times with the gun's butt. Harding was bleeding even before they went outside.

He hadn't fired a shot—which was all that saved the Georgian from a prison sentence. On a possible assault-with-a-deadly-weapon charge, he spent the night in a cell. The cell was "flea-ridden," he complained, unfit for a dog.

Griffith, a deacon of the American League, left Detroit hastily. Assistant butcher Harding decided not to take legal action. He told Bethune Station police that he was amazed by the berserk attack, but since it was Ty Cobb he would settle for an apology to himself and to Carpenter, repair of shop damages, and payment of his doctor's bill. Detroit team attorneys were alleged around town to have quieted the victim by paying him something like one thousand dollars, as they had done to resolve other eruptions by their client. It was a cheap settlement; Cobb's 1909 Cleveland knifing of a detective had cost Detroit ten times that much.

Carpenter wasn't placated, however. He resented the claim that his fish were "rotten" and didn't let it pass. Less than a week later he filed a disturbing-the-peace charge, and again his assailant was jailed. It was said that policemen drew straws to determine which of them would have the "honor" of making the arrest after a game at Navin Field. No handcuffs were used in this instance. Cobb spent another night in a smelly hoosegow, appeared in magistrate's court next day, and at the advice of his attorney, James O. Murfin, pleaded guilty. If he hadn't done so, observed the Detroit press, he faced a probable jail term of six months for using a deadly weapon.

Cobb stood silent before the bench with his right hand bandaged. He did no talking other than to identify himself. "He regrets this incident to the bottom of his heart," stated Murfin. "He regrets it exceedingly on account of management of the Detroit team and his teammates. He feels that as they are struggling he should be in the game . . . He believes that he made a mistake and has promised to control his temper in the future. He has had his lesson."

Discussing *Carpenter v. Cobb* in his old age, Cobb remarked, "I had some good contacts at magistrate's court." He was fined a paltry fifty dollars, with the warning that if he caused more such trouble he would be heavily penalized. As the judge may or may not have known, this was his fifth known assault on a black person, three of them coming inside Detroit jurisdiction.

In the fish fight Cobb fractured the thumb of his throwing hand. For fifty-two days, through June, July, and until August 7, he was sidelined. Up until then the Tigers had a chance to take the pennant, or come close. Frank Navin was enraged; without his number-one man the club turned stale, lost seven straight at one stretch, and finished far out of first place. There would be no World Series money, no pay raises for 1915. Hard words were passed when pitcher Hooks Dauss and an aging Sam Crawford flatly let Cobb know they realized what he was doing after his thumb healed—that is, hitting to boost his own average, not for the team's general welfare. When a sacrifice fly or bunt was needed, instead of providing it he would place-hit a ball just over the infield. Many of these "nibbly" punched hits were worth little in a free-scoring game, failing to produce runs. But without him the Tigers were sluggish, lacked belligerency, and were not a contender.

What would he do next? According to several players, Navin had come genuinely to wonder whether Cobb's repeated bizarre rages meant that he was not mentally sound. What else could explain it? Cobb's reply was the usual: "Trade me."

It was maddening to be caught in a situation in which one man was so essential to finishing even in third or fourth place that he could not be dealt away. Hughie Jennings thought he was managing a winner—"then in one hour in a butcher shop Cobb ruined us." It wasn't funny, but a Detroit quip went, "Lucky it wasn't a porterhouse steak—he'd have killed somebody." The convicted Cobb's rationalization of his broken thumb was, "Everybody gets hurt sometime. It's up to the others to take up the slack. And nobody around here did that."

His own performance stood up well. With a hand still tender, he was held to about a .340 average before getting hot in the final months of 1914. In August he trailed the persistent Joe Jackson of Cleveland by 18 to 21 points. With one of his most superlative stretch of runs yet he moved ahead of Shoeless Joe and Eddie Collins of Philadelphia. His concluding .368 mark was enough to capture one more championship trophy—easily. Collins finished at .344, and in a tie, Speaker and Jackson hit .338. Joseph Jefferson Jackson had complained in the past, and now the South Carolina country boy moaned to writer Harry Salsinger, "Ah wonder what it takes around here to win somethin'? Ah did .408 in 1911 and Cobb did .420. Ah did .395 the next year and he did .410. Now he's did it again. Ahhh-hell!"

Intimations by American Leaguers that Cobb was a looming case for the psychopathic ward faded for the time being. No one yet had battered pitchers so hard over a sustained period, none had shown such base-path craftsmanship. Signs seen in him earlier that year by the *Sporting News* of a "decay from glory" went unmentioned—no doubt much to the regret of the trade sheet—at the October finish. "He's weird, all right," said Rebel Oakes, manager of the Federal League's Pittsburgh club. "He's a nutter, but, by god, there's nobody nearly so competitive. When he's at bat you can hear Cobb gritting his teeth."

General opinion was that Cobb was headed for a fall. But George Tweedy Stallings, highly respected New York and Boston Braves manager, college-bred Georgian, and Cobb's companion on game-hunting expeditions, was protective and optimistic; "Kings don't take orders. If Ty wasn't so fiery and out to beat you, he wouldn't be half as great a player."

Detroit's front office, along with Mrs. Cobb, expected him to return to Augusta that fall, and was startled when he turned up in Shelby, Ohio, playing with a nondescript team of minor-leaguers. The reason: he was paid $150 per game. It was precisely like Cobb to go after every loose nickel, no matter where located.

The "straw hat affair" demonstrated just how much Silas Marner there was in him. A custom had developed in Detroit on Labor Day for the more rabid fans to scale their straw hats onto the field when the Tigers were going well. Cobb ordered the grounds crew to collect and store the skimmers for him. In his book *The Detroit Tigers*, author Joe Falls told of how Cobb shipped hundreds of hats home to his Georgia farm at season's end, where they were worn on the heads of his field-hands and donkeys as protection from the sun. "Each day after the players left," wrote Falls with a grin, "Ty also would pick up pieces of soap left in the showers. These, too, would go back to Augusta with him—soap for the hired hands."

Concerning the tipping of waiters and cab drivers, a practice then catching on, he was just as thrifty. Upon one cabby's asking for a tip, Cobb snapped, "Sure, don't bet on the Tigers today."

"Mister Ty"—the salutation he came to prefer—had as his long-term aim to become the highest-paid player in history—and to take off from there. For the 1915 season, despite his transgressions, he negotiated a salary raise from roughly fourteen thousand to twenty thousand dollars, plus certain bonuses. That made him number one in the game for pay, ahead of Tris Speaker, Christy Mathewson, Walter Johnson, and other golden names, and he set out to buy land and expand his sideline interests. At the Pontchartrain Hotel bar he had come to know such auto men as John and Horace Dodge, Ransom E. Olds, J. W. Packard, and David Dunbar Buick. From 1905 to 1914 Cobb had lacked investment capital. Now he was better prepared when Charlie Hastings, manager of Hupmobile, proposed, "Everybody down south knows you. I can arrange for you to take over an agency for us in

Atlanta or Augusta. You'll have to put up fifty dollars for each car we deliver, which will be twenty-five hundred dollars initially. Then you'll need another twenty-five hundred for stock in the company."

At first Cobb thought it was too big a deal to handle, but finally he signed on with Hupmobile, and in his first two years sold some 125 "Hups" under an ad banner strung near Augusta's Broad Street: "TY COBB DRIVES ONE, THE GEORGIA PEACH SAYS SO SHOULD YOU." His profit averaged 30–35 percent, money that he plowed into additional cotton-market shares. It was a thrill for some pecan farmer to have Ty Cobb motor into his place, accept a cup of homemade corn liquor, and sell him a car. Sometimes he would make sales on the sidewalk in Macon, Decatur, Kenesaw, or Savannah, with his autograph as a nice bonus.

On his native ground he held a wide edge—"and the edge in this world means everything," he said—over other auto salesmen, even those offering Henry Ford's product, by combining sales technique with his national image. When less than halfway through his major-league career, he was close to equaling his player's salary in ancillary income. Prior to the Hupmobile dealership, Cobb had received all the free bats he wanted from Hillerich and Bradsby Company of Louisville, in return for his endorsement etched in the wood of Louisville Sluggers. When a customer wavered about buying a Hup, he would mention, "Of course, partner, a bat with my name on it goes with the purchase." Kids and fathers hung around the Cobb Agency to stare at the strapping prince of ballplayers. Salesman Cobb gave the kids lessons on how to grip a bat with hands six or so inches apart.

In what he saw as a peacemaking move by Detroit's front office, Cobb was invited to join Navin, Bill Yawkey, and Hughie Jennings in buying ["a minor partnership on my part"] the International League franchise at Providence, Rhode Island. Meanwhile, he was able to increase his shares in the Lavonia, Georgia, bank where he was already a director. By his growing affluence he had also been able to retain sixty-odd acres of the one-time hundred-acre Royston family farm, in danger of loss by foreclosure after his father's death ten years earlier. At the time, Cobb's low earnings had prevented forfeiture of some of the land. By 1915 he was able to clear all debts. More than most gains, this gave him satisfaction—in his revered father's name he had saved the homestead.

Until the second decade of the century, few books "written" by major-league stars had been published. The most notable was Christy Mathewson's popular ghostwritten *Pitching in a Pinch* of 1912. Seeing profit in a "confession," Cobb came out in 1914 with *Busting 'Em and Other Stories*. Readers who claimed that his overblown ego—"monumental," said most reviewers—lay behind this drive to succeed in yet one more field, found just about what they had expected. The preface of the book by ghostwriter John N. Wheeler of the North American Newspaper Alliance gushed with:

"Ty Cobb is an institution like the President of the United States."

"He is a speed flash who makes lightning look slow."

"He is the fastest thinker in the game . . . He makes players not as fast as Cobb look foolish."

"A mechanical marvel . . . Cobb is the most sensational player the game has ever produced."

"Cobb is a born reporter and would have been a star in the newspaper trade if he'd adopted the business. He is an intellectual blotter."

And, finally, "Readers, meet Mr. Cobb—author!"

As usual with such books, Cobb's authorship, of course, actually amounted to relating anecdotes and gossip to Wheeler and, as he later conceded, "giving Wheeler a hand with the technical stuff."

Cobb's first-person tribute to himself began modestly with mention of a seventeen-game batting slump he once had, then drifted into negativism, wherein he advised American boys not to seek a pro baseball career. It was too tough a line of work at the top. Plenty of men went broke. Stardom was largely "accidental." You had to make money quickly or not at all. The injury rate was fierce. Under pressure Cobb was losing hair, turning gray, and growing bald at age twenty-seven. He regretted that he had never attended college to become a doctor or lawyer. As for his own son, he wasn't particularly anxious that Ty junior become a ballplayer, and certainly he'd attend a university.

Contradictorily, the most heated of fighters in the big leagues for player salary increases felt that players were earning so much that teams could not support heavy payrolls. Income couldn't keep up with outgo, the way things were going. Underpaid leaguers who read this must have wondered; was the Georgia Peach on their side, or management's? Was the vice presidency of the rebellious Base Ball Players Fraternity that he had accepted in 1912 a sham?

NOT LONG after the book was released, the Peach took his biggest step toward security. In Atlanta he had met Robert Winship Woodruff on a golf course. Woodruff was involved in marketing a flavorful drink invented by a southern pharmacist, and felt the concoction would sell well nationally and internationally. He was expanding widely from the South and wanted home-boy Cobb to buy ten thousand dollars worth of shares. The home boy said he'd think about it. The drink was called Coca-Cola.

In the 1920s, Coca-Cola stock would make him wealthy beyond his dreams—better than a millionaire before he was thirty-five. By then he was commanding the greatest income of any athlete in the world with the possible exception of Spanish bullfighter Juan Belmonte.

CHAPTER SEVENTEEN

UNRECONSTRUCTED OUTLAW

I was a phrenologist back then," Cobb told me in retirement, "and I still am . . . The shape and contours of a man's skull tell you plenty about his intelligence and general character . . . Barney Johnson was an ideal example."

"Barney"—Walter Johnson—in a prime lasting for a dozen years, was as great a right-handed pitcher as ever lived. Tousle-haired, with a noble brow, pleasant facial features, and warm blue eyes, he revealed himself to Cobb upon first sight as too decent for his own good; that is, history's fastest pitcher (416 lifetime wins, 3,508 strike-outs, 110 shutouts) would not turn loose his fastball with malice afore-thought. Phrenology said so to Cobb. (In point of fact, phrenology was based not on appearance but on the bumps on a man's skull.)

Hanging over the plate, inviting a beanball, Cobb got away with usurping "pitcher's space" for long years. Especially with someone he liked, Johnson was forbearant, afraid of seriously injuring the batter. When the Tigers and Washington Nationals played each other, T.C. hosted Johnson at dinners at the Detroit Athletic Club and with thea-ter tickets. A rare photograph exists showing Tyrus with one arm thrown around Johnson in a proprietary manner. The two grew friendly enough that in 1914 Cobb helped dissuade Johnson from jumping to the upstart, doomed Federal League when the big man already had six thousands dollars of the Feds' advance money on the table and his mind about made up to defect. T.C. refused to jump; Johnson followed.

In all, Cobb faced the Big Train 245 times for a .335 bat average. "If I hadn't been able to read him, it would have been about .290," he willingly admitted.

COBB WAS less successful in sizing up an opponent by his appearance in 1914–15 when, given some of his first looks at a hefty left-handed rookie pitcher with the Red Sox, he was not impressed. "He's overweight and balloon-headed," judged Cobb. "Just another fresh kid from Double A" was how he initially saw nineteen-year-old George Herman "Babe" Ruth.

Ruth, who was blocky-headed, had been pitching fairly well since the Red Sox brought him up from the Providence Grays of the International League that spring. Wasting no time, he'd beaten the Yankees with a five-hitter, while incidentally hitting a home run. The new boy-man with the brush haircut would hit four homers in this break-in season. He would also, and primarily, win 18 games with controlled fastballs and sweeping curves.

In late August the Tigers were locked in a close pennant race with Boston and the Chicago White Sox. A decisive four-game series began for Detroit at Boston's Fenway Park, at which time Cobb and Ruth came to know each other. Carl Mays, who would deck a man with a grin, was on the hill for Boston. Novice bench-jockey Ruth yelled to Mays when Cobb came to bat, "Knock him on his ass!" Many of the twenty thousand local fanatics liked the suggestion and yelled it. Mays knocked his man down twice running. Dodging a third beanball, Cobb threw his bat at Mays and charged him. Umpires broke it up. "Duster" Mays followed up by hitting his target on the wrist and hand. Again going for Mays, this time carrying his bat, T.C. was stopped by Jennings, the umpires, and some of the Tiger bench. Cobb stood on first base after walking to call Mays a "dirty scum yellow dog." And: "Step outside and meet me."

Riot impended. Beer and pop bottles flew from the stands, one of them grazing Cobb's shoulder. Behind sharp pitching by Hooks Dauss, Detroit won, 6–1, and when Cobb made the final out with a fly-ball catch, hundreds of Beantowners leaped over railings to get at him. Special park guards and a police squad armed with batons partially restored order, helped by a few Tigers who circled their teammate with whirling bats. During this melee Cobb walked, not ran, to the clubhouse. Young Ruth was seen to rush onto the field—the first hint of the repeated confrontations he and T.C. would enter into off and on for the next thirteen seasons—but by then Cobb was behind locked doors.

Along with most American Leaguers, Cobb had not the slightest idea that in Ruth he was observing a player who would develop into much more than a pitcher. His "hard one" smoked; from 1915 through 1918 the Babe would win an impressive 78 games against 40 losses for Boston, with a pair of 20-wins-plus seasons, earned-run averages of 1.75 and 2.02, and 450 strikeouts included. He was a born thrower. Further, the rookie from an industrial school for orphans and waifs in Baltimore was just learning his trade.

Home runs? "His hitting never crossed my mind then," admitted Cobb in time. From 1914 through 1917 Ruth hit but nine homers, quite good but not significant in a day emphasizing science over power for a public schooled in the "old Army game" of place-hitting, bunting, singling behind runners, the steal and delayed steal, the hit-and-run, and the infield-bounding "Baltimore chop." The very long ball was nothing more than an occasional feature.

In the 1916 World Series the Babe would pitch a wonderful fourteen-inning, 2–1 victory over Brooklyn, without blasting a ball out of the park or even hitting safely. He would hit no homers while appearing in three World Series as a Red Soxer. "He did some pinch-hitting," reflected Cobb, "and he was below average. Ruth fooled me. I didn't think he had the hand speed to do what came later."

THROUGHOUT THE 1915 campaign, when he first became vaguely aware of Ruth, the Tigers' prima donna was playing at such a tempo that there was talk of the U.S. mint striking a coin for him. "Make it a hundred-dollar gold piece, that's fitting," suggested Hughie Jennings. All that he did was lead the league's batters for the ninth consecutive time with a .369 mark—his average for the past five seasons was almost .390—and as customary leave everyone in the dust. The next best was Eddie Collins, with .332. In the National League the leader, Larry

Doyle of the Giants, at .320, was far behind. In his tenth anniversary season as a big-leaguer, nearing age thirty, Cobb grouped his second-highest-yet number of runs (144) to lead the league in scoring, along with making the most hits (208) while raising the most hell yet on the bases. Still as fast as ever, he beat all of his past steal statistics. Since 1907 he had stolen per season 49 (led league), 39, 76 (led league), 65, 83 (led league), 61, 52, and 35 bases.

In the winter of 1915 he had resolved to achieve a number not to be beaten during his career. With that in mind he had gone to a leatherworker in Atlanta to have weights installed in his shoes, his latest innovation. All winter he walked the fields hunting game birds—"maybe five hundred miles," he guessed—while wearing ten-ounce impediments. In spring-camp games, without informing anyone but Jennings about the leg-toughening weights, he seemed to be slowing up. Writers fussed about his "decline." Upon removing the lead, he stole four bases in one day against the Athletics, then three each against St. Louis and Cleveland. Six times in 1915 he stole home base. When on third he would say to the baseman, "Want to bet, bo?" Nobody did.

Cobb ended the season with an all-time high of 96 steals. Close to fifty years would pass before anyone would top that, and then Maury Wills of the Los Angeles Dodgers, with 104 in 1962, would do it in nine more games than were played in 1915, on far smoother base paths, and with improved shoes and camera techniques to aid him. "I've always regretted I didn't go for a hundred or more steals," T.C. said to me in 1960. "But in that month I was saving my sore legs . . . in case we went into the World Series."

That the Tigers did not do, and in a most unusual and frustrating way. Never in American League history had a club won 100 games on the season and missed the championship. Largely due to the Peach, the Tigers won 100 and lost 54, but even so were nosed out by Boston, with Ruth a growing factor on the mound, at 101–50. New York and Philadelphia critics, always glad to knock Cobb, attributed Detroit's failure to his eighteen-game hitting slump in August. He retorted that the loss was due to a two-inch piece of foreign material that cooperative umpires had allowed Red Sox pitchers to use on their baseballs all season. At Boston he had tripled off Ernie Shore, then suddenly an already blackened ball was having convulsions. "Because," he fumed,

"Shore got some emery board, taped it inside his glove and roughed the ball into dipping a good six inches." That day Cobb had gone to the Red Sox dugout to let loose at manager Bill Carrigan: "I'll punch in your head if you don't stop loading up!" he threatened.

"Now, Ty," broke in umpire George Hildebrand, who, gossip had it, was a friend of Carrigan, "don't start something or you'll be gone."

"Go ahead and sock me!" cried Carrigan.

"You want me out of here, you bastard," came back Cobb. "You won't get me. But I'll see you out in the alley after this is over."

Carrigan didn't keep the date, which was intelligent of him.

Around the Motor City there was talk, murmurs really, that T.C. and not Jennings should be field-managing the Tigers. Cobb discouraged it. For one reason, he liked the peppery Jennings. For another, the Irishman with the red hair and sideline whistle was building a 1916 team seemingly equipped to bring home a championship for the first time since 1909. With Cobb acting as his counselor, Jennings had recently added southpaw pitcher Harry "Giant Killer" Coveleski, who had just won 22 games for the Tigers and in 1916 would win 21. A crackerjack new second baseman, Ralph "Pep" Young, a former prep-school star, became an asset. Jennings traded third baseman George Moriarty, one of the team's persistent Cobb-haters, and acquired Oscar Vitt, an acrobat at third base. In the outfield was strong-armed Bobby Veach, a .300-plus hitter who would contribute 143 triples and doubles in a coming three-season stretch. Hulking in the wings stood a two-hundred-pounder from the Pacific Coast League who was personally scouted by Cobb. "A slow outfielder, but he hits a ton and a half," reported T.C., thereby coining a fresh baseball expression. Harry "Slug" Heilmann had the fast hands that Cobb felt rookie Babe Ruth of Boston lacked; after hitting .282 in his baptismal Detroit year of 1916, Slug moved up to .320, .394, and finally .403, and one day into the Hall of Fame.

How Detroit landed one of the greatest batsmen of all time was a story Cobb enjoyed telling: "Frank Navin, as usual, was sitting on his fat butt when this boy came along," he snorted. "Fielder Jones [former manager of the "Hitless Wonders" White Sox of Chicago] called me from the coast to tout Heilmann. The price on the kid was only two thousand dollars. Navin hemmed and hawed. In the off-season I went to San Francisco and tested him long and hard. He hit the cover off everything we threw at him. His father was the problem—he couldn't believe his Harry would be paid a fifteen-hundred-dollar bonus for just knocking a ball around. I told the old man I was making twenty thousand a year—and his boy was a natural. Finally I convinced him that we didn't want Harry to join a bank-robbery gang back east."

But with all their rebuilding the Tigers came in third in 1916, and simultaneously a thunderbolt hit—Ty Cobb impossibly lost the league batting crown. You had to go back before the U.S. financial panic and depression of 1907 to call up a time when he had finished out of first place at the plate. With nine back-to-back titles, Cobb was the only man to take over so implacably one department of any sport. The closest behind Cobb in "king of clubs" ranking stood Hans Wagner, with four straight championships, and Nap Lajoie, with two.

Cobb gave no answer to the question, *Is he losing his grip?* nor did he concede he was slipping. Since opening day he had known trouble. Two bouts of intestinal flu had hurt. Umpires, tired of his grandstanding complaints on calls, were said by him to have formed a covert coalition against him. The story went that he and Charlie Cobb had quarreled. It was gossiped that his wife wanted a fur coat to wear at such places as Detroit's Whitney Opera House (Ignace Paderewski had performed there) and he had refused to buy the garment. On the diamond, losing all control in Chicago, he had thrown his bat into the stands after being called out sliding, almost injuring people who were slow to scatter. Ban Johnson's office suspended him for three days for that, even as he was raising his average close to .360. He trotted out an old line for the press: "There are two kinds of umpires—idiots and big-league idiots."

The Cleveland Indians had paid a record fifty thousand dollars to the Boston Red Sox for Tris Speaker in the spring of 1916, and Speaker's efforts to unseat the Peach finally paid off. Cobb, in September, at times limping, broke out with three base hits (and three steals) against Washington, but it was too late. One of the closer duels yet staged for preeminence ended:

	Games	Batting Average	Hits	Runs	Doubles	Triples	Home Runs	RBIs
Speaker	151	.386	211	102	41	8	2	83
Cobb	145	.371	201	113	31	10	5	67

To be stripped of the batting championship was a blow. Cobb was reckless enough that winter to promise his Georgia connections that it would not happen again.

HE WAS vainglorious. Carlyle's definition of self-esteem as embracing "the sixth insatiable sense" fitted him as well as the custom-tailored clothing he wore. The transcendent figure of a game drawing 16.5 million fans in 1916 and expected to surpass 20 million in 1917—unless President Wilson and the Congress were foolish enough to plunge the nation into a foreign war—the Georgian dressed the part. His suits were of the best tweed and twill, his boots were costly. He wore colorful bow ties. He wasn't seen at such fashionable restaurants as New York's Delmonico's in the cloth caps worn by many ballplayers; for him it was a fine felt hat. Cobb combed his thinning hair to make it seem more abundant, and spoke of the Tigers as "my ball club." He adopted pipe smoking and wore a diamond stickpin when visiting at the White House. He was rather steadily a guest there in prewar years.

He was dudish on the golf course, where he employed both a caddy and a forecaddy, a mark of affluence. On extended hunting trips to Dover Hall, a twenty-five-hundred acre game preserve in which he had a financial interest, Cobb brought along two gun-bearers. Widely published humorist Irvin S. Cobb (no relation), asked for an introduction and was much pleased when it was granted. Cobb missed a business date one day because he was "with MacArthur," meaning Colonel Douglas MacArthur, a one-time West Point shortshop and a fast-rising officer soon to lead the Army's Forty-second Division into combat in France.

When meeting a stranger Cobb would bark, "How *you*?" and thereafter dominate the conversation. Tris Speaker recalled that Cobb kept his hands in his pockets when a banker, doctor, Wall Streeter, club owner, or whoever approached him, as if not to pick up germs. George Stallings, ex-big-league manager and associate of Cobb, said, "Players spoke of him as 'Mr. More.' Meaning he had more hits, more runs, more steals, more records, and more money than any of them. There wasn't one of them who wasn't jealous."

Oddly-named Luzerne Atwell "Lu" Blue, a .300-hitting rookie with the Tigers in postwar years, contributed, "You should have seen other teams before a game . . . They'd circle around to cross his path, to give him the 'How are you, Ty? How's the Peach?' Oh, how they sucked around! The idea was to keep him friendly and in no mood to go on one of his wild sprees and beat the hell out of you."

For Cobb, the seasons of 1917 and 1918, against a setting of fourth- and fifth-place finishes by Tiger teams that again failed to jell and on which only one other man hit .300 or more, were a whirlwind tour. Before long his face would appear on billboards of many of the country's thirty-thousand-odd movie houses as an actor. He addressed several state legislatures, putting in a word for modification of the game's octopuslike reserve clause; he sold war bonds here and there. His absence from home and family in Augusta brought on talk of marital discord.

Baseball Magazine's Frank Lane, on one of his periodic visits to the Cobb homestead, heard whispering that Charlie Cobb was more than miffed when "Mr. Cobb"—as she called him—did not appear for the birth of their third child, Roswell Herschel, in late 1916, because he was at a movie company's stages in St. Louis, taking a screen test. While awaiting the result of that, he collected eight hundred dollars for playing in a prohibited winter game in Connecticut, which was blacklisted because the Detroit club did not share in the receipts. That cost him one more league fine. He bylined press copy on the 1917 Chicago White Sox–New York Giants World Series, adding a tribute to Hans Wagner, who was retiring from a wonderful twenty-one-year career at age forty-three.

Killing game was the most fun for Cobb. Sources reported that in a week he bagged three deer, two wild pigs, a bobcat, a few turkeys, and some one thousand squirrels for the pot with his new five-hundred-dollar shotgun and benchmade rifles. In between, he played golf at Augusta Country Club. Hooked on the game since 1913, he began at the club by shooting a 69; a few days after the splendid 69, he blew up to an 89. Poor putting by the master of the accurate ballpark bunt annoyed him so much that he had a putter blade fastened to the end of the baseball bat and went at it with this weirdest of implements.

At home, 2425 William Street in Augusta, as Lane discovered, his host had a second-floor "secret room," always kept under lock and key. Allowed a brief look into the sanctum, Lane found it a jumble of silver- and gold-plated trophies won by the Peach, racks of guns, contract and bank-dividend paper, portraits of Cobb's father but not of his mother, the first bat he'd owned, autographed photos of U.S. presidents, a library of books about Napoleon, boxes of Havana cigars, baskets of unanswered fan mail, and a supply of whiskey. "Moonshine whiskey— I always patronize home products," remarked Cobb. Napoleon? "I have all the books on his life that I ever heard of. He knew how to win against the odds." With Bonaparte he felt a rapport.

In his kennels he kept some of the finest bird dogs—pointers and setters—in the South. Cobb's Honor was a field trials champion. It had stung him that earlier, in one of the rare instances of a Dixie journalist criticizing him, he had been accused of viciously kicking and whipping one of his dogs. The accuser was Ralph McGill of the *Atlanta Constitution*. McGill wrote that T.C. lost his temper when the animal broke on point and lost a trial that his owner had expected him to win. Cobb denied every "foul" word of it. McGill, later publisher of the *Constitution* and a Pulitzer Prize–winning editorial writer, allegedly never retracted the story, but stood by it.

New York writer Fred Lieb, who followed T.C. closely for years and was a tough but fair critic, investigated and wrote as follows: "A number of hunting dogs were stabled around the Dover Hall lodge and everyone had been told not to pet them. Newspaper guests told me how while Cobb sat on the porch, one of the dogs started up to the porch . . . Cobb sprang from his chair and kicked him so hard that the squealing hound landed some 15 feet away. 'That damned dog is a hunter and knows he doesn't belong here!' he explained to my news-paper friends." Oh, yes, assured Lieb, Ty Cobb had a cruel streak, one he never bothered to conceal.

Another off-season hangout for the first citizen of Augusta was a dentist's office. Located on a back street, the place was a front for a pri-vate group of merrymakers. Behind drawn drapes the boys held "smokers"—drinking, joking, enjoying female companionship. Scan-dalous stuff, said insiders, but since the Georgia Peach was a member, not to be mentioned on the outside. Supposedly wives didn't know of it. Whether Charlie Cobb was aware of its existence was unknown. While he golfed, hunted, played exhibition ball, tried his hand at polo, drove race cars, fished, and "visited the dentist," she sat at home with three small children.

Even while asserting his need for peace, quiet, and physical recovery time, he was off in all directions. In 1917, the Sunbeam

Motion Picture Company offered him the star turn in a film titled *Somewhere in Georgia*. The melodrama's script was by Grantland Rice, his longtime admirer, and Rice pressed him to accept the offer to turn film actor. His acting in the 1912 play *The College Widow* was either a "stinker" or not too bad, depending upon which reviewer was believed. *Widow* had returned a fair profit. Said Rice, "You'll be seen all over the country and the money's very good. Ask for twenty-five thousand dollars and I think Sunbeam will pay."

By signing he would score another "first"—first pro athlete of any type to star in a Hollywood feature. John McGraw was coming out in something called *One Touch of Nature*. *Somewhere in Georgia* would beat McGraw to the screen and would overshadow all baseball three-reelers made to date.

In Los Angeles and in the East, where the movie was shot in under a month, and where he did well with the fast-action sequences, he met Douglas Fairbanks. Film idol Fairbanks came by the set to meet his favorite sport star. When shooting, Fairbanks earned fifteen thousand dollars per week. Cobb said, "I gulped when I heard that figure." The two partied, became friends, and Fairbanks suggested that he direct a first-class movie on Cobb's *real* life. Nothing ever came of it.

By early 1918 Cobb regretted the *Somewhere in Georgia* venture. He should have known better, he decided, than to lend his name to a potboiler that was in part biographical of himself. He played an ambitious young bank clerk of Atlanta who is signed by the Detroit Tigers, is hazed by the players, and miserably slinks toward home a failure . . . along the way to his hometown lady love, he is kidnapped by desperados, roped up, and left in a barn to die . . . he escapes, commandeers a mule train . . . dashes home just in time to hit a home run that wins the big game for his town's team . . . in glory marries his sweetheart . . . curtain. Playing the girl of the clerk's fancy was Elsie MacLeod, a blond ingenue.

Somewhere in Georgia struck out like Casey in "Casey at the Bat." Ward Morehouse, a Broadway critic, called it "absolutely the worst flicker I ever saw, pure hokum." One difficulty was that director George Ridgewell could not get his leading man to kiss Elsie MacLeod any more passionately than he had kissed his co-star in *College Widow*— he just pecked at MacLeod and that was it. But the $25,000 fee and expenses he received from Sunbeam exceeded his Detroit season's salary and was compensation enough for the knocks. Many years afterward, in a conversation at his California home, Tyrus lit a cigar, sat back, and with a smile related, "Out in L.A. I got to know a girl who became a great movie star. Spent two nights with her. Most beautiful woman I ever bedded." He offered few details. "Did you know," he went on, "that they smoked opium all over Hollywood back then? Some damnfools offered it to me."

IN 1917 the Tigers trained in cotton-growing Waxahachie, Texas. Navin and Jennings were not much surprised when Cobb did not report. He was in South Carolina, working out alone and with no intent of showing up in "Waxy," particularly after he learned it was raining so hard there that cows were swimming in from pasture. When he did appear, the Tigers and New York Giants were scheduled in an exhibition at Dallas. "Immediately, brother," reported one of two dozen sportswriters on hand, "the fur began to fly!"

Hostilities got under way when Cobb delayed the game—he'd golfed that morning and was cleaning mud off his spikes in the clubhouse—and Charley "Buck" Herzog, second baseman for the Giants, made an issue of it. "Well, well, the big shot finally got here!" shouted Herzog to the crowd. "The big redneck from Georgia doesn't want any part of us."

"Go get yourself a banana, you ape," returned Cobb.

Herzog kept it going and the Peach notified rival manager John McGraw that he had better quiet Herzog—"or I'll send him back to you on a stretcher." McGraw said something like, "Hurt Buck and you'll need that gun of yours to get out of here."

Herzog was a tough individual. He'd scrapped his way through stints with the Giants, Boston Braves, back to the Giants, at Cincinnati, and yet again back to the Giants in a dozen years. Claiming not to have lost a fight, he was fierce in executing the double play.

Leaving his bat at the plate before the first inning, Cobb strolled out to Herzog and his double-play partner, shortstop Art Fletcher, to notify them, "Sometime in this game I expect to get on base. And I'll be down to see you two baboons, never fear." McGraw ran onto the field to yell back.

Singling to right field, Cobb called down from first base to Herzog, "Now I'm coming, you whore's son." Herzog, taking catcher Lew McCarty's throw, advanced up the line to tag him. Cobb went for the baseman rather than the bag, ripping Herzog's pants from thigh to ankle and drawing blood. Herzog threw punches. T.C. reciprocated, then both teams got into it. Dallas fans saw a fine scrap wherein Indian Jim Thorpe, the Olympic Games celebrity playing outfield for the Giants, was knocked on his backside. McGraw and Fletcher tried to pin Cobb's arms behind him and were flattened. It concluded with umpire Bill Brennan ejecting the Peach, but not Herzog or any other Giant.

"The fight made me hungry and I ordered a big dinner at the Oriental Hotel that evening," recounted T.C. "I was eating a fine meal when Herzog suddenly showed up. He growled at me 'I want to see you—in your room, alone.'" Cobb was agreeable, "Would thirty minutes from now suit you?" he asked.

"In his room he moved the rugs and furniture back and sprinkled the floor with water for good footing with his leather shoes," said Herzog. The hallway outside soon became crowded with Giants and Tigers, eager to witness the rematch. A referee ruled everybody out except for two seconds. Herzog asked that the room "be swept of guns and swords," and it all built dramatically. One Texan offered one hundred dollars for a ringside seat and was refused. For Waxahachie the fight was rated the most interesting thereabouts since General John J. Pershing had arrived in 1916 en route to search for border guerrilla leader Pancho Villa.

Although Buck Herzog had once been an Army boxing coach, it ended quickly. Given a choice of style by Cobb, he elected for a rough-and-tumble match, with Marquis of Queensberry rules ignored. "That's where he made his biggest mistake," T.C. said later. "I had no training in boxing science."

Numerous versions of what happened were told, until eventually it began to sound like a James J. Corbett versus Bob Fitzsimmons match for the world heavyweight title. The most widely accepted account was that of Oswin K. "Jake" King, publisher of *Uncle Jake's Sport News*, who was standing in the doorway of room 404. King recreated it this way: "They exchanged a few blows, Cobb knocked Herzog against the foot of the bed and had him bending backward over the footboard at his mercy. Then it was stopped to save Buck a beating."

That was accurate in abbreviated form. The victor told Grantland Rice, who had not been a witness, "First I used some psychology on Herzog. Told him, 'You're going to get good and licked.' He showed nervousness. That was what I wanted. The fact is that I backhanded him to the floor after missing a right hook . . . then I tore a handful out of his shirt, clipped him on the chin and he flew backward . . . got to his knees and said he'd had enough. I called to the Giants in the hall that if any of them felt ambitious to step right in. Nobody did."

McGraw, in the hotel lobby next morning, cursed Cobb and threatened to have him suspended. What followed is a story that was wildly exaggerated, but was confirmed by Bugs Baer, to the effect that Cobb bent over the pudgy, forty-four-year-old, five-foot, seven-inch McGraw and pinched his nose until McGraw howled. Cobb said, "Go back to those crooked New York betting shops you run! If you were a younger man, I'd kill you!"

McGraw was a man of position and power, and he was humiliated. The producer of four World Series teams and with five more coming up, he was a manager-politician with close ties to the ruling National Commission. His Giants established New York City as the nation's sporting capital, and the "Little Napoleon" operated pretty much as he pleased. He owned stock in a Havana gambling casino, was seen in the company of big-time gambler Arnold Rothstein, and was a partner in betting shops near Herald Square. "McGraw gets away with anything he wants"—so it was said. And Cobb had twisted his nose and threatened him with homicide.

McGraw also was possessor of one of the newfangled motion-picture machines recently developed by Mutual Film Corporation, to be used for photographing his Giants in action and improving their play. McGraw had the machine on display in the hotel lobby. On the way out, Cobb kicked it over.

Having disposed of Herzog, Cobb refused to play against the Giants, and left Dallas. He foresaw the possibility of a gang attack on him. He moved his training routine to the Cincinnati camp, where Christy Mathewson managed the Reds. Legendary thirty-six-year-old Matty, or Big Six, had reached the end of throwing his fabled fadeaway pitch—good for 373 wins against only 188 losses for the Giants in seventeen seasons—and on July 20, 1916, had been traded to Cincinnati in a multiple-player exchange. Mathewson welcomed Cobb cordially.

He had inherited a Reds team with a record of two seventh-place and one last-place finish from 1914–16 and saw an opportunity to improve his situation.

"I heard about the Herzog thing," said Mathewson, according to T.C. "Did you get some help from the boys?" He meant Cobb's team, the Tigers.

"Not much," answered Cobb. "They love me on payday, but damn few were around me on the field the other day."

"If you can get loose from Detroit, Hermann will pay you more here than you're getting," offered Mathewson. "A lot more."

"Hermann" was Gary Hermann, wealthy owner of the Reds, a wily Ohio politician and big party-thrower, who would enjoy stealing the American League's single best attraction and bringing him into the National fold.

"I'm too tied up in business around Detroit," Cobb said with regret. "My contract with Navin runs out in January. Let's talk about it then."

That never came about. Mutual admirers Cobb and Mathewson would next see each other in 1918 in a U.S. Army camp in France.

McGraw's Giants were not finished with him that 1917 spring. En route home from Kansas City to open the season, the entire team telegraphed him: "It's safe to rejoin your club now. We've left Texas."

The Peach said he wired back: "How's McGraw's nose?"

IN 1917 and in 1918 Cobb was more short-tempered than usual, mostly because at ages thirty and thirty-one he twice dislocated his shoulder diving for outfield chances. Detroit's revamped pitching staff, headed by Hooks Dauss and Bernie Boland, was inadequate. No Tiger moundsman won more than 17 games in either of the two years, and the team limped in at fourth and seventh places. There was "Cobb for manager" noise from the stands at Navin Field.

His injuries healed and nothing was changed—he led the American League in almost everything. In 1917 his 225 base hits, 44 doubles, 23 triples, 336 total bases, .571 slugging average, and 55 steals stood in front. Regaining the batting title at .383, he far outhit the field. George Sisler, the young St. Louis star, was 30 points behind him and Tris Speaker 31, while the National League's leading hitter, outfielder Edd Roush of Cincinnati, trailed by 42 points.

In the war-shortened 1918 season, Cobb didn't pause. His .382 average was well ahead of ex–Tiger first baseman George Burns's .352 at Philadelphia. According to Cobb, an argument he had with Navin earlier, in March of 1918, went as follows:

Cobb: "Don't lose Burns. He's just learning to hit."

Navin: "I'm dealing with Connie Mack."

Cobb: "No! No! No! Burns is only twenty-five, for Chrissake, and he's big and can run . . . and . . . oh, for Chrissake!"

Away went Burns to the Yankees, who immediately traded him to the A's for outfielder Francesco Stephano Pezzolo (or Pezzullo), playing as Ping Bodie. Burns hit better than .300 for Mack's Athletics and other teams in seven of the next nine seasons, and in 1926 was voted the American League's most valuable player.

Unable to relax when benched by his injuries, Cobb suggested that Hughie Jennings restrict himself to coaching only on the first-base line, while Cobb took over the more-important third-base pathway. Umpires hated him even more at close range. He invaded the batter's box to kick dirt and dispute calls. He would go into an act, putting the ball through a semimicroscopic examination, slowly turning it, claiming that it had been doctored. Some said that Cobb carried a little glob of pine tar in the palm of his hand, which he would apply during the ball testing. When the pitcher was angry enough to lose control, Cobb would toss the ball on the grass nowhere near the batterymates, and say, "Well, pitch it—what the hell are you waiting for?"

About home runs he was phobic. Except when the bases were loaded, homers carried much less value than the single base hit ringing clear, he claimed, followed by more singles and concomitant stealing. Yet one of his own hits he liked best was a homer struck in St. Louis, following a long triple in his previous time at bat. This one soared out of sight over the left-field bleachers—so far that writers judged it as even longer than earlier blasts by Shoeless Joe Jackson and Babe Ruth, which had carried an estimated five-hundred-odd feet. When he felt like it, this percentage player could hit for distance.

After going 7 for 9 in a Cleveland doubleheader in August 1918 and behaving like a good guy for weeks, Cobb took on an unlikely opponent: the U.S. Customs station at the Canadian-American border. There he threw a tantrum so obnoxious that Customs considered arresting him. Jack Miner, a Canadian big-game guide, famous for his woodcraft and a close friend of Cobb, came across on a ferry to be the Peach's guest at a ball game. Customs closely checked Miner's luggage for illegal booze. Cobb, fuming over the delay, got into a squabble with ferryboat passengers, whom he felt crowded too closely around him. Most of them only wanted to shake his hand.

He threw elbows and yelled, "Goddammit, nobody pushes me around!" A Customs man suggested that jail might cool him off, at which point the Greatest Ballplayer on Earth make a complete fool of himself. "I can lick any son of a bitch here!" he raged at officials. Finally, Miner, much embarrassed as a guest in the United States, calmed Cobb and they proceeded to the ball game.

"I never could understand why he would do a thing like that," said Miner when long later a Canadian newspaper asked about it. "I liked Cobb, but never could understand him."

The United States was at war now, and Cobb knew it was inevitable that he would join one of the services. But before he signed up, he wanted to be guaranteed a commission, preferably with the Army. During a late-season 1918 road trip with the Tigers to Washington, D.C., he set out to wear a captain's bars.

CHAPTER EIGHTEEN

POISON GAS AND THE BABE

As Ty Cobb saw the waging of war, it was inevitable and natural to mankind—and could even be beneficial. He planned martial arts training for his sons when they reached prep-school age. Early in 1918, lecturing American patriots on warfare at a rally in Atlanta, he declared, "When you have a winner and loser, it settles disputes over territory. That might not last long. But after the Germans get their asses kicked in the one going on now, you won't be hearing from them for quite a while."

His combative nature and his intelligence made Cobb ideal officer material in World War I. Yet as the United States entered the second summer of conflict against Germany's massive forces, he surprised the public by staying on the sidelines. Through some of the heaviest fighting, from late 1917 until well in 1918, Cobb remained a noncombatant.

In so doing, he was far from alone within baseball. So many big-leaguers elected not to join up that charges of slackerism were leveled against the game. In the summer of 1918, while 600,000 American troops were pouring into French ports and the Great War's outcome hung in the balance, Cobb and other stars called unwelcome attention to themselves by continuing as civilians and playing out an abbreviated big-league schedule.

The Georgian put on his usual brilliant show. In a 1918 season shortened by War Department decree, he outhit everyone in the league. That was not surprising. But then, suddenly, belatedly, he reversed himself and made headlines by joining the Army.

FORTY-TWO YEARS later, at a 1960 social get-together of Cobb and Casey Stengel at Cobb's home in the northern California millionaires' colony of Atherton, the two old friends spoke of their World War I experiences and other matters. Stengel had come to visit a man he had always idolized. In the past, during crises in Stengel's career, Cobb had given helpful advice and practical assistance. He had been there with counsel on where Casey could find another job when the Brooklyn Dodgers fired him as manager in 1936. And he had recommended the Dutchman for employment when the Boston Braves let him go as field chief in 1943. In both cases, Cobb's word in the right ears had helped the vagabond Casey—he was with thirteen teams as player or manager in fifty-six seasons—survive in baseball. Then, six weeks before Stengel came visiting at Atherton, it had happened again: the Old Perfesser had been ousted by the New York Yankees, even though he had just won another pennant for the owners. After the Yankees narrowly lost the ensuing World Series to Pittsburgh, Stengel had been dropped by owners Dan Topping and Del Webb.

Over whiskey sodas at Cobb's mansion, the two talked at length. An aging Stengel was confused and hurt. He wondered if at this point he should retire. "I win ten pennants for the Yanks and I'm out on the street," he said gloomily.

"I tried managing," said Cobb. "It's the shits."

"For twelve months of the year," said Stengel.

The practical Cobb asked, "Did New York pay you off in full?"

"Every dime," said Stengel. "I was makin' a hundred and sixty thousand and that's what I got upon leavin'."

Said Cobb, "Oh, well then . . ." He meant that with his friend paid off, Casey really had no big problem. Baseball managers were born to be fired. In Cobb's view, $160,000 should relieve the pain Casey was feeling.

"The mayor of New York and some rich people are startin' up a new club, the Metropolitans," mentioned Casey. "They are talkin' to me about comin' in to manage."

Aware of the formation of the Mets of the National League, Cobb disliked the idea. "They have about a dozen bosses and damned few players," he warned. "Don't touch it." However, the Old Perfesser did make a comeback with the Mets in 1962, lending his quaint personality to the most hilarious and inept band of losers yet to step on a major-league field. During the four seasons in which Stengel led them, the Mets finished in tenth and last place all four times. Finally they jumped all the way to ninth place. By then, Stengel had beaten his critics to it; he had retired, permanently. "What I needed with those Mets," he informed Cobb later, "was an embalmer."

As I listened in on their rambling conversation in 1960, the seventy-one-year-old Stengel and the ailing seventy-three-year-old Peach fell to recalling World War I. Casey remarked that he had experienced an easy war. "Remember Eddie Grant?" he asked. "Got himself killed in France with the artillery."

"Grant of the Giants," said Cobb. "Third baseman. Good field, fair hitter. Too bad about him."

"I never heard a shot fired," carried on Stengel. "All I did was hand out baseball equipment to some fellas when they made me sports director at the Brooklyn Navy Yard. I just waited it out until I could get back playin' with Pittsburgh."

"Well, I heard some shots," retorted Cobb. "Once I almost got blown up coming out of a toilet."

Casey found that funny. "You should have stayed out of the war like so many baseball guys did."

"For God's sakes, Casey, how could I do that?"

"No, I guess you couldn't," said Stengel.

Cobb's point was obvious. If he had not voluntarily enlisted in the armed forces, his public reputation would have been permanently blackened. He was too famous, and too well known for supporting President Woodrow Wilson's declaration of war with Germany, issued back in April of 1917, to remain an observer. Americans were dying by the thousands on the western front. The country's watchword—"every able-bodied man should do his bit"—had become more and more a critical issue. As 1918 wore on, editorial writers, seeing how few professional athletes had responded to the call, urged a crackdown by the government.

Cobb's status as the father of three children, ages two to eight, left him ineligible for conscription by his Georgia draft board; he was rated Division Two and exempt. Yet from spring training time on, he had felt uneasy about staying out. While not singled out as a war-dodger, he was included by association in press broadsides directed at organized baseball for its reluctance to part with prominent talent. During pre-season spring training, teams had marched in infantry-type formations, with bats on their shoulders simulating rifles. Army sergeants in some cases handled the drilling. Players found the exercise both a waste of time and deceiving. Eventually the program was cancelled.

It would not suffice for Cobb to stand on dugout roofs with movie stars and other celebrities and sell Liberty Bonds and war stamps before games. Nor would the Peach take a war-connected job in a shipyard or munitions plant, as some big-leaguers had done. It was not his style.

Still, there was nothing precipitous about Cobb's way of doing things when away from the ball field. He took his time about enlisting in the Army, and prepared for a possible long absence by turning over his complicated business affairs to safe hands. "I figured on maybe a year or more of war," he said. His principal investments were in auto shares, among them Ford and Cadillac, in textile buying, real estate, cotton futures, and in product endorsements. Much of this activity was concentrated in Detroit. The City on the Straits had grown from 488,766 citizens in 1910 to more than 900,000 by 1918. In (or out) of a wartime boom, people were approaching Cobb with a new financial proposition every few weeks, "some of them hard to turn down."

One outstanding offer came from Carl Fisher of Fisher Auto Body Company. Back in 1904, racing driver Fisher had put acetylene lamps on his Packard, thereby introducing the night driving of cars, and became a millionaire. As of 1917–18, Fisher had the Indianapolis 500 event going, drawing large crowds, and he had invited Cobb to buy in and join his board of directors. Cobb had held off on accepting, since he was unable to give Indy much time and his future was so undecided.

OTHER COMPLICATIONS preceded his departure for the war theater. One of his children, Herschel, had been ill and might need him around. And in a small way, or so he said, he had already contributed to defeating the German war machine. He told an odd, unconfirmable story of the French running short of recoil mechanisms for their big-cannon 75s, and their appeal to the United States for help. This led to War Department armorers visiting John Dodge, of Dodge Motors in Detroit, to determine whether Dodge had the manufacturing capability for such precision parts. "Dodge was having trouble making the deal," claimed Cobb. "I wined and dined them and showed the government boys such a good time at the ballpark that they decided Dodge was okay . . . and finally signed a contract." So he told it. Malcolm Bingay's history, *Detroit Is My Own Home Town*, reports the incident, but does not include Cobb as a go-between.

The decisive factor in the summer of 1918, convincing Cobb that perhaps he had delayed too long in signing on with the American Expeditionary Force, was public opinion. The press renewed attacks on the maneuvering by ball-club owners to keep their rosters as intact as possible through draft-exemption loopholes. "With only a few boxoffice names in uniform," the *New York Times* declared, "the so-called 'magnates' have proclaimed their adherence to the sleazy fallacy of 'business as usual,' a policy not calculated to make us proud of the game as an American institution." *Stars and Stripes* spoke coldly of the notion of baseball as an essential American recreation. "Bullets, not bats" was the way some put it.

The crunch began for team owners on May 23, 1918, when Provost Marshal Enoch Crowder issued a "work-or-fight" order, setting July 1 as the deadline for players to enter needed war work or face induction into service. Slackerism was charged, not just hinted. Secretary of War Newton D. Baker held firm, brushing aside exemption requests by owners, even when Woodrow Wilson, on July 27, 1918, issued a letter stating that he saw "no necessity" for stopping or curtailing major-league play. But Baker did give the owners until September 1, or through Labor Day, to finish a shortened schedule of 126 to 128 games.

The World Series remained imperiled. About to win the National League pennant, the Chicago Cubs, fearing drafts of men before the Series, asked for a written federal guarantee that the Classic would be saved. A special two-week grace period was granted to the Cubs and their likely opponent, the Boston Red Sox, to meet in the Series.

Between the months of June and October many of the top big-leaguers went off to war. Among them—poorly trained for the battlefield in the short preparatory time available—were Eddie Collins, Grover Cleveland "Old Pete" Alexander (who would be badly shell-shocked in trench combat and have his hearing permanently impaired), Jimmy Dykes, Sam Rice, Ernie Shore, Harry Heilmann (injured aboard a submarine), Herb Pennock, Wally Pipp, Eddie Grant (killed), and Rabbit Maranville. "They gave the boys a short-arm inspection, handed them a gun, and that was it," Cobb recalled. Some men reached the front, while others staged exhibition games for the troops. Reportedly, 124 American Leaguers and 103 National Leaguers entered the armed forces. Three ballplayers were known to have become fatalities. Such commitment was seen by most citizens as considerably more satisfactory than the thousands of bats, balls, and mitts earlier sent overseas by the leagues, and the declared $7 million in Liberty Bonds and for the Red Cross raised by sixteen teams.

Teams could field only patchwork lineups. Other than reactivating recently retired players, the only source of resupply in late 1918 was the minor leagues, themselves playing shrunken schedules. Records disagree, but one source shows that of nine lower leagues starting the 1918 season, only one, the International League, completed it in full. Class AA and A talent moved up to fill holes. If the war continued into 1919, there might be no baseball at all, at least not of a caliber worth watching.

Ban Johnson, head of an American League that he had personally created in 1901 and toughly, inflexibly ruled thereafter, saw little or no profit ahead. On May 24, one day after the work-or-fight edict, he had announced that the AL would close for the duration. The member clubs, however, defied Johnson and—in a strong indication that his power was slipping—kept going to Labor Day. Cobb was able to get into 111 games, where he finished first in AL triples and second in runs scored. His .382 batting average handily led both leagues. Zack Wheat of Brooklyn topped the National League with .355 in 105 games. Toward the truncated season's end, in Boston, the Peach hammered a home run—"about the longest I ever hit"—into a brewery across from Fenway Park. The story went that workers were bottling beer when the ball crashed through a window, hit a tub, and sprayed suds around. Cobb's "beer-buster" was almost as impressive as his nine base hits in three games at St. Louis.

Income from the World Series, which began September 5, withered to the extent that each Boston Red Sox player was paid an $890 winner's pittance, while each losing-side Cub drew $535. What went down as the lowest Series payout in history was caused in part by a controversial new format dictated by the National Commission, whereby second-, third-, and fourth-place teams of each league shared in the division. That peremptory ruling—players were not consulted by the commission in making it—cut the already meager pie into so many pieces that the Red Sox and Cubs demanded that the split be postponed until after the war.

Commission members met to settle it with some forty players of both sides under the stands before the fifth game at Boston. Beginning as a shouting match, it blew up into a near riot. Shoves were exchanged. Police with paddy wagons had to be summoned. Players threatened not to take the field and shut down the Series. Ban Johnson of the National Commission was of no help. Known to be a hard drinker, Johnson showed up half-intoxicated and made a maudlin appeal to "you boys" to play ball.

For an hour the field remained empty of contestants, while a crowd of some twenty thousand booed and irate umpires considered an unprecedented double forfeit of the proudest pageant of American sports. Cobb, seated in the press box as a guest of Boston, did not join the brannigan. "I might have punched someone," he said later. He saw the rebellion as presaging wholesale strikes in the future against the owners' greed. Ballplayers he thought, would be forced to take drastic measures in future labor-management negotiations.

The commissioners held fast on the division of money, until finally, with wounded soldiers in the stands as guests, the game began. Cobb cagily advised the teams to have a public statement from them read before the first pitch was made. Commissioners objected, but ex–Boston mayor John F. "Honey Fitz" Fitzgerald stood at the home plate with a megaphone to announce the teams' message: "We will play not because we think we are getting a fair deal, which we are not. But we will play for the sake of the public, for the good name of baseball and for the wounded Army and Navy men in the grandstand."

"The owners are entirely to blame," Cobb charged in an Associated Press interview. "The teams were not doing their best out there today, and that's deadly for baseball." In confirmation, the Red Sox won the Series with an incredible .186 team batting average in six games, against a .210 for the Cubs.

Players were angered by another management tactic. Those who were not absent at war or engaged in war-related industries were hit by an owners' scheme for avoiding payment of the balance of their salaries for the shortened season. This was done by the blatant subterfuge of "releasing" all of those still in baseball uniform with ten days' notice. Normally, such releases would have made them free agents, but the owners of franchises avoided that with a gentlemen's agreement not to deal with other clubs' players. The early releases saved owners an estimated $200,000. Cobb thought it an unconscionable act and said so, terming it worse than slicing up World Series receipts among clubs finishing far out of first place: "Some logic that is." As for himself, Cobb was paid in full by Detroit.

In the fifteenth, war-spoiled World Series, Babe Ruth, who remained out of the Great War, pitched a six-hit, 1–0 shutout for the Sox. During the regular season of 1918, the Babe, who had begun to play outfield when not pitching, had hit 11 home runs to tie Tillie Walker of the Athletics for the league title. He thereby established himself as the foremost two-way threat since mustachioed little John Montgomery Ward won 158 games as a pitcher for Providence, the New York Giants, and others from 1878 through 1894, while batting .371 and .348 in good years. On the mound against the Cubs, Ruth carried with him a mark of 13 consecutive scoreless innings pitched in previous Series competition. In this Series he extended the record to a phenomenal 29⅔ shutout innings, which would stand until Whitey Ford, the superb southpaw of Casey Stengel's Yankees, topped it in 1961.

Cobb happened to be on the same New York Central train that was taking Ruth to New York on a business matter after the Series. Out of curiosity, Cobb asked Ruth, "Why were you throwing at Max Flack?"

"Flack, hell," said Babe. "That was that other fielder—Mann."

"No, it was Flack you got right between the eyes in the first game," corrected Cobb. "Les Mann is a right-hander. Flack is a lefty."

"Jeez, whattayaknow," said Ruth. "I was throwing at the wrong monkey all afternoon!" (This same story has been told by others, with variations on Cobb's version.)

These and other events were of lesser interest to the masses of Americans. In August and September, German forces retreated in Flanders, U.S. troops eliminated the Saint Mihiel salient, attacked in the Argonne, and helped break the powerful Hindenburg line. As a theme song, "Over There" sounded more and more optimistic. By the time that Germany gave up on November 11, 1918, the United States had embarked 2,045,169 men for European service, and suffered 320,710 casualties.

DURING THE weeks before the 1918 season ended, Cobb made four long-calculated moves. He notified Frank Navin that he would never be interested in field-managing the Tigers, if offered the post, but only in a front-office position—perhaps as chief operations executive—provided the salary was right. Secondly, he moved his wife and children from Detroit back into the family's comfortable Augusta residence on William Street, with its two black houseboys and cook—"Mr. Ty's mansion," as townspeople called it. Further, in consideration of going into battle, he wrote a will (later on the testament was canceled and eventually a new one substituted). Fourthly, in August, with the baseball season still on, Cobb voluntarily enlisted in the Army. His activation was to come on October 1.

"I did a little negotiating," he said of his insistence upon becoming a commissioned officer. Cobb generally got what he wanted and, while the Tigers were playing at Washington, he met with a general involved in recruitment. "We talked," said Cobb, "for about an hour." He was recommended for a captaincy. With that arranged, he underwent a physical and a standard psychological test. "Funny result on that," he remembered. "The doctors made the finding that I was normal, but on the *shy* side. I wasn't an ego type because of the '*shyness.*'" That gave the Peach a wry laugh.

For an assignment Cobb requested and received duty with the Chemical Warfare Service. It was a puzzling choice. With his expert eye for distance and experience with hunting and guns, the Field Artillery would have best suited him. Why become involved with notoriously deadly gas when other options existed? German strategists had introduced airborne poison gas at the second battle of Ypres in 1915 and thereafter employed it widely. Use of the weapon horrified neutral nations and set the U.S. high command to seeking counter-measures. Chlorine-based "mustard" gas seared the lungs and often asphixiated its victims. Phosgene gas was as bad or worse; before they died, soldiers turned a livid purple in the face.

Gas knew no rank: six weeks after Colonel Douglas MacArthur reached combat, his eyesight was threatened by gas exposure and he went around blindfolded for a week. "Silent death" attacks were all the more terrifying because the available gas masks were distrusted by the men in the trenches. "I knew the masks were not much good, but they were working on improvements," Cobb said.

Cobb was well aware of the high risk with chemicals. Charlie Cobb and many Georgians had urged him to enlist elsewhere. At the time, Cobb offered only one explanation: "Christy Mathewson and Branch Rickey are in Chemical—they are guys I like and friends." Another reason could have been the hard criticism by newspapers of sports figures not in uniform for the United States, so that he felt the need for an act of bravado. Still another reason might have concerned the amount of publicity he attracted in the press; Cobb habitually checked out newspapers and magazines, assuring himself that his notices came regularly and in prominent type. Sometimes he would approach editors of sports periodicals with ideas for punchy articles, such as "How I Flash Signals from Center Field." The resultant ghost-written pieces would appear in the form of "as told by Ty Cobb" or as mislabled straight byliners. "Cobb of Chemical War" was sure to make a newsplay. Poison gas carried a special image. Finally, there was reason number four: he was absolutely fearless.

His Army orders were to report to a troopship on October 1 and be given crash training in France as a technical advisor attached to the so-called Gas and Flame units. Before leaving, he turned over one of his businesses—selling Bevo, a soda pop—to friends in the South. His franchise for Bevo covered an area containing numerous Army camps. In dry-state Georgia a soldier could not legally buy a hard drink. Cobb recalled, "The local boys introduced them to 'White Lightning' [native liquor so potent it could lift a man inches off the ground] and my Bevo sold well as a mixer." At least it reduced the wallop.

In the weeks before his embarkation for Bordeaux, he was at his playing best—and at his most waspish. There had been steady friction through 1918 between Cobb and a majority of the Tigers. Many of them complained to Jennings, and thus to Navin, that Cobb was more and more undermining existing methods, and that he had caused at least three semiregulars to lose their jobs through his influence with team stockholders. Recently he had "demoralized" Harry Heilmann. That highly promising twenty-four-year-old outfielder, discovered by Cobb in the bushes in 1916, was in T.C.'s doghouse for not hitting .300 from the start. Cobb had loaned Heilmann some of his special-model, thirty-nine-ounce black bats, but a defiant Slug seldom used them. He liked his own clubs. "Stubborn goddamn hayshaker," Cobb called Heilmann, for whom he had predicted so much, and who in the 1920s would arrive to deliver no less than 640 doubles, triples, and home runs, and gain stardom.

A dispirited group, the Tigers had reacted poorly to Cobb's steady prodding to snap out of it and at least make a pass at a pennant. As Jennings became increasingly ineffective on the bench, his captain at times took over as surrogate manager, going so far as to call time-out, run in from center field, chew out the pitcher, and with arm-gestures correct his throwing motion. By custom, mound conferences were quiet, private affairs. Cobb humiliated pitchers in public view.

Pitcher Happy Finneran, in retirement, thought that Cobb incited spite to make himself more visible. Finneran and others also pointed out that, although without military training or a college education, he was soon to become an Army captain. It did not hurt to have played poker with U.S. presidents.

Except for the Series, the baseball season shut down as a wartime casualty on September 2. Fred Lieb, in *The Detroit Tigers*, noted, "In a dismal team season, only Tyrus kept the old batting eye aflame. He was two things—fierce and fiercer." Opponents searched for signs of slow-down in him thirteen years from the start of his career, and found none, other than a drop-off in stealing output. There were intervals when he went hitless in doubleheaders. Usually that came when he was recuperating from an injury. In May he missed ten games with a torn right shoulder, in July he was out for six more with a left shoulder jammed in sliding. A shinbone bled and he played on in a bandage. Overriding his latest list of setbacks, his double and triple beat the Yankees that fall. He went 6 for 9 against Cleveland in a double bill, a blazing 9 for 12 in a St. Louis series, and against the battery of catcher Cy Perkins and pitcher Scott Perry of the Athletics stole home base twice in nine innings. "I watch the catcher's eyes on a steal," he explained.

"He can't fake me waving his mitt. Where he looks will be the ball and I come in accordingly." In effect, Cobb was playing both offense and defense simultaneously. "His secret is," said Connie Mack, "that he thinks two plays ahead of everybody else."

His home-plate stealing was based on more than speed and surprise. He had the ability to swivel his neck, see the ball's course, and react. Another tactic was to wear extra-long uniform sleeves, which flapped and distracted the pitchers and also protected his elbows while doing a "deep slide," one in which he dug up a curtain of dirt to confuse basemen and umpires.

In stretching hits he still had no master. Among his more show-stopping feats was a play at Boston in which Cobb, at second base, scored on an infield out without an error being involved. This one he conjured up by taking an extra-long lead, so that when the ball was bouncing along—a slow roller to shortstop Everett Scott—he had nearly reached third base. While Scott was routinely throwing out the batter to first baseman Stuffy McInnis, Cobb sped onward, reached home in a tie with McInnis's fairly good throw, crashed into catcher Sam Agnew, deflected the ball with his hip, and was safe. Cobb's postgame analysis: "It took six separate actions by three players to get me, didn't it?"—the shortstop's catch and throw, the first-sacker's catch and throw, the catcher's reception and tag. In combination the ball had to travel some 320 feet, as Cobb had long before calculated. For other fast base runners this would not work. They saw the odds as much too long. As Cobb viewed it, other base runners were not in the right frame of mind to face long odds and beat them. It was a matter of confidence defeating geometry.

New players up from the minors as wartime replacements, who until then had not seen Cobb in action, were amazed. Even some old pros still fell for his sleight of hand. In a Washington game, he caused Clyde "Deerfoot" Milan, the base runner at second, to presume that a seemingly sprinting-in Peach could not reach a humpbacked liner hit to him in center field. Milan thought he saw Cobb running hard, but too late to make the catch. He hesitated, then lit out for third. Suddenly making the catch, Cobb easily doubled Milan off second base. Explanation: T.C. had been pumping his legs up and down, with glove outstretched, depicting a missed catch and practically running in the same spot—applied pantomime. It was all in the deceptive timing.

Old tricks or new, the war-bound Georgian left them something to remember him by in two 1918 season-ending games with the defending league champion Chicago White Sox. Cobb especially enjoyed beating the proud Sox. He held a low regard for the methods of their manager, Clarence "Pants" Rowland, and maintained a holdover dislike for the Sox's fine pitcher, Eddie Cicotte, with whom he'd fought with fists in their minor-league Augusta days. T.C. suspected that during Tiger appearances at Chicago, fans were encouraged by Cicotte to curse him and throw junk. Formerly losers, the Sox had advanced by the season from third to second during 1915–16, until in 1917 they had wrested the league championship from the Boston Red Sox. But for now, at the end of 1918 play, Cobb was motivated by the Chicagoans' fall from the top to a sixth-place finish. He took the opportunity of catching the Sox on a downswing to even up old scores. Any Detroit–White Sox series was played up because it might mark the end of his career. Cobb broadly hinted of retirement, saying that chronic back and leg pain left him unable to concentrate; he sensed that it was time to get out. He confided this to St. Louis columnist T. C. David that September. David wrote a sob-story piece—"Is the Fabulous One Lost to the Game?"

On Labor Day before the start of the season-ending home doubleheader with Chicago, Cobb walked past the White Sox bench, singled out Cicotte, and growled, "You'll get it today, bo. That's for sure." Helping to knock Cicotte out of the box early, he had three hits, two triples included, in each of two games. The aroused Tigers pounded their opponents, 11–5 and 7–2. One field fight broke out. Cobb stayed out of it. He was concentrating on Cicotte.

WHILE PREPARING to report to the Chemical Warfare Service in October, Cobb issued a statement that seemed to reflect his sensitivity to arriving at such a late date in his country's service. His statement, published by *Baseball Magazine*, was headlined "Why I Went Into The Army" and was subheaded by the publisher "What Induced The Great Star To Renounce A $20,000 Job For A Difficult And Dangerous Commission In France." His explanation was written in the first person. In tone it sounded like a defense against recent newspaper slaps at ballplayers. He wrote: "A few more days and I shall have played my last big league game. I am bowing out. Some years ago I signed a long-term contract [with Detroit] which expires this Fall. Ordinarily I would be interested in renewing that contract on favorable terms. Now it doesn't occasion me the slightest concern. For I have signed another contract. I have taken another job."

In his rambling announcement he said, "By the time my bit in the Army is finished I shall probably be too old and used up to resume my former profession." And then came: "After a good deal of deliberation I came to the conclusion that I could not afford to stay out of the war. And when I say afford, don't think that I mean anything in a business sense. I am surely not taking the job for the money there is in it, as everyone must know."

Then: "The public has knocked baseball unmercifully. This knocking has been uncalled for. Anyone who calls me a slacker is dead wrong. That I am going in as a captain will be criticized . . . but none can say that I will be protected from danger more than the humblest private in the trenches. If I were a general, it might be different. As a captain I shall be in the same position as an enlisted man." Cobb also called attention to the fact that he had chosen chemical warfare duty, "which," he mentioned, "is well known to be the most hazardous of just about any service."

In a well-tailored uniform and trench coat he wore for photo-taking, the captain was off to France by ship on October 6. He carried with him his own pistol, his "varmint" gun.

Cobb's fame counted for little in the way of earning him special treatment after he arrived and was assigned to Hanlon Field, near Chaumont, France, southeast of Paris. Hanlon was an auxiliary airfield not in a combat zone, but vulnerable to aircraft attack and night infiltration by Boche raiders. In three cases Cobb had close escapes. In one instance, a party of Germans crept in to hit the Hanlon installation with grenades thrown at parked U.S. aircraft; Cobb, jumping from his nearby bunk, fired shots with his revolver. "Don't know if I hit anyone," he spoke of it. "But with the whole camp shooting back, the bastards pulled out in a hurry."

At Hanlon he took instruction in the use of a developmental charcoal-filtered mask effective against aerial spraying of several different gases. In the trenches, doughboys never knew when and where the killer vapors would be concentrated. The AEF's Gas and Flame section was protective, not offensive; it required clamping of the mask onto the face upon first smelling an assault. Masking had to be done immediately, if not sooner.

Cobb described what happened near Chaumont. "We had hundreds of soldiers to train. We wound up drilling the damnedest bunch of culls that World War I ever grouped in one outfit. And the masks were very awkward. They were attached by a tube to a canister dangling around the neck . . . The soldier inhaled clean air through the tube held in his mouth and which was filtered through a charcoal-soda lime . . . A nose clip was supposed to prevent breathing through the nostrils. But men forgot and sometimes they panicked.

"One day we marched about eighty of our culls into a dark, airtight chamber for practice. Real mustard gas was to be released right after a signal was given warning us to snap masks into place and file out in an orderly way. Then we were to dive into trenches as if under machine-gun fire. Well, the warning signal was poorly given and a lot of us missed it, including Christy Mathewson and me. Christy was an instructor in Chemical, too. So were Branch Rickey and George Sisler."

Men screamed when they breathed a smell of death. Crazy with fear, they piled up to escape, a hopeless tangle of bodies. "As soon as I realized what was happening," went Cobb, "I fixed my mask . . . groped my way over to a wall, and worked toward the door. I fell outside . . . was damned lucky. Most of the poor bastards were trapped inside. When it was over there were sixteen bodies stretched out on the ground. Eight men died within hours of lung damage. In a few days, others were crippled."

Cobb had been exposed to enough poison gas that for the next weeks a colorless discharge drained from his chest; he felt weak and had a hacking cough. He remembered Christy Mathewson telling him, "Ty, I got a good dose of the stuff. I feel terrible." Mathewson had not only been in the chamber with Cobb, but earlier had inspected trenches for gas residue.

Following illness and hospitalization, Mathewson was shipped home, where in 1919 he became John McGraw's right-hand man with the Giants and in 1923 president of the Boston Braves. Developing tuberculosis of both lungs, he was sent to a sanatorium at Saranac Lake, New York, known for its work in dealing with the "white plague." Four years later, Cobb went to visit Mathewson. Big Six was a cripple, unable to move anything but his fingers and forearms. He died at Saranac at the age of forty-five on October 7, 1925, on the day the World Series opened. Thirty-six thousand Series fans stood as the flag was lowered to half-mast and sang "Nearer My God to Thee."

Cobb usually avoided funerals, but that one he attended. "Big Six looked peaceful in his coffin," he said. "That damned gas got him, the doctors said. Almost got me."

Within days of the gas episode, and still not fully recovered from his own exposure, the Peach had another close escape when a stray shell exploded close by the Hanlon encampment. He had just left an outdoor latrine when the shell burst and a sliver of metal grazed his head. The fragment missed one of his eyes, but not by much. He envisioned the headline that might have made—"TY COBB KILLED LEAVING CRAPPER." A bit closer and he could have been half-blinded.

Germany capitulated on November 11, and he was aboard one of the first troopships home, the *Leviathan*. Douglas MacArthur, winner of nine medals in the war, sent one of his aides to the dock at Brest to bid a lightly bandaged Cobb bon voyage. En route to New York Cobb visited the wounded, saw men die. He reached New York on December 6. He had been at war for sixty-seven days—"a cup of coffee" in baseball parlance.

Sportswriters waiting at the dock asked for verification of his startling earlier word that he had swung his last bat. "That's right," replied Cobb snappily. "I'm retiring. I've been in eighteen hundred games and sixteen thousand innings in fourteen years. That's enough at my age." He was just turning thirty-two.

Skeptical Damon Runyon of the *New York American* told readers that he much doubted that "a legend," Cobb, was bowing out. Runyon thought he needed strife and the crowd's roar too much to leave the stage.

WHILE THE nation celebrated the coming of peace, Cobb, the inveterate investor in prime business properties, made good use of his threat to leave baseball. During the war years his financial portfolio had steadily expanded, and after 1918 he systematically increased it. Possessing an independent fortune placed him in an all but unique position among ballplayers, giving him bargaining power against stipulations of his holdover Detroit contract. By now his overall holdings had reached approximately $700,000. Cotton shares that Cobb wisely had bought in the past half-dozen years had tripled in value because of wartime demand and current shortages. Furthermore, he had retained his United Motors and Timken Roller Bearings blue-chip stocks, and he remained partner in a consortium building housing for low-income whites and blacks in Georgia and Alabama.

Magazines and feature syndicates paid him up to two thousand dollars for "signed" articles. Some of baseball's first bonus clauses had been shrewdly designed by Cobb back in 1915. One bonus covered his averaging .300 or more at bat in subsequent seasons ("which was like stealing the Detroit organization's money"). Another concerned his playing in at least 120 seasonal games (he missed this only once between 1907 and the war year). He also demanded payment for certain team public-relations appearances.

Before gaining sophistication, Cobb had been a poor platform speaker, self-conscious and stumbling over multisyllabic words. By attending speech classes financed by the Wheeler Syndicate, which acted as his booking agent, he gained sureness on his feet. At one postwar banquet held in his honor at Detroit's Hotel Statler, T.C. spoke to six hundred people with such lines as "Out where the grass is green I feel best placed to express myself. I am a hitter and fielder, not an orator. However, since you have seen fit to stage this appreciated affair, I shall do my best to accommodate your interest—which, like mine, is baseball." He ended to an ovation.

He was among the first, as far back as 1910, to answer letters from his fans. Using the green ink he favored, Cobb scrawled notes to anyone from a barber in Iowa to a small boy in California. Often worshipers writing in would be startled and overjoyed to receive from him a whole letter, signed, "Your Friend—Tyrus R. Cobb." (In later years his practice would be very different.)

He was home in Augusta in December 1918 for his thirty-second birthday celebration and to resume mowing down more wild game. He bagged thirty turkeys in one shoot. Team owners, meeting that winter for the purpose of recouping wartime losses, voted to place limitations on club payrolls. The cuts, in some cases, ran deep—several thousand dollars per man. Colonel Tillinghast L'Hommedieu Huston, wealthy contractor and partner with brewery millionaire Jacob Ruppert in ownership of the Yankees, was quoted, "The players can sign at the new salaries offered—or not at all." Payroll realignment meant reductions across the board.

Frank Navin barely had broken even on Detroit receipts (or else lost forty thousand dollars, as he claimed) in 1918, while finishing seventh and being forced to use as wartime stopgaps six different first basemen and such nonentities as Joe Cobb (no relation), Tubby Spencer, Archie Yelle, and Art Griggs. Navin joined those owners who feared a continuing recession at the gate. The number of roster players per team was lowered from twenty-five to twenty-one. Spring-training time was shortened. Cheaper road hotels were used, and both leagues set the schedule at only 140 games.

The short-scheduling proved a costly mistake. The big leagues rebounded in 1919 to attract 6,432,439 customers, a major gain; had the "wise men" promoters been perceptive enough to foresee the trend and return to the traditional 154-game format, they would have drawn another estimated 650,000—a lost opportunity. American show business, by contrast—Broadway shows, Hollywood movies, cabarets, and concert halls—was bulging at the seams in 21,897 houses nationally. Its operators had seen the spendthrift Jazz Age arriving and did not retrench on capital investment.

Cobb was not retrenching. He was casing ventures right and left. "Any bright guy could see," he spoke of the period, "that this was the time to get going. I had a friend, a movie stuntman named Claude Graham-White. He bought Rolls-Royces during the war for as low as four thousand dollars each. Owners couldn't get the gas for them. Afterward, Whitey sold the cars for up to eleven thousand dollars per copy—and I had invested with him. Cleaned up."

Preposterously, the payroll slashes of preseason 1919 included Cobb as an intended victim. Detroit had not stood in the winner's circle for nine years, and evinced no sign of becoming even a contender. Fans were bored. In December 1918, Navin wrote to Cobb that, due to the pinch, he must take a pay reduction. Navin named eighteen thousand dollars as the figure—a two-thousand-dollar cut. At eighteen thousand the Peach would remain the game's number-one earner.

Cobb ignored the offer. He let other communications go unanswered. Silence, as he had often demonstrated in holdouts of the past, truly could be golden. The American and National leagues' trading markets were operating briskly after the war. Cobb was worth at least $100,000 to Detroit in a sale, but only if he remained in uniform. After a long silence, T.C. put out a story that he was serious about quitting to enjoy life, as he had promised the previous September. He had long wanted to travel abroad, see the Colosseum, the Louvre, and Leaning Tower, go grouse hunting in Scotland. At a family reunion in hometown Royston—two-hundred-odd of the Cobb clan attended—he spoke out about Navin: "Eleven [batting] trophies, and Navin tries this on me. He goes to the race tracks and loses thousands and then goes out to shaft me."

Defiance was one thing; the shackling, unbreakable reserve clause, permanently tying an employee to a single franchise, was another. In his wish to leave Detroit, Cobb was in a bind. The owners reportedly had agreed to strengthen the reserve by refraining from signing another team's players. The new one-for-all action by employers was a reenactment and reaffirmation of the closet plots of the past, tightening the indenture of employees. A disgusted Cobb was interested in moving to Cincinnati of the National League for more money. Under new manager Pat Moran, the Reds had powerful hitting from Jake Daubert, Edd Roush, and veteran Heinie Groh (of the famous thick-barreled "bottle bat"). A strong pitching staff was headed by Hod Eller and Slim Sallee. Cincinnati was set for a pennant and, as it turned out, would easily defeat McGraw's Giants for first place in the 1919 race and beat the White Sox in the World Series.

Cobb persisted as a holdout. Shifting strategy, he stopped speaking of retiring and hinted that he would jump to the Reds or not play at all. "A bluff by me," he later called it. "A way to shake up Navin."

Emphasizing his point, the Peach was far away from the Tigers when they opened spring training at Macon, Georgia, in March. He did his campwork with Clark Griffith's Washington Nationals at handy Augusta. Word circulated that owner Griffith was plotting to steal Cobb in an outlaw act against the reserve. "That story was a fake, too," Cobb long afterward explained. "I did talk to Griff . . . but he would have had to pay Detroit a hundred thousand dollars and players to get me . . . which he didn't have . . . and I didn't care for Griff's bunch of .250 hitters." Griffith did not have a World Series contender, and the Series was an arena to which T.C. very much wanted to return.

Throughout March he left Navin waiting to resolve their dispute. In that month came the death by heart attack of William Hoover Yawkey, timber baron and multimillionaire chief stockholder in the Tigers. Yawkey had intervened in previous Cobb holdouts over salary, usually favoring the player whom he greatly admired. Yawkey was a big, florid-faced, lumbering man, naive about baseball and an ornament of Detroit's fun-loving set—"he never passed a saloon unless it was closed." Tipsy or sober, he was on Cobb's side, and Navin had to jump when told to do so by the boss. At a later time, T.C. said that Yawkey gave him "a very nice present" when Yawkey's $100 million (or so) will and testament was privately read. Cobb didn't say how much the gift amounted to, but with a lavish spender like Yawkey it could have been $50,000.

Although Navin now had complete control of a next-to-last-place, stumbling team, on April 1 he backed down, reinstating the $20,000 salary that his main attraction commanded and agreeing that established bonus payments remain intact. Cobb informed Navin that if and when they talked contract for 1920, it would be in the $35,000 to $40,000 range.

And yet, to inside observers, a measure of doubt remained. His headlong, brutal style of play meant more injuries, reducing Cobb's longevity. It was wondered if his black rages—outbreaks that several times had come close to causing his disbarment—could ever be controlled. Attention was drawn to his outside business distractions, and the discouragement of being stuck with a Detroit team that was going nowhere. Any or all of these could detract from Cobb's ability to remain a dominant force. And there was another consideration: new young stars were rising across the leagues, including one named Ruth.

Away from his Georgia homestead for seven months of the year, and in his sexual prime, Cobb became involved in a love affair in 1919. He had fame, money, and lean good looks and had to fend off women. He did not like "used goods"—girls recommended to him by his associates—and found his fun while making his own social rounds. Secrecy prevailed.

One romance of the late season backfired. "Met her in Boston at a society dance," he remarked one day to Muddy Ruel, the one-time Yankee, Boston Red Sox, and Washington catcher who in 1960 would help Cobb assemble his memoirs for publication. "I was doing a lot of ballroom dancing in those days in my time off. She was a redhead, a hot number."

"Did you—?" inquired Ruel.

"Well, what do you think, Muddy? We had open days on the road schedule and I was tired of going to banquets."

"What happened?"

"She wanted me to get free and marry her. When she made trouble about it, I cut her off my list. Never spoke to the bitch again. She married a tennis pro."

"So what did you do then?"

"Oh," said Cobb airily, "there were plenty of others around."

CHAPTER NINETEEN

"I FIGHT TO KILL"

fter the Great War the elastic in Sam Crawford's throwing arm showed wear, and in 1918 the veteran of nineteen major-league years was dealt by Detroit to Los Angeles of the Class AA Pacific Coast League. Wahoo Sam left behind an important record, one that in 1994 still stands—312 career triples. No hitter since Crawford has surpassed him in cumulative three-basers—not even Cobb (297), Ruth (136), or Willie Mays (140).

Crawford's durable feud with Cobb continued after he left the Tigers. When I asked Cobb why the breach never healed, he said, "Crawford was a hell of a good player. Hall of Famer. But he was only second best on our club—a bad second. He hated to be an also-ran."

However, in Los Angeles, the normally mild-mannered Sam told Bill Henry of the *Los Angeles Times*, "If a blind man rattled his cup on the corner, cheapskate Cobb might throw in a dime. I spent fifteen years in the same outfield with him. He never helped any of us with a loan, even when we were broke. And he had a rotten disposition, too."

The widely held opinion was that Ty Cobb was a tightwad. He would share a stock-market tip with a few teammates, but that was the extent of his generosity. As a youngster he had seen his schoolmaster father find it hard to subsist on modest earnings, and die in debt; now the son was out to become independently well-off as soon as possible. Ancillary income that came his way was plowed back into low-risk investments. He once said to me, "Fuck luck. Those who depend on it wind up busted. I go out and make my own luck."

Only in one case, Cobb said, did he fail to cash in on a bright new idea. "Bright" was the precise word for the invention of George Y. Cahill of Holyoke, Massachusetts, who in 1916 produced a system for illuminating outdoor events such as night baseball. Cahill's assembly of twenty lights flooded fields with nearly two million candlepower. Although players were expected to object that under such brilliance they would go blind, the majority of them liked the innovation. Yet it was so radical and experimental that major-league officials passed up the idea until 1935, when Larry MacPhail of the Cincinnati Reds installed lights and with President Franklin D. Roosevelt turning a switch in Washington, D.C., presented the first nocturnal major-league game in history. "I tried to buy into Cahill's business [in 1918–19]— hell, lights revolutionized the game—but got there too late," regretted Cobb.

Soon afterward he came close to losing out on another venture, one that in the 1920s made him financially secure, then rich, and, finally, put him in the millionaire bracket. It was perhaps the largest commercial coup made by any athlete in any sport. "My ace in the hole," he termed it; "my annuity."

Cobb's gold strike went back several years, to Augusta, where he had regularly golfed with entrepreneur Robert Winship Woodruff. Woodruff's company bottled a beverage that had been originally sold as French Wine Cola Nerve and Tonic Stimulant. The drink was the 1885 creation of John S. Pemberton, an ex–Civil War cavalry officer, later an Atlanta pharmacist. As the legend went, Pemberton sat on a three-legged stool, stirring tubs of homemade batches with an oar. In 1889 Georgia businessman Asa Candler bought out Pemberton, patented a "soda fizz" now named Coca-Cola, and franchised it out in the South. Everybody wanted to know the recipe, but Candler wasn't talking. So the ultra-secret Coke formula became a permanent mystery.

Cobb had known of Coca-Cola's history since he broke into the majors. Back in 1908, when he had won the second of his AL batting titles, he had posed for photos on the bench with a Coca-Cola carton conspicuously at his side. After the war, Robert Woodruff came calling with offers to sell company stock to his fellow Georgian at a very favorable figure.

"You have to remember that things were balled up afterward . . . nobody knew how the cat would jump on some propositions. I wasn't interested in Coke right then." So Cobb described negotiations that followed.

A key discussion came at New York's Ansonia Hotel on a day when a Detroit-Yankee game was rained out. Cobb quoted himself as telling Woodruff, "Bob, I can't afford to go in with you. I'll pass on it." His real objection was that Coca-Cola was then unlisted on the Big Board of the New York Stock Exchange.

"Ty, you've just got to buy some of this," insisted Woodruff. "We've formed a syndicate to buy out Asa Candler entirely. We're capitalizing the company strongly. If you buy now, the price to you is only thirty-six dollars per original share." Woodruff predicted the stock would rise sky-high.

A banker and director of important Georgia companies, Woodruff revealed that his syndicate was paying $25 million for all Coca-Cola rights, the largest financial transaction to date in the South. That was how much he thought of the product.

"That made me sit up and whistle," Cobb recalled. "I could get in at three hundred shares for ten thousand, eight hundred dollars. And Woodruff offered to loan me the money through his bank, Georgia Trust, payable back through Coke dividends."

Through a rainy New York afternoon, T.C. stalled, until, finally capitulating, he set himself on the road to financial independence, though with little enthusiasm. Within eight years his annual income from Coca-Cola would reach $350,000, and would triple that figure as time passed and he made more stock purchases. At various points the value of his Coca-Cola holdings would reach $181 per share. In time he came to own twenty-two thousand shares of a company selling its drink almost everywhere on earth. "Played golf one day in the fifties with Ike Eisenhower," T.C. would relate. "Ike told me that during the second war soldiers drank five billion bottles of Coke." With his other investments, particularly in oil, cotton, and motorcars, a ballplayer whose highest team salary never passed $85,000 reached millionaire status and more when he was still well under age forty.

It was not so much eccentricity as gratitude showing in him when in later years Cobb would patronize only those service stations selling Coca-Cola, not some other soft drink. If necessary he would detour out of the way to order a Coke. One day in 1960 I was driving with him from San Francisco to Los Angeles, and on Highway 99 he left the route and veered off to a gas pump. Ordering fuel for his Lincoln, he told the attendant, "And I want a Coke." The attendant said he carried only Pepsi. "The hell with you!" barked Cobb and drove off.

It became baseball lore that as much as he hoarded money, and as little as he tipped waiters, hack drivers, and Pullman porters, Cobb would share inside dope on stock-market buys with people he liked. According to one of his brokers, Elmer M. Griffin of Beverly Hills, California, his timely advice made considerable profits for retired ballplayers with small incomes or in distress. "I can name you a dozen or so of old big-leaguers that Cobb rescued through speculations which he often financed," stated Griffin in 1940. "He'd buy you a house if you hadn't crossed him in the past, if you didn't have the rent and he liked you."

One of the beneficiaries was Paul Cobb, his two-year-younger brother. Few athletes have stood in deeper shade than this Cobb. Almost as tall and heavy as T.C., Paul had played outfield at Georgia Tech, then spent nearly a decade trying to reach the majors and always falling short. "*You're* Ty Cobb's brother?" managers at minor- and semi-pro-league stops would ask. Paul Cobb's only substantial accomplishment as a player was to be drafted from Joplin, Missouri, in Class C ball by the St. Louis Browns of the American League in 1909, where he failed to make the grade.

"Having the Cobb name hurt Paul when it should have helped him," grumbled his older brother. "Hell, I taught him to hit and steal. He'd have hit .290 or more if given the chance." Some felt it was Ty Cobb's unpopularity with the game's ruling powers that mitigated against the "other Cobb's" chances. T.C. believed that to be true. Hates and jealousies impeded the boy's efforts to advance, he was convinced. Eventually Paul went into Florida real estate, helped, T.C. said, by the bonanza accumulating after the Coca-Cola tap was turned on.

Bob Woodruff of the bottling empire remained so close a friend of his celebrated stockholder that the two always hugged each other when reunited after a long separation. "I was never so tight with any man," Cobb declared. Woodruff owned a forty-six-hundred-acre cattle spread in Wyoming, formerly the homestead of Buffalo Bill Cody. An expert horseman since his farm-boy days, the Peach rode the high trails there, shot bobcat and elk, and soaked naked in outdoor mineral springs, letting his scarred legs heal for the seasons ahead. His body was nearly hairless and the regional Arapaho tribe gave him the honorary name of "Smooth Eagle." Once Woodruff remarked, "Ty could trap game with anyone. I think he was part Injun."

Reminisced Cobb, grinning: "There were plenty of Arapaho girls around our camp . . . they didn't go neglected."

High in the remoteness of the Grand Tetons may have come an obsessively driven man's happiest times. "Goddamn, how I loved it," he said of those expeditions in 1919 and 1920. Out there he was temporarily free of family obligations, pressure from fans, salary wrangles, beanballs, business and legal troubles, and the matter of staying ahead of rivals named Speaker, Jackson, Sisler, Heilmann, and the rising, right-handed-swinging Rogers Hornsby of St. Louis. That Hornsby could *hit*. And in Boston was a twenty-five-year-old pitcher with an outstanding fastball, who was converting to playing the outfield. In five Red Sox seasons, Babe Ruth had compiled an impressive 80–41 win-loss mound record, while simultaneously averaging well over .300 at bat. The large, moon-faced left-hander was a rarity, a pitcher-slugger. Ruth hit plenty of doubles and triples, but when he connected fully, the ball disappeared from sight.

His 11 home runs of 1918 had tied for the league lead. Since the all-time American League record was 16, by Ralph "Socks" Seybold of Philadelphia in 1902, this was an eye-opener. Veteran critics could see him striking as many as 20 homers if he concentrated on batwork.

Opponents' scouts studied his six-foot, two-inch and close to two-hundred-pound body up and down. The Babe was as peculiar as the mythical Hippocameleopard. No one else had his ability to be a star on the mound and be abnormally powerful on offense. Pitching seemed to be his calling—but, then again, perhaps not. In one week he had pitched two wins over St. Louis, while also pounding three homers. Ruth had what insiders called "unknown potential." How much brandy he could drink at a sitting was also unknown.

RELUCTANTLY COBB left the Wyoming plateau in February to prepare for 1919 play. His mind was divided. "I was thinking more of Jackson and Sisler than this Ruth," he told Bob Woodruff when they met in March. "And how much longer I could go on playing twelve hundred innings [per season] with bad legs." He considered the idea of buying a ranch like Woodruff's—something smaller—and taking early retirement.

ONCE THE season began, there were plenty of signs that young "two-way" Ruth was far more than merely another good ballplayer. On July 15, at Detroit's Navin Field, Cobb, in center field, played Ruth extra deep. The Babe poled one so far over his head that it cleared the bleachers and landed in the street, the longest home run ever seen in Motor City. It might have traveled five hundred and some feet. In the next few days, at Boston, Ruth added two more mammoth homers in one game.

Before that, in June, pitcher Ruth had beaten Walter Johnson of Washington. Four days later, against Cleveland, he had thrown a shutout. At Detroit, Cobb faced him with two men out and the bases loaded. Ruth's big hands gripped his fastball loosely, which was unorthodox. Not so unusual on this day was that his first pitch took off, sailing so widely that umpire Billy Evans threw the ball out as probably illegal. On the next pitch, Cobb loudly complained that the ball had to be doctored with a foreign substance, to veer a good eighteen inches as it had done. Again Evans threw out the ball.

"Here comes one down the middle!" Ruth shouted.

It started straightaway, then dived for a strike. Evans let that one stand, but tossed out the following pitch and then another, until during a single Cobb at-bat, six deliveries were declared suspicious and not counting either way. Cobb ended the farce by striking out. It was one of the most satisfying "fanners" of Ruth's mound career to date; he rubbed it in by saying, "Cobb's easy." And Babe added a home run as the Yankees won by just that margin, 1–0.

In this immediate postwar season, Cobb watched and wondered as Ruth upped his batting average from a previous .300 to .322, while also pitching nine victories to five defeats. Yet those feats seemed insignificant when he also went on to produce 29 home runs that season, breaking the modern major-league record of 24 set by Gavvy Cravath of the Phillies in 1915. There was no question now about where

Ruth's talents would be best used. He was a star, and the now well-heeled New York Yankees were maneuvering to buy him. Price didn't much matter.

Ruth's batting average of .322 might not be close to Cobb's .384, but the Babe had something new to sell: propelling the long ball—the *very* long ball—in quantity. The boisterous, fun-loving Ruth was on his way to turning ballparks into theaters of tumult. His most spectacular seasons were coming up, and one of them, 1920, was just around the corner. On January 3, 1920, he would become the property of the Yankees, acquired in a $400,000 transaction in which Ruth represented $125,000 of a sum embracing cash, credits, and a loan to Boston owner Harry Frazee. That record investment would be justified when that season Babe drove an unbelievable 54 balls over fences, close to four times as many as National League home-run champion Fred "Cy" Williams of the Phillies collected, and roughly five times more than any other Yankee delivered. The next-best Yankee power men—Wally Pipp, Bob Meusel, and Aaron Ward—had 11 apiece.

At first Cobb had nothing much to say about Ruth. But when Babe was mentioned as a possible successor to his crown, he visibly reacted. When Ruth appeared in Detroit, Tyrus would be seen looking in the other direction, boning his bats or making some other sideplay. To a growing number of fans around the league, Cobb was beginning to come off as no longer so uniquely colorful, not quite so enjoyable to watch. In press boxes it was felt by some Cobb-watchers that perhaps he had met a man he couldn't beat. Perhaps.

"We are alike in only one way," Cobb said in his sparing public comments on Ruth. "We're both hard losers."

But that wasn't entirely true. T.C. notched some of his bats with the initials of pitchers he did particularly well against: "W.J.," "E.C.," "F.B.," and so on. Ruth cut "win" notches in his close to three-pound bats. In temperament they would on occasion turn out to be equally combative. In May of 1923, against the St. Louis Browns, the Babe threw dirt into the face of umpire George Hildebrand. Kicked off the field, he climbed into the stands after hecklers. Scaling a dugout roof, a frenzied Ruth invited everyone present to a fight. "You're all yellow!" he hollered. "Come on down here!"

In that same month, the reigning record-holder for misconduct in a ballpark was similarly occupied. During a Detroit–St. Louis Cardinals exhibition, Cobb threw dirt into the face of umpire Harry Pfirman and offered to fight anyone at all. Ejected, he refused to leave, resisting the umpires so long and hard that at last the game was forfeited to the Cardinals.

Ruth was suspended and fined two hundred dollars. Cobb was suspended and fined one hundred dollars, apparently receiving a discount as a longtime customer.

BEGINNING IN 1920 and continuing for the better part of a decade, the Cobb-Ruth rivalry was a close matchup of Old School versus New School, not to be equaled in intensity until the 1940s, when Joe DiMaggio and Ted Williams competed for batting honors. As a delighted press played it, here was Cobb's flashing rapier against Ruth's cannon. Ruth would scratch his groin, glance at the fences, tap the plate, flick his bat, and launch another of the 113 home runs of his first two New York seasons (54, then 59) out of the park. Cobb would shift around in the box, feet together, eyes fixed on the pitcher, crouch slightly, and slash a single or double to the opposite field.

In total bases, T.C. had led the American League six times, but after 1919 it became more and more a matter of George Ruth reaching the most stations. What else, when the "big baboon" would during his lifetime average a home run every 8.5 times at bat?

Cobb's base-stealing skill could not be matched by the less swift, less expert Ruth. This was particularly true of successive, multiple steals. Defensively they were close enough not to matter. Ruth's arm was stronger; his opponent could catch some balls beyond the heavy-set Babe's reach. Ruth made fewer errors.

They were not really comparable. It was a matter of taste—clout or scientific tactics. Sportswriters doted on a situation in which they could carry on at length about "a whale versus a shark." Casey Stengel joined in: "Nah, it's a bomb against a machine gun."

For a time, Cobb evinced little outward concern, looking upon Ruth as vulnerable to baseball's inexorable forces. He had met such challenges since 1907, and beaten back all of them. "Ruth's unfinished," he said to Detroit writer Harry Salsinger. He meant incomplete, lacking. Cobb felt that the contender was too fixed in his style to adapt, even partially, to Cobbian baseball philosophy, and that it would prove his downfall. The hard-line, traditionalist Cobb was convinced that pitchers would soon adjust to such an undisciplined free-swinger, a muscleman whose bat control was limited by its big, uppercutting arc. Here was no Shoeless Joe Jackson, with the ideal, flowing, level swing. Ruth, swinging from his heels, was flawed. Through impatience and guess hitting, he would strike out and pop up too often. He was a sweep-hitter with stiff arms and wrists. He had a curveball weakness.

And he would grow fat early. Along with everyone, Cobb had heard tales of the Babe consuming six club sandwiches, a platter of pig's knuckles, and two pitchers of beer at a sitting. It was publicized that he breakfasted on three-pound steaks, six eggs, a heap of potatoes, and a quart of rye whiskey with a ginger-ale chaser. He became renowned, with the Babe not particularly objecting, for his ability to outdrink anyone in the American League (the National had its own good bottle men). Immature, everyone's hero hit Prohibition beer and rum hard, avoided bed-checks, and habitually stayed out all night. Supposedly, during these sprees, Babe was with a pickup girl or in a bawdy house with ladies of the demimonde. Around 6:00 A.M. one morning, when the Tigers were in New York for a series, Cobb was up and doing roadwork on Park Avenue when he ran across Ruth arriving home. "Been having a good time?" asked Cobb, pleased to see him breaking curfew.

"Pretty damned good," replied Babe. "There were three of them." He was tipsy.

Yankee manager Miller Huggins and his spies often caught Ruth in the act, and a body of reportage, some of it much exaggerated, came to picture the former Baltimore bartender as a Falstaffian character who could combine dissipation with getting base hits to a degree never before seen—or imagined. In part this was true. And Ruth was slow in reforming his ways. Another instance that Cobb said he knew to be a fact was that Babe had rented hotel rooms in Detroit after an important win over the Tigers and threw a team party at which all of the invited females were bluntly told to "put out" or depart.

Ruth's vital juices overflowed. His legend was building. In his first Yankee years he flipped and wrecked a car, was jailed for speeding, lost forty thousand dollars within days at a horse track, ate most of a straw hat as a gag, and had a fifty-thousand-dollar paternity suit filed against him. Fans everywhere loved him no less for his infractions; vicariously they were right with him.

"Most of the American League figured he'd eat and fuck himself right out," said Cobb in later years. It was an admission of poor judgment that he would heartily regret.

Within a few seasons Cobb tempered his view with an observation: "After Ruth had been around awhile and no longer was pitching, I could see what made him so different. *His pitching days made him a hitter* [of home runs]. As mostly a pitcher, he didn't have to protect the plate as I did and other regular hitters had to do. He could try this and that. Experiment. Learn timing. As a pitcher, if he flopped [at bat], nobody gave a damn. Pitchers always had been lousy hitters. Now and then over those six years at Boston one of his big swings was good for four bases." (Between 1914 and 1918 at Boston, Babe hit 0, 4, 3, 2, and 11 home runs.) "Once he got smart and grooved his cut, he had a whole new career." He averaged 45 homers a year for the next ten years.

John McGraw, not known for his extensive silence on issues, and whose word was considered gospel truth by multitudes, agreed that Babe Ruth was a perishable commodity. Early in 1920 the Giants manager was quoted as telling New York writers, "Ruth is a bum. He can't play the inside game. Can't hit and run. If the Yanks use him every day the bum will hit into a hundred double plays before the season is over." Like Cobb, the Little Napoleon was confronting a phenomenon who was threatening to change the way things were done on offense.

A NEW, uninhibited breed of ball fans showed no such reservations. "Built like a spinning top" or "a bale of hay," Ruth had arrived at the ideal moment, the saturnalian 1920s. Not even Jack Dempsey with his knockouts, or touchdown-running Red Grange, better suited the decade. After the war the U.S. adopted Prohibition and then defied it, drove fast cars, speculated wildly in a bull market, erected skyscrapers, made sexual freedom commonplace, and let crime lords run loose. Prosperity, and the need in urban centers for thrills, created $2-million boxing gates and filled such cavernous arenas as sixty-five-thousand-capacity, $2.5 million Yankee Stadium, opened in 1923 and soon to showcase Ruth at $2.20 per grandstand seat. As of that year, fifteen of the sixteen parks housing major-league teams had an average capacity of thirty-five thousand. The Giants could accommodate fifty-four thousand. Brooklyn's updated Ebbets Field held thirty-five thousand.

The size of parks brought new touches: electric scoreboards began to replace rickety wooden ball-and-strike indicators. Hot showers for players came along. Teams were required to provide canvas infield coverings in event of rain.

Babe, now paid twenty thousand dollars per season, hit balls "into the next county," and there was a wonderful go-for-it defiance of gravity in his act. Yankee attendance in 1920, 1,289,472, broke the record by a 380,000 margin. With Ruth, Bob Meusel, Wally Pipp, Ping Bodie, Carl Mays, and Bob Shawkey in the lineup, the perennial also-ran Yankees were edging toward becoming a pennant winner, a goal they would reach in 1921. Detroit, meanwhile, sputtered along in fourth place, purportedly up for sale by Navin.

Not overnight, but very rapidly, Ruth popularized the new focus and form of attack. His connect-or-bust style, so wholly opposed to the Cobb school of finessing runs, advancing base runners by pre-plotted degrees, and using his spikes freely, changed the central object of the game, the official ball. Three hundred to 400 home runs were registered in the majors in prewar seasons; by 1930 the figure would be 1,565. Ruth in 1919 was only one year away from smashing more homers in a season than any entire American League *team* other than the Yankees. He and other young power specialists were a main factor in the 1920 introduction of a more tightly wound "rabbit," "kangaroo," or "cannon" ball of Australian wool. At least, that's where the leagues said it came from; apparently nobody traveled down under to verify it.

Announcing the end of the deadball of past years, the Wilson Base Ball Equipment Company came out with an advertisement on its version of the new baseball:

THE ACE OF DIAMONDS
Conforms to specifications of the National and American Leagues. Due to a special winding process the balls are ABSOLUTELY SPHERICAL and guaranteed NOT TO BECOME LOP-SIDED FOR 200 GAMES.

For fifteen years of the deadball period, Cobb had faced balls more befitting the sandlots than the majors—dented and "soft," blackened from overuse and by original poor quality, causing "twilight blindness" in some games starting at 3:00 or 4:00 P.M. in unlit parks.

Cobb to date had been painfully beaned three times, and on each occasion he had completely lost sight of the ball as it neared the plate. Now, at long last, umpires were instructed to discard balls every few innings and throw in glossy new ones to replace the "mushy potatoes." As the lively ball took preeminence, several club owners, as an aid to higher scoring, pulled in their fences. Consumption of baseballs was convincing proof of what was transpiring. In 1919 the National League alone used 22,095 balls; by 1924 the total went to 54,030. Another indicator: the World Series had been replete with 1–0, 2–1, and 3–2 total scoring; from 1920–30 the Series produced twenty games with nine or more runs tallied by the sides, even with such superior pitchers on hand as Walter Johnson, Pete Alexander, Sad Sam Jones, Rube Marquard, Stan Coveleski, Lefty Grove, Waite Hoyt, and Herb Pennock.

COBB WAS truly trapped by the arrival of the Big Bang epoch. It went against everything he practiced and believed, opposing his conception of knitting together team offense. "The home run could wreck baseball," he warned. "It throws out a lot of the strategy and makes it fenceball." Originally he had believed that the craze epitomized by Ruth would go away as fans regained their senses. But when the Tigers traveled to the Polo Grounds one summer day, he met more evidence that he had miscalculated Ruth's influence on the man on the street. Like the battleship admirals after World War I who lobbied for bigger hulls and eighteen-inch firepower, the customers wanted noise. Babe homered, his twenty-sixth of the season. But Cobb homered, too. He also cleverly maneuvered as the runner at second base to be hit by a pick-off attempt, allowing Heilmann to score the winning run. In the outfield, racing far back, he leaped and robbed Ruth of another homer. It was inspired play. Yet it was Ruth whom the crowd cheered all day.

Detroiters knew that, in 1919 and at times thereafter, their man was playing at a distinct handicap. At Chicago he cut his toe upon colliding with an outfield fence, and the toe swelled up. Later on, also at Chicago, he was carried off the field, all but unconscious, after colliding with teammate Ira Flagstead in the field. A knee ligament was ruptured, and for a while the Peach was out of it and on a cane. Just as throughout the pre-1920s era, he continued to be in one sort of physical distress or another. The knee, reinjured while sliding, caused hospitalization, costing him twenty-seven days on the sideline. What he feared was happening: his resilience was diminishing. In his "memory book," Cobb describes his ordeal as "the worst I ever went through. I thought for a while that this was it. Surgeons couldn't help me I was so bad off."

He came back, as always. As a boy he had accidentally shot himself in the upper chest with a rifle. In Canada he had fallen down a steep slope while hunting and been on crutches. He had, by count, in 1919, two dozen stitches in his lower legs. From all these injuries Cobb had recovered with a swiftness that greatly impressed his doctors. "Mind over matter, I guess," he said. Somehow, after a serious setback he always regained good form.

In August of 1920, while he was still limping, the Yankees came to Navin Field. His competitiveness and rare recuperative power led T.C. to insist on playing in the four-game series. He managed eight hits in the set before sellout crowds, and no man could say how he did it. "I was just getting it along . . . hoping to come back," he spoke of his distress. Ruth, however, upstaged him with three home runs in two games to reach number 46 on the season. When the Babe next appeared at the plate, Detroit gave the enemy player a standing ovation lasting several minutes. The Tigers' honorary captain had to wait in the outfield in his home ballpark and endure hearing the cheers of thirty thousand being accorded a man who had yet to win a league batting title.

Ty Cobb's emotion at that moment was revealed to me in 1960 at his California retirement mansion: "Well, I had to stand there and take it. That was it. In Detroit or anywhere the fans were treacherous bastards. I knew Ruth couldn't hit with me — that is, *real* hitting — or run bases with me — or [play] outfield with me. As long as the guys in the league knew that, I didn't care very much."

That last assertion is, to say the least, questionable. In repeated ways over the years he displayed his distaste for and jealousy of Ruth's flamboyant rise. In the 1924 off-season, Ruth was invited to Dover Hall in Brunswick, Georgia, a rich man's hunting spa long patronized by Cobb. The mistake of housing the two in the same tent was made. Cobb openly objected to the campmaster. "I'm not living with any nigger," he announced. Cobb left camp and did not return for several years. Ruth stayed on, possibly unaware of the intended insult. Ballplayers who had seen the Babe's pale body in the showers knew that despite his flattish nose and rather thick lips, he was German-American. Still, rumor circulated among white supremacists, and Cobb's words were quoted. During Tiger-Yankee matches, T.C. would call Ruth "nigger," "ape," "polecat," and so on, as he sauntered past the New York dugout, holding his nose. A fight between them was shaping up. T.C.'s bench-jockeying was as crude as he could get, and by 1924 the two would come to blows.

Jimmie Reese, who had been a coach with the California Angels and once Ruth's roommate on the Yankees, said of the Dover Hall affair, "It was just like Cobb to call Ruth a black man. Because back then it hurt a fellow. Cobb was no good in the opinion of almost everyone in the league."

THERE WAS no bending to him, no mellowing with age. Perhaps pressure from Ruth made him only the more Draconian. Yankee outfielder Ping Bodie told of an incident showing Cobb as incurably out of control as ever. During the warm-up before a Detroit game, Bodie left his bat on the sideline. Cobb tripped over it. He grabbed the bat in a rage and threw it into the stands, which, luckily, were not occupied. Bodie had witnesses who heard Cobb call him "a dirty damned wop."

In one of his worst flareups he made the notorious statement of "I fight to kill." In every dugout it was known that the Georgian did not like Billy Evans, a respected American League umpire since 1906. Feelings heated up in 1919 and thereafter when Cobb questioned many of Evans's ball-strike counts. He jawed away until Evans drew a line in the dirt; if his critic stepped over it, he would be "run," or ejected. Along came a late-season game with the Washington Nationals in which Cobb twice was called out on close base-stealing attempts. Evans, a former semipro boxer and Cornell University athlete, made the second of these decisions. He left after the final out for the umpires' dressing room. Close behind him came Cobb, his face mottled. He banged on the door, cursing and yelling, "Come out of there or I'll come it and get you!"

Evans, emerging, was heard to say, "Take it easy." His hands were out in a peacemaking gesture. But Cobb demanded a fight and Evans obliged him. They met under the stands and players stopped dressing to watch. Walter Johnson of the Nationals tried to stop it and failed. As reported by Rogers Hornsby in his autobiographical *My War with*

Baseball, Evans asked Cobb how he wanted to fight. "No rules," was the reply. "I fight to kill."

For forty-five minutes the two punched and gouged it out. Evans was badly cut at the outset and had his nose broken. An orthodox fighter, he found himself up against blows below the belt, rabbit punches, and knee kicks. Evans had Cobb down at one point. They rolled in the dirt, both bleeding. Cobb's eleven-year-old son, Tyrus Junior, allowed to watch, danced about, crying, "Hit him harder, Daddy! Hit him harder!"

Hornsby called it as vicious a scrap as had happened. Cobb pounded the umpire's head into hard ground. He was still pounding away when players and groundskeepers mercifully broke it up. Evans was carried off to see a doctor. Observers felt that had the brawl continued, Evans could have been gravely hurt, perhaps had his skull fractured.

Cobb had broken his own rule about turning violent against officials, who had the power to expand the strike zone on a hitter. Evans made no protest to the league office. He took his humiliation silently. But somebody talked, and Cobb was suspended for the balance of a season all but ended.

"I wasn't proud of it," said Cobb to newspapermen who headlined the fight. "But Evans had it in for me and his calls were prejudiced. I had to stop that."

THE TIGERS complained that it had been hard enough to live with him before Ruth came along; now it was becoming impossible. After a Navin Field game where he went hitless, home fans booed loudly. One fan invaded the field to jeer. Cobb kicked him in the stomach, then the groin. And kicked him again. An angry crowd grew so dangerous that Frank Navin ordered an escape car to be rushed to the players' gate. Grouped outside were some two dozen Detroiters leaving the park. A white-faced Cobb walked down a line of fans. To each of them he called, "You want to fight? You want to settle this?" He was alone, no teammate backing him up, while he sought to take on someone—anyone. "I never saw anything like it," marveled veteran Bobby Veach. "All alone like that, he could have been murdered by that crowd."

"If you're all cowards—then fuck you!" was the Peach's last word. He walked to his own parked car and drove away. Detroit had plenty of tough truck drivers and steelworkers, but the insane look to Cobb held them back.

His rampages were senseless, ongoing, and frightening. His warpath included his home territory of Georgia. There would be a pathetic scene in Atlanta in 1924 involving a paddywagon and another trip by him to a municipal jail. He was many miles from the big league that winter, but when a waitress at Atlanta's railroad station restaurant handed Cobb his luncheon bill, he threw a tantrum, "That's a dollar-fifty too much!" he objected. When the waitress replied that the bill was correct, she was subjected to a cursing. The $1.50 matter became a yelling match with the house cashier and manager, during which Cobb tore up the check and used ballpark guttertalk. He raved so wildly that the cashier, until now a Cobb admirer, broke a heavy glass platter over his head, staggering him.

Policemen arrived. Outside on the street the Georgia Peach felled one cop with a punch to the head. A crowd gathered to watch him wrestle with other officers. Overpowered, he was removed to a nearby jail, where he ranted at a desk sergeant while authorities debated what to do with him. It was all too sad, and after a few hours he was quietly released from custody on his personal bond and without incurring a formal booking.

Word of his latest outbreak reached Detroit's front office. Navin was said to have shrugged. It was only one more instance of a destructive neurosis in Cobb whereby he stood above the crowd, enabled by some twisted thinking to inflict pain as he went, to assault people, and feel himself justified. Behavioral scientists didn't exist in baseball then, but if they had been on the scene, Cobb might well have been found to be suffering from some form of grandiosity or advanced megalomania, or perhaps delusions of persecution. Modern medical men might trace it to the boyhood trauma of his father's killing by Cobb's mother—accidental or otherwise. Whatever motivated—or possessed—him, he was the most chilling, the eeriest of all American sport figures.

His 1919 season performance was more than satisfactory, considering. Although Cobb had been plagued by a succession of injuries, his bat, along with those of Veach (.355 average) and Flagstead (.331) had lifted the surprising Tigers to a fourth-place finish behind the champion Chicago White Sox. For once he had a few members of the team responding to his own standard, a league-leading .384 average—the seventh time he had topped .380—his twelfth batting title, and 161 runs produced. His springtime doubters agreed that he was as difficult as ever to put out, to catch in a rundown, or to deal with on well-placed bunts. Navin had made a reported profit of $110,000 at the gate.

The dark notes were Ruth's sustained progress with the radical home run, and unsubstantiated rumors that the Chicago White Sox had thrown the World Series just ended to Cincinnati. The early "buzz" on a fixed Series reached T.C. in October, when he was back hunting and fishing at Bob Woodruff's ranch in Wyoming. He was notified by President John Wheeler of the Wheeler News Syndicate in New York that manager Kid Gleason's White Sox had played to lose in an eight-game Series believed to have been choreographed by big-time gamblers.

Cobb did not need Wheeler's information. He had attended that Series, once more in the role of press commentator, and came away fully convinced of crooked work. Privately, he told Woodruff, "Fixes have been going on since 1910 . . . when they tried to beat me out for the batting title." He had always seen the hand of gamblers behind that attempt to make Nap Lajoie the champion, a scheme that came close to succeeding.

In San Francisco that winter he predicted to Yankee pitcher Frank "Lefty" O'Doul, a Bay Area resident, "This is going to cause a lot of hell." The American public did not learn of the Series scandal until almost a year after the fact, when stunning disclosures were made and, finally, eight White Soxers were banned for life.

BEFORE LEAVING Wyoming, Cobb bought a dozen head of white-faced cattle for a beef herd he planned to develop on land outside Augusta. There was still some farmer in him. In San Francisco for part of that winter he managed the local Seals club of the four-team Pacific Coast Winter League. This was a sort of Ringling Circus operation. Fans walked right into the dugouts—to chat with players—and were kicked out by an irate Cobb; gamblers laid bets at fieldside; the Los Angeles entry in the PCWL had a chimpanzee mascot, "Hairy Harry," who wore a little umpire's cap. Phil Douglas, a pitcher with the New York Giants in the regular season, was assigned his own private detective to keep "Shuffling Phil" out of saloons.

In the PCWL he experienced local scandal. On October 20, 1919, the deputy district attorney of Los Angeles County charged before a grand jury that some of the PCWL clubs and the parent Pacific Coast League were controlled by a powerful gambling ring "which has cleaned up enormous sums and distributed thousands of dollars to ballplayers who did their bidding." The accusation named other league members, but not the San Francisco Seals, led by Cobb. In the end, four players were thrown out of baseball, a regional prelude to the "Black Sox" affair now brewing in Chicago. Cobb quit the Seals soon after, fearing that the infection might have spread into his camp.

On top of everything else, there was gunfire in the still-untamed West. Cobb reported, "I did okay in California in 1919 and 1920 [when he returned to again manage San Francisco] except when gamblers got to shooting at each other in the stands . . . Bullets were flying around the park." Quarreling gamblers used pistols in this league. "But I stuck around for a while. I was paid twelve hundred dollars for every game I appeared in as a player, too, and I hit those western boys for about fifteen thousand dollars in a few months." In the minor league, any game with Ty Cobb in it was a sellout or close to it. Against the Los Angeles club one afternoon, he toured fifteen bases—three home runs and a triple.

Enjoying the California weather, he considered moving there when retirement came—if he could sever his Georgia roots. He was still out west in November of 1919 when several Detroit businessmen called to say that Hughie Jennings would not be retained much longer as Tigers' manager. Twelve seasons in a hot seat had driven the Scranton Irishman to frustration and to drink. He might last one more season. Cobb was deep-sea fishing off Catalina Island with author Zane Grey when he was advised that Navin was thinking of offering Jennings's job to him. Cobb replied informally that he would not accept the Detroit post, if it was offered. "I made that clear to Navin," he noted in his memoirs. "Running a team like Detroit was a trap."

Yet he couldn't go on hitting at a .380 pace indefinitely, and Detroit people hoped he would change his mind during the coming months. He wrote to a friend, "What I figured was that I'd get a manager offer somewhere else. Maybe at Philadelphia. Connie Mack was in terrible shape—five straight last-place finishes."

No offer from Philadelphia appeared in late 1919, nor in 1920.

The Peach's soaring averages would fall by 50 percentage points to .334 in the latter of those two years, and his steals would diminish. He would be advised by specialists that he again needed to consider eye surgery. Eye trouble of the past, which came and went, had left him prepared for an operation someday. Time for a thirty-three-year-old to reconsider his future.

CHAPTER TWENTY

NEW DECADE—
NEW ENEMIES—
NEW JOB

Bell Syndicate of New York City, a sports-promotion agency, arranged a vaudeville tour for Cobb early in 1920. In Michigan, Pennsylvania, and Ohio small towns he stood onstage and hit balls fastened to a cord suspended from above—out over the audience. When the ball returned he would whack it again to the bang of a drum. A brief lecture by Cobb on grip and follow-through ended the performance. In the hustings it filled theaters. "Made me two hundred, three hundred dollars per night," he said.

Frank Navin and the ace of his team reached an uneasy peace in 1920. For his part, Cobb, in the clubhouse, laid off disparaging his boss's knowledge of baseball. Insiders were surprised when they stopped barking at each other and appeared to be amiable. Navin even left his private train compartment when on road trips to play poker with Cobb, Harry Heilmann, Jennings, and others. "Navin couldn't play poker any better than he knew ballplayers," related Cobb. "We cleaned him out at cards."

Regarding his then-current contract, Cobb was jaunty in recollection: "I had Navin whipsawed. The town would have boycotted the Tigers if he tried to deal me away . . . so the fat man was paying me twenty-five thousand dollars without too much moaning and groaning."

Median salary of a team of also-rans was an estimated $6,500, or about average pay in the two leagues. The lowest-paid Tiger received about $2,000. Navin often quoted a survey that showed that 60 percent of American families existed on $2,000 or less yearly. Players had no complaints, he argued.

But if Cobb were to agree to take over field-managing the depressed Tigers for more money—$40,000 was a bruited-about figure—one person who would not be pleased was Charlie Cobb. Her marriage of 1908, at age seventeen, was disintegrating. Her husband habitually didn't return home for dinner, while using his rooms at the Detroit Athletic Club as a social and business-conference center. Charlie, delicate of health and needing his companionship, was distraught. Once the 1920 season opened, she packed up and left Motor City with their four children, Ty junior, eleven, Shirley, nine, Herschel, three, and Beverly, just a few months old, for the family home in Augusta, an act of independence now becoming habitual with her.

Reconciliations would follow, during which another child was born. Yet it had been a mismated marriage from the beginning—a girl from the well-bred, affluent Lombard clan of Georgia tied to a brawler from a world of foul-mouthed roughnecks. "Mr. Cobb," as Charlie still called him, provided well, but offered little more in the area of shared enjoyment, of companionship.

Cobb became a bachelor during much of this season. He hired a cook, but took most of his meals out and kept part of his wardrobe of tailored suits and shirts at the Detroit Athletic Club, located off mainstreet Woodward Avenue. It became a regular sight to watch him drive his Hupmobile from Navin Field to such fashionable restaurants as Churchill's and the Pontchartrain Hotel. His companions at dinner often were from the field of entertainment, such as songwriter-playwright George M. Cohan, and from industry, especially the auto moguls. He would dine early and be in bed by 11:00 P.M.

UNTIL NOW Cobb had mainly taken criticism in stride. After years of it, however, he had become tired of his constantly harped-upon reputation as a base-running villain. Now, not for the first time, he set out to modify his image, to get it across that he was as much the attacked as the attacker. It was chiefly Cobb who had altered baseball's running game by introducing the idea that the base paths primarily belonged to the runner, a man confined to a stipulated strip of the field. He wished it to be understood that he simply was one who went at it harder, more recklessly and violently than others when facing a blocked-off bag. If enemies were spiked or had bones broken while interposing themselves between Cobb and his destination, the blame was not with him, but with what he called "basehogs."

"I'd had more bad raps in New York than anywhere," he complained. "I'd protested [verbally] before. So I began sending letters to the writers, beginning with that damned Bugs Baer."

Arthur "Bugs" Baer of the *New York American* was among sporting reporters and cartoonists who pictured Cobb as fiendish in preparing his spikes in advance to cut down infielders. Baer proclaimed that the Peach used a barbershop strop to apply a sharper edge to his steel. Cobb's letter to Baer—clearly he had a little help in composing it—went:

> Dear Bugs:
>
> May I ask you to furnish me with the names of any individuals, even you, who like criticism? I think we all try to attain—with our hearts in the right places—certain goals. What is criticism, may I ask? Criticism is breaking down, a destroying influence.
>
> As to my sharpening my spikes in a barbershop, no, Bugs, I did not. There is no equipment for such an operation in a barbershop. It calls for a file—not that I am well-acquainted with the filing process. The story of my spikes-sharpening springs from a prank hatched by members of our club, Detroit.
>
> As you know, Bugs, baseball is not a pink-tea party. I have been handed more injuries in the heat of play than I have caused.
>
> Now that I have unbosomed myself, with every good wish for your health and happiness, I am
>
> Ty Cobb.

In other volunteered correspondence to critics he insisted that the false barbershop story began with Tiger rookies on the bench, rasping away at spikes with files while the New York Yankees passed by before a game. Cobb tried to explain, "It was only horseplay by a bunch of bench-riders . . . It wouldn't have been a story for Baer and other writers if they didn't put me in it.

"I have been roughed up more in print on this than on anything."

Bobby "Kentucky Rifle" Veach, who played the outfield in company with the Peach from 1912 to 1923, dissented. "Maybe Ty didn't hone his spikes," Veach testified later, "but he used to yell at me in the field that he was going to get so-and-so the next inning. Then he'd give the works to someone like Cy Morgan [Red Sox], Home Run Baker [Yankees], and Harry Bemis [Cleveland]. He'd draw blood. Liked to go for shins and kneecaps." Veach died in Detroit in 1945, maintaining that such incidents—some of them exaggerated—were mainly true. Was Veach prejudiced? "Some," he conceded. "I hated Cobb's guts from 1912 on for what he did to us."

A practical reason for Veach's stand was that for much of the 1920s, an epidemic of dirty base-running had existed across the American League. As Veach explained it, a symbiotic relationship exists between opposing forces—whatever takes place with one component is bound to set off a mirror reaction in the other. "Clubs got even," said Veach. "Our base runners paid for Cobb's doings." A steady .300 hitter, Veach in one season got into only 114 games, partly due—he claimed—to injuries received in retaliation for his teammate's slashing. Cobb cut twenty-odd men that Veach knew about.

Cobb's suggestion that he should be seen in a more enlightened way mostly resulted in scoffing. The record was plain to see. "I'm afraid," once said Grantland Rice, pro-Cobb among the press, "that he'd too often hurt someone for any forgiveness later." (Rice, however, did not print this at the time.)

In January of 1920, returned from managing San Francisco in the Coast League, the Peach vacationed for a few weeks. He had switched to a thicker, heavier bat of forty-two ounces (up from thirty-seven), theorizing that at age thirty-three his swing was no longer extra quick and that he needed more contact surface. Against popular thinking on this, he felt he could still get around in time and that, on in-tight, strike-zone pitches, the added wood he could get on to the ball would produce a share of clubbed slow infield rollers—"hand hits"—that he could beat out. Further, a thicker bat helped on bunts. He was one of the first bunters who slightly withdrew his bat to "smother" a fastball and so turn a rocket into a precisely placed twenty-foot dribbler. He weighed his new sticks each week to make sure that friction and chips off them had not altered their heft.

ONCE AGAIN, for the fifth springtime, in 1920 he avoided the Tigers, who trained in Macon, Georgia. It poured rain in Macon. Writer-catcher Eddie Ainsmith's poem encouraged him to work out in damp but not soggy Augusta, on the Warren Field where he had broken in as a pro and where semipros were available to pitch to him. Ainsmith's ode went:

> Away down South in the land of cotton
> Where the sky is high
> And the grounds are rotten,
> Stay away! Stay away!
> Stay away! Stay away!

Frank Navin was angry that T.C. had stayed dry while the rest of the club barnstormed through terrible weather. Needing to speak with him about a contemplated change in Detroit team management, Navin tracked him down to an Augusta golf course, where he was trying to break 80. Cobb kept Navin waiting, then recommended that the owner take up golf for his big belly.

Finding it difficult to beat 195 pounds on the scales, Cobb showed many of the symptoms of a man lulled by his own accomplishments and—he admitted this later—coasting for the first time. Rising at 7:00 A.M. had been his habit from farm-boy days. Lately his clock had been set for nine-thirty or ten. Golf had become something of a harmful habit. He had found a game difficult for him, and went at it for thirty-six holes per day. Members of the Augusta Country Club were warned to stand clear when partnering with him—he threw clubs upon missing a putt. He remained away from his job, not bothering to join the Tigers until April 10, only four days before opening day in Chicago, where he had four hits in two game-losing Tiger efforts. After that he went into as prolonged a slump as he had ever known.

"I beat myself," he later put it. "Too much horsing around, too much anticipating. I'd averaged almost the same in the past three years—.383, .382, .384. My legs were in better shape. So I was grooved and saw no reason why it wouldn't go on the same."

Sharing his slump, the Tigers lost their first thirteen games. Few worse starts were on record. Defensively they were a joke. Cobb's inspiration was gone. He developed a hitch in his swing—the heavier bat hurt, not helped—and well into the season he was struggling to reach .200. He injured a knee and, reinjuring it, was sidelined for weeks. There was the strange sight of the mighty Tyrus taking extra batting practice in the twilight after games. Hughie Jennings had largely a stand-pat lineup carried over from 1919, one with infield leaks, and had but one pitcher, Howard Ehmke, able to win as many as 15 games in the season. Catcher Oscar Stanage batted .231, new infielder Babe Pinelli .229. Lefty Dutch Leonard lost 17 games, Hooks Dauss lost 21. Only the Philadelphia Athletics of the long-suffering Connie Mack were a worse aggregation.

The American League was tougher than ever, with Cleveland, Chicago, and New York the class. Pennant-bound Cleveland had Jim Bagby en route to a 31–12 pitching year; New York had Ruth batting .370 and compiling a fearsome 54 home runs (10 against Detroit), and effective throwing from Carl Mays and Bob Shawkey. Detroit had Cobb, averaging .265 all spring long, a horrible sight. At length, in June, Cobb found his stroke, reaching .300, then .334 toward the end. His recovery came far too late, and for the first time since 1916 he lost his league's batting championship. That trophy fell to compact, 170-pound, left-handed George Sisler of St. Louis.

Sisler had been scouted in college by Cobb, but Navin irrationally had failed to sign him. In 1920 he finished with a stunning 257 base hits—the most blows struck to date in the modern majors—for a .407 average. Nobody except Shoeless Joe Jackson, who in 1911 averaged .408 to Cobb's .420, had hit .400 or more since Cobb's 1912 mark of .410. Leg-sore Tyrus had appeared in but 112 games in 1920. Shoeless Joe at Chicago rubbed it in with a .382 mark, and 58 more runs driven in than Cobb.

There was a bit of consolation for T.C. one July day against the Yankees. He made a racing-in catch of a screaming line drive by Wally Pipp and with Ruth carelessly wandering off second base, continued on to tag him out. He applied a vicious blow to Ruth. "Oh, did that hurt the poor boy?" asked Cobb. "Maybe you should take up pattycake."

Casey Stengel, long afterward, said, "I was playin' for Pittsburgh that year, but I saw Ty a few times. He was goin' through hell. He's really burnin'. He tells me that maybe he'll hang them up. But I knew better. Losing was about to make him as good as ever."

Sparing the sympathy, much of the press was of the opinion that his loss of speed—in bat velocity, running the bases, and particularly in chasing fly balls—was so evident that it foreshadowed his end as the Peerless One. Harry Salsinger of the Detroit press was more circumspect, but did comment that Cobb's tremendous drop in steals, from a league-leading 68 and 55 a few seasons back to 14 in 1920, pointed to his doing more pinch-hitting than playing regularly in the future. Further, a seventh-place Detroit finish was seen as the last chance for Hughie Jennings as the club's manager. Jennings now had finishing marks over a decade of second, sixth (twice), fourth, second, third, fourth, seventh, fourth, and seventh.

In September during a series in Boston, weeks before Cobb came in only tenth-best in the American League batting race, Jennings held a private meeting with Cobb. They met in a Boston bar; Jennings's hands were shaky. As Cobb later described it:

"Ty, I can't go on. I'm not thinking straight," admitted Jennings.

"Stop drinking so much," replied Cobb bluntly. "I can smell your breath from six feet."

Jennings would not confess that he had become an alcoholic. "I never drink before games. It's just that I'm worn out, tired all the time. Navin is always on my back."

"How about yesterday's game?" demanded Cobb. "You were out of it, not thinking."

In the ninth inning, the Tigers had trailed the Red Sox by three runs, Detroit had runners on first and second and no outs, with hard-hitting Bobby Veach at bat. Jennings flashed the bunt sign. The Tigers protested. They appealed to Cobb to stop Jennings from such a bonehead play. So Cobb had run out to the coaching box. He had dropped to one knee, pretending to be tying his shoelace. Jennings stared back blankly when reminded by him that there were no outs and that Veach hammered Boston pitching. When he failed to react, Cobb removed the bunt sign. Swinging away, Veach poled a home run, tying the score. The Tigers went on to win.

"Go on the wagon, Hughie," urged Cobb. "Go to a health farm this winter. And take 1921 out."

Jennings, a college man, the National League's champion fielder in his heyday, at age fifty-one was in bad shape. For the 1921 season he would be a coach with the New York Giants; after a nervous breakdown a few years later, he would retire. The once-boisterous "Eeee-yahhhh Man" who blew whistles, honked horns, and capered on the coaching line, would die young, in 1928, at age fifty-eight—looking like seventy-five.

WHILE COBB'S statistics dived sharply—he had failed to stand first in his circuit in any of the thirteen statistical categories, even as Ruth led in runs scored, home runs, and runs batted in—organized ball was headed in the 1920s Jazz and Nonsense Age to a boomtime in which overall annual attendance would reach 9.5 million and then 10 million. Across the leagues, fan turnout would rise 50 percent over the draw of 1919. Some owners boasted that they could fill a 100,000-seat arena if they had the seats. The Yankees, to name one case, even while failing to win the 1920 pennant, doubled their 1919 figure with 1,287,422 paid attendance. Now that more than 8 million automobiles were on U.S. roads, fans could come a far distance to attend a game.

The World Series was first broadcast in 1921—the Giants edging the Yankees—and within four years the Chicago Cubs' owner, William Wrigley, made the revolutionary move of allowing his games to be aired on the radio. Ladies' Day, with admission free, was introduced, to much acclaim. Parasols, cloches, and bobbed hair were seen scattered throughout ballparks.

Equipment changes were overdue. A glove with a pocket replaced the old flat "pancake" glove, thinner-handled bats became the vogue, the pitchers were allowed to use a resin bag—coarse powder—to obtain a better grip on the ball.

More than that, the spitball was outlawed in 1920. An advisory council of the National Commission, in the process of abolishing spitters and freak pitches in general, ruled, however, that those who heavily relied on wetting the ball could finish their careers using saliva, but saliva only. Pitcher Bill Doak of St. Louis had argued that an outright ban would deprive at least seventeen veterans of their earning power.

But once these men had retired, the ancient, controversial pitch would be out—at least legally.

ON AUGUST 16 of the 1920 season, the Tigers were in Boston for a Red Sox series. Cobb, in his hotel bed with bandaged legs, received a phone call from United Press. A reporter asked, "Did you hear what happened in the Yankee-Cleveland game today in New York?"

"No, I didn't," replied Cobb.

"Ray Chapman was hit on the head by Carl Mays and he may not survive."

"That's bad," said Cobb.

Continued United Press, "There's a lot of feeling over this . . . The Washington club has stated that it won't play the Yankees again while Mays is pitching. They claim he throws at hitters deliberately. Cleveland says it'll boycott, too. I'd like to ask you—what about Detroit?"

Careful about how he answered, Cobb said, "Well, I'm only a member of the Detroit team. I don't set policy. Anyway, I'm here in Boston and didn't see it."

Obviously out for a headline-making quotation, the United Press man pushed him to say more. Cobb grew irritated. "Look here!" he snapped. "Under no circumstances will I comment on it . . . Even if I'd been there I doubt that I would have commented." With that he hung up on the caller. So he remembered it years later.

His phone began ringing again, and within the hour Cobb knew that in the fifth inning of a Cleveland-Yankee game at the Polo Grounds, the Yankees' submarine specialist, Carl Mays, had badly beaned Cleveland's shortstop, Ray Chapman. The ball had caromed off Chapman's left temple with an audible *crack* and bounced back toward Mays, who fielded it and threw to first for the out. Later Mays was to submit that he thought the ball had hit Chapman's bat, which had caused the deflection. The *Washington Evening Star*'s report went: "Chapman collapsed . . . was lifted to his feet by players . . . staggered and crumpled . . . was carried to an ambulance . . . An operation was hurriedly decided upon shortly after midnight, when a portion of Chapman's fractured skull was removed by surgeons.

"Chapman died at St. Lawrence Hospital at 4:50 o'clock this morning." Major baseball had its first fatality. Incredibly, it would never experience another.

Outside New York, Mays was lambasted and found guilty, without proof, of purposely beaning Chapman. When it was reported that the victim, before his hospitalization, had murmured in the clubhouse, "Tell Mays not to worry," anti-Mays feeling expanded. The burly 195-pound Mays, while performing for the Boston Red Sox prior to becoming a Yankee, had built a reputation for throwing close to or at batters. His brushbacks and knockdowns had long brought complaints. At the moment Mays was working on a 26–11 season, helping the Yankees toward what could be their first pennant since the team's founding in 1903. Three times the former Highlanders had finished second; recently they had not done even that well—fourth in 1918, third in 1919. Suspending Mays could kill their chances for 1920.

Cobb was well acquainted with Mays's style. The "slingshotter" never hurled dangerously close to him. If he ever went that far, Cobb let it be known, there would be reprisal of a strong nature. "Mays threw at others with a rising fastball—right at the chin," Cobb had noted to a few sportswriters, off the record. "We call him Bean-O."

Cleveland, headed for a pennant it would win, had a popular player in the twenty-nine-year-old Chapman, a fielding flash and a .303 hitter when he died. The Kentuckian had averaged .267 and .300 in the two years before that. He kept the Indians loose by such things as putting garden snakes into his teammates' hotel beds.

Forty-eight hours after his death the Tigers came into New York for a four-game series with the Yankees. Cobb found the city's newspapers blossoming headlines: "COBB SAYS MAYS THROWS KILLER PITCH" and "MAYS SHOULD BE BANNED, SAYS PEACH." At least five papers were saying it. From his Commodore Hotel quarters he issued denials. He had said no such thing. But the headlines were believed, and Manhattan fans in large number were set to make it the hottest yet for an old enemy when the teams squared off.

Grantland Rice, always a "friendly," visited the Peach at the Commodore. An irate Cobb greeted him with, "United Press lied and now everybody is doing it. They're saying that Chapman was slow in ducking and avoiding blame on Mays. Off the record, I'd like to see Ban Johnson run that bastard out of the league. But you know Johnson—always protecting the pitcher." League president Johnson confusedly announced on that weekend that Mays might not pitch again, then exonerated him; big Carl was back at work within a week and won his next game with ease.

Rice's subsequent account of his Commodore meeting with Cobb on a Friday, published hours before a Saturday opener with the Yanks, went, "I found him in bed with a temperature of 102. He was as mad as I'd ever seen him. Both of his thighs were a mass of adhesive and torn flesh, testimony to some rough base-stealing. It was enough to turn your stomach. Ty was up to his chin in morning papers—all blasting him for that interview back in Boston . . . I told him the first thing he needed was a doctor.

"He said never mind the doctor, he had to be at the game tomorrow and face the wolves." He asked Rice to file a wire story that he had not criticized Mays. Rice did so, but it was too late.

"On Saturday," described Rice in his 1953 autobiography, *The Tumult and the Shouting*, "33,000 stormed the old Polo Grounds—Yankee Stadium wasn't completed until 1923. Cobb didn't take batting practice, in fact didn't appear on the field until ten minutes before the game. When he did show . . . making the long walk in from the center-field clubhouse, the crowd stood as one and booed."

On his way in, he roughly shoved out of his way the Yankee batting-practice pitcher. He stopped near home plate, stared at the audience, and bowed toward the press box, as if saying, *There are the people responsible for this*. Among those yelling crudities at him from the bench was Babe Ruth.

Old New York gave him the worst jeering of his career. The Polo Grounds rocked. In a return gesture, seemingly aimed at his teammates for not speaking up in his support over the Chapman-Mays matter, he did not sit in the Tiger dugout. Until game time he sat in a lower grandstand seat, as if inviting physical attack.

Detroit drubbed the Yankees, 10–3. Cobb had one single, one stolen base, and scored one run. He made a racing catch of Ruth's long line drive. Next day, Sunday, before thirty-six thousand, he gained more substantial revenge. In an 11–9 slugout won by the Tigers, the Peach was next to unstoppable: five base hits in six times at bat, two RBIs, and another run-saving catch. Some Polo Grounders cheered him for that retaliation. One day later, facing a Carl Mays returned to duty, he added two more hits, even while Mays coolly delivered a 10–0 shutout. In the series' fourth game, Detroit was the 5–3 winner. Cobb starred afield and doubled.

Fans noticed no incidents between Cobb and Mays. But there was a concealed one. In his autobiography the Peach spoke of walking past Mays during the game and piping, "Hello, Bean-O, old boy." Wrote Cobb, "I wanted to upset him."

His satisfaction was incomplete but pleasant. "The three games we won out of four killed the Yankees," he pointed out. New York finished the 1920 season precisely three games out of first place.

BACK IN Detroit to conclude a wasted season, Cobb awakened on the morning of September 28, 1920, to glaring headlines: "CHICAGO SOX PLAYERS CONFESS SELLING GAMES—EIGHT ARE INDICTED: ALL SUSPENDED." The "unholy octet," named by a Chicago grand jury, stood indicted of laying down to the Cincinnati Reds in the 1919 World Series, allowing the Reds to win the playoff, five games to three. All but one were still on the White Sox, who at that point were trailing Cleveland by only 6 percentage points in the standings, with a full week's games remaining to be played. Chicago owner Charlie Comiskey had no choice but to suspend the dirty players, even though it brought a decisive end to the club's pennant hopes.

The news itself was not surprising to Cobb, who had long realized that the 1919 Series had involved rottenness to the core. What may have been astounding even to baseball insiders like himself, however, was the magnitude of the operation. The stunning fix had been wholesale. Those facing prosecution were two starting pitchers, Eddie Cicotte and Claude "Lefty" Williams, almost the entire White Sox infield—George "Buck" Weaver, Swede Risberg, and Arnold "Chick" Gandil—along with outfielders Shoeless Joe Jackson and Oscar "Hap" Felsch and utility man Fred McMullin. They had committed the incredible frameup for gamblers' money. Cicotte, one of the more artistic of pitchers, and celebrated slugger Jackson confessed all, leading to implication of six others. The main gamblers involved were identified as New York's gangland-connected Arnold Rothstein, ex–boxing champ Abe Attell, John "Sport" Sullivan of Chicago, and Philadelphia's Billy Maharg. Investigation would indicate that the fixers had offered sums ranging from a reported $10,000 to $100,000, with some portions of that paid to some of the players. Rothstein, later shot and killed in

1928 by unnamed underworld parties, left behind in his files affidavits showing that he put up $80,000 in bribe money.

In the role of commentator for the Wheeler Syndicate, Cobb had attended the "bagged" Series and for the past twelve months had known what had happened. He had no comment to make to the press after the scandal broke. Privately Cobb remarked to Jennings, "When they get to the bottom of this, Charley Comiskey's cheap pay will come out." Jennings didn't need a reminder that the Sox owner paid Cicotte, after his fourteen years in the league and recent won-and-lost marks of 28–12 in 1917 and 29–7 in 1919, $5,000 per season. Happy Felsch and Buck Weaver were at $4,000 and $4,500. Joe Jackson, currently hitting .351, drew $6,000. Cobb knew that the White Sox—now universally called the Black Sox—had quietly been talking team strike. Comiskey's payroll was said to be the lowest anywhere in the majors. (In point of fact his salaries were not markedly lower than other owners', but that's what people thought.)

Drawing 236,928 customers, the infamous Series had richly rewarded Comiskey and some other franchise holders. It grossed $722,110, or nearly one-quarter of a million dollars above the former record set in 1912 for games between the Boston Red Sox and New York Giants. Cobb claimed that it had been only a matter of time until the Sox found relief through the Rothsteins and Attells. "A dead lock to happen," he said later on.

Cobb remembered certain on-the-spot observations made before the dirty work began. He had registered at Cincinnati's Sinton Hotel the day before the opening game. The Sinton's lobby teemed with flashy types—not only the usual ticket scalpers, but gamblers in number. Although no New York team was involved, he noticed that a large eastern contingent had showed up. Cobb recognized Sport Sullivan, odds-setter and bookie. Six or so years earlier, Sullivan had been banned from Detroit's clubhouse area. Arnold Rothstein, too, was greeting people in the lobby and laying bets. This was Cobb's first tip that the Series' outcome might be predetermined.

Another tip was that early odds strangely favored the White Sox only slightly, and then moved, in a rush of money, to favor the Reds by 6–5 and 7–5. That didn't add up. Chicago definitely was the stronger team, with a club batting average on the season of .287 against Cincinnati's .263. The winner needed to take five of nine games of a Series that had been extended from the usual four of seven—and the Sox had a 29-game winner, the knuckleballing Cicotte, and Lefty Williams, a 23–11 pitcher.

Cobb was warned away from making a bet. White Sox manager Kid Gleason, who had once tried to obtain the Peach for his team, remarked to him, "Some funny things have happened to us [over the past season]. Damned funny." Cobb replied, "Yes, Kid, I've noticed." He sat in the press box as an observer and watched the Reds in game number one knock Cicotte out of the box in the fourth inning and win 9–1. In game two, the Reds won, 4–2, over Williams. Some writers were suspicious about the White Sox's erratic play. Then Cobb learned by the grapevine that Gleason secretly had gone to Comiskey to report something fishy going on. Comiskey reportedly consulted National League president John Heydler, who refused to believe the story. Other alarms were sounded to high officials. Nothing was done to stop the Reds from closing out one of the greatest of upsets in eight games. Cincinnati won twice by shutouts and once by a score of 10–5.

"Another thing I heard before the rats got busy," recalled Cobb, "was that it had been arranged for Cicotte to hit the first batter up in the first inning with a pitch. That was the signal that the fix was on . . . Well, Cicotte hit Maury Rath right off . . . so I knew for sure we had a stacked deck.

"Any ball game can be easily fixed," mused Cobb as an elderly man. "All you need is a pitcher to take a little off his fastball and a shortstop–second base combination to mess up the doubleplay."

In Cobb's book and that of many others, Comiskey was as despicable as the Black Sox. Much evidence accumulated in the winter following the Series indicated that Comiskey had to be aware of the facts. Yet he dismissed all the evidence as hearsay. Before exposure came, he signed suspected players to 1920 contracts, and in fact gave salary raises to Cicotte, Williams, Jackson, Felsch and others.

The "Square Sox," those players who had been guiltless, had to play the 1920 season alongside teammates they loathed. Honest Sox second baseman Eddie Collins, a future Hall of Famer, one day confided to Cobb, "I almost quit the game, Ty. Everytime I looked at a guy I wondered if he was trying." Yet such was the talent on the team that they almost won again, before the suspensions were announced.

NATIONWIDE, THE reaction to the news of the fix was shock, disillusion-ment, and disgust. The World Series had attained such a devoted, quasi-religious mass following that in the century's second decade it outranked all native sports classics—heavyweight title fights, the Indi-anapolis 500 auto race, the Kentucky Derby, any tennis event, and even the Olympic Games when the U.S. was heavily represented. A leading historian of baseball, Harold Seymour, years later quoted a pre-1920 sports-journal poem to show how naive the public had been:

> For the baseball season is so soaring
> High above all, serene
> Unaffected by the roaring
> For the grand old game is clean!

But now conspiracy of a high degree had been uncovered, and public faith tottered. Cicotte, Shoeless Joe, Felsch, and Williams signed confessions. On September 28, 1920, a Chicago grand jury brought in indictments against eight Black Soxers. But then the paperwork and confessions were stolen—perhaps by the state at the probable instiga-tion of Arnold Rothstein—and cases against the accused were so weakened that the state's attorney general admitted that he could not win in a trial proceeding. After legal and other delays, on August 2, 1921, a jury returned a decision of not guilty of intent to defraud for all the Black Sox, along with some of the gambler-fixers. It was said that some of the jurors, after the verdict, threw a courtroom party, bringing in drinks and carrying the acquitted players around on their shoulders. To much of the U.S. press, the decision was a terrible mis-carriage of justice, an official whitewashing from the league's top on down.

The rejoicing was of short duration, for organized baseball was now being run by a man named Kenesaw Mountain Landis. Even before the Black Sox came along, a struggle had gone on among own-ers and league presidents to reshape the game under a commission of no more than three men, able to rule broadly over everything that occurred. The three-man idea was dropped after long wrangling, and the magnates hit upon hiring a single czar who would prevent more scandal, with its potential to cause fan boycotts and reduce receipts. Fifty-four-year-old federal court judge Ken Landis, small in stature and without a college degree, was a famously tough jurist, incorruptible, and a lifelong baseball fan. He was also a notorious egotist, a prohibitionist, and a man who hated gambling in all its forms.

Landis took office as the game's first high commissioner in January 1921. Owners ceded him unlimited power. By contract Landis had the authority "to take punitive action against leagues, clubs, officers and players found guilty of detrimental conduct." Among his first acts as suzerain was to disregard the jury's verdict and banish all of the Black Soxers from professional ball for life. Landis was a law unto himself. Beyond his initial crackdown, Landis threatened to blacklist any player found taking part in a game in which one of the ineligibles appeared. "Landis batting cleanup," went the expression; "God help the unholy."

LANDIS'S OBVIOUS intent to investigate ballplayers' habits worried Cobb in the winter of 1920–21. The commissioner's office interrogated various prominent players on many teams, including Cobb. He was clean. Other Tigers were checked out. It was clear that Landis's purge was far from ended. One result was that John McGraw and owner Charles Stoneham of the Giants were forced to divest themselves of the ownership of the Oriental Park and Jockey Club racetrack in faraway Cuba. Any form of gambling was out for management and players. Cobb had plans to buy stock in a Canadian track at Ontario, but this was now prohibited by Landis.

He wasn't talking, but Cobb knew of corruption in locations other than Chicago and Cincinnati. He was not surprised when Landis, between 1921 and 1924, after a lengthy survey of conditions, excommunicated four New York Giants—outfielder Jimmy O'Connell, pitcher Phil Douglas, outfielder Benny Kauff, and coach Cozy Dolan—for gambling and other violations. Still more fell, among them infielder Joe Gedeon of St. Louis and infielder Eugene Paulette of the Philadelphia Phillies.

The fixed 1919 Series seemed more and more to be a backdrop to what went on behind scenes at ballparks, bars, and poolrooms. "Back then anything went you could get away with," Cobb stated in 1960. "There were crooks all over the place . . . I advised Navin to hire himself a detective." One day in 1921 Cobb walked past a Detroit poolticket room where for a dollar and up you could buy a chance on who won or lost, an Americanized form of parimutuel betting. Three Tigers were there, just leaving.

"Get the hell away from here," ordered Cobb.

"Oh, we're just looking around," they protested.

"Get away now and don't come back or I'll turn you over to Navin's cop. Or would you rather talk to Landis?"

Navin, indeed, had employed a detective, a huge, retired policeman named "Sheriff" Crowe. The Tigers were said to resent Crowe, but with Cobb maintaining his own watch, there were no Detroit scandals in the early 1920s.

Weighing heavily upon Cobb in 1920, and inexorably gaining in popularity, was the figure of George Herman Ruth, who was upstaging all of the four-hundred-odd men in the big time. The Babe in his beginning Yankee years was moving more and more into the national consciousness, collecting more columns of press space than any individual other than Cobb had produced. Moreover, Ruth was coming along in the role of savior of scandal-wracked baseball. His clubbing *was* helping in a major way to minimize the damage done by the 1919 World Series, although that damage was ongoing, as evidenced by Judge Landis's ejections of more players. The Babe hit more homers than entire ball clubs. He provoked an atavistic longing for someone not confined to the old game of science, and who blasted five-hundred- to six-hundred-footers into "Ruthville," wherever the park might be. He was lovable and magnetic. People dogged him on the streets. United Press would soon run a newspaper box feature each time he furiously lofted a ball out to the Knothole Kids waiting in the streets and parking lots.

It would become news when a bee stung the Babe, when he was jailed for speeding, when a "crazed" fan threatened him with a knife, when he bought his wife a mink coat, arrived at work with a hangover, smashed his bat in two after striking out, had lunch with a movie star, or even lit a big Havana cigar. Following 1920, in which Ruth averaged .376, with an unbelievable 54 homers and a record slugging average of .847, Cobb's detractors in effect told him to step aside. Hercules had arrived to take over.

Veteran baseball people still saw the Peach as the best in the business. Tris Speaker declared that "it goes without saying that Cobb still is the greatest ballplayer around." Yankee manager Miller Huggins, of the old school, also stuck to his view that to those who knew inside baseball, Ruth still had a way to go to catch Cobb for ability to start a rally and sustain it, to supply the clutch base hit, lay the bunt, and generally disrupt the defense. Although he was Ruth's manager, Hug confided what he believed to insiders. At the approach of 1921, as Cobb perceived it, Ruth was not yet totally proven, and things might change to the Peach's advantage. Greatness, to him, meant something that came after only ten years of performance.

Yet the Bambino's prowess undoubtedly figured in a crucial change of mind on Cobb's part. At various points since 1918 he had brushed off Navin's offers to him to replace Hughie Jennings and assume the position of player-manager. Yet to take over as manager would obviously center fresh attention on Cobb. Where Ruth would be confined to hitting, fielding, and spot pitching, Cobb would have the status of commander of the whole show. Should the Tigers start winning—that chance was there, if not likely—he might top anything he had yet achieved. Acquiring new personnel would be the key to a comeback. That, and kicking some lazy Detroit tails or trading them.

He had gone on turning down Navin until late 1920, when Walter O. Briggs, an auto-body millionaire of Detroit, made an emotional appeal. Briggs had recently bought an estimated $250,000 interest in Navin's franchise, and was pledged to make Detroit once again a contender. It was Cobb's duty, he declared, to save the Tigers by taking over as manager.

Said Cobb to Briggs, "I don't want the responsibility. Also it would hurt my hitting and I won't have that."

"Give it a try," urged Briggs. "It could lead to a partial ownership in the franchise." Briggs knew that Cobb very much wanted that.

"Hire Kid Gleason," advised Cobb. "He's a winner and you can forget the Black Sox thing. He had no part in it, as everyone knows." The fifty-four-year-old Gleason, nonplaying manager of the despised Sox, was tactically as smart as they came.

Cobb continued to say no to managing while off game hunting in the South. Then, at the Roosevelt Hotel in New Orleans early in December 1920, he ran across E. A. Batchelor, a Detroit sportswriter in town to cover the University of Detroit–Loyola football game. "There's no two ways about it," coaxed Batchelor. "The whole town wants you to manage and, if you don't, Navin will give the job to Pants Rowland."

That disturbed Cobb. In his ghostwritten book, *My Life in Baseball*, he stated, "Big leaguers considered Rowland a bush-league manager. He'd never appeared as a player in a game of major league ball. He was a lucky phony . . . had been released at Chicago to bring in Gleason. I hated to think of Rowland in charge."

Batchelor went on, "If they sign Rowland, could you play under him?"

"I'd have to think that over," returned Cobb.

Batchelor phoned Navin in Detroit to report that his man seemed to be wavering.

Cobb summarized what followed. "I was in a unique position for a ballplayer. Newspapers had a stock line, 'Ty Cobb, the only millionaire ballplayer in history.' By 1921 I had added investments in the auto industry, stocks and bonds, real estate, cotton, and Coca-Cola . . . had accumulated a fortune outside of baseball. I was independent of my salary and not tempted by the pay raise accompanying the manager's position. But the reputation of the Tigers as steady losers did bother me. I could see many things that had to be done."

Two weeks before New Year's Day of 1921, he made the carefully considered decision to accept. His takeover would mean that Rowland would not get his hands on two dandy Tiger newcomers: catcher Johnny Bassler and infielder Lu Blue, both with .300 potential, both defensively solid. Nor would Pants Rowland be in charge and mismanage Harry Heilmann, by now a feared power hitter—one in a million, said Heilmann fans. He could play first base as well as the outfield. Another motive for Cobb was to show his versatility. Tris Speaker, his longtime rival for all-around honors, had managed the Cleveland Indians into the last World Series while hitting a big .388 in his role as player, a true mark of greatness. In the past there had been others who doubled as player-manager and won pennants: Frank Chance, Fielder Jones, Jake Stahl, Jimmy Collins, Fred Clarke.

All factors duly weighed, Cobb agreed to talk with Navin, who in December was in New York for the American League winter meetings. They conferred at the Hotel Vanderbilt. Cobb insisted on a one-year contract. He would not commit beyond that. This appeared to be cautionary, in the event that the Tigers flopped ("It was for that reason— and because I didn't get along with Navin," he said in later years.) In negotiating, he required that Navin agree not to interfere with his direction of the team, and grant to him all decisions on scouting of minor-leaguers, accept his primary say-so on who would be signed, traded, or sold, and give him a voice on salaries paid. ("Otherwise Navin would have tried to tell me who to pitch and when.")

It was a lot to demand. Navin deliberated for most of a day at the Vanderbilt. A deadlock was broken when Walter Briggs sided with Cobb. He would be paid $35,000 per year—up from his present $20,000-with-bonuses player's salary—and given the private office Jennings had enjoyed, along with expenses paid for the odd trip home to Georgia. At $35,000 and a few thousand more in previously established bonuses, he would become the highest-paid director of field operations in the game, other than part-owner John McGraw of the Giants and, possibly, Speaker in Cleveland.

On his birthday, December 18, he signed to boss the Tigers in 1921. "I had my lawyers read the contract three times," he wrote in a memoir. "I didn't trust Navin."

Thereby he also became, along with Speaker, one of only two player-managers then active in the majors. In the lobby, newsmen waited for the official word. "Well, I did it, boys," announced Cobb, while Navin and Briggs stood smilingly by. "I feel like I've undergone a change of life." To questioners he replied, "I'll expect a hustling club. If I have to crack down on players, that will be time to clear them off the roster."

Damon Runyon of the *New York American*, who no longer wrote about baseball regularly and was gaining fame with his fiction, thought enough of Cobb's signing to join the press turnout. "That's quite a birthday present you're getting—thirty-five thousand dollars," Runyon said. The Peach had always liked Runyon, who as a sportswriter had not been one of the New York sect who attacked his every aggressive act. Yet now he was short-tempered with the writer: "You're wrong. It's anything *but* a present. This thing has been forced on me!"

At a moment that called for a celebration—how many men ever got to manage in the big leagues?—he was experiencing doubts that he had made the wise move. His reputation would be on the line. "I had signed away my independence," he told me, forty years later. "Up to now I'd been judged on what I did, alone. But no manager who ever lived could beat the blame when his men fucked up—didn't give it everything they had, boozed it up, alibied their mistakes, faked injuries. There were enough of that kind on Detroit's contract list to give me a headache. I'd be judged by what they did. And there wasn't much time before training began to hang a price on some and run them off."

Asked by Georgia friends that winter what would happen to his career, Cobb pulled a long face. "My hitting will get back to normal, because this time I'll be bearing down," he predicted to his cousin, Harrison Gailey. "But I won't stay more than one season as manager if Veach, Sutherland, Young, Bush, Jones"—naming 1921 roster men— "lay down on me and we finish far out. I won't be associated with quitters." He told Robert Woodruff of Coca-Cola, "It will take three years for me to rebuild this team. Seventh place was where they belonged last season. The first thing I'll do is teach them to hit for percentage, not for the fences. I expect to see that job through."

In February he traveled to San Antonio, Texas, to inspect the Tigers' new training camp. Breckenridge Park was rutty, but no worse than the poor fields where Detroit had worked out in the past. If Navin wanted to save money in renting the place, Cobb did not propose to begin their changed relationship by putting up a squawk.

Back home, he met with associates who were negotiating to buy the minor-league Augusta franchise and physical plant. Cobb's end of it would be nearly fifty thousand dollars. He could afford the investment. When the deal went through, it meant he was co-owner of minor-league teams in two states, Rhode Island and Georgia, the wintertime manager of the San Francisco Seals in the Coast League, player-manager in Detroit, the owner of auto dealerships, cattle and cotton acreage, and holder of what he hoped would be a continued strong position on Wall Street.

One busy fellow . . . and pushing his luck.

CHAPTER TWENTY-ONE

"WHY CAN'T THEY DO IT MY WAY?"

"How much help are you prepared to give me?" *I asked of Navin and his partners at the start of 1921.*

"Everything you need to win," *Navin came back.* "My partners go along with that."

. . . . . .

"His weak spine showing all the way, Navin did nothing of the sort. He sabotaged his own ball club. In my six years as manager, I had the worst ownership any manager ever suffered. At the same time, Navin wasn't giving the government an honest tax account on his gate receipts."

Ty Cobb
My Life in Baseball: The True Record

Thunderstorms and lightning off the Gulf of Mexico slowed spring-training workouts for a while. Some observers joked that Cobb had brought the stormy weather with him. He arrived early in San Antonio in 1921, took a suite at the Alamo Hotel, and called in the press. The "pussycat" Tigers, he declared, would be a different group than the one the fans had been seeing. Item: they would reform their off-field habits. Item: infielders would turn more double plays or be benched. Item: the Tigers would come out fighting.

"Anyone not hustling will be gone," said Cobb. "If we don't finish better than last year, I will give up the job—that I guarantee."

New York and other eastern writers were not overwhelmed by his offer. The seventh-place squad he had inherited was by no means hopelessly deteriorated in all categories. It still had some strong bats, in Heilmann's, Veach's, and Cobb's, and an improving Howard Ehmke among the pitchers. A miracle worker wasn't needed to elevate Detroit from a previous 61–93 in 1920 to sixth place or better.

A harsh boss laid down new rules. Before the full roster had assembled and while he was playing golf at a local course, he was asked by Harry Bullion of the *Detroit Free Press*, "What about golf for the players?" Under Jennings they had been allowed a game now and then. "That's out for everyone," he said. "I'll confiscate the clubs of anyone showing up with them. It's a totally different swing from batting, and fouls you up." Yet Cobb, who planned to play 140 or so baseball games himself, could swing drivers, two-irons, and niblicks in his spare time.

He also ordered practice on Sunday. Everyone was confined to camp on weekends except the boss, who was often gone from town, checking out minor-leaguers of the Southwest and visiting Texas-born Tris Speaker at his Cleveland Indians camp in Fort Worth. Cobb and Speaker had become mutual admirers, and that spring the Peach hosted a party for the Indians' manager, a rock of a man who had pushed Cobb to some of his records and in 1916 briefly had usurped his batting championship. At the party, talk turned to the best way for a player to prepare for retirement.

"Buy Coca-Cola stock for sure," Cobb advised Tris and Philadelphia sportswriter Tiny Maxwell. "Don't sell for a little profit. Forget about it for a few years and live off it when you want to retire." By not taking the tip, Maxwell estimated, he lost out on $240,000 to $300,000 by 1929, when Coca-Cola, despite a national depression, declared three major stock dividends. Speaker did buy in, Cobb told me, and prospered.

Speaker found the Peach to be more tense and nervous than ever before. He advised Cobb to slow down or he would burn out by mid-season. In the mid-1950s, Speaker recalled to me, "He was taking it all too big, determined to make something overnight of a weak team." Cobb's hair had thinned out to about one-third of its former growth. Worry lines furrowed his cheeks. He had a new habit of clenching his hands during conversations. He took several more drinks than was usual. The gossip among the Tigers was that T.C. had become a closet drinker. That rumor was superfluous; by habit he had been taking on extra bourbon rations in private after games.

Imposing a midnight curfew on the club at San Antonio, he drove the Tigers harder in the next weeks than clubs normally are goaded. Bunting practice by the hour was ordered for all. He worked long hours to infuse some of his passion for winning into an organization known for its malingering under Jennings. Cobb made no pretense of feeling anything but contempt for a confirmed second-division bunch. "All we hear from morning to night is baseball," groused such veterans as Donie Bush, known at Navin Field as Error-every-other-inning Bush. Sport-page critics wrote laudatory columns about how Cobb was lighting fires under .230 hitters and "reorganizing" the whole team. They were intrigued by the way he passed out cigars to men who did well in exhibition games. To be seen smoking a "Cobb stogie" meant you were doing well.

But seasoned hands such as pitchers Dutch Leonard and Hooks Dauss and fielders Veach and Heilmann liked a night out on San Antonio town, and Cobb's device of hiring hotel bellhops to report on what time they checked in was considered lowdown-sneaky. Cobb said that he jumped on Leonard with, "The report shows you got in at two A.M."

"No," protested Leonard, "I was inside the hotel at midnight."

"Where in the hotel? In some cunt's room?"

"No, in the bar—by myself."

"You were drinking from midnight to two A.M.?"

"Well, I had a couple," admitted Leonard. "Just to make me sleepy."

"You're fined fifty dollars!" roared Cobb. And he made the penalty stick.

John McGraw's New York Giants, also training in San Antonio, lived across Alamo Plaza from the Tigers' hotel. No Tiger was permitted to cross that square to visit with the Giants. Cobb refused unconditionally to schedule even one training game with his neighbors. Although San Antonio citizens were eager for such a pairing, and everyone from the mayor on down protested, Cobb was adamant. In part it was a case of reverberations from 1917, when the Giants and Tigers had staged a springtime brawl at Waxahachie, Texas, ending with Cobb twisting McGraw's nose. McGraw had seethed ever since.

To complaints that the feuding was unfair to San Antonio fans, Cobb said, "I have no use for that bigmouthed McGraw. He and his team don't exist." McGraw sent a messenger across Alamo Plaza to notify the Peach that the Giants would play Detroit only if Cobb personally apologized. "Tell McGraw he can go to hell!" jeered Cobb.

It seemed silly, but if you looked closer, the matter ran deeper than a single vendetta. Baseball tradition as far back as the 1880s held that an opponent remains your enemy at all times. No fraternizing permitted. If Detroit met the National Leaguers now, the next thing you could expect was that the players would be *talking* back and forth. That would violate a precept fundamental to Cobb. His standing order for all preseason games, although inconsequential affairs, was that hostility prevailed, as in the proverb "Take not notice of the despicable enemy."

He held fast on this point for all of his retired life. "I can't believe the hearts-and-flowers stuff I see in modern baseball," he wrote. "Rivals practically stroll arm-in-arm. A runner on first base chats back and forth with the baseman. Hitters ask catchers how they're feeling, and not to distract them. Off the field they play cards, have drinks together. The feuding, combative spirit that made the game idolized is washed up now. Pro football, where they don't kiss each other, is taking over as the No. 1 sport. For shame."

So the two clubs never crossed swords in 1921. Casey Stengel was about to be traded by the Phillies to the Giants, and was in San Antonio. "We wuz old friends," Casey recalled, "but when I passed Ty on the street, he wouldn't speak to me. He had a lot of road apples [unskilled bodies] on hand that March. I understood how he felt."

Cobb banished his bull pen from open view and concealed it behind the grandstand. With logic he explained, "Why distract a pitcher by showing he might get the hook at any moment?" In Detroit he also ordered the pen situated out of sight. His mound staff already lacked confidence. His three best holdovers from 1920 had posted disappointing win-loss numbers: Dauss, 13–21; Howard Ehmke, 15–18; and Leonard, 10–17. "Far better for my men to see the other side warming up a new arm. Helps us in reverse."

COBB HAD not neglected getting in shape and tuning his own batting during the spring. At twilight in San Antonio he often was seen practicing, spraying hits to right field, then hitting a sizzler to center field, then a line drive to left field, followed by an hour of bunting drill. His mastery of hitting to all fields was at a lifetime peak. He demonstrated as much in the regular-season opener with the Chicago White Sox, who were now engaged in rebuilding themselves after the Black Sox debacle. On a chilly April 14, before twenty-six thousand at Navin

Field, the rookie manager doubled in a run and scored a second run in a 6–5 nip-and-tuck victory. Harry Heilmann helped clinch it with a run-scoring double.

Now there began one of the most captivating races for the American League batting title since Cobb versus Lajoie in 1910. This one, uniquely, was pupil against teacher. Slug Heilmann, age twenty-seven, Cobb age thirty-five. Since 1914, Cobb had coached Heilmann in the science of applying a bat's center of percussion to a ball in or close to the strike zone. Because of the astronomical figures they achieved in their duel, fans everywhere were entranced. "I told Harry that I'd give him a fine whiteface breeding bull from my herd in Augusta," Cobb said, "if he outhit me for average on the season. He was that far advanced."

Their intramural rivalry began with Cobb off to a poor start and far behind. Their chart from early to midseason read:

	Cobb	Heilmann
April 27	.317	.513
May 18	.395	.465
June 15	.395	.465
June 15	.394	.431
July 23	.394	.432

Within that span, and with Heilmann well in front, another use was found for heavyweight Harry by his boss. Momentarily the Tigers stood in the league's first division. Cobb's stratagems of platooning, using pinch hitters, playing the waiting game, laying the bunt, and stealing were working better than expected. But, seeing no pennant in sight, he contrived a scheme. Outfielder Bobby Veach was too easygoing to suit his manager. Veach came to bat with a smile on his face, a friendly fellow to one and all—even to umpires. Said Cobb to Heilmann, "I want you to make him mad. Real mad. You are batting behind Veach, so while you're waiting, call him a yellow-belly, a quitter, and a dog. Call him everything in the book. Ride hell out of him. Take that smile off Veach's face."

Heilmann objected. He liked Veach, did not want to lose his goodwill. Tearing into a teammate was not the amiable Harry's style.

"Just do it," ordered Cobb. "No arguments."

Only upon Cobb's promise that at season's end he would inform Veach that it had been a setup done for his own good did Heilmann reluctantly agree. In his history, *The Detroit Tigers*, Fred Lieb quoted a source, *Detroit Times* sports editor Bud Shaver, on the result of Operation Veach:

"Heilmann abused Veach as a bush-leaguer with no guts who feared enemy pitching. And he kept it up. Veach was puzzled at first, then infuriated. A slim, 160-pounder, the Kentuckian wanted to fight the burly, 210-pound Californian. Heilmann, of course, declined. But in not many days the harassment made a better competitor of the targeted Veach. From a .308 average, 113 runs-batted-in and 11 home runs of the previous season, he jumped to .338, 128 RBIs and 16 homers in the current affair."

Cobb cold-bloodedly added to his reputation as an agitator. According to Lieb and Shaver: "He did not honor his promise to Heilmann, but at season's end left for home without bothering to lay it out for Veach on how it had been an experiment in psychology. Heilmann tried to explain to Veach, unaided, but Bobby snarled, 'Don't come sucking around me with that phony line.' And a feud which had started as a trick grew into a genuine one that lasted season after season."

Cobb was full of such acts that summer. It was said that he left open his office door so that Dutch Leonard, struggling in an 11–13 season despite a 3.73 ERA in 1921, could hear him on the phone, faking a call—"I'm putting that damned Dutchman on waivers." In June the Tigers lost all five games of a Yankee series. Breaking several clubhouse windows with a bat, smashing chairs, Cobb all but wrecked the visitors' clubhouse. The Detroit front office was reported to have received a bill for $120 damages.

Further along in June, it was said that Cobb—his batting race with Heilmann remaining a close one—deliberately did a low-down thing. He changed his batting order without informing the long-suffering Heilmann. That left his best man batting out of turn when Slug hit a home run against Washington with one man on base. Umpire Billy Evans called Heilmann out when he crossed the plate and voided both runs. That cut a bit off Heilmann's hitting average.

Questions were asked about T.C.'s ability to handle two dozen individuals of varying makeup. Salsinger, with irony, wrote in his "The Umpire" column in the *Daily News*, "Some weeks ago, Tyrus Raymond

Cobb made a flat denial of reports that he intended to use the iron-hand policy in managing the Tigers. He stated emphatically that his aim was to use tact and diplomacy, considering the human element as well as playing ability. Well?" Salsinger's reminder was printed the same week that Cobb, in center field, called time-out, ran in, wrested the ball from pitcher Red Oldham's hand, and gave him a dressing-down before calling in a reliever. So much for his concealed bull pen to protect his pitchers' sensibilities.

Meanwhile, back at the Polo Grounds Babe Ruth was solidifying his status as the young prince of baseball. He was on the way to a 59-home-run year. Whether at Detroit or at New York, Cobb's behavior toward Ruth was what Robert Creamer, in his biography *Babe*, called "cruel and humorless." Ruth became vulnerable to jockeying after a story leaked that he did not bother to change his underwear from week to week. During pregame activity, the Georgian held his nose while edging close to Ruth and asking the Yankees, "Say, do you smell something? Something around here smells like a polecat. Oh, hello, Babe." As an aside to Yankees on the bench, he would inquire, "Who's that blackie you got? Who's the nigger boy?"

Customary bench-jockeying or on-field exchanges didn't often go that far; there was a limit to the jibing. In particular, opponents went easier on Ruth. If you really irritated him he could make you regret it with one swing of his king-sized bat.

The Yankees wanted him to use his fists. "Sock Cobb on the nose, Babe," urged catcher Wally Schang.

"Ahhhh, go fuck yourself," said Ruth to Cobb.

Ruth was not notably handy in a fight, whereas the Peach was known to be an expert. Ruth went on taking the barbs, mainly retaliating by citing home-run power. To reporters at the batting cage, when Cobb was within earshot, he would guffaw, "Why, I could hit .400 every year if I just knocked out those little singles like him."

One day at New York, after a Cobb triple beat the Yankees and a shoving match occurred between the teams, the Babe blew up and charged into the Detroit clubhouse.

"Where's Cobb?" he asked.

"Right here," said T.C., appearing from around a corner.

"You old bastard," yelled Ruth. "If you ever call me a son of a bitch again, I'll choke you to death!"

Cobb calmly replied, "What's the matter, big stuff? Can't you take it?"

"I can take it!" Ruth was jumping up and down in a fury. "But I won't take that from anybody!"

"Ah, that's nothing," said Cobb. "You have no case after what you called me yesterday."

"I didn't call you anything much yesterday—just a Georgia prick."

"You're a goddamned liar," Cobb came back.

Ruth went for him, several Tigers moved between the two, and Babe was escorted (i.e., thrown) out the door. He left huffing and puffing and challenging Cobb to a fight outside. Nothing more happened, according to witness Bob Veach. "I always knew that in a real fight with Ruth," Cobb often said, "I'd be the loser with the crowd. They might lynch me."

In 1921 Ruth was emerging as a full-fledged colossus. Bookies could not guess what the Big Fellow would do next. He was so hot that he had 25 home runs by July; even his pop-ups were so towering that fielders gathered under them reminded Tris Speaker of a union meeting in progress. Babe averaged around .380 most of the season, and if he did not score and drive in 285 or more runs in 150 games, it was said, it would be a shame (he did). Behind him the Yankees might at last reach the World Series (they did, and lost to the Giants). Elsewhere he overshadowed Cobb in notoriety. In a quarrel in a roadhouse, a man pulled a gun on him and Ruth's career came close to an early ending; his movie, *Headin' Home* premiered at Madison Square Garden; *Current Opinion* saluted him as a national hero, a designation matched only by New York writers' nickname of "His Royal Nibs," who was more successful with his "whammer" than Toscanini with his baton.

Cobb's problems at Detroit were basic and manifold. To begin with, his infield of Lu Blue at first base, Ralph Young at second base, Donie Bush at shortstop, and Bob Jones at third was no prize crew—a "swamp of despondency" as the press derided it. Things were so bad that he was forced to play outfielder Ira Flagstead at short, deal away Bush to Connie Mack, and introduce two raw rookies into his inner defense. Most of the team, schooled hard by T.C. in the springtime, was hitting far above expectations, but they lacked fighting spirit, the will to win. Cobb railed at almost everyone because men could not perform at his own level. "If I can get eight hits in eleven ups," he stormed after losing a doubleheader, "why can't guys fifteen years younger?" The answer was self-evident, but he failed to make allowances. Setting himself as a model was Cobb's main managerial weakness.

In late midseason, figures in the batting-title race between Cobb and his protégé Heilmann read:

	Cobb	Heilmann
July 27	.389	.431
August 10	.387	.417
August 24	.392	.403

The manager's state of mind was not improved in August upon his receipt of word from Atlanta gynecologists that his wife, Charlie, was dangerously ill. On July 23 she had given birth to their fifth child in eleven years, named James Howell Cobb. Postpartum complications left her doctors much concerned. The Peach had not gone home for the delivery. Now, ready to resume play after recovery from a six-stitch wound in his knee sustained while sliding against Cleveland, a cut that had become infected and had cost him weeks on the sideline, he left Detroit for Charlie's bedside.

Childbearing had been an ordeal for her before this; it was another case of a young mother—she was twenty-six—separated from her husband at a crucial time. A still-healing Cobb spent only a few days with Charlie before hurrying back to Detroit. "It was hard to forgive Ty for the way he handled that," a family friend once responded when asked about this brief visit; "Detroit wasn't going anywhere in the league." As it was, Mrs. Cobb had been considering divorce for some time.

By a wide margin the Tigers were out of the running. Upon rejoining them in New York in the first week of August, however, the Peach evened things somewhat with Ruth and the Yanks. With his knee still hurting, he got into an argument with Bob Shawkey, on the hill for the Yankees. Shawkey, a 20-game winner in two past seasons, had an odd pitch that fluttered. "Illegal," said Cobb. "He's using something on the ball."

Two umpires examined the ball, found nothing but a small nick in it, threw it out, and ordered play to proceed. Cobb walked off to his dugout. He conferred with its inhabitants and drank some water for a good five minutes. Once Shawkey was sufficiently angry and Cobb was about to be disqualified, he returned and drove a triple to deep right field. For the day, he scored three runs in an 8–3 drubbing of the home team.

All season long he lashed his second-divisioners, to the point that rumors were heard of a team strike. In New York, he rode Dutch Leonard after Leonard missed two bunt attempts, benching him to send up a pinch hitter with one strike left in the count. Leonard yelled a protest. Somehow the Tigers beat Ruth and the Yankees, 4–2.

NAVIN, AT the finish, was cool to his manager. He had expected much more. Cobb was disgusted at his charges' concluding sixth-place finish, with a record of 71–82 (.464). He blamed Navin, who had been ineffective in repairing Detroit's defense and pitching by way of trades, or bringing up outstanding minor-leaguers. Cobb told business associates that owners Navin and Briggs were a "lost cause." He doubted that he would ever again take on two tasks at once. Most critics sided with him, citing the superlative job he had done in upgrading Tiger hitting. Here was a losing team that, painstakingly taught, had just averaged .316 at bat as a team—the highest offensive showing in modern history. The Tigers' .316, in fact, was the best since the Baltimore Orioles' batting spree back in 1897. For the only time in American League history before or since, all three Tiger outfielders—Heilmann, Cobb, Veach—hit better than .300 and drove in 100 or more runs apiece. Not even the 1927 "Murderers' Row" of Ruth, Lou Gehrig, Tony Lazzeri, Bob Meusel, and Earle Combs, possibly the finest lineup ever assembled, would match Detroit's combined hitting; the Murderers would average .307. Two other great Yankee teams, those of 1926 and 1928, would average .289 and .296. Moreover, the Cobbmen's hitting had led both leagues.

It was a conspicuous tribute to Cobb's tutelage from spring training on; his instruction had improved the batwork of almost every one of the regulars and some subs, so much that the Tigers had climbed by 10½ games over their 1920 standing. But their fielding had been third-rate, near the league bottom for errors. Howard Ehmke's 13 wins to 14 losses had been the pitching staff's best showing. Counted-upon reliever Jim Middleton had gone 6–11.

All that was left to be salvaged was the AL batting crown—Cobb's or Heilmann's? The race was coming down to the wire:

	Cobb	Heilmann
September 7	.390	.403
September 14	.394	.398
September 28	.390	.395
October 2	.389	.394

Heilmann went hitless on the final rainy day of October 2, while Cobb, suffering a league suspension for bad behavior, did not play. The pupil seemed to have narrowly won. But unofficial statisticians working for newspapers had a different tabulation. The *Cleveland Plain Dealer*, for instance, reported:

Tyrus Cobb Heads League in Hitting for Thirteenth Time
By Francis Powers

For the 13th time since his sensational entry into the majors, the American League batting diadem rests on the thinning locks of Tyrus Cobb. Figures give Cobb an average of .391 to .390 for Harry Heilmann, also of Detroit. The indomitable Georgian and Heilmann have been waging a neck-and-neck battle since midseason.

Official results had not yet been issued when Heilmann conceded victory to the man who had taught him not to lunge at pitches, to grip the bat away from his body, and not to swing at bad balls. He walked up to Cobb in the Navin Field clubhouse and before newspapermen said, "Congratulations—you're the best hitter the game has known." Heilmann was hurting, but did not show it.

"Wait a minute," said Cobb. "Your congratulations are not in order. Wait for the league office to settle the matter."

Heilmann returned, "Well, it's official to me. The better man won."

To the assembled reporters, Cobb went into what appeared to be a prepared explanation, a not-too-subtle reminder that 1921 had been an anomaly. He said, "I've been pulling for Harry to win all season. He is one of my few players who came through for me. He's a grand chap. He served on a U.S. submarine in the war and won medals. But there is no doubt that managing has hurt my hitting. I have had many concerns and did not have time to make a deliberate effort to take another championship." Without all of his distractions, Cobb strongly implied, he very well could have been number one again.

The twelve batting titles he already held were his proudest possessions, something he foresaw as lasting for decades, and to make it thirteen was important to him. And it was almost as if he knew what the official standing would be. He mentioned, "I have a little man who keeps the figures for me. His book mark shows Heilmann is the winner."

When the official statistics were announced two months later, Heilmann had hit .394 to his manager's .389. It was only the third time in fifteen years that anyone but the Georgian had stood on top. Heilmann also struck a blow for right-handed batsmen. Not since 1905 had anyone but a left-hander led the American League—"because," pointed out Cobb, "the best pitchers have been right-handers, with their natural advantage over those batting from the same side."

Heilmann was happily convinced that his manager appreciated his victory until he made a trip to San Francisco weeks afterward, when Cobb's true reaction to losing was confided to him by a businessman friend of both men. The "friend" told Heilmann, "Cobb isn't the gracious loser he makes out. He was in my office the other day and on the phone to the American League Service Bureau back east. He was yelling into the phone, 'Dammit, I tell you there must be something wrong with those batting statistics! The figures are wrong! What the hell kind of service are you running anyway?'" For years Heilmann took pleasure in telling that story around Detroit.

There was consolation in other data. Cobb's season had been next to sensational by any measurement. In the first year in which he led the league—1907—he had scored 97 runs; now, one and one-half decades later, he scored 124. His total of extra-base hits went from 49 back then to 64 in 1921. His average at the plate went from a twenty-year-old's .350 up by 39 points to .389. His 22 stolen bases of 1921 were second highest in the league. This was accomplished while leg tendons and ligaments were twice injured. He was in no way in decline; rather, he was improving—except in the desire to continue managing the Tigers, about which he was skeptical.

HE WAS back in San Francisco that winter, once more managing the local Seals in the Coast League at the same $1,200-per-game salary of 1920. This time the Seals drew poorly at the gate. That affected Cobb's tentative plan to buy the Golden Gate franchise. "The asking price was two hundred and fifty thousand," he told Muddy Ruel. "I doubt that I could have broken even with Frisco in less than two years." He had the needed investment money and more, but he passed up taking on an owner's burdens.

He did spend forty thousand dollars of Navin's money while out west on a likely pair of Portland, Oregon, pitchers, Herman Pillette and Syl Johnson. That didn't guarantee his return to run the Tigers on the field in 1922. "I'm just scouting players as an accommodation for the ball club first in my heart," he explained. In private, Cobb commented about Detroit to a Los Angeles writer: "Navin is a two-bit loser."

He was far from home base, yet he easily arranged to stay in the headlines during the Coast League winter. One of the Seals' opponents, the Los Angeles–Vernon team, employed the services of a cross-eyed umpire named Steamboat Johnson. Johnson had set a league record when a count of bottles showed that some three hundred beer containers had been thrown at him after one of his decisions. Fans had presented Steamboat with a seeing-eye dog to guide him from the park to home. He was one of the richest characters that baseball had produced on any level.

Cobb took an immediate dislike to this sideplay. When Johnson called a San Francisco runner out on a close play at the plate, Cobb burst from the dugout to put the blast on Steamboat. After a verbal exchange, he ripped off Johnson's face mask and said, "You're blinder than a potato with a hundred eyes!" And hit Johnson on the nose.

If he thought that his fame would carry him past such behavior in a minor league, his judgment was wrong. Frank Chance, the one-time Peerless Leader of the Chicago Cubs and a tough man, was president of the Coast League. Chance was no admirer of Cobb's way of running the bases and his history of molesting umpires.

"You're fined one hundred and fifty dollars," said Chance. "One more infraction and you're finished on the coast."

"I won't pay it," said Cobb. "Your umpire is incompetent."

"Then go back to Detroit, where they put up with you," declared Chance.

Cobb did leave for home, but by way of New York, where before a conclave of big-league owners he reintroduced the need for a pay scale enabling players to live "decently" and a system whereby permanently and totally disabled players would be supported for life by a system similar to the Workingmen's Compensation Act. He had been lobbying along this line for some time. But he could not obtain an affirmative vote on either of the projects. Baseball operators saw him as a chronic malcontent who had repeatedly put salary squeezes on Detroit and was talking a fifty-thousand-dollar package, should he elect to again perform in 1922—acts that would have the effect of forcing bigger paychecks for premium players throughout the leagues. Owners who soon would draw a record two-league seasonal total of 9.45 million fans also agreed that the ten thousand dollars they annually donated from World Series receipts to support the game's disabled was sufficient. Cobb's reaction was: what can you expect from a monopoly?

At home in Augusta he found Charlie still sickly. That condition would linger through what remained of their marriage. Father stayed at home for several weeks before leaving on one more big-game hunt. One of his daughters, the late Shirley Cobb Beckwith, who died at eighty in 1991, said in remembrance, "Mr. Cobb would line up us children like soldiers, review our school grades and piano playing—then he'd be gone for months. We never knew him except as a great man. We were afraid of him—afraid of his awful temper."

FORTY YEARS later, in 1961, sitting in an easy chair on the patio of his home at 48 Spencer Lane in Atherton, California, Cobb added a footnote to 1921: "It was right about then that I wrote a new will. Tore up the old one [written before he left for France during World War I]. One of the bequests at my death was for twenty thousand dollars . . . to go to a worthy Georgia student who couldn't afford college. I'd always regretted that I missed college. My students had to meet strict standards. Later on I enlarged on the Cobb Scholarship Fund to take care of several hundred kids."

Ty Cobb would not go out of life known as a tightwad.

SHATTERED DREAMS

Babe Ruth, twenty-seven and approaching his peak, underwent what was seen as his comeuppance in 1922. He had a miserable season. After sweeping the league one year earlier in runs scored, home runs (59), and runs driven in, he now failed to place first in even one category.

By comparison, and though hard used at thirty-five, Cobb was a joy to watch that year. He would hit .401—the third time he had averaged past .400. No man had hit so high on three occasions; only one man, Rogers Hornsby, would equal him in .400 seasons.

The Babe's flop was seen as a retribution for whooping it up in bars, hotels, and clubs, where he broke most of the codes against drinking, gambling, night-owling, and sexual reveling. He turned off his bosses and many of a nation of followers when he let his physical condition slide. His behavior opened the door to a renewal of the feeling that the sober, fanatical Cobb was the greater player, the most consistently effective and probably the most valuable of his or any time.

Even before his home run output and other contributions nosedived, Ruth was suspended by Commissioner Kenesaw M. Landis for six weeks, beginning on opening day. Landis further fined the Yankee captain his share of the past autumn's World Series purse—in the amount of $3,362—for violating a rule dating to 1911 prohibiting players of World Series games from appearing in exhibitions after the Series. Babe Ruth's All-Stars had appeared in 1921 from Buffalo, Elmira, and Jamestown to Scranton, partying as they went.

When Landis was a federal judge in Chicago, he was noted for his iron-handed decisions. He had sent men to prison for twenty years for violating the antidrinking Volstead Act. Hired to crack down on baseball and sanitize it, Landis cited other codes being ignored by Ruth. He hit the bottle with enthusiasm, gambled heavily at Jamaica and other racetracks—he once lost $25,000 on a single race in Havana—and at Hot Springs, Arkansas, casinos. "His horses finish about 5:00 P.M., but still he backs them," jested Bob Considine of the Hearst press. Amidst it all, baseball's Falstaff refused a $50,000 salary offer, insisting on $1,000 per week, or $52,000, for 1922. Yankee president Jake Ruppert paid it. Reading of his demand in the papers, Cobb informed Georgia friends, "It's like I thought. Ruth hurts himself every time he opens his mouth—or a bottle."

Fifty-two thousand dollars, a huge sum compared to the $8,500, $10,000, and $6,500 annually earned by other Yankee stalwarts such as Wally Schang, Bob Shawkey, and Wally Pipp, caused a negative public reaction. New York writers spoke of fans from Manhattan to the Bronx to Queens asking, "Why should Ruth break the bank when everybody else is paid so much less?" The playboy was too damned greedy. Nor should he have brawled with Pipp, one of the best men with his fists on the Yankees. Ruth in midseason fought at fieldside with the hefty Pipp. The first baseman slapped him around, leaving Ruth with welts and the embarrassing disclosure that he was not much of a fighter.

When the Babe came off the suspension on May 20, the Yankees stood in the league's first place. They appeared not to need their key run producer. Five days after that, he was suspended for throwing dirt at an umpire and cursing fans who booed him for striking out too often. A second suspension followed on June 19, for similar malfeasances. Two more suspensions came atop that, until Ruth had lost $1,500 in unpaid salary while benched. Not finding his groove for weeks, he did not reach the 14-home-run mark until July 6, and he trailed powerful Ken Williams of the St. Louis Browns in what had been Ruth's singular specialty. Also set back by a tonsil operation, a discouraged Ruth was on his way to a final 35-home-run season, a drop of 24 from his 59 of 1921. Williams would become the new home-run champion with 39. Babe's hitting would fall to .315, a plunge of 63 points from his previous mark. The same was true for runs batted in—down from 171 to 99. His games played dropped from 152 to 110.

While Ruth was engaged in faltering, fans and writers who had dropped off Cobb's bandwagon after the Babe's arrival on the New York scene were again paying close attention to the Georgian. If he had another big year personally, and somehow managed the Tigers to a better finish, Cobb might well find himself back on top in general opinion. Grantland Rice thought as much. Other writers followed his lead.

"WHAT RUTH did concerned me not a damned bit," said Cobb years afterward. "I had enough habitual dead asses on my second Detroit team to make a second-division finish almost guaranteed. The only reason I returned for another try was that I hated to go out with a loser. I was looking ahead to 1923 and 1924 when the right trades and deals with the best minor-league clubs could change everything."

Reading between the lines, it was evident that one reason why Cobb remained as manager was that he stood on the threshold of monopolizing the all-time record book as no man had done. *Baseball Magazine* editorialized, "His have been monumental achievements. Now he is about to break every longtime offensive mark ever set. Honus Wagner still is chief in total hits with 3,420 safe hits. Ty's total is 3,055. In one more time around he will be all but assured of surpassing Wagner. He is also close to most seasons with an average of .300 or better. By 1923, Cobb no doubt will wipe that out with 18 straight years at over .300. It would be a tragedy were fate to deny him the crowning touches to his epic career."

He didn't believe in fate. In luck, yes, to a degree, but fate was for the mystics. At Detroit's spring camp at Augusta, he used fear as a motivator. Applicants for Tiger jobs who didn't go all out were in town one day and aboard a train to elsewhere the next. In some people's opinion, he was much too tough. "He suspended me three days without pay for missing one fly ball," nineteen-year-old rookie outfielder Floyd "Babe" Herman went about saying. "And this was just in training." Herman would leave Detroit before long for the Brooklyn Dodgers, his talent unrecognized by Cobb. There he would average

.340, .388, and .393 to become, as one of the "Daffyness Boys," the toast of Flatbush.

Dutch Leonard cursed Cobb to his face during their running dispute over how to pitch to such batting machines as Sisler and Speaker. Leonard quit the team in the spring, terming Cobb "a horse's ass," leaving to run his Fresno, California, fruit farm and await his day of vengeance. He would return in 1924 in explosive form.

A picturesque former border-guarding Texas Ranger, Harry "Rip" Collins, who had won 14 games in two of the previous three seasons for the Yankees and Red Sox, joined Detroit, and almost at once lined up with the disgruntled players. Collins's published contribution later was, "Cobb stirred up bad blood in the club. I would say that more than half of us hated him. I couldn't figure out what he was trying to accomplish as Simon Legree. Finally, I stopped talking to him except when I couldn't avoid it."

Within the next twenty-four months, fifteen Tigers would parade into Navin's office, asking either for a trade or Cobb's dismissal. Complaints ran from the tongue-lashings he handed out, to their disgust at having to supply water buckets in hot weather to Cobb's pet dog. A cur who had wandered in that March had been adopted by the boss. Each player was under instructions to pet the dog at least once a day. Why such a requirement? Veteran players saw symbolism in it—they were a "dog" of a team. When the pet disappeared, Cobb replaced him with an ocelot cub from the South American jungle, who scratched people.

It was evident to opposition scouts visiting Detroit's camp that Cobb was desperate to restore the Tiger glory of the 1907, 1908, and 1909 championship years any way he could. If he achieved a turnaround, he could retire in satisfaction. In interviews he missed few openings to point the finger at Navin for the caliber of talent supplied him. "A ball team is like a machine shop," Cobb was quoted as saying. "It's a business. When you have a high state of efficiency, things run smoothly. You are turning out a good product, the workmen are happy. But if you fail to produce, if you are indifferent to quality, you can only blame the management. It is precisely the same problem of the field manager who takes a losing team and tries to make it over into a winner. The Tigers, when I took them over, were like a broken-down machine shop . . . filled with the losing spirit."

That lackadaisical condition, he strongly implied, was due to the failure of Navin and Briggs, over the winter, to sign infield replacements and dependable pitching. When the Yankees beat them to two sure-handed infielders, Jumping Joe Dugan and Everett Scott, they had to settle for three unproved infielders in Fred Haney, George Cutshaw, and Topper Rigney. Next, pitcher Howard Ehmke, a former 17-game winner for Detroit, asked to be traded. Ehmke's relationship with Cobb stood at the breaking point. The seven-year veteran found his manager too frantic, too hypercritical. His wish to go elsewhere was rejected. For now, Ehmke stayed with Detroit.

The Tigers lost their season's opener to the Cleveland Indians, 7–4, before dropping six straight games on the road. A little later, rubbing it in, on April 30 rookie Charley Robertson of the White Sox beat them, 2–0, with a rare, perfect, no-hit, nobody-reached-first-base gem. It was only the fifth such blanking in big-league history. In game footnotes, the Peach was portrayed as raging on the sideline, kicking bats and jockeying Robertson in an attempt to unsettle him. His temper was heated all the more because that spring Cobb was on the disabled list with injured leg ligaments, torn again when he tripped over a divot in the grass. Laid up for a month, walking with a cane, he returned on May 1, with the Tigers seemingly sliding out of contention.

PERHAPS THE club was fed up with his ranting. Perhaps it was the example he set, beyond fiat, through his own performance, with a hitting outburst that put him close to the .400 mark in June and July. Perhaps the American League, with the exception of the Yankees and the surprising St. Louis Browns, was not as strong a league as judged. Possibly, too, it was gross overemphasis on the Ruth-style home run and neglect of all-around, timely hitting, as suggested by the 1,050 homers blasted in the majors in this season against 339 hit only a few years earlier. Whatever the causes, the Tigers righted themselves, went on a tear, and became a wholly different organization. Happiness gripped the clubhouse in June when they won twenty-two and lost only four. In July and August, the Cobbmen had a pair of eight-game winning streaks. They climbed to only five games behind the Yanks and Browns for first place. "I can taste the pennant," said Cobb, who was swinging at .415 and leading the league, 13 points above Sisler of the Browns.

But the Yankees and Browns kept winning steadily, too, and yielded less ground than was needed for the accomplishment of a

Detroit miracle. It was a dogfight. One of Cobb's more unusual acquisitions, the blimp-shaped Bob "Fatty" Fothergill—five feet, ten inches, 260 pounds—responded outstandingly as a pinch hitter. Fothergill, wearing a size-52 uniform, came from the International League. His eating habits approached Ruth's. In one Yankee game, when Fatty waddled to the batter's box, New York pitcher Lefty O'Doul called to Cobb, "The rules say that only one man can bat at a time!"

Cobb replied, "So what?"

"Then why are there two men standing at the plate?"

Despite his bulk and slowness afoot, Fothergill batted .322 on the season. The team's climb to the first division brought on a rush for tickets. People lined up a block away to obtain favorable seats in a Navin Field about to be expanded to thirty-seven thousand capacity. Hundreds camped at the gate all night, sitting by bonfires. "Of course," reported Fred Lieb, "Navin quietly raised the seat prices by two bits." By October, Navin's paid attendance would set a franchise record of 851,000 paid admissions, ranking with the leading teams.

Cobb's $50,000 contract was structured to pay him an override of ten cents for every ticket sold beyond 700,000, and he was also paid $2,500 for public-relations appearances during the season. That left him, according to several sources, slightly ahead of Babe Ruth in baseball-only income, with endorsements not included. "Ruth," Cobb later caustically noted, "endorsed whorehouses by word of mouth. He talked a lot. I advertised milk and Cobb candy."

But misfortune arrived as the season moved along. During a dispute at St. Louis, Cobb tromped on umpire Frank Wilson's foot with his spikes and was suspended by officials for three days. Harry Heilmann, with 21 home runs to date, fractured his collarbone in August; the big slugger was gone for the season. Two pitchers, Lil Stoner and Carl Holling, were caught drinking in Boston at a late hour; Cobb fired them on the spot. Team hitting cooled off. Only one pitcher, rookie Herman Pillette, threw well, and by September the back-to-normal Tigers were out of the race.

Having been given the opportunity to reach the World Series and failing to have made it there, a frustrated Cobb left for Georgia within hours of closing day. His whip-cracking, punitive methods had worked for a while, but not over the long run. Detroit had barely beaten out

Tris Speaker's Clevelanders for third place, with a 79–75 final mark. However, a few bright spots encouraged him. The team had won eight more games than in 1921. Navin's record box-office draw and Cobb's personal batwork meant that he could negotiate for more money in 1923, if he elected to stay on as manager. His ability to improve a man's hitting was again evident. Detroit as a unit had batted a spectacular .305, which was 18 percentage points above the pennant-winning Yankees, who averaged .287.

Against that, the Yankees, now on the way to compiling a dynastic sweep of American League championships—in 1921, 1922, 1923, 1926, 1927, and 1928—had been 22 percent more effective on defense than Detroit. Cobb could only wish he had such double-play mechanics as New York's second baseman Aaron Ward and shortstop Ev Scott. Despite the prevailing home-run mania, the cutting off of enemy runs remained as vital as it always had been.

His other comfort was his own .401 bat average, at an age when most men were winding down careers as reserves and nearing retirement. Leg injuries in his thirty-sixth year had limited him to 137 games, but he made them count, with 99 runs scored and 99 runs driven in. His 211 base hits in 526 trips to the plate computed into a mark topped only by Sisler's .420. In just one way could the Peach be seen as slipping—his stolen-base totals of the 1909–15 period had stood at 76, 75, 83, 61, 52, 35, and 96. Now he could steal only 9 times on battered legs. At the same time, few men in their prime could match Cobb's 42 doubles and 16 triples of 1922.

However, it was an ordinary ground ball struck by him in May that after the season ended caused more furor than anything involving Cobb and a Louisville Slugger stick since the ugly Larry Lajoie affair of 1910.

At the Polo Grounds on a soggy field, Cobb had pushed a grounder to Ev Scott at shortstop. Scott juggled the ball and Cobb beat out the throw by part of a step. Fred Lieb, scoring for Associated Press, ruled it a base hit. John Kieran, the official league scorer, called it an error. In his *Baseball As I Have Known It*, Lieb explained, "Irwin Howe, who was the American League statistician, took his figures day by day from the Associated Press box scores. Howe did so in this case, and in October it meant the difference between a .401 for Cobb as against

.3995, using Kieran's scoring." Lieb quite properly offered to defer to Kieran, since Kieran held official status. But Ban Johnson, for once taking Cobb's side in a dispute, stood behind the AP's judgment and certified the Peach at .401.

With almost anyone else the dispute would have faded out. With Cobb it spread nationally. Some members of the Baseball Writers Association of America loudly condemned what became known as the "Case of the Two-Point Base Hit," insisting that Cobb be given a .3995. Lieb reported, "Vitriolic telegrams were exchanged among the BWAA." Balloting of the eleven chapters of the BWAA was held and the vote, two chapters abstaining, was 5–4 in favor of lowering Cobb's average so that he would miss another .400 season.

Cobb was furious. He saw his long-running feud with the New York, Philadelphia, and Boston press exemplified in this attempt to deny his just rights. From Augusta he spoke contemptuously of the BWAA: "Why should I give a damn what those twenty-five-dollar- and thirty-five-dollar-a-week newspaper sons of bitches think?" Visiting New York in November, he played host at a dinner for a few famous sportswriters and editors whom he had found supportive—Damon Runyon, Ring Lardner, Granny Rice, Gene Fowler, and Bill Phelon. Their competitors were not invited. During the evening he was chided by his guests for abusing their fellow journalists. As the Georgian remembered it decades later, Runyon said, "They're all for Ruth, of course, in picking the greatest player. I say they're wrong. But you have to live with these writers."

"Not me," said Cobb. "I'm fed up with those phonies and I may file a lawsuit."

"Worst thing you could do," counseled Ring Lardner. "In a pissing match with the big daily papers, the press always gets the last splash."

Cobb claimed that a secret conspiracy existed to rob him. "In May of 1921," he fumed, "the scorers took three safe hits away from me and added two more times at bat that I didn't have. That happened in New York. It's just one more example of knifing me." He recalled 1913, a season in which he should have been credited with a .400-plus mark. Some "fancy pencilwork" had made it a .390.

Long after, in the 1950s and 1960s, several retired eastern sportswriters I consulted pretty much agreed that, whenever made at home in Detroit, questionable hit-or-error decisions often went in the Peach's favor; on the road it was the opposite. This was 1920s baseball, when unsupervised official scorers sometimes showed their own form of civic boosterism in reports they turned in. A little padding also gained the statisticians some favor with certain players.

Umpire Billy Evans, once the loser in a bloody fistfight with Cobb, felt that Sir Tyrus arrogantly went out of his way to antagonize the game's officials, scorekeepers included. It was then the standard practice of team managers to present the umpires and the evening newspapers with their starting lineups some ten to fifteen minutes before game time, which was usually 3:00 to 3:30 P.M. That enabled beat writers to wire their downtown sport departments and catch early editions with the nominated batteries. Almost alone, Cobb refused to cooperate. His starting nine was "confidential," his own business, until the last moment.

Ban Johnson's office sent Cobb a memo, insisting that he release his pitcher's name in time to accommodate the press box. "Again Cobb called us writers two-bit sons of bitches," wrote Lieb of the *New York Evening Post*. "I gave him some good roasts in the paper in 1922 and 1923. And then he called me into his dugout. He challenged me to fight it out, man-for-man. I declined. Nobody in his right mind would tangle with that wildcat. He fought by no rules and had maimed too many people with his Jack Dempsey stuff. Not to mention his Wild Bill Hickok act with a loaded gun."

However, Cobb did finally disclose his concealed reason for not supplying pregame information. "It's the bookmakers," he revealed. "Unless the bookies know ahead of time who I'm pitching, they can't form a betting line. They're only guessing."

As for the crowds, lacking the advantage of stadium public address systems, they learned the names one or two minutes before the first pitch. A man in a derby hat, standing at home plate with a megaphone, typically would bellow, "Pitching for Washington—Walter Johnson! Catching—Patsy Garrity!" Usually the complete lineups were given. This served well enough with such easy names as Bill Doak, Joe Judge, Snooks Dowd, Max Flack, Addie Joss, and Ivy Wingo. But when the megaphone man had to deal with such twisters as Pembroke Finlayson, Dominick Mulrennan, Ossee Schreckengost, Grover Lowdermilk, Val Picinich, Elam Vangilder, Jefferson Pfeffer, and Ivy Higgenbotham, the pronounciations drew laughs. So did such oddities as Pickles Dilhoefer, Chicken Hawks, Yam Yaryan, Kaiser Wilhelm, and Baby Doll Jacobson.

CHAPTER TWENTY-THREE

A NEAR PENNANT WIN

Charlotte Marion Lombard Cobb—"Charlie"—was a long-suffering wife. By 1923, she had undergone one miscarriage, one premature birth, serious postpartum complications, and was warned by doctors never again to become a mother. "She's not built for the strain," said Ty Cobb's mother, Amanda, who knew about such things. Amanda had been only fifteen years old herself, when, after long, difficult hours of labor, she delivered the seven-pound son christened Tyrus Raymond.

According to family sources, Charlie Cobb's parents were offended by the fact that her husband was not in attendance at three of the births. Al Ginn, part-time chauffeur for Cobb and his favorite relative, felt that Charlie was unprepared and poorly suited for life with such a fast-moving, tempestuous mate. Somehow Charlie, the convent girl bred into a society of garden parties, cotillions, and southern gentility, stayed on, bore children, and was discreet about anything she said to the inquisitive press. Cobb became even more withdrawn from and unavailable to her in the 1920s. If Charlie had not been able to retreat for long periods to the Lombard clan's estate in Augusta, she might early on have become an unusual woman in her circle, a divorcée. "When Tyrus wasn't going around making baseball people hate him, he could be sweet to his wife," attested an old Georgia friend. "I guess he sort of loved her. With Charlie, I think she was mostly scared. For sure she wasn't happy."

FACING OVERLAPPING troubles—domestic, occasional business-venture setbacks, an elusive pennant—Cobb disappeared early in 1923 into the backwoods of Wyoming, Colorado, and Canada and the mountains of northern Mexico. His aim was to kill the rare "Big Three" of bighorn sheep, the Rocky Mountain, Mexican, and Canadian varieties. He had bagged the first two as of 1923, lacking only the third.

Cobb's hunting expedition was motivated in part, that spring, by off-season rumors that he might be fired as manager and replaced by an old Detroit favorite, Bill Donovan. Cobb maintained an office back of the third-base stands at Navin Field and there he read in a Boston paper that the colorful forty-seven-year-old Donovan, now managing New Haven in the fast Eastern League, was "likely" to take his job. When Navin came by his office, Cobb asked, "What's this about Donovan?"

"Nothing to it," said Navin.

"Suppose I don't believe you?" came back Cobb.

"Well, if you're not happy . . . ," replied Navin, seeming to give his highly paid club leader an out, if he wanted one.

"Happy? Damned right I'm not!" barked Cobb, releasing his frustration. "We're headed for third or fourth place again, and I don't see you doing anything about it." He handed Navin a list of players that he urged be obtained. "Get me those boys and we can do some good."

On the list one year earlier had been the name of twenty-two-year-old Henry "Heinie" Manush from Tuscumbia, Alabama. Cobb had been tipped off to Manush by a hardware salesman who had seen him play in the Western Canada League, and the Peach had put out inquiries. Navin had not heard of Manush. Nor was he much impressed. "Get me Manush and stop wasting time," went on Cobb. "All he did last season was hit .376 with Omaha, with forty-four doubles and twenty homers."

The Manush case was decisive to Cobb's plans. If Navin had failed to land left-handed outfielder Manush, he said in later years, almost certainly Tyrus's career would have ended in Detroit and he would have retired, waited a year, and signed with another team—probably

Cleveland—or quit baseball to expand his two automobile dealer-
ships, buy Coca-Cola franchises, or, a growing possibility, run for the
Georgia state senate. All this was forgotten when Cobb, brushing aside
Navin, personally signed Manush.

Heinie Manush was young and raw, exactly the type that T.C.
enjoyed rebuilding. His bad habits were not fixed. In 1923 spring training, Cobb converted Heinie from a dead pull-hitter to using the entire
field, taught him patience at bat and how to keep a notebook—as
Cobb did—on rival pitchers' tendencies. Rookie Manush responded
with 25 doubles and triples and a .334 average; within three seasons
he became the American League's champion hitter at .378. One day he
would become a Hall of Famer. "Ty Cobb was always on my ass," reminisced Manush before his death in 1971. "If I went without a hit on
Friday, he wouldn't speak to me on Saturday. I couldn't like him as a
man, no way. He ran things like a dictator. But as a teacher—well, he
was the best."

Shortly before training began at Augusta, Cobb disappeared. In
Toronto, the Great White Hunter met Jack Miner, a game guide with
whom he had explored the wilderness before and who knew where
bighorn sheep and caribou were to be found. They rode horses into the
northern mountains, where Miner proceeded to get them lost. After
three days of wandering with a defective compass, they were running
short of food. The weather grew very cold. "I saw us being discovered
frozen stiff," related Cobb. "We climbed a tree . . . saw smoke in the
distance. Turned out to be a Canadian ranger's station. He put us right
and we got out over fifteen tough miles by foot just before a blizzard
hit." On the way back to civilization, Cobb shot a caribou, but not the
bighorn ram he wanted.

GOING INTO his eighteenth season, heavier about the thighs and chest
at 205 pounds, he was greeted by a poem whose author's name he
soon forgot. The verse would be resurrected or imitated in the next few
years, each time to the repeater's regret:

> The curtain's going to drop, old chap
> For time has taken toll
>
> . . . .
> You might go on and play and play,

But why go on for folks to say
There's old Ty Cobb, still on the job
But not the Cobb of yesterday.

"They've got me ready for the pipe and shawl," he observed. "We'll see." And then he predicted that Detroit would win the pennant.

The overwhelming opinion was that his forecast was a promotional stunt, nothing more. Gamblers saw it as a come-on, an attempt to boost Detroit's preseason ticket sales. Mammoth Yankee Stadium, opening in April, was where a third straight pennant was almost certain to fly. Man for man, the Yanks had as solid a lineup as any assembled since the New York Giants of 1911–13 had swept three straight National League titles. In a new, $2.5 million baseball palace, a chastened, sober Babe Ruth surely would recover from his weak 1922 performance and keep fans busy trying for souvenirs in Ruthville, the park's right- and center-field bleachers, where Babe would be lofting most of his home runs. By comparison, Detroit had added no players more helpful than a few journeymen infielders, such ordinary pitchers as Rip Collins and Dutch Leonard (who had returned), and promising but untested rookie Heinie Manush. Cobb's stiffening legs were another factor. He was expected to drop somewhere around the .330 mark at bat, and probably to two dozen or fewer steals.

Disorderly as ever, Cobb caused the loss of a game one spring day when he was thrown out for using prohibited language with umpires. He refused to leave the field for so long that the officials forfeited the game to St. Louis. On another occasion, league president Ban Johnson received complaints that Cobb, standing in the coaching box, encouraged the home crowd to hurl coins at the visiting Philadelphia A's. His catchers Johnny Bassler and Larry Woodall would wait until a batter was starting to swing and then drop sand into the back of his shoes. In a bunting situation against the Yankees one day, Cobb revived his old maneuver of placing the ball down the first-base line, forcing pitcher Carl Mays to field it. Timing his arrival, Cobb slammed into him, tearing his pants, bruising Mays, and starting a field brawl.

The handicappers were in for a surprise. A determined bunch, the Tigers turned truculent that summer of 1923 and began a steady climb toward the top. They reached the first division, with an outside chance at the pennant. Accusations were made that Cobb had turned the Tiger players into thugs who freely overused the beanball, ran bases with spikes flaring, and intimidated umpires past the usual limit. Cobb himself was a constant presence, pacing the dugout, talking it up. His bench was an uncomfortable place on which to sit if you had muffed a double play or walked two men in a row. Fred Haney, an infielder, reported, "We could hear him gritting his teeth." Looking into a man's eyes, Cobb would command, "Fire up! Show me some fire!" Once he slapped second baseman Del Pratt across the mouth. According to Haney, who long afterward would become the general manager of the Los Angeles Angels (later renamed the California Angels), Pratt owned an extraordinarily large male sexual organ. Cobb—said Haney—yelled at Pratt, "You're all prick and no hit!" Wisely Pratt did not strike back. He improved his average to .310 and returned to the old man's good graces. On another day, when Navin brought a party of team stockholders to visit the dugout, Cobb refused to greet the investors. He was busy.

The aroused Tigers played .640 ball in the final third of the race. Scouts from other teams, watching a trick played by the Peach on Ruth in New York in September, called in the best such of the season. Haney reported that it began with Cobb, playing center field, whistling a signal to pitcher Hooks Dauss to give Ruth a base on balls when he came to bat. A walk was an obvious move. But Dauss threw a called strike past Ruth. Cobb raced in to bawl out both Dauss and catcher Bassler for disobeying his order. Ruth grinned, thinking it an oversight.

Back in center field, Cobb whistled another reminder. But again Dauss shot a called strike past Ruth. A furious Cobb ran in, stomped around, removed both Dauss and Bassler from the field, and brought in a new battery. After warming up, reliever Rufe Clarke fired a called third strike past an unprepared Ruth. On three straight pitches, Babe had struck out without moving his bat from his shoulder. Cobb doubled up with laughter, rubbing in the ruse. "A once in a lifetime setup play," he called it. "I flattered Ruth with that walk-the-man stuff and he fell for it."

Fred Haney named another Cobb play as the most fiendish he ever saw. In 1920, when Carl Mays of the Yankees had beaned Cleveland's Ray Chapman with a pitch that may or may not have slipped, and Chapman had died of a skull fracture, an outcry against "Killer" Mays had lasted for months. The tragedy marked Mays for life. "We went into Yankee Stadium, three years after Chapman's death," testified Haney, "and Cobb called me aside. He instructed me [as the hitter] to crowd real close to the plate. Then I was to fall down and writhe around if Mays's first pitch was close, a duster. I did so and Ty called for time-out and walked out to the mound. I thought he intended to jump all over Mays. But to my surprise he only said, 'Now, Mr. Mays, you should be more careful where you throw. Remember Chapman?' Cobb walked back to the plate, shaking his head. Mays was actually trembling . . . he was so unnerved that he couldn't get anybody out. We scored five runs off him to beat New York easily."

The good-hitting Tigers were acting like a team at last. Cobb directed them with a complicated puppet act, shouting orders in code, flashing signs, and pulling strings from the outfield and dugout. At Shibe Park, Philadelphia, he punched a groundskeeper for using a telephone when Cobb needed it. Since the groundsman was black, his act revived the old issue of his racial bigotry. The *Cleveland Plain Dealer* spoke of his "wanton wickedness." He ridiculed the Indians' pitcher, Guy Morton, until Morton was so nervous that he walked the Peach on four pitches with the bases loaded to force in the tying run; the Tigers won, 4–3. The importance of this game was that while Detroit could not by then catch the mighty Yankees, they could nose out Cleveland for second place, a finish worth about one thousand dollars per man to the Tigers in the coming World Series money division.

Seemingly, late in the schedule, the Tigers were in a hopeless position. They were required by the weird scheduling of the day to play no less than six doubleheaders within six days—108 and possibly more innings, and during a heat wave. Yet they stayed in the race, winning 33 of their last 53 and 11 of their final 14, to edge out Cleveland for the season's runner-up position behind New York. Cobb was limping on the last day but he hit two doubles against St. Louis for a 7–6 victory. The long-shot Detroit club ended with an 83–71 figure.

The 1923 season went into the records as the Georgian's finest managerial accomplishment, the product of his willpower, seizing opportunities, goading his men, and playing dirty tricks. He had no right whatever to second place. His infield's 103 double plays were the fewest of any team in the majors. His pitching staff's earned run average of 4.09 was second worst in the American League. Although Cobb's own batwork slipped to a .340 average—with a strained lower back he sometimes needed help from a trainer to lace his shoes—he entered two all-time records into the book. On May 25, he scored his 1,741st run, replacing Hans Wagner's career mark for all of modern baseball. Then, on September 20 he passed Wagner's major-league high for cumulative base hits with 3,455. Meanwhile, Heilmann was hitting .403 for his second batting title.

Cobb came out of it exhausted and dejected over not winning. He had played in 145 games, had 189 hits, 40 doubles, 7 triples, 88 runs batted in, 6 homers, 9 stolen bases, 362 putouts, and 12 errors. The daily pressure aged him more than had any season to date. "Couldn't sleep, had a bad stomach," he spoke of the aftermath. "My old eye trouble came back." After attending the Yankees-Giants World Series, in which Ruth's three home runs helped win it for the American Leaguers, he visited both an orthopedist and an optometrist.

Given two more skilled pitchers and infield help, Detroit just might have raised a pennant. The public set a Navin Field attendance record of more than 900,000. Only the Yankees, with seventy thousand or so seats and standing room available as against compact Navin Field's thirty-five thousand, sold more tickets. On the road, in drawing power, the Tigers almost matched the Yanks of Ruth, Meusel, Pipp, Herb Pennock, Sad Sam Jones, Waite Hoyt, Bullet Joe Bush, and company. Estimates were that Detroit, in franchise value, now stood among the leading half-dozen operations in the majors. For the moment, Navin, Briggs, and their shareholders had no complaint, and were constrained from considering Bill Donovan as a field-chief replacement for the baddest man in sporting history.

PRESENT-DAY baseball's free agency and salary arbitration systems were unheard of in the 1920s, but Cobb did not need such bargaining assistance. His stature was so high that for years he had virtually set his own price tag. For his 1924 salary, management suggested $55,000, not much of a raise over the past. "I got well above that," he said long afterward. "There were those long-term bonuses in my contract. And I bought stock in the club on the quiet. I worked this through a banker friend, who acted as my beard [stand-in]. My name didn't appear on any documents and I doubt that anyone in the organization knew about it. In New York they claimed that Ruth was paid more than me. But that was wrong. In combined ways I was making more than anybody." To Cobb's recollection, his pure baseball income for 1924 approached $60,000. His outside investments all but matched that.

At the Pontchartrain Hotel, a favorite hangout of Detroit's moneyed sportsmen and place where a painting of Ty Cobb hung, the betting was that he would not serve as player-manager for a third time. Enough was enough. Handling two responsibilities was hurting his statistics and his health. Another reason for that assumption was the lack of credit given Cobb by Francis Navin. The big-bellied Navin presented himself around town as the main reason for the 1923 surprise success. Navin was not a "baseball man," and Cobb had come to hold him in all but open contempt. Earlier, Navin had pulled political strings to have old Bennett Field renamed for him. ("Cobb Field" would have sounded better.) President Navin showed little ambition to see his team reach a World Series, but appeared content to sell one- and two-dollar tickets at a near-capacity rate. He was not a builder.

At horse tracks, Navin was a notorious plunger. One afternoon in 1924, Cobb was wagering conservative twenty-dollar amounts per race at the Windsor Jockey Club when writer Fred Lieb informed him, "Navin is here and he just lost twenty thousand dollars. He didn't turn a hair—just looked at his program and said, 'Let's see what's good in the next race.'" That kind of gambling was a high crime to Cobb.

He and Navin clashed time and again over player needs. A typical instance came midway in the 1924 season, after first baseman Lu Blue hurt a knee and was lost indefinitely—for thirty-eight games, it turned out. No roster replacement was available. But Johnny Neun, a hard-hitting star fielder with St. Paul of the American Association, could be obtained. "I wanted to shoot Navin," Cobb sketched the story. "He claimed he couldn't afford Neun at a fifty-five-hundred-dollar selling price. At the time we were in a close fight with Washington for first place. I told Navin that if he was so cheap, then he could take the fifty-five hundred out of my salary to buy Neun. He still wouldn't get me a guy who could help us win." Eventually Detroit signed Neun, but too late. The Cobbmen slid to third place in 1924, while Washington beat out the Yankees for the league title.

Comedy spiced the Cobb-Navin wars of 1924–26. The egos of two millionaires were equally matched. They could come to work at the Cherry Street park, hang their hats on pegs not far apart, and not speak to each other all day. Players told how one afternoon at Detroit, the visiting Yankees were joshing with Cobb during pregame warm-up about his famous ability to place-hit balls to any chosen field. "Bet you can't put one in our bull pen," challenged Yankee pitcher Bob Shawkey. Adjusting his bat, the Peach hit three straight pitches into the bull pen, scattering players in all directions. Then Navin walked past, curious about what was happening.

"Jesus Christ!" Shawkey was exclaiming hours afterward, "That Cobb drove one right at Navin, just missing him! Could have bumped him off!"

No one present had ever heard of a player doing anything so vicious. Asked in 1960 if the story were true, Cobb replied, "Could have been."

Navin hired a private detective to keep track of straying players. Cobb fired the sleuth. At the Grand Ballroom of the Book-Cadillac Hotel in Detroit, city fathers tendered a banquet honoring Cobb's long reign as Mr. Baseball, attended by two thousand people. The crowd filled two rooms. Navin was given a secondary seat to Connie Mack, Henry Ford, World War I air ace Eddie Rickenbacker, Mayor John W. Smith, and songwriter George M. Cohan. While guests were dining on roast pheasant and lake trout, Navin approached Cobb to speak of a ten-thousand-dollar check he was carrying in his pocket. The check, made out to Cobb, represented a final bonus payment under his season's contract. As Cobb explained the incident in his autobiography, "Navin said, 'Would you mind if I present this ten thousand dollars to you as a direct gift of the Detroit ownership?' He meant it, too." Cobb was taken aback by Navin's effrontery. "Of all the brazen, phony acts this man had put on," Cobb wrote, "this one took the cake. He *owed* me the money, yet wanted it to look like a big, generous present from him." The audience cheered while Cobb, for once silent in a public situation, allowed Navin to hand him the "gift" check. He always regretted doing it. With recalled bitterness, he said, "I should have exposed the faker on the spot."

ANOTHER STRESSFUL season affected Cobb's diet. Stomach pains forced him to eat bland foods, such as eggs, fish, oatmeal, and mashed potatoes. He gave up eating meat. He was steadily on the road to banquets and testimonials in his honor and cooks were required to serve him special dinners. Developing a cough, Cobb stopped smoking cigars, but by early 1924 he was back to consuming six or more Havanas per day. His drinking of hard liquor, never immoderate, remained unchanged. He signed one of his most lucrative outside contracts—$25,000 per annum to promote General Motors automobiles—and appeared across the eastern seaboard.

Long vanished now were the days when, as a hazed, ostracized rookie, his bats were sawed in half by Detroit veterans. In those days, Tyrus, on team road trips, would kill time by going off, alone, to tour the Statue of Liberty, Boston Tea Party docks, Ford's Theater, Mount Vernon, and other historical sites. Once he had stood in the crowd outside the White House. Now, three presidents—William Howard Taft, Woodrow Wilson, and Warren Harding—had invited him inside, and they had exchanged autographs. He had played golf with Taft and Harding. He remembered, "I attended Masonic rites with Taft in Augusta. He interrupted it with his snoring. He weighed about three hundred. Sounded like a buzz saw. I had to nudge him awake."

Not in the best of health, Cobb persisted in staying on in 1924–25 as the Tigers' player-manager, hoping to find a combination that would end the Yankees' three-year reign as champions. Time was running short. Headed toward middle age, Cobb had grown jowly and had developed liver splotches. In civilian dress he resembled a prosperous merchant or banker—or so he appeared until you saw him stripped; then he became 210 pounds of hard muscle. Damon Runyon of the Hearst press called him "Tire-us, the Jewel of Jawjah" for his endurance. Runyon said a good many observers felt that, contrary to widespread opinion, Ruth did not overshadow him except in power hitting. Other writers cited the judgment of some American League players in contending that Cobb still possessed more offensive and defensive abilities than the glorified Babe. For one basic consideration, he struck out far less than Ruth, the chronic fanner. (Over their careers Ruth compiled 1,380 strikeouts to Cobb's mere 357.) And the Peach personified fine points of American baseball that did not much interest the distance-obsessed Ruth. He held fast to his doctrine that games were meant to be won with a tight defense, by exploiting the hit-and-run, the disguised bunt, sacrifice fly, the squeeze play, hitting through holes, and the steal in its various forms—the delayed steal, double steal, stealing off the pitcher, the fadeaway slide into base, the "suicide" long lead off base, the spikes-high "threat" steal—along with the psychological upsetting of opponents. You got the job done with daring, thinking two or three plays ahead, and outfoxing and outgaming the other team—and you commonly did it by small margins.

Yet sometimes a hero remains on the scene overlong, and the feeling grew that the game was passing by Cobb's methodology. "Ty is living in 1905," said Bill Donovan. In the past ten years, home run totals in the big leagues had exploded. A bigger, stronger generation of players had emerged. In no consistent way could Cobb's approach offset long-ball hitting.

Cobb discouraged his men from taking a full swing most of the time. Homers were an incidental factor; bat control was everything. Assembling the Tigers for spring training in 1924 in Augusta, he stressed meeting the ball sharply for singles and doubles and going to the opposite field. And he wanted pitchers who could throw knee-high strikes—making batters hit into the dirt—and catchers who could fire throws to second base without leaving their crouch. He wanted base runners quick enough to execute the double steal. Bunters were instructed to put hard-to-handle backspin on the ball. The Tigers were told to spoil pitches with deliberate fouls until the pitcher made a mistake. Cobb valued men who were willing to crowd the plate and deliberately, painfully, let themselves be hit by pitches.

When he failed to have most of his needs filled, Cobb took matters into his own hands. For the first few weeks of the campaign he averaged a blazing .450 at bat. He was unable to steal in his former style—9 steals were all he had managed in 1923—but within five days in April he stole home base twice, against wily Ted Lyons of the White Sox and Bill Bayne of St. Louis. It was wonderful to see the old-timer work that most difficult of plays. Against the Yankees at Detroit in June, Cobb exchanged hard words with Babe Ruth and followed with a pair of triples and a single as the Tigers walloped New York, 10–4.

One day later came what fans everywhere had waited to see: a physical clash between Babe and Cobb. Not just a pushing match, Cobb later revealed, but the real thing, a release of four years of hostility. As could be expected, Cobb started it. Bob Meusel, a strong, silent type, came to bat against Detroit's relief pitcher, Bert Cole, with the Yankees leading 10–6 in the ninth inning. Ruth had batted just ahead of Meusel. Babe had fouled out after Cole threw a fastball at his head. He warned Meusel, "Cobb signaled Cole to bean me. So watch out."

From the outfield came another whistle from Cobb to Cole and Cole obediently hit Meusel in the ribs with a second fastball. Meusel threw his bat at Cole and charged the mound. "Before you knew it," wrote one correspondent, "every player on both sides was involved." Cobb raced in from the outfield and Ruth met him at the plate. Descriptions disagreed, but it was like two football fullbacks colliding head-on. They crashed, bounced off each other, and started exchanging punches. More than one thousand rioting Tiger fans attacked the Yankees, swinging seats uprooted from concrete. Police finally broke up the worst brawl of the season. They escorted the teams to their clubhouses through a mob gone wild. Cobb tried to reach Ruth again on the way out, but his blows were blocked. "You're a rotten cur dog!" yelled Meusel at Cobb. "Ruth would kill you if he had a chance."

"Bring him around to the pass gate!" shouted Cobb. "I'll beat the hell out of both you and that nigger!"

The umpires forfeited the game to New York, Cole and Meusel were suspended for ten days each, and Meusel drew a hundred-dollar fine. Cole was fined fifty dollars, as was Ruth. Cobb was gleeful—he came out of it with no punishment, although his beanball signals had been intercepted by umpire Billy Evans and reported to Ban Johnson's office, and even though it had been the Peach who ran in 350 feet to collide with a waiting Bambino.

Seeing a possible Detroit pennant, Cobb performed at close to the same pace in succeeding weeks. His play and that of Harry Heilmann and Earl Whitehill, a left-handed addition to the pitching staff, put the Tigers into first place on June 23. The Yankees and the surprising Washington Senators were right on their heels. In a Boston series, Cobb scored four runs and stole four bases, one of which was home base. In a 13–7 beating of the Red Sox, he made obscene gestures to a hotheaded Boston-Irish audience. Fans littered the field with junk and, invading the diamond, tangled with the police. "Lurking beneath Cobb's uniform is a pyromaniac," charged the Boston Globe. "He loves to start fires."

Thereafter the Tigers faded. They could not keep up the pace. Ultimately they dropped out of contention. In late September, in Detroit, the Tigers faced the Yankees in a three-game series. Cobb's team couldn't win the pennant, but could ruin New York's chances. Navin ordered a special two-hundred-man police patrol to control the expected trouble. But fans were peaceful enough while their team swept the series, ending the Yankee's title chances and their three-year domination of the league. Cobb, who made three timely hits in the set, was as big a pain as ever. He razzed New York's manager, the five-foot, four-inch Miller Huggins—"Hey, who's the midget?"—and verbally abused Ruth. Ban Johnson, in the league president's box, sent Cobb a note to stop the profanity. Ladies were in the house. "Tell the ladies to plug their ears," came the reply.

It was not Ruth who retaliated in this series' last game, but Lou Gehrig. At the time, Henry Louis Gehrig was an insecure twenty-one-year-old from Columbia University, used as a pinch hitter. The muscular left-hander had failed a Yankee tryout in 1923 and had been farmed back to Hartford of the Eastern League. ("He couldn't field a lick then," said one-time Yankee infielder Jimmie Reese, "but could use the bat. Nobody suspected that Lou would become one of the greats.")

Fed up with Cobb's abuse, Gehrig and shortstop Everett Scott ran from the bench. Cobb ducked and their punches missed. Umpire Tom Connolly threw Gehrig and Scott out of the game. The Peach went unpunished, since he had not fought back. "We won eighty-six games that year," Cobb was to characterize 1924, "and some of them came by getting the other side too mad to think."

Cobb had acted throughout the season as if he had tasted from Ponce de León's mythical fountain of youth. His pitchers once more failed him. There were injuries. And the Tigers fell back to a third-place finish, six games behind Washington and the equally ageless Walter Johnson. But with 625 at-bats, T.C. broke his personal record of 605, and appeared in every one of the club's 155 games. Only three American League base stealers surpassed his mark of 23. "Stealing is becoming a lost art," he complained. His batting average of .338 was 40 points above his team's aggregate average. Most pleasing of all to Cobb was that he led all league outfielders in fielding, committing only 6 errors for a fine .986 fielding percentage. He could still go and get them.

There was criticism that he would not have lost a championship by six games had he recognized that the home run was implanted to stay, and allowed the Tigers to swing freely for the fences. Under restraint, they had collected a total of 35 homers to the Yankees' 98 and St. Louis's 67. Cobb's prejudice in this regard, however, never would change. So fixed in stone was "Cobb's Law" that in 1925 the Yankees and St. Louis each would knock 110 balls out of parks to Detroit's 67. "I wouldn't want Ruth's number of strikeouts against my name," he said. That also went for most of the other sluggers coming up.

Detroit, the factory-workers' town with high auto-industry employment, set another sensational record at the box office. More than 1 million turned out, only thirty-eight thousand less than the Yankees could show. Navin was prospering, and he stopped hinting about replacing Cobb as field chief. Two men so opposite in goals would need to reach some concordance whereby they could live side by side. Gate revenue, and Cobb's solid support of the fans of a baseball-happy city, outweighed their personal differences and the petitions of Tiger players who could not live with their manager's driven, despotic ways.

SLUGGING IN A CAREER TWILIGHT

As 1925 came around, Cobb's threatened eyesight became his most pressing concern. He needed the surgery, delayed since 1923, when his vision had become clouded, particularly during twilight games starting at 3:00 or 3:30 P.M. or on gray-sky days. Printed material such as small agate type used in newspaper box scores had become difficult for him to read.

He disclosed to his ballplaying brother, Paul, "The ball looks a bit fuzzy . . . Sometimes I don't pick it up until it's near the plate. That's too late."

One of his quips became applicable—in reverse. Until now, when asked about his hitting, he had used a lighthearted crack: "Sure, I hit .400 against the fastest pitchers. They have great speed and stuff—for the first sixty feet." But by mid-1925 the final six inches to the batter's box no longer was a joking matter.

Specialists at the Wilmer Eye Clinic at Johns Hopkins Medical Center in Baltimore, in an examination conducted two years earlier, had been unable to complete their work. The fact that his condition had not been fully identified was the patient's fault. Distrustful of the medical profession ever since his botched tonsillectomy back in 1906, he called off the eye tests before doctors had reached a conclusive finding. His fear of the result might have entered into that decision. Eventually he explained, "I wasn't ready for it then."

Opposing pitchers, hearing rumors out of the Tiger camp of Cobb's possible trouble, disbelieved it. That the most hawklike eyes the game had known were not quite perfect was dismissed by opponents as one more Cobb trick, a fake. From opening day the Tigers played poorly, but he ripped everything—beating out bunts, driving screamers down the baselines, handling breaking pitches as well as ever. Still delaying eye tests, he stood among league leaders at a .390 average. He drove in four runs to beat the White Sox, 8–7, and homered twice to help beat the Yankees. "And he says he's going blind," said rookie southpaw Bob "Lefty" Grove of the Athletics. "There's nobody in the league I hate to pitch to more."

Despite Cobb's drumbeat hitting and that of Harry Heilmann and others, the Tigers never were in the championship chase. It was the most paradoxical of situations. Taught by their manager to hit and advance correctly, the Tigers were a batting circus in 1925. They scored far more runs than any of their competitors, with an output of 903 as against the 829 runs of second-place Philadelphia. The sixth-place Yankees, with Babe Ruth ailing and out of action for seven weeks, and with only 706 runs, were 197 behind Detroit's production.

Yet with all that offensive strength, the Tigers were on their way to a third- or fourth-place finish at best. Cobb was back to kicking around office furniture. It was a classic case of imbalance. He threatened to resign his job if his "misbegotten" pitchers did not begin winning and his infield did not shape up. His pitching staff went on failing collectively, so that by October only one member, a tired, thirty-seven-year-old Hooks Dauss, would win as many as 16 games. The club's ERA was 4.61.

Yet not everything was depressing that summer. After the Tigers blew a fifteen-inning game to Cleveland, and after Cobb singled twice and doubled in a St. Louis defeat, he made history by putting together the most astonishing number of long hits of the century, setting marks that are still in the 1994 record books. Furthermore, he did it after calling his shots in advance, before some dozen witnesses.

It had begun on May 5 during batting practice at St. Louis when Sid Keener of the *St. Louis Star* and Harry Salsinger of the *Detroit News* approached him for an interview. Cobb was cold. He frowned at the reporters. "I'm surprised you boys want to talk to me," he said, "since you're so impressed by the home run."

"Now, Ty," said Keener. "We know things are rough right now. But we just want to ask about how you're feeling."

Cobb had just come off the sick list—influenza—and it showed. He replied for everyone within earshot to hear, "Gentlemen, pay close attention today. I'll show you something new. For the first time in my life, I will be deliberately going for home runs. For years I've been reading comparisons about how others hit, as against my style. So I'm going to give you a demonstration."

His challenge was as explicit as one could get. In the first inning against St. Louis, dropping and closing his hands from the Cobb spread grip to use the whole bat, the Peach hit a Bullet Joe Bush fastball (and none were faster) into the right-field pavilion. In the second inning, he drove a slow curve by Elam Vangilder completely over the pavilion and onto Grand Avenue. In the eighth inning, he homered for the third time against reliever Milt Gaston. Mixed in with the four-basers were a double and two singles. His 6 for 6 set a major-league record for total bases of 16 in one game. That remains the American League record today; through sixty-nine years it has not been beaten, only tied.

All of this came on that May 5 in a "warm-up" way. His home-run eruption had given Detroit a 14–8 win. The next day he singled his first time up, running his string of consecutive base hits to nine. Then he homered twice, off two left-handers, Dave Danforth and Chet Falk, while Detroit pounded the Browns, 11–4. Five home runs in two straight games has not been surpassed since then, through more than six decades, whether by Ruth or any other batsman. It remains a modern-day record, equaled by only five other hitters. In the third game of the St. Louis series he missed a sixth home run by a matter of inches. In accumulating 25 total bases in two successive games, he set another still-existing mark. Years later, historians would peer at the old typeset and whistle at what they read.

Coming at the dusk of his career, this may have been Cobb's most resplendent hour. For impact, it stood in company with his season averages of .420, .410, and .390, bunched between 1911 and 1913. In forty-eight hours of 1925 he made his point, massively, that home runs were not difficult to accumulate, that he could wallop for long distances with anyone when inclined to do so, but that superior, inside ways to play the game existed.

After his "Big Five," he returned to spraying his hits, and at the 1925 season's conclusion, had but 12 homers in all, but his average was a soaring .378. His message went: It could have been five times that many round-trippers if he had so determined. "There's no doubt in my mind that Ty is the best all-around hitter who ever lived," reiterated Tris Speaker. "He can bunt, chop-hit, deliver long drives, or put balls out of sight."

COBB HAD not been immune to boos from a minority of fans at Navin Field since the Tigers' third-place ranking in 1924. Even after his awesome 1925 outburst at St. Louis, he drew a sprinkling of jeers in June and July, a reminder that Detroit had yet to win a pennant. Conditioned for a fight, he got into more trouble when a customer dressed in tiger stripes ran onto the grass and spit at him. Cobb kicked the fan in the pants. Park guards pulled him away.

At Cleveland in July his leg was wrenched and he was carried off the field when second baseman Joe Klugman fell atop him while avoiding a sliding Peach's high spikes. In mid-July, in a leg bandage, he came near to repeating his forty-five-minute fistfight with Billy Evans of 1921, which had bloodied that umpire. Against the Indians, Cobb badgered umpire Clarence "Pants" Rowland over a third-strike call. Bumping Rowland around the home-plate area, he almost knocked him down. Ejected, Cobb was handed a five-day league suspension. In Washington he drew the anger of the Nationals' president, Clark Griffith, for his overt stalling tactics. Old Fox Griffith, a prominent league executive who prided himself on being a leader since the 1890s in reducing rowdyism at parks, was fed up with Cobb's constant, obnoxious turning of games into brawls, and with his extensive delays while playing to the stands. The Old Fox issued a long list of complaints. In return, Cobb called the Nationals' president a liar. He publicly charged Griffith with encouraging the East Coast press to slander him and force him out of the league. The Georgian further took the opportunity to repeat his stand against team owners for their monopolistic grip on the industry.

Walter "Big Train" Johnson, of the Nationals, a peacemaker in controversies, asked Cobb why he caused so many disturbances when he came into Washington. The national capital incited the worst in him. He gave Johnson two reasons: "Griffith is one of the main men behind the reserve clause." And, "People like him have blocked me from leaving Detroit."

IT WAS in September 1925, with the Tigers in fourth place, that a man who would have much to do with Cobb's remaining baseball career was heard from in north-central California. Hubert Benjamin "Dutch" Leonard, a temperamental, in-and-out left-handed pitcher, had walked out on the Tigers after a dispute. Leonard was also a well-to-do farmer, owner of Fresno, California, citrus, melon, and vegetable acreage, who could afford independence when he quit the team. He accused his manager of overworking him to the point that his arm would be ruined. Although he did such things as keeping the thirty-three-year-old Leonard in a Boston game to take a 12–4 beating, Cobb disagreed. In a confrontation, Cobb called him "another of my goddamn cowards and Bolsheviks." Leonard then refused to pitch at all. He was placed on waivers, no team claimed him, and Cobb arranged his sale to Vernon, California, of the Pacific Coast League. Out there, rumor circulated that an enraged Leonard was claiming that he "had something" on his former boss and might make it public, to Cobb's great detriment. What Leonard had to reveal that could hurt the Peach was not specified. It remained vague—supposedly it had something to do with gambling. Nothing developed just then, but Cobb's enemies were titillated and remained curious. Muddy Ruel warned his friend, "Look out for this Leonard guy."

IN AUGUST and September, the Tigers pepped up enough to win ten straight and finished in fourth place, sixteen games behind a champion Washington club for which Johnson, Stan Coveleski, and Dutch Reuther won 58 games, and down the track from second-place Philadelphia and third-place St. Louis. In a closing-out doubleheader at St. Louis, Cobb staged another offensive show. He went 6 for 10, stole two bases and even pitched one shutout inning, just for the fun of what was left of another dull season. His .378 average was up with the circuit's leaders—this was his sixteenth campaign at .350 or better—but fatigue was evident, in that Cobb played in just 121 games.

At the ensuing World Series between Washington and Pittsburgh, when the Pirates became the first participant in history to come back from a 3–1 game deficit and win, he encountered a depressed George Herman Ruth in the press box. Ruth did not bristle, nor did Cobb. Neither felt well. They were photographed shaking hands unsmilingly.

"Had a hell of an off year, Cobb," said Ruth. "Got sick, couldn't hit my hat." (The reference was to his notorious "bellyache heard around the world" of the past April, rumored to have been caused by a venereal disease, but more likely to have been an intestinal abscess, for which he was operated upon. Whatever the dismal truth, Babe had batted a low .290, with 25 home runs, by far his worst production as a Yankee.)

"You're no kid anymore," said Cobb. "Got to take care of yourself."

"They pinch-hit for me a couple of times," said Ruth.

Cobb shrugged. "That's happened to me." (It had not—not yet—but for some reason Cobb felt empathetic toward Babe.)

"I'll take the hot tubs, get in shape. See you next season," ended Ruth.

"Next season," said Cobb. "I'll be there."

ON THE morning of March 2, 1926, two weeks before spring camp opened in Augusta, Cobb was wheeled into surgery at the Wilmer Clinic at Johns Hopkins in Baltimore. Dr. William H. Wilmer had finally prevailed upon him to have his vision trouble pinpointed and treated. Wilmer, a fellow Georgian, was known as one of the country's foremost doctors of ophthalmology. Operations would be performed on both eyes. After tests, Wilmer explained, "This would be serious if you had let it go much longer. As it is, you should make a full recovery."

"How soon is that?" asked a jittery Cobb.

"Within a month, probably. But you'll need to wear smoked glasses for a while," replied Wilmer. "And do no batting for the time being."

Cobb's ailment was caused by a filmy substance, termed pterygium, brought on by an accumulation of fine dust particles over the eyes, which had formed through more than 2,700 games. The surgical procedure would be to slit the growth, bury its terminals with tiny sutures, and allow the "cloud" to grow away from the pupils.

When he awakened from the anesthetic, Cobb discovered his head swathed in a full mask. He was left blind for four days and ordered to make no abrupt movement of his head. It was tormenting. The immobility was the second-hardest part of it. Cobb: "I lay there waiting for the decision . . . tried to think of something other than the coming season . . . and failed. I diagrammed plays in my head . . . that didn't work, either. All I could think of was that one word—*blind*."

When the bandages were removed, everything looked blurry to him; as he began panicking, his vision slowly cleared. Wilmer declared the surgery to be a complete success. Wilmer then left on other business, assigning a nurse to medicate his patient. Foolishly, Cobb got out of bed and insisted on leaving the clinic. His nurse protested, "You can't do that! Your eyes need to be treated for several days."

"Lady, I've got a ball club in training!" snapped Cobb. "I'm leaving. Get me my clothes."

Nurses were hunting for Wilmer when Cobb felt "a small twinge at the back of my eyes." It worsened. Within minutes, he was in agony. The pain was head-splitting, intolerable. He ran down a hall to the head nurse's station, screaming that his head was on fire: "Get me that medicine fast!"

Rushed to first aid and medicated, he was relieved of the worst of it. "From then on, I was the most cooperative customer Johns Hopkins ever had," he said to me in his sixtieth year.

He arrived, shakily, in Augusta on March 13, two weeks late. An unsympathetic Navin asked why the operation couldn't have been performed over the past winter, and not left the Tigers temporarily without leadership. "Because I make my own schedule!" returned Cobb. And that was that.

His recovery was slow. Wilmer had warned him not to take batting practice for at least one month. Any accidental beaning or abrupt swiveling of the eyes was to be avoided. Wearing smoked glasses, the patient began hitting line drives within two days of his arrival. Photographers crowded around, eager to record his ability to hit in the same way—or not. He took a dozen or so swings and quit. He gave no explanation, but that night he left camp, was driven to his Augusta residence by Charlie Cobb, and stayed in bed for several days. Any exposure to bright light or even smoke from a cigarette or cigar caused a sharp stinging of his eyes. Wilmer, meanwhile, had wired him: "STOP AT ONCE. USE PRESCRIBED TREATMENT."

Years later, in Nevada, Cobb wrote to me of this time: "How I dreaded the first fastball I'd have to face on a sunny day when regular play began." What he should have dreaded even more was Dutch Leonard, a man with information that seemingly revived 1920 and the perfidious Black Sox of Chicago.

CHAPTER TWENTY-FIVE

"REPREHENSIBLE— BUT NOT CRIMINAL"

For someone as calculating, opportunistic, and well known as Cobb, it figured that he would form advantageous friendships with sports-minded politicians. During the short but marred Harding administration he had developed a strong, profitable White House connection. Warren Gamaliel Harding, twenty-ninth president of the nation, had been a first baseman–outfielder with the Marion (Ohio) Base Ball Club. Later he owned the Marion minor-league franchise. Harding loved the sights and sounds of a ballpark. He treated Cobb as the most honored of guests. In March of 1921, Harding had invited the "Great Agitator" to attend his inauguration; thereafter, when the Tigers were scheduled in Washington, Cobb became a poker-playing insider at the White House. "I saw as much as ten thousand dollars on the table in one stud game," he recorded in his retirement. "Harding was popular enough, but he was surrounded by crooks. I sat back in card games, and went easy on the drinking . . . His pals hit the bourbon hard, so I had a good payday for myself about a dozen times a year."

By 1926, Harding was long dead, but T.C.'s continued clubbiness with national political leaders would now stand him in good stead. Events began to build around him, off and on the field, that cast Cobb in such a bad light that he was to need all of the support he could get in top Washington circles. Without these defenders his career might end in the most shocking form of disgrace known to a ballplayer.

THE YEAR 1926 was another case of Tiger failure: one more sixth-place finish, during which the manager, nearing forty but still carrying a Maxim gun to the plate, showed signs that after twenty-one years he and Detroit were about to part company. His suitability as a manager was widely questioned. That feeling mounted with the formation of statewide "Fire Cobb!" factions. Michiganders with less than perfect memories even threw overripe peaches at him.

An example of what fans saw as his worst flaw came at Yankee Stadium in September. His pitcher-switching act that day exposed him as possibly unfit to deal with circumstances under pressure. It came when his pitcher, Lil Stoner, breezing for a Tiger victory behind a four-run lead, walked two men in a row. Showing signs of panic, Cobb jerked him. In came Augustus "Lefty" Johns in relief. Johns was about to win the game for Stoner in the ninth inning when he gave up one hit. Cobb rushed in from right field, jerked the ball from Johns's hand, and benched him, too. Johns objected to joining Stoner in the showers and he and Cobb exchanged words. The next hurler, Wilbur Cooper, an old-timer of fading ability, gave up more hits, and within minutes an almost sure win for Detroit became a defeat.

With few exceptions, those who worked under Cobb's direction felt smothered—he expected them to think as fast and imaginatively as he did, hit for an impossible average, and approach the game with his fire. None of the Tigers came close to his requirements for mental agility and obsessiveness; some—Heilmann, Manush, Gehringer—were greatly gifted, but were not in their leader's class. He rode his players so hard that some spoke of living in a nine-inning hell. "We thought that Cobb would crack up any day," said intelligent infielder Fred Haney. "One day he would be riding high and working well with his lineup, next day he'd go around with the whites of his eyes flared and be the meanest guy you ever saw. He had spells, fits. Unimportant things made him blow. Some of the boys thought it was a case of brain fever."

IN EARLY November, Frank Navin loosed a thunderbolt—Cobb would not be retained as manager or player in 1927. Navin blamed him for "demoralization" of the Tigers, a situation showing no sign of improvement. Cobb had handed in his resignation on November 3, briefly stating that he was "bone-tired" and had planned to resign back in August. But his main reason for leaving, he let out, was Navin, who demonstrably did not understand how to build a winning team through trading, scouting, using the waivers process, stealing other teams' stars, and bringing along talent through patient development in the minors.

Then, while Cobb and Navin were placing the blame on each other, Tris Speaker, thirty-eight, the highly admired Cleveland manager, also resigned, to enter the trucking business. This came on November 29.

The public's reaction to the departure within weeks of two of the biggest box-office names in the game was surprise, then suspicion. Was something going on that had not been disclosed? Why, for instance, had Cobb dropped from view, unavailable to the press at a climactic moment? How was it that Speaker had quit just weeks after leading the Indians to a second-place finish, only three games behind the Yankees? Texas Tris, now at a peak of popularity in Ohio, was being paid close to forty thousand dollars.

A few days before Christmas, a stunning explanation came from Commissioner Kenesaw Landis. He verified as true the rumor that Cobb and Speaker had been permitted by him to resign in the face of accusations made against them of fixing and betting on a game played between Detroit and Cleveland seven years earlier, back on September 25, 1919.

THE STRONGEST evidence against the pair of a gambling conspiracy consisted of two letters in Landis's possession. One had been written by Cobb in 1919 to Hubert "Dutch" Leonard, who had pitched for Detroit during the time he alleged the fix was on; the other letter was written in 1919 by Smoky Joe Wood, a Cleveland outfielder, which also was sent to Leonard.

For a reformer as dogged and as much a headline-hound as Landis, the correspondence was pure gold. It was widely reported, and not denied, that American League owners had paid Leonard between $15,000 and $25,000 to buy his letters and perhaps to suppress them. By 1926, Leonard was a well-to-do fruit farmer in central California. His motive for disclosing the letters was identified as revenge on Cobb for cutting him from the Detroit roster in 1925 and effectively ending his big-league career. As for Speaker, he had let Leonard slide down to the minors by not picking him up on waivers after Cobb's rejection. It would have cost Speaker's club only $7,500 to take him on waivers, cheap for a pitcher who had posted some good seasons.

Long before Landis took over the investigation in late 1926, when American League president Ban Johnson began to look into the matter, Cobb denied everything. Now he demanded that Leonard be brought from California to Chicago to meet him face to face. Leonard, refusing, was widely quoted as saying, "They got guys in Chicago who bump people off for a price." Yet Leonard, earlier in 1926, had come east and tried to sell his incriminating letters to a newspaper.

What had happened, claimed Leonard, was this: before the 1919 Detroit-Cleveland game in question, he, Speaker, Cobb, and Wood had met under the stands, and a conspiracy was hatched. Leonard quoted Speaker as saying that, since his Indians had clinched second place in the closing-out season and Detroit was in a battle with the Yankees for third place and a piece of World Series money, why not make sure the Tigers collected it? "Don't worry about a thing," said Speaker, according to Leonard.

To take advantage of a sure thing, Cobb offered to put up $2,000 of a pot collected then and there by the four men. Leonard would gamble $1,500 and Speaker and Wood $1,000 each—$5,500 in all. Cobb, added Leonard, provided a Detroit groundskeeper named Fred West to lay the wagers with chosen bookies.

When Landis placed Leonard's documentation on record on December 21, 1926, he touched off the most lurid sport scandal since the 1920 Black Sox affair and the excommunication of Shoeless Joe Jackson, Eddie Cicotte, Buck Weaver, and friends. "I am going to expose that bastard Cobb," Leonard had promised Pacific Coast baseball men. "I'll ruin him."

Newspapers gave a heavy play to the course of events:

CHICAGO, Dec. 22—[Associated Press]—The attention of the base ball world centered today on a seven-year-old game, that between the Detroit and Cleveland American League teams on Sept. 25, 1919, around which charges of fixing, involving two of the greatest players known to the game, have been made.

The long smouldering bombshell, the subject of many recent rumors, broke yesterday and sent fragments into many places, but today those accused came back quickly with denials of wrongdoing.

Ty Cobb and Tris Speaker, idols of thousands of base ball fans, and holders of many base ball records, declared they were innocent of assertions that they were involved in a conspiracy to "throw" the ball game and to benefit by betting on the outcome of the contest.

DETROIT NEWS, Dec. 24—Fred O. West, Navin Field employee of the Detroit Tigers, mentioned in testimony before Kenesaw Mountain Landis, Commissioner of Base Ball, as the man who placed the alleged bets for Ty Cobb, Tris Speaker, Joe Wood and Hubert (Dutch) Leonard on Sept. 25, 1919, made the following statement to The Detroit News today:

"I took a sealed envelope from one place to another on the date mentioned. The following day I called at the second place, got another sealed envelope and delivered that."

West refused to mention the name of the player who handed him the sealed envelope, although admitting it was one of the four involved in the scandal. He refused to say where he took the envelope that he picked up on the following day.

"I can't say what was in the envelope," said West. "It was sealed and I'm not in the habit of opening sealed envelopes.

"I was called to Chicago by Commissioner Landis. I saw him Monday. I told him what I have just told you. It's all I have to say."

Hughie Jennings, the manager under whom Cobb broke in at Detroit in 1905, and usually pro-Cobb in Cobb-versus-establishment clashes thereafter, worsened the crisis for the Peach—now facing possible expulsion from baseball—by speaking of how easy it would be to fix a game and issuing a "no comment" on the questioned game, played when Jennings was Detroit's manager. His "no comment" sounded like he was avoiding the issue:

CHICAGO, Dec. 26—[United Press]—Hughie Jennings issued a statement yesterday on the base ball plot averred by Commissioner Landis. He said, "I have no knowledge of the matter whatever. My slate has been clean base ball for 35 years. This is the first inkling I have had of this case. Whatever I have done in base ball has been of such a nature that I would be ready any time to go before anyone and place my case before them. I do not feel that I should comment on the case. These things are all very well to bring out if you have the goods and can prove them.

"Judge Landis has probably been investigating for some time and would not make any such statement unless he had proof to back it up. As for the complicity of the game of base ball it would be an easy matter for players so inclined to throw a game without the manager having any knowledge of it. It would be a very easy matter to cover up. But if I had any inkling of the thing during my time as manager of Detroit, or since, I certainly would not have covered the matter up but would have given the facts no matter what the cost."

One of the offshoots of the alleged plot was the disclosure of the longtime covert practice of teams playing "good fellowship" games in late season. Basic to this scheme was the bribe. If Team A, fighting to collect second- or third-place money, needed help, Team B, finishing out of the money, would provide it by trying extra hard against Team A's chief rivals. Team B's *quid pro quo* was the gift of a suit of clothes or cash from A for each of its regulars.

Cobb candidly told me in 1960 that he had shared in such secret subsidizing on occasion, when the Tigers "broke our backs" to help out a team after Detroit was eliminated from the World Series race. "Once I got a dozen shirts from the Boston Red Sox," he said offhandedly. "It was just a thing we all did."

But this time there could be no cover-up:

DETROIT NEWS, Dec. 27—"I am not surprised," said "Bernie" Boland, former Tiger hurler, who pitched the "good fellowship" game of Sept. 25, 1919. Boland is a paving contractor, living at 11833 Wisconsin Avenue.

"I hope everything comes out about it. I was a pick and shovel pitcher, working like a miner, taking the games as they came. Dutch Leonard was a star, wasn't he? But he picked the soft spots. If he had to pitch against Walter Johnson he was sick or something. He never showed up in the spring and I and others had to pitch these small town games where they lay the diamond out the night before. I got tired of it and then when I tried to get in shape too quickly I hurt my arm. They ran me out of the American League.

"There are a lot of these friendship games at the tail end of the season, when they give the boys hits to fatten their batting averages and help them get good salaries. I do not remember this particular game, but you can bet I had nothing to do with the matter. This is all news to me. The only player I ever gave a hit to was 'Stuffy' McInnis. He used to plead so hard so he could make a .300 average. In that newspaper report of the game in question they say I gave Speaker three triples. That is not so. I never gave Speaker anything in my life.

"The way I figure it, about one in every 300 games is crooked, and those at the tail end of the season.

"This is bad for baseball, for practically all of the players are honest, but I am glad some of them are getting justice at last. It's mighty hard to keep going when the boys quit behind you."

One corrupt game in every three hundred? Club owners blanched at that news. They had covered up the rewards systems, allowing it to pervade a game believed by millions of Americans to be on the square. Now the outcome was a shameful disclosure. Landis called players of past and present to his Chicago office to be grilled. Swede Risberg, one of the exiled Black Sox of six years earlier, swore to God that a whole series of games between Detroit and the Chicago White Sox—two straight doubleheaders of September 2 and 3, 1917—had been "greased" to aid Chicago in its struggle for first place. Risberg said Detroit helped Chicago win all four crucial games and the pennant. According to him, each White Sox player put up forty-five dollars toward purses of one hundred dollars as a bribe for Detroit pitchers and others.

But Cobb testified that he had no part of the 1917 dirty work and Risberg verified that. Landis cleared Cobb of any wrongdoing in 1917.

Landis possessed an embarrassment of riches. He paraded forty witnesses at a January 5, 1927, board of inquiry session, and everyone wished he had not done so. Disillusionment grew as players confessed to fixed games arranged by the idolized New York Giants of John McGraw, whose infielders had a habit of sidling up to opponents and whispering, "You wanna kick one today?" A few years earlier, Landis had warned, "If I catch any crook, the rest of his life will be a hot period!" At the moment, in early 1927, with a new scandal arising, Landis became more moderate, telling the press, "Team pools or incentive money offered others is an act of high impropriety, reprehensible and censurable, but it is not criminal."

The infamous letter written by Cobb to Leonard, offered retroactively as evidence, read:

Augusta, Ga., Oct. 23, '19

Dear Dutch:

Well, old boy, guess you are out in old California by this time and enjoying life.

I arrived home and found Mrs. Cobb only fair, but the baby girl was fine, and at this time Mrs. Cobb is very well, but I have been very busy getting acquainted with my family and have not tried to do any correspondence, hence my delay.

Wood and myself are considerably disappointed in our business proposition, as we had $2,000 to put into it and the other side quoted us $1,400 and when we finally secured that much it was about two o'clock and they refused to deal with us, as they had men in Chicago to take the matter up with and they had no time, so we completely fell down and of course we felt badly about it.

Everything was open to Wood and he can tell you about it when we get together. It was quite a responsibility and I don't care for it again, I can assure you.

With kindest regards to Mrs. Leonard, I remain, sincerely,
Ty Cobb

These rather vague references would not have identified Cobb as a gambling man and possible fixer, had he not mentioned two thousand dollars and Joe Wood as partner in a "business proposition." Wood's letter to Leonard was more specific, reading:

Cleveland, O., Friday

Enclosed find certified check for sixteen hundred and thirty dollars ($1,630).

Dear Friend "Dutch":

The only bet West could get up was $600 against $420 (10 to 7). Cobb did not get up a cent. He told us that and I believed him. Could have put some at 5 to 2 on Detroit, but did not, as that would make us put up $1,000 to win $400.

We won the $420. I gave West $30, leaving $390, or $130 for each of us. Would not have cashed your check at all, but West thought he could get it up to 10–7, and I was going to put it all up at those odds. We would have won $1,750 for the $2,500 if we could have placed it.

If we ever get another chance like this we will know enough to try to get down early.

Let me hear from you, "Dutch."

With all good wishes to yourself and Mrs. Leonard, I am, always,

Joe Wood

When Cobb was summoned to explain himself, he appeared at Landis's office with two costly Detroit and Chicago lawyers. But Landis did not allow them to interrupt his rapid-fire interrogation. A transcript of the Cobb questioning, in main part, reads as follows:

Q. What is your full name?
A. Tyrus Raymond Cobb.
Q. And your residence?
A. Augusta, Georgia.
Q. And you were connected with the Detroit club in 1919?
A. Yes, sir; I was.
Q. In what capacity?

A. As a player.

Q. Who was manager of Detroit through 1919?

A. Hughie Jennings.

Q. You became manager?

A. 1921.

Q. You managed the team from 1921 to 1926, inclusive?

A. Yes, sir.

Q. Mr. Cobb, I hand you a document, dated Augusta, Ga., Oct. 23, 1919, addressed to "Dear Dutch" and signed, "Sincerely, Ty," which will be marked Exhibit One. And I ask you to look at that document and tell me if you wrote that letter.

A. It is my letter.

Q. I call your attention to the letter which you have just identified as having been written by you and ask you if you recall the occasion of having written that letter.

A. Yes, I wrote the letter.

Q. And what was it about?

A. It was in response to a request by Leonard that I ascertain from Wood [Joe Wood] the amount of money that was wagered on this game in question.

Q. The amount of money that was wagered on what?

A. On the game in question.

Q. That is the game of Sept. 25, 1919?

A. Yes, sir. He stated—you want me to relate what he said?

Q. Yes.

A. He stated that he was leaving and wanted to check up on the amount that had been wagered.

. . . . . .

Q. Give me the conversation, as near as you can remember it, just what was said.

A. Well, he was leaving, could not be there after the game, and he wanted to find out as quickly after the game as possible—he wanted me to ascertain from Wood, the amount that was paid. That is, to the best of my knowledge.

Q. When did you first hear that a bet was to be put on the ball game?

A. Leonard came to me and wanted to know who would be a man they could trust, and that is where I figured that the—

Q. What was your answer to him?

A. I told him I would get a man for him.

Q. And what did you do along that line?

A. I pointed out West, a man that was employed at the park.

Q. Where was West at the time you pointed him to Leonard?

A. Well, to the best of my knowledge, he was either close to the edge of the playing field or was inside the field.

. . . . . .

Q. What did you understand Leonard to mean when he asked you the name of somebody he could trust, or you could trust, whichever it was?

A. Well, I figured that he wanted to bet on the game.

Q. What made you think so?

A. Well, that is the only inference that I could gather from what he said.

Q. Had you any conversations with him before about betting on ball games?

A. No, sir.

Q. Was there anything else in his inquiry to you that you have not mentioned here that would indicate to you the kind of trust he wished to repose in somebody?

A. Well, there might have been other conversations. I am only relating what I can remember—away back there. And there might have been other things. For instance, he talked about ascertaining what amount of money would be put up by Wood, see? He wanted me to inquire.

Q. Did you have any conversation with Wood about this bet?

A. I did not. I did not until after the game. That is—wait a minute. I did not until I asked him concerning the amount of money bet.

Q. Did you have any conversation with Speaker about this game?

A. None whatever.

Q. Betting on the game?

A. No.

Q. Did you bet any money on the game?

A. Positively did not.

Q. Did you intend to?

A. I did not.

Q. Did you have any conversation with anybody whatever about betting on the game?

A. I did not.

Q. You played in that game?

A. I must have. I have never seen the box score yet.

Q. I now hand you the box score, taken from a paper of Sept. 26. Does that box score refresh your memory as to whether you played in that game?

A. It indicates I must have played in the game.

Q. Well, after this conversation with Leonard, if you had not played in the game, you probably would remember you had not been in the game, wouldn't you?

A. At this time, I would not. I don't know anything about it; I don't remember any of the details concerning the game.

Q. You have no recollection of the game?

A. No.

Q. How it was played?

A. No.

Q. It appears from this box score that Detroit won, 9 to 5.

A. Yes.

Q. I wish you would look at your letter, and, calling your attention to the language of that part of the letter starting with "Wood and I."

A. Yes, "Wood and myself."

Q. Now, make any statement you desire to make respecting the language which you used in that letter to Leonard.

A. In writing this letter to Leonard, it is apparent that I, in a way, tried to veil the betting end of it as a betting proposition. I stated to Leonard just what Wood had told me. The amounts of $2,000 to $1,400 quoted by the other side was entirely different from the information that Wood conveyed to Leonard in his letter, which indicated I was not in on the betting proposition, that Wood merely put me off by giving me the wrong information and a fictitious amount.

Q. Now, in this statement that Leonard made to me in California and which I have read into this record, he tells of a conversation under the stands after the game played the preceding day. Was there any such conversation between you, Wood, Speaker and Leonard?

A. Positively no. If such a frameup were true, why should we stop for a few minutes under the stands and arrange such an important matter? The players—both sides—come to the field through a dugout from their respective club houses. Where would we have the time and where could we go for just a few minutes, as Leonard has stated, to frame up such an important matter?

Q. Do you remember what the position of the Detroit club in the pennant race was at the time?

A. From memory, no. Indications were that it was in third place.

Q. That is, you were fighting for third place?

A. Yes, that is the indication. I don't remember the details.

Q. Why was it you mentioned West to Leonard as a man he could trust?

A. He is the only man that I knew of that was handy, and I figured he could be trusted.

Q. What made you think West was familiar with this sort of thing?

A. No other reason in the world except as I have stated.

Q. Had you ever had West place any bets for you on anything?

A. No, sir.

Examination of Joe Wood, by then the head baseball coach at Yale University, brought out the admission that he had written the letter dated "Cleveland, O., Friday," addressed to "Dear Friend 'Dutch'" and signed "Joe Wood."

Q. Now just tell me all about that bet.

A. The day before the ball game Leonard came to me and said, "Boland is going to pitch against you fellows tomorrow; we are fighting for third place; you fellows' position

in the race is settled; you can't move up or down. Now
the Detroit ball club is fighting for third place money, and
it looks like a good bet. You want to go in on a bet with
me?"

I thought it over and I asked him how much he
wanted to bet. He said he wanted to bet about $2,500. I
told him I didn't feel as if I wanted to put up that much
money, but I said: "I have a friend here. I will mention it
to him. If we can split that bet three ways, I would be willing to go in that way."

Q. Did you have any conversation with Speaker about a bet
on this ball game?

A. I never had any conversation with Speaker about a bet on
this game. I had a little conversation with Cobb about this
ball game when he stopped me and asked, "How much
did you bet on this game today?" I didn't think it was any
of his business, I gave him an anonymous reply. I said I
had an opportunity to put up $2,000 against $1,400 but
didn't get it up in time.

Landis then questioned Cobb further:

Q. Mr. Cobb, have you in mind any possible reason why
Leonard should have made this statement to me about
you and Wood and Speaker and Leonard being together
under the stands and framing up this ball game?

A. I cannot imagine a human being with any sort of honor or
ideals having the spleen that Leonard has for me. The fact
of the matter is, when I became manager of the Detroit
ball club, I believe at that time he was under suspension;
either then or later he was under suspension and I did
everything I could with Mr. Navin to have that suspension
lifted; I got him back to the Detroit ball club because its
pitchers were very weak and we needed all the help we
could get.

I gave him every possible break that a veteran pitcher
could expect. I gave him his rest, we were down in the
race, and were fighting our way up again. We had 12

games of ball in six days. I called a meeting of the pitchers and told them we had a real hard test facing us and that I might have to call on them out of turn.

Cobb then told of asking Hooks Dauss to pitch out of turn, and said he then called on Leonard and that Leonard flatly refused to go to the mound after being ordered.

Continuing under oath, Cobb added:

A. I had a talk with Mr. Navin and it was decided we would get rid of Leonard. The whole team was upset over it and he had the reputation in the past of being a bolshevik on the club.

I released him to Mr. Navin. Mr. Navin asked waivers and did all the other things. It was the only thing in my whole acquaintanceship with Leonard that I would figure would make him do such a thing as this.

Cobb, coolly, did not admit to anything more heinous than acting as an intermediary in laying a bet. Landis took his testimony under advisement. Cobb demanded that Leonard come to Chicago from his California home to face him directly. Leonard declined. He said that he feared a physical attack from "that wild man" or that the gun Cobb was known to carry might be pulled on him.

THE BASEBALL world now awaited Landis's verdict. Cobb reminded fans, "I could buy myself a major-league franchise right now. Why should I bother with a few dollars gained through a damned fool bet?"

Another point: Leonard claimed that Speaker's Cleveland Indians had agreed to let Detroit win (which the Tigers did, 9–5); if so, would not Speaker have gone easy with the bat, and Cobb been fed some soft pitches? In actuality, Speaker tripled twice and singled, while the Peach produced just one scratch single.

Lawyers retained by the two advised them to sue Landis and organized baseball for a sum in the six figures.

THROUGH HIS White House connections, which dated back to the presidencies of Woodrow Wilson and Warren Harding, Cobb arranged a meeting with Charles Evans Hughes, former U.S. Supreme Court justice and recent secretary of state. Several wealthy men in Georgia offered to meet Hughes's fee for handling Cobb's libel and slander suits, in which he sought $100 million in damages. Some law experts felt that Cobb's case could be won on the strength of his unmatched playing record alone. National newspaper columnist Will Rogers was caustic, writing, "I want the world to know that I stand with Ty and Tris. I've known them for 15 years. If they have been selling out all these years, I would like to have seen them play when they wasn't selling."

Babe Ruth had something to say. His attitude surprised some people—normally the Babe would just as soon punch Cobb's nose as not—when he spoke from a vaudeville stage in San Francisco: "This is a lot of bull. I've never known squarer men than Cobb and Speaker. Cobb doesn't like me and he's as mean as [*censored*]. But he's as clean as they come."

Ruth, observed New York journalist Henry L. Farrell late in December, was a beneficiary of any dirty work that had gone on. He wrote, "You hear it in the streets here, in the subways, on the trolleys, in the clubs of drinkers and from the Park Avenue aristocracy: 'Well,' the general comment runs, 'Cobb is in a big jam, worse than usual, but Babe never would do that. Babe has human frailties. But never would you find him involved in anything as messy as this.'"

In Augusta by torchlight, a large crowd, three bands, and local and state leaders gathered around Augusta's historic Confederate Monument on Broad Street to swear allegiance to a favorite son. Landis was hung in effigy, while the favorite son was proposed as the next mayor of Augusta.

Landis continued to delay his decision. To lose Cobb's box-office draw would make the judge unpopular with most owners. Meanwhile, the man on trial was applying pressure where the leagues were vulnerable. Cobb hinted to newspapers that he had inside information on how certain club officials filed false ticket-sales figures to tax collectors and scalped World Series tickets. "I may say a few words on how the boys handle turnstile counts in a number of cities," he threatened. He would "tear baseball apart."

"It's amazing how 40,000 paid admissions can become 36,000," he told the *Philadelphia Daily News*. "Evidently he is in a position to blow the top off a game already riddled with knavery," U.S. senator Hoke

Smith of Georgia predicted. "If they force out the grandest player of them all, he will take with him his pound of flesh."

During his first four years as commissioner, Landis had barred some fifteen players for life, including the eight Black Sox. Now, without explanation, he held the Cobb-Speaker-Wood case in abeyance until late January of the new year. A distinct danger existed that he would throw the book at Cobb, leaving him an even sorrier sight than the great Shoeless Joe Jackson, banned from baseball forever. Or the commissioner might do nothing—in which case the suspensions of Cobb and Speaker that American League president Ban Johnson had pronounced would remain in effect.

ON JANUARY 26, Landis ended a month of delay. He prefaced his decision by casting doubt upon Dutch Leonard's reliability as an absentee witness, then ruled, "This is the Cobb-Speaker case. These players have not been, nor are they now, found guilty of fixing a ball game. By no decent system of justice could such a finding be made."

His ruling glaringly omitted any mention of gambling on baseball games. Still, it amounted to a full acquittal for both men, and in effect constituted an admission that one man—if his name was Tyrus Raymond Cobb—could force the clearing of his name.

There were other repercussions. Ban Johnson was ordered to take a leave of absence and, after a brief reprieve, to resign as American League president, mostly because he had hounded and prejudged Cobb. Navin, who wanted Landis's $65,000-per-year job, was discredited. To many fans Cobb was plain guilty.

BOTH COBB and Speaker were reinstated, but neither would play for their former clubs again. Teams came at Cobb with rich, record offers. He said in February, in private to some relatives, "I'll play one more season, bad legs and all, to make my vindication complete."

John McGraw was coming off a fifth-place finish with his New York Giants. His offer was a reported $60,000 per season for two years and a private hotel room for Cobb on the road. McGraw had bad-mouthed Cobb for years; Cobb brushed off the bid. Clark Griffith of Washington promised to equal any other offer, and threw in a $10,000 bonus for signing. The Brooklyn Dodgers were heard from, too. But Connie Mack outmaneuvered everyone. According to Cobb, Mack, his long-ago hatred of the Peach having receded, came to Augusta, handed Cobb a blank check, and said, "Just fill in the amount, Ty, and sign it. Whatever you say it will be is it."

"Now," Cobb related to me many years later, "Philadelphia was the place where snipers had threatened to shoot me from the bleachers and where Mack once had campaigned to have me thrown out of the league. But a blank check was unheard of, and I gave it careful consideration." The contract he finally signed included $70,000 in salary and bonus, 10 percent of spring-training gate receipts, and $20,000 more if the Athletics won the pennant. It worked out at $85,000 for 1927. Since Babe Ruth did not enjoy a share in Yankee preseason income, that left Cobb still the highest-paid individual in the profession.

"So," he told me, "I broke into ball with a sixty-five-dollar-a-month contract in the lowest form of the bush league down in Alabama. My deal with Mack was worth $555.55 *for each game* of the Philadelphia schedule. My father—how proud he would have been if he hadn't left for the other side."

CHAPTER TWENTY-SIX

FINAL INNINGS

"The honorable and honest Cobb blood . . . never will be subjected. It bows to no wrong nor to any man . . . The Cobbs have their ideals and God help anyone who strives to bend a Cobb away from such."
Cobb in a 1927 letter to U.S. congressman Robert H. Clancy

So he came to historic Philadelphia to play out his string—"one final season"—his twenty-third. It was inconvenient for him to sell his home in Detroit, to lease another in the exclusive Philly suburb of Bala-Cynwyd, and to have the bushels of mail he received rerouted. Connie Mack made the move psychologically easier by arranging for the local chapter of the Baseball Writers Association of America to sponsor a welcoming banquet for Cobb at the Hotel Adelphi. The affair sold out. Seven hundred Philadelphians wanted to hear him strip some hide off those who had demeaned him and by inference harmed the Cobb clan.

The writers heard him declare, for the first time, that his lawyers had actually dictated the terms of his reinstatement by Landis, thereby making major-league history, and he reminded the press that behind him stood a "baseball bloc" in the U.S. Senate. "I want to thank," he said, "Senator Pat Harrison of Mississippi, Senator George Wharton Pepper of Pennsylvania, Senator James E. Watson of Indiana, Senator James Couzens of Michigan, and Senators William J. Harris and Hoke Smith of Georgia for their actions in my behalf." The senatorial bloc had less proof of his innocence than the prosecution had of his guilt in conspiring to gamble on a game (or games), yet to the politicos the "witch-hunting" of Landis, Johnson, and others was outrageous, a travesty of justice.

Philadelphians, sensing this might be a pennant year for them, toasted their new man for hours at the Adelphi. Detroiters were equally effusive. In an odd act on "Cobb Day," when the Athletics played their first series in Motor City, fans presented their former outfielder and new opponent with a Packard sedan and a fine silver service. He drove the car around the field. Then he lined a double into the roped-back right-field crowd, helping clinch a win for the Athletics.

He had always believed that Detroit fans were cuckoo. The Packard proved it.

SPECULATION RAN that two such seasoned strategists as Mack and the Georgian would inevitably clash. Mack's autocratic way of shifting his outfielders about like chessmen—by semaphoring with his scorecard in or out, left or right, into the alleys—was seen as infringing on Cobb's judgment. Skeptics could not see Cobb surrendering the critical matter of positioning, which he alone had handled through almost three thousand games. In no way would he be likely to play second fiddle. Said the local *Bulletin*: "Poor gentlemanly Connie Mack has caught a tiger and an angry old tiger by the tail."

That sensitive matter was not settled until after Cobb had been measured at the Fort Myers, Florida, training camp for the first uniform of his big-league experience that did not carry a Gothic *D* on the shirt. As long as he was working for Mack, he stated, he would obey all orders given him. Just let Mack flash the sign and he would respond. His own background as a manager did not apply. In a remarkable concession, he bowed to Mack—and he soon learned that the sixty-five-year-old ex-catcher knew the league's hitters, park air currents, and the sunshine factor so well that against power pull-hitters Cobb was able to catch balls that he otherwise might not have touched.

Mack, at about $300,000 in expense, was pennant loaded. He had burly young Jimmie Foxx—who would hit 266 home runs in seven coming seasons—at first base, Mickey Cochrane behind the plate, Al Simmons in center field, Max Bishop and Joe Boley as a keystone combination, and pitchers Lefty Grove, Rube Walberg, Howard Ehmke, Eddie Rommel, and old John Picus Quinn, who had been around since

1909 with his spitball and who would win 33 games in 1927–28 when past forty years of age. They were a blend of power and intelligence. On paper the club figured to challenge Old Fox Griffith's dangerous Washington team and the defending champion Yankees.

Cobb sucked in his forty-four-inch waist and began what was one of his most improbable campaigns. In April in Boston the Athletics were trailing the Red Sox 7–1, and Mack was cleaning off his bench in an effort to get some runs. That day he used eight infielders, five out-fielders, three catchers, and four pitchers—twenty men in all.

By the seventh inning, he was still behind 7–3. Cobb singled, stretched it to a double when the Red Sox outfield failed to hustle, and stole third. Bill Carrigan, managing Boston, relieved Whitey Wiltse and brought in Tony Welzer to pitch. Cobb studied the situation. In some ways, it resembled the setup in the World Series of 1909, when he stole home plate on pitcher Vic Willis of the Pirates. Welzer, like Willis, had a batting rally to put down, and he wasn't thinking specifically of Cobb.

However, in 1909, Detroit had a right-handed batter at the plate, his body screening the catcher's view of third base and somewhat blocking his movement. This time a left-hander was up. It gave catcher Slick Hartley of the Red Sox all the space between the plate and the incoming runner to make the play.

Despite the odds, Cobb opted to go. The A's needed something flashy to happen to ignite a rally. As Welzer coiled into his delivery, the Peach took off and Welzer all but ruptured himself reaiming to throw low to Hartley. Cobb's slide was a fall-away with just a toe there for the catcher to touch. Hartley handled the steal of home a split second too late.

That made it 7–4. The Athletics picked up two more runs in the next inning. At the beginning of the ninth, the game was tied 8–8. With Jimmy Dykes on base, Cobb doubled him home. The A's had the game won, 9–8, if they could stop the Bosox in their half of the ninth.

Alertness beats sheer speed—a Cobb maxim. With one out, Boston got a man, Baby Doll Jacobson, on first base. Phil Todt, a streaky line-drive hitter, came up. Right fielder Cobb crept in per-ilously close behind Jimmie Foxx at first base. Todt, as if working from a script, lined a low looper over Foxx's head. Catching it on the dead run, Cobb kept going to touch first base and double up Jacobson, ending the game. It was his last unassisted double play in a big-league game.

IT FELT mighty good. The warhorse seemed to be able to run and catch and hit with abiding usefulness. In two four-game series with the Browns and White Sox, he hit for a .722 average. After early games, the American League superstar race looked like this:

	At-Bats	Hits	Batting Average	Fielding Percentage
Cobb, Athletics	62	25	.403	1.000
Ruth, Yankees	48	15	.313	.962
Speaker, Senators	48	14	.292	1.000

Cobb held no hope of adding another batting title to the twelve he already owned—not after nearly three thousand games and more than eleven thousand at-bats, and not with the coming of Heilmann, Gehrig, Sisler, Simmons, Foxx, and Manush. His goal was to finish well up in the statistics, contribute substantially to the Athletics' offense, and teach hitting to the rookies and second-year men. And there might be a pennant for him, a long eighteen years after his last World Series appearance. He had about given up hope of that. "Tell you something never printed," he remarked to me one day in 1960. "If Mack hadn't put such a hell of a lot of fine players under contract, I'd have been gone in 1927. A pennant shot was the only reason I stayed on."

True statement or not—let us not forget the $85,000 he was collecting—Cobb avoided any serious injury and by May cartoonists no longer portrayed him as a tottering character with a white beard down to his belt and a scythe. "How can they?" asked Westbrook Pegler of United News Syndicate. "Why, that poor old guy! His vision is failing and the other day at Cleveland you could see he was slipping when all he got was five hits in five trips to bat, including a homer, triple, and double, which brought his lifetime average to only .372. The poor old guy!

"Down in Washington a few days later, there was another occasion to jerk loose some tears for poor old Tyrus Cobb. He went to bat 11 times in a doubleheader and, to save his life, he couldn't make more than seven hits and drive in five runs, the poor old guy! And what he did earlier in St. Louis makes it all the more evident that the ancient swatter is ready for the boneyard—merely five home runs and 25 bases toured in two games."

Only Mack and a few others knew what it cost him to suit up each day and face New Age fastballs. By June he was playing on a fast-dwindling reserve. He weighed 215 pounds at midseason. He cut back on drinking bourbon. As during past emergencies, after games he was driven straight to his home or hotel bed. He was served dinner in bed and answered his mail or read a book until lights out at 10:00 P.M. He remained in bed until late morning of the next day. After breakfast, a trainer would arrive to wrap medicated gauze on recent spike cuts, with tape applied over that. Only when it was time to leave for the park would he rise. Often he would turn on a portable phonograph and relax to thirty minutes of Fritz Kreisler's violin music.

Describing an Athletics-Yankee game of 1927, New York writer Joe Williams commented that Cobb's theories on batting remained as valid in the jackrabbit-ball era as they had been in deadball 1910: "History was made at Yankee Stadium yesterday. Ty Cobb went around the bases in the sixth inning. It marked the 2,087th time he had circled the bags, but more enlightening was the method he used—old-fashioned stuff scorned in the Era of Ruth. No home run figured in this.

"He laid down a bunt, perfectly, which caught third baseman Joe Dugan totally by surprise. Cobb slid into first, beating Dugan's hasty throw. How long since you've seen a first-base slide?

"Next, Sammy Hale hit a short rap to center field, and when anyone else would have stopped at second, Cobb pumped his aged legs and went for third. Earle Combs' throw to third had him out cold. Locating the ball with a quick glance over his shoulder, Cobb slid left, then contorted himself to the right. He had Dugan faked out from here to Hackensack. When the geyser of dust cleared, he was seen to have half-smothered the throw with his body, and while Dugan scrambled for the ball he was sitting on, Cobb was up and nonchalantly dusting himself off. Dugan? He wept."

It had been thought that the combination of his age and Mack's calming influence might make him less a Torquemada of the ballpark. Instead, in an earlier exhibition match, umpire Frank Wilson canceled a game and forfeited it to Boston after exchanging shoves and slurs with old enemy Cobb. When a replacement game was arranged, Cobb refused to play and sat in the stands. He was fined one hundred dollars and suspended for a week. But that brawl did not compare to the Emmett "Red" Ormsby affair. Hard-boiled ump Ormsby, who had no use for Cobb and advertised it, had once sounded off that even Cobb's mother must hate him. Ormsby was on sensitive ground; after Amanda Cobb's killing of his father, her son for a time provided for Amanda, but well before her 1936 death he had sent his mother to live with others and largely eliminated her from his life.

Ormsby committed the further indiscretion in a game at Philadelphia of calling a ball driven by Cobb out of Shibe and onto Twentieth Street not a home run—as everyone else saw it—but a foul ball. A homer would have beaten the Red Sox. Cobb shoved and struck Ormsby, setting off a bottle-hurling riot that needed a squad of twenty police to put down. Ormsby had a split lip and a fat eye. Ban Johnson, not yet permanently retired as American League president, suspended "constant offender" Cobb without a stated time limit—that is, indefinitely. Johnson did not get around to lifting the penalty formally before he left office, giving Cobb, at the ages of sixty and seventy, the pleasure of boasting, "I'm still under suspension—the longest blacklisting in big-league history." After a while everybody ignored the suspension.

Then Ruth and the Yankees came into Philadelphia. Babe strutted to the plate. He waved a handkerchief to the Athletics' fielders, a signal to move back. He swung three times with full power and struck out. Cobb came to bat. He took out a handkerchief and also waved the boys back. Then he bunted, beat it out, and stole second and third. Ruth and the Yankees cussed him each step of the way.

PERCEPTIVE FANS of the 1990s, if they are history-minded and informed enough, see surviving traces of Cobb on 1994 base paths. In the early century he had created or improved upon such stratagems as the drag bunt, squeeze play, safety squeeze, suicide or running squeeze, and his specialty, the now-you-don't-see-him-now-you-do delayed steal. The last-named stunt looked next to impossible on paper, but now and then he made it work. In 1927 Cleveland's second baseman and shortstop were playing well away from the base, with Cobb the runner at first. He did not break for second as the pitcher released the ball. Instead he waited until the ball had just reached the hitter and then he made his break. Since Cobb had not started with the pitch, the two infielders were sure that no play was on and relaxed mentally and physically. Cobb was now well on his way to second base. Cleveland catcher Luke Sewell raised his arm to throw, but nobody was covering the base. Sewell had to wait to throw until the shortstop arrived in a rush, and the timing of the toss was so difficult that the ball shot past him into center field. Center outfielder Bill Jacobson's hasty return throw was wild. Cobb scored a run on what had been accomplished by the world's slowest steal. He had never seen this play timed correctly before first using it himself in 1905. "So maybe I invented it," he speculated.

Surprisingly, he felt so frisky during the season's second half that he moved into demanding center field, and batted cleanup in the order. In a four-game White Sox series, he stole four bases. After a barren offensive spell—no hits in twenty attempts—he rebounded in September with seventeen base hits in twenty-five at-bats. But his best work could not stir the Athletics to catch the 1927 Yankees, the best-balanced group ever seen in any league, winners of 110 of 154 games to the runner-up A's 91–63 mark. The Yanks' Ruth, Gehrig, Bob Meusel, and Tony Lazzeri amassed 133 home runs, 200 doubles and triples, and batted in 544 runs. Ruth's fabulous 60 homers for the year had the baseball world agog. Gehrig's challenging presence was an important factor. At age twenty-four Columbia Lou had been 3 home runs ahead of Ruth on August 10, with 35. Ruth met his challenge with 25 homers to 9 by Gehrig the rest of the way. Gehrig finished with 47 homers. In his appraisal of the two, Cobb rated Gehrig as the more durable and slightly more valuable batter-fielder. Until a large belly and age slowed Ruth in the early 1930s, very few persons would have agreed with that analysis.

It pained Cobb to have missed what he assumed was his last chance to appear in a World Series. He had made no plans to continue into 1928. His weak collective average of .262 in seventeen games of the three World Series of his young "learning" days, 1907, 1908, and 1909, had been galling. He had assumed that somewhere along the line of his remaining career with Detroit the Tigers would capture another title or two, at which time he would—a favorite expression—"set the record aright." It had not happened. Additionally, he had missed out on the twenty-thousand-dollar bonus guaranteed by Mack if the A's won the pennant. Or so it seemed.

Mack had backed himself into a difficult spot regarding the twenty grand. In a quarter-century of formalized big-league baseball, no man had ever recorded 4,000 career base hits. Honus Wagner had piled up 3,430 during a twenty-one year span; Tris Speaker, still active, would finish at 3,515 over twenty-two years. Cobb, on July 19 of the summer of 1927, stood at 3,999. On that date he slapped a double off Sam Gibson of Detroit to reach a unique 4,000-hit milestone. He stood at that peak alone. "Unbelievable," said the *Detroit News*. Connie Mack was to live to the age of ninety-four and in 1956, the year in which he died, the 4,191 mark of Cobb still stood. It would continue to stand long after Mack's passing.

Mack believed that he was looking at the best player he had ever seen—as fast as Eddie Collins, as physical as Wagner had been, as a psychologist matched by none. He had just turned in a marvelous season. He remained one of the most feared of base runners. His 22 stolen bases were topped by only two American Leaguers, Bob Meusel and George Sisler of St. Louis. His .357 batting was a hair above Ruth's .356, and fifth in the American League, behind only Simmons, Heilmann, Gehrig, and Fatty Fothergill of Detroit. ("Sure, he's a prick, but God Almighty, how that old man can still hit and run," Ruth commented.)

One day that summer there had been a rundown play at home plate. Who raced all the way in from right field to cover it but Cobb?

Few in 1927 drove in or scored Cobb's 197 cumulative runs, which figure also led his team's statistics. Beyond that, in a new environment he got along fairly well with teammates. His characteristic choler was tempered while he was employed by the sedate and big-paying Connie Mack. "Here it is September," joked one of the A's, "and Old Hellfire hasn't slugged a pitcher with his bat or gone to jail yet." He had clashed with Mack only once. Mack ordered a pinch hitter for him and he yelled, "No one hits for Cobb!" Then he singled.

Pennant or no pennant, the proper thing to do, Mack felt, was to pay the twenty-thousand-dollar bonus. Wrote Mack in his autobiographical *My 66 Years in the Big Leagues*, "I gave him the extra amount. I never regretted doing this."

TO THE battered but still breathing and belligerent Base Ball Players Fraternity, formed eight years earlier largely for the purpose of breaking the reserve clause peonage system, the approximate $100,000 grossed by the Peach was a cause for rejoicing. In a book he published Cobb wrote, "Slavery was ending. From now on ownership had to pay for what it got. The day when contracts were dictated by front offices and not negotiated was going." He could easily afford to increase his cotton-growing acreage in northern Georgia and in Alabama, continuing to use itinerant blacks as crop harvesters. "I make as much off my cotton as two World Series shares," he wrote to friend Bob Clancy late that year. In that case he was making around twelve thousand dollars from this source per season.

But cheap labor had become a critical issue in his own profession. Together, he, Ruth, Speaker, and Rogers Hornsby were taking down close to $260,000 per season. The wide pay gap between a top drawing card and an average member of the labor force could not be maintained much longer. Paying off in comparative peanuts had to end, now that two-league attendance had jumped 52 percent over what it had been in the previous decade. In large part the American ballplayer was undergoing metamorphosis from rural hayslinger, uneducated factory worker, and town handyman to a Halls of Ivy product. As 1927 was ending, 107 men representing seventy-nine colleges and universities held one-third of the regular positions on major rosters. Better educated and advised campus-bred athletes might alter the odds around negotiating tables. So, anyway, went speculation.

Yale University had approached Cobb months earlier to coach Old Eli's baseball team, Cobb said in later years, and he left Philadelphia before the season ended to discuss the offer. Yale had some kids who could swing a bat. But how could he be interested, when Yale didn't pay its players a thin dime and a fine prospect could wind up by graduating on you? Slush funds for big-college sports were forming around the country in an era of building huge stadia, but the Ivy League, to which Yale belonged, was pledged to the concept of amateurism.

After Yale, Cobb detoured to Chicago to watch a longtime friend, Jack Dempsey, attempt to recapture his world heavyweight boxing title from Gene Tunney, who had beaten him in 1926. The fight on September 22 grossed a world record $2,658,660. The Peach, introduced from ringside, drew mixed boos and cheers. Afterward, he always remembered, the bloodied, defeated Dempsey laughed about it in his dressing room. "What's funny?" asked Cobb. "You could have licked him if you'd used your brains." He came away disgusted.

In October, he spent the best part of a month on the ten-thousand-foot Wyoming plateau, a repeat visit. His compulsion to kill big game remained as strong as ever. By now he had a trophy room filled with preserved heads of the largest North American specimens. He maintained a photo library of what he had shot to the end of his days. A Pacific blue marlin he caught weighed a near-record 1,266 pounds. Garland Buckeye, pitcher by trade, remarked that he had shot seventeen varieties of wildlife, including some rarities; Cobb reckoned that he had killed more than that, from bear to wolverine to Canadian moose and elk. He planned a safari to Africa soon. In Wyoming, he and Buckeye strayed upon private land. Cowboys across a canyon fired rifle shots into the air—a keep-out warning. Buckeye left immediately. Cobb, according to Buckeye, fired an equal number of shots upward. Then he left.

Mack and the press were kept guessing about any plans he had for another "final" tour in 1928. One day he would intimate that he might return, the next day he would be considering a round-the-world cruise. Meeting with him at Shibe Park in Philadelphia, Mack confessed that he was unable to come close to matching the record sum he had lavished on Cobb the year before. The recipient countered that he did not expect that much, but might settle for, say, two-thirds. The Great Holdout Artist was—at the end—a reasonable man. Mack agreed to that figure. Their deal provided that Cobb would make every effort to play a minimum of one hundred games.

"My arm and wind were still pretty good," he diagnosed himself years afterward to me. "My legs were bad—rheumatic knees, old muscle tears." He did not show at the Athletics' springtime camp in Florida, but, as in previous years, worked out only a few miles from his Augusta home on a field being used by the New York Giants. John "Muggsy" McGraw remained manager of the Giants. He and Cobb had not spoken to each other in years, nor did they speak now. "Fucking McGraw," remembered the Peach. "McGraw and his pals met King George V and the Earl of Chesterfield at a game in London. The next day the earl's ruby tie pin was missing. McGraw and other bums once were arrested in Arkansas for crooked bookmaking."

Frank O'Doul of San Francisco, the jolly Giants outfielder known as "The Man in the Green Suit," was a guest at Cobb's home that spring. O'Doul's view was, "Ty was a cold fish . . . had no sense of humor. About once a year he got off a funny line, like the one about the umpires being blinder than a potato with a thousand eyes. As for his returning to play for one more year, the reason for that move was obvious. Baseball was in his bones—he couldn't stand to watch other guys doing something he had damn near invented." O'Doul didn't need to cite a second motive. Like almost all veteran pros, Cobb was mercenary. O'Doul: "He couldn't leave five dollars on the table."

Charlie Cobb underwent further serious surgery before the season opened. Her husband stayed only briefly at her bedside. He was due to open the season in right field at Shibe Park, and the job came first. Long afterward, his eldest daughter, Shirley Cobb Beckwith, spoke of her father's priorities: "What else could we expect? He always put himself ahead of the family. What it came down to was that he needed the crowd's adulation."

THE ATHLETICS, in no way resembling the Philadelphia clubs that had finished in last place seven times straight after the 1915 season, got off to a promising start in 1928, challenging the Yankees for the lead. Their senior member was hot at bat in April and May, although not so hot at fielding. He had two hits and two runs scored against the Yankees, but fifty-six thousand New Yorkers booed him for losing a fly ball in the sun and for getting put out while trying to stretch a base hit. He had a double and single against Detroit, a home run against Cleveland, a bases-loaded triple in a defeat of Washington. But his fielding, like that of his forty-one-year-old teammate, Tris Speaker, acquired by Mack from Washington that year, was wanting. Tyrus and Tristram were—sad to see—slow afoot. No longer could Cobb race in one hundred feet for a shoestring catch; Speaker, who by his swiftness had played the shallowest of center fields, was now forced to set up much deeper. Fly balls dropped between them often enough that the *New York American* cartooned it as "The Philly Phollies."

Cobb drove himself unsparingly to reach a .330 batting mark by late May. At one juncture he was sidelined with a "bad boiler"—stomach trouble, vomiting. He played hurt as the Athletics streaked to twenty-one wins in twenty-five games and trailed the Yankees by only three and a half matches. Speaker was benched with ruptured blood vessels. His stomach calming, Cobb gave crowds estimated as the largest in the game's history—up to eighty-five thousand—something to remember him by. On June 15 at Cleveland, in the eighth inning, he demonstrated how much ability he had left. "A little Cobb telepathy," he called it.

It began when he hit a grounder to first base, a twisting ball that baseman Lou Fonseca bobbled. Meanwhile he raced to second base. On a following groundout by Max Bishop, he advanced to third. A roar went up—"There he goes!"—when he caught pitcher George Grant off guard. Before catcher Luke Sewell could handle Grant's snap throw and apply the tag, Cobb was in there safely.

It was the thirty-fifth steal of home base of his career—and the last. Since that June day no one has tied or beaten that number, or even come close. Casey Stengel considered the feat to be the most demanding, dangerous single act in any sport, and informed people that of all of Cobb's records surviving into the 1960s (and the 1970s, 1980s, and 1990s) this one was the hardest earned and at least the third-most important. Casey: "Ya got to remember that he went for the plate like a freight train. Ooooooo, he was scary!"

Setbacks came. On July 18, Sam Gibson of Detroit hit Cobb's right wrist with a pitch that laid him up. Days later he twisted a knee ligament; on July 27, Sarge Connally's pitch knocked him out of a White Sox game—a fastball to his breastbone. Accumulated injuries forced him to miss much of the fun of a late-season Athletic-Yankee fight for the pennant. "I'm not much to look at," he told *Baseball Magazine*. "I'm black and blue from my ankles to my hips."

On September 7, Mack's men tied the Yanks for first place and one day later took over the league lead by a half-game margin. By now Cobb had been replaced in right field by twenty-five-year-old Mule Haas, who was born in Detroit. Cobb overheard Haas joking about how he had watched the Georgia Peach playing in the Detroit outfield when he was a baby in arms. Not many years earlier Cobb might have punched Haas for that. Now, to keep the peace for Mack in a championship race, he let it pass. But a bigger incentive was that if the Mackmen won the pennant, Cobb would get another crack at the World Series.

According to Cobb's very good memory, he was headed down a passage to his dugout at Yankee Stadium during a September series with the Yanks when he encountered Ruth. On a hot day Babe was wearing his summertime home remedy, a wet cabbage leaf atop his hair and under his cap.

"Does that help?" asked Cobb.

"Cools me off, you bet," replied Ruth. "Stops heat prosecution [sic]."

There was an awkward pause. By habit the two men had been jockeying each other with foul language during this series.

"Too bad about Shocker," said Cobb, speaking of former Yankee pitcher Urban Shocker. A fine control pitcher who had won 37 games to 17 losses in his last two seasons, Shocker was from Detroit and had known Cobb there. Days earlier, on September 9, Shocker had died of possible heart failure.

"Yeah, Shock was a good guy," agreed Ruth.

"He got me on the slow stuff," said Cobb.

"Uh-huh," said Ruth.

They parted on that note, and never again spoke to each other during a game. There would be no opportunity for them to exchange incivilities again. Cobb's final appearance in the American League came before forty thousand on September 11, at "The House That Ruth Built" in the Bronx. Thirty-three-year-old Babe struck a home run so high and so far that you needed a telescope to follow it. His blow won the game, 5–3. Cobb, coming off the bench in the ninth inning as a pinch hitter for infielder Jimmy Dykes, lifted a blooper back of third base off Hank Johnson. Shortstop Mark Koenig caught it for the out. Cobb ran as fast as he could to first base on the play . . . and a career dating from the turn of the century ended. An era dating from ragtime, umpires with waxed mustaches, and cars you started with a crank passed into history.

He wore the uniform a bit longer. Connie Mack needed the money, so the schedule was interrupted for an exhibition game on September 13 against the Albany, New York, club of the Eastern League. Cobb played and had a pair of singles. Next day came an exhibition affair at Toronto. A small crowd of about twenty-five hundred Canadians witnesses his last appearances at bat in a big-league uniform. Once more he hit two singles. He was truly finished—3,033 games, 11,429 at-bats, 4,191 hits, and 2,244 runs on the official record. Lifetime batting average: .367, to this day the highest ever registered.

In his final season Cobb played in 95 games and batted .323. Only nine other American Leaguers averaged better than that. Only two regular members of the National League champion St. Louis Cardinals of

1928 did as well as forty-two-year-old Cobb. The Yankees clinched the pennant on September 28, two days before the season ended, then walloped the St. Louis Cardinals in four straight World Series games. By then Cobb was retired and looking for something with which to occupy himself for the rest of his days.

A NUMBER of seasoned baseball beat reporters doubted that anyone still able to hit well over .300 had reached the end of the line, and they were skeptical about his retirement plans almost to the end. At a press conference he called in Cleveland on September 17, Cobb reaffirmed his departure, while thanking those supporters who had stood behind him during his worst times. "Not that there were very damn many," he said later, privately. Someone remarked that the man who stood first in so many playing categories had been last in making friends.

Once more he expressed regret at having seen so little of his children while they were growing up—the eldest, Tyrus Cobb, Jr., was eighteen, preparing to enter Princeton University—and noted that this would be corrected. The boy had caddied some golf games for him.

His retirement notices were worthy of an abdicating high government official or crime lord. "Say farewell to the most admired, envied and hated of ballplayers"—New York Evening Post. "There never has been a player who brought such intelligence, audacity and ferocity to the game"—New York Evening World. "Pitchers walk Ruth to dispose of trouble . . . if they dare give Cobb a base on balls, their troubles are just beginning . . . He has been every bit as dangerous on offense as Ruth"—Literary Digest. "Hell in spikes"—Police Gazette.

Ty Cobb set marks that, approaching the year 2000, no major-leaguer has equaled. "He put them so high that a cannon couldn't shoot them down," said Casey Stengel. As of 1994, more than sixty-five years had passed since Cobb's retirement. No ballplayer in Cobb's time, and none to this day, could come close to matching his .367 lifetime batting average, the most eminent single statistic in sports. Ted Williams, probably the best of modern hitters, finished at .344, 23 percentage points behind the .367 (he might have reached .360 but for two war-service interruptions).

Joe DiMaggio says simply, "Ty was too much for everybody." DiMaggio stands in awe of the doctored baseballs faced by Cobb—illegal today—and the low-visibility parks of his day, compared to the ideal lighting conditions after World War II. Despite that major handicap, Cobb ranks first of all-time with 2,244 runs scored, well ahead of Ruth. Cobb's feat of leading his league in batting average twelve times is no less than staggering. Ruth did it once, DiMaggio twice, Williams six times, Hornsby seven and Wagner eight times. In the category of hitting .300 or more per season, the Georgian still stands far in front of everyone, with twenty-three seasons.

He accumulated 5,863 total bases and rang up 3,052 singles, both still existing records. His 5 home runs in two consecutive games tie him with others. His career 892 stolen bases stood for decades. Young baseball-card collectors can tell you which hero stole home base the most times—"Ty Cobb, thirty-five!" In his career he had set 123 records.

ALL ALONG Cobb had professed that relief from pressure and finding time for a normal family life were his goals. That autumn his children hoped to enjoy their father's company, perhaps to travel with him from their home on William Street in Augusta to places they had never seen. Sticking to his promise, Cobb sailed for Japan in October aboard the SS *President Jefferson* with his wife and three young Cobbs—Herschel, Beverly, and James Howell. The trouble was that almost everywhere they traveled, Cobb had been booked by promoters to hold baseball clinics for the Nipponese. The hosts were eager to learn the game. And time-consuming clinics made the tours less a matter of shared fun and sightseeing than a method for selling Father's name. He was paid one thousand dollars each for staging fifteen instructional sessions from Tokyo to Nagoya and Kobe. In Kobe, someone stole his uniform from his hotel room, added proof of his popularity in the Orient.

Upon the family's return to Georgia, he was not to be seen at home for a time while his prize bird dogs were competing in field trials in two states. And after that the jaunting paterfamilias scheduled a European hunting tour extending from Scotland to Germany to Spain. Cobb's children would not be coming along.

PAYBACK TIME

B ack home in April of 1929, with time on his hands, Cobb took off in another direction—Europe and the British Isles. He had not been abroad since he was Captain Cobb of the Gas and Flame Division of Chemical Warfare in World War I. He was in good spirits when he and Charlie sailed aboard the SS *Roosevelt* for London.

Charlie was eager to tour the palaces and cathedrals of the Continent. Cobb wanted to test himself against the fast-flying grouse of Scotland and to hunt by foot the fierce boars of Germany. It turned into a lengthy tour of half a dozen countries and so much scenery that he complained to the Ty Cobb Fan Society of Augusta-Atlanta upon their return that he had been dragged from the halls of Versailles, King Ludwig's castles, the Colosseum and Vatican to the canals of Venice to the Tower of London and the Swiss Alps. They even made a side trip to the Pyramids in Egypt.

Between inspecting holy *reliquiae* and the art of the Louvre, he hunted grouse at Keith, Scotland, by invitation of Sir Isaac Sharpe, one of the world's top trainers of retrieving dogs. In *My Life in Baseball*, he wrote, "Keith was the big league of game birds, a pilgrimage place for the finest of shotgun artists. The challenge of trying my luck there in

80,000 acres of moor and heather had been gnawing at me since I was a young man." The Scots wondered if the American could hit one of their rocketing grouse. He knocked down two on his first shot, and had a full bag for the day. Down in north Georgia, where he had hunted quail since he was knee high to a hedgehog, they had fast birds, too. In Germany he had one shot at a boar—and missed.

BEFORE GOING abroad, and afterward, he put out feelers to American and National league teams, expressing his interest in acquiring a majority stockholder position and top executive post with one of them. He had come to feel that he could not just walk away from something that had been his life since 1905. At midlife, he needed to practice what he knew best. His name still could sell tickets. His ability to handle money in large amounts was well established. But the dual brotherhood was unresponsive. Both leagues could use a ready-made multimillionaire in their ranks—if he abided by the rules. But applicant Cobb had made a shambles of competition in its normal meaning; he had played as if in some kind of primal heat, and as a manager had not led his players so much as intimidated them. No offers were forthcoming above the AA level.

Through 1929 he persisted in trying to buy his way back into the Big Show. A possible opportunity developed at Redlands Park, Cincinnati. Ticket sales there were down, leadership was weak. The city that had introduced professional baseball to America in 1869 had not won a pennant since 1919. Longtime club president Gary Hermann had retired and the new boss, Sid Weil, a used-automobile dealer, had a limited knowledge of team promotion. Weil enjoyed suiting up with his players and chasing fly balls with them.

However, according to Cobb's files, opened by him to this researcher in the early 1960s, their negotiations never became serious. Cobb offered $325,000 for the franchise, including seven of the players currently under contract, the ballpark and furnishings, clubhouse equipment, ticket boxes, flags, and ground equipment. Weil was shocked. His price was $500,000 and he wasn't budging. Weil asked about the rest of his players—why was it that Cobb wanted only seven of twenty-eight?

"Because the others aren't major-leaguers," Cobb said he told him. "Some are stiffs."

"Stiffs!" exclaimed Weil. "They are veterans."

"Veterans of the Spanish-American War," said Cobb coldly. The deal fell through when he refused to budge above the $325,000 or buy any "stiff."

Detroit, one of the American League's steadiest money-makers before and after Cobb's years there, was another possibility. Frank Navin, now co-owner of the Tigers in partnership with auto-chassis maker Walter O. Briggs, would lose much of his fortune in the 1929 Wall Street crash, and entertained bids for the club. However, co-owner Briggs remained angered by the Cobb-Speaker-Leonard fix scandal of a few years earlier. He suspected that Cobb had been guilty of conniving in the fix of a ball game while in Detroit uniform. A prominent citizen and churchman, Briggs privately spoke of Cobb as "Houdini" for working his way out of expulsion from the game. Taking that attitude, Briggs refused an offer of $2 million for the Tigers from a syndicate headed by Cobb and Atlanta businessmen, and he stepped in to block Navin from making a deal. Navin declined in health, dying of a heart attack in 1935.

Cobb continued his futile search for a baseball home. Repeated refusals by teams of any takeover by "the Georgia crowd" led by Cobb indicated to the public that he was *persona non grata* in both leagues in the role of owner, co-owner, or front-office executive. The assumption was entirely correct. Press critics proclaimed this the price of making enemies from New York at the top to Boston at the bottom of the leagues. How many bottles and seats had been thrown at a raving Cobb, or in his defense, during park riots? He would almost certainly be as difficult to live with as a policymaking owner as he had been as an outlaw with the bat and his filed spikes.

Another Cobb-led bid to buy a franchise, an offer for the San Francisco Seals of the Pacific Coast League, was rejected in 1930. As it worked out, not only that turndown, but equally those before it, proved a disguised blessing. In the ruinous national depression of the 1930s, with its unemployment, breadlines, and bank failures, organized baseball at every level took a beating. Total major-league attendance in the 1920s had been 92,652,885; in the 1930s depression decade it slumped to 81,013,329. Even the Yankees were badly down, from a 10.5 million draw in the 1920s to 9.1 million in the hard times. Clubs cut ticket prices, but with jobless men out begging for food, how many could afford even a ticket costing seventy-five cents? It would have been the worst of timing for Cobb to have invested a few million in sport.

Along with many speculators playing a bull market during the Roaring Twenties, Cobb had more than doubled his wealth in the period from 1920 to 1930. When the market slumped, aside from American Can, which fell from 182 to 86 in the crash, Cobb's major holdings stood up well. "He was smart and damned lucky," said Elmer Griffin, a Wall Street broker. "He continued buying Coca-Cola, General Motors, and Anaconda Copper, and the Depression didn't hurt him heavily in the long run." In a crash that ruined more Americans than all previous money collapses combined, Cobb emerged in good shape.

Yet not even his kind of available cash and bank credit could buy him a seat on the inner councils of baseball. "There were crooked lawyers and Tammany Hall ginks and bootleg whiskey smugglers who held important jobs in the game, but Cobb couldn't get in," he said later about himself in those years. "Even using my own money and not a bank's, I couldn't buy in."

VISITING CALIFORNIA in the spring of 1930 to scout talent for Connie Mack and to play golf, Cobb discovered the quiet little rich man's town of Atherton, twenty-three miles south of San Francisco. He had expected never to live anywhere but Georgia. Yet it had been so blazing hot there in the past summer that, in those pre-air-conditioning times, the Cobbs had kept electric fans running for two straight months, and had still sweltered. At Atherton, with cool weather year-round, he found an elegant Spanish Mission–period home priced at $110,000 in an idyllic setting—three oak-shaded acres, with a swimming pool and guest quarters. There were fifteen rooms in the main house, and space for stables to house Cobb's polo ponies. Lately, he had resumed playing polo after a long lapse. He was a first-rate horseman and scored well, but was regarded as undisciplined and too rough. Every few chukkers he would cause a collision and a rider or two would be spilled. Cobb never seemed to get hurt, only his opponents. The San Francisco Chronicle noted, "Tommy Hitchcock, the famous 10-goal poloist, calls Ty Cobb a wild man and menace . . . He also regrets to say that baseball's toughest guy has been known to whip the hide off his ponies."

COBB'S FIVE children were growing up in a hurry, and continued to see little of their widely invested father. Cobb admitted that he was gone from home most of the time. Ty Cobb, Jr., at eighteen, stood almost as tall as his father's six foot one. The redheaded eldest son had been raised by his mother and private-school teachers. "I blame her for the way the kid behaved," Cobb flared in conversation with his close friend, Elmer Griffin. The girl-chasing Ty junior had been in one scrape after another while enrolled at Richmond Academy in Augusta, then at Princeton University. He drew traffic tickets for speeding, dated fast girls, and missed classes. Showing no baseball ability, Ty junior wound up as a member of the Princeton varsity tennis team. The senior Cobb, thinking tennis to be a pitty-pat sport for the white-flannels set, winced. "Here's a boy who has grown up privileged to visit big-league clubhouses and training camps," he told Griffin. "But he would rather watch Bill Tilden than see his father win games." (Tilden, U.S. tennis king in the 1920s, was a known homosexual.) Paternal bitterness ran deep.

In the late spring of 1929, receiving word that Ty junior had flunked out of Princeton, Cobb had caught a train to the New Jersey campus and called at his son's lodging house. He carried a black satchel. He removed from the satchel a blacksnake whip "and then I went to work on that boy pretty hard," he told this writer. "I put him on the floor and kept it up . . . tears and some blood were shed . . . but Tyrus never again . . . never . . . failed in his grades."

Cobb never thought of the act as repulsive. When he mentioned the horsewhipping to the few people of his inner circle he did so with an air of satisfaction. He said, "You can look at it two ways. Teaching Ty a lesson hurt both of us. On the other hand, it did some good . . . he grew up in a hell of a hurry. In the end he made something of himself."

That was true—for a while. Since Princeton no longer wanted him as an undergraduate, Ty junior entered Yale University. He improved academically and became captain of Yale's tennis team, a star singles player. However, in 1930 he was arrested for drunkenness on two occasions and failed to graduate with a degree. Cobb provided lawyers to handle the police charges, then informed the twenty-year-old that there would be no further communication between them. Cobb senior was finished with Cobb junior. This was not just a threat. An unbending father meant it, to the extent that they remained alienated until near Junior's death at the age of forty-two, in 1952, of a malignant brain tumor. It was all very sad, Griffin reported. "Ty paid for the young man's sickness and death," said Griffin. "But that was all."

On April 10, 1931, his plan to move his family across the continent to the wine-and-roses country of Atherton was blocked when Charlie Cobb filed a divorce suit in Augusta. It appeared that a troubled marriage had ended. She deposed that her husband had treated her cruelly, had done so repeatedly, and she could take no more.

Under Georgia law, Charlie would become a very wealthy woman of thirty-nine if a divorce was granted. Cobb, who was playing golf on the California circuit when her charges were announced, expressed shock at his wife's action and predicted that there would be no divorce once he returned to Georgia and they reconciled their problem. Asked if their differences over how Ty junior had been raised was a factor, Cobb had no comment.

He must have been persuasive, for before the month was out, Charlie withdrew her suit. Comment was withheld by both sides. The move to California was on again, and after delays, by May of 1932, the Cobbs were in residence at their fine new establishment. He named it "Cobb's Hall."

While Charlie and the young children were attempting to adjust to new neighbors and the California way of life, Cobb was off and running again to distant parts. He added to his big-game hunting territory the Alaskan island of Kodiak, where he shot a bear, and the Snake River country of Idaho, for salmon fishing. Cobb was back on the golf circuit that summer.

If ever a sport had been created for which he was wholly unsuited, it was golf. He had fooled around with the game earlier. Now, in the 1930s, he entered into it seriously. Hitting a small ball into a small hole is so frustrating that it drives normally calm men into blowing their fuses. As might be expected, the fiery Georgian, in pursuit of par or better, was in a class by himself for temper explosions.

What with his perfected bat swing and ability to concentrate, he should have been a natural at golf and won senior tournaments. However, consistently and inexplicably he lost to ordinary 80-shooters. He played in the mid-80s and low 90s. Although he consulted the best teachers—Bobby Jones, the number-one amateur in the world, was one—and used the most expensive handmade clubs, he was beaten at

Pebble Beach, California, in 1930, 8 and 7, by the women's champion, Babe Didrikson. With a roar, Cobb threw his driver to an adjoining fairway, almost beaning people playing there.

Within a few years' time he had become unwanted at some of the nation's most prestigious country clubs. It was not more Cobb apocrypha but fact that he was forced to resign from three clubs for offensive behavior. As of the late 1930s, he had been a member of eight clubs, from Georgia's Augusta National Golf Club, home of the Masters, to San Francisco's Olympic Club.

He *needed* to win at a surrogate game, but could not. His most humiliating moment came in 1939 at the Olympic Club, when in the club championship event he was paired with a twelve-year-old boy, Bob Rosburg, a local prodigy. "I wiped him out, beat him badly," said Rosburg in 1992, when, as a noted professional, he was asked to comment. "Cobb didn't say a word at the horselaughs he drew. He cleaned out his locker and never returned to Olympic."

Ballyhooed matches with Babe Ruth were another matter. In June 1941, Fred Corcoran, the Professional Golfers' Association manager, challenged Cobb to meet Babe over fifty-four holes in a charity series that would draw galleries of thousands. Cobb at first declined. He saw it as a sucker trap. Ruth was a six to eight handicap and hit balls three hundred yards when serious and sober. Corcoran kept the pressure on. Ty received a telegram from his former ballpark rival: "IF YOU WANT TO COME HERE AND GET YOUR BRAINS KNOCKED OUT, COME AHEAD. SIGNED, RUTH." Rather than appear to be ducking the issue, he agreed.

Newspaper buildup centered on the forty-six-year-old Bambino's power versus the fifty-four-year-old Peach's "craftiness." Cobb found himself a popular underdog. "I don't have much of a chance," he moaned to the press in a persuasive way. "I just had a lucky eighty-six back home at Lakeside."

Ruth was all confidence—until he lost the first match at Boston's Commonwealth Country Club, 3 and 2. That night Cobb revealed, "Not once did I jockey him, as he expected. Just mentioned that the Fat Man was getting fatter and looked off-balance. Like an egg standing on toothpicks."

Ruth won the second match in a one-hole playoff after both shot 43-42-85 at Fresh Meadows in New York. The rubber match was held at Detroit's Grosse Ile, a mass of traps. Cobb the schemer now did three things: he hired Grosse Ile's assistant pro as his caddie, he brought in the veteran international champion Walter Hagen as his coach and, en route to the course by boat, he saw to it that the Bambino had plenty of Scotch to drink.

At tee time, Ruth, with a jeweled bobby pin holding back his hair, was feeling just fine. At the turn, underdog Cobb was five strokes ahead. He distracted his opponent with such questions as, "Do you think Japan wants war with us?" After earlier refusing a wager, Cobb suggested a bet "for any amount—fifty thousand, you name it." The size of the bet—Babe was a big gambler, but not that big—and the smoke from Cobb's cigar on the tees bothered Ruth. He lost the deciding match, 3 and 2. Cobb walked off to gallery cheers.

Until his death, the trophy he won shared close to equal space on Cobb's mantle with his Baseball Hall of Fame plaque. He might not have mastered golf, but there was consolation in owning the "Ruth Cup."

COBB'S SCHEDULE appeared overfilled, but it was artificially contrived. Beyond golf, polo, shooting game, and reading extensively on world history, he had not enough action to occupy him, and in times of idleness he was bored with life. He was far from ready for the pipe and slippers, although he had a collection of some two hundred briar pipes and smoked them. Time grew so heavy on his hands that he wadded up newspaper and tossed it from a distance into a wastebasket—by the hour.

Players he had competed with and against did not visit him at Atherton in any number. Fred Haney, who had played for the Tigers, told of leaving a Detroit game with Cobb one evening in the mid-1940s and encountering players waiting for taxis. The boys were play-wrestling and laughing. "I wish I could have done that," said Cobb wistfully. "Had some pals on the team and kept them. But I didn't."

His most influential fans, the baseball reporters, in general opposed what amounted to a blackballing by a majority of owners. The Baseball Writers Association of America called attention to this in 1935–36 when they devised a formula to nominate, vote upon, and elect to a Hall of Fame the greatest players that the game had known since its modern-era inception in 1901. Candidates selected by the BWAA to the Hall at Cooperstown, New York, had to be named on 75 percent of the ballots. The maximum number of votes available was 226. Ty Cobb received 222, or close to 100 percent. Babe Ruth and Honus Wagner were tied for second place, each with 215 votes. Pitchers Christy Mathewson and Walter Johnson filled out the First Five, with 205 votes for Matty, 189 for Johnson. The balloting probably was as accurate and honest as any such rating could be.

That sweeping victory, coming at a time of displacement and frustration, delighted the Peach more than any event of his professional life except for his $100,000 season at Philadelphia in 1927 and his lifetime .367 batting average. He seemed to foresee that fifty or more years from now he would remain recognized as the best ever to wear spikes, because the Hall of Fame said so.

A little more than three years after the voting, in June of 1939, the red-brick National Baseball Museum and Hall of Fame Building was dedicated at Cooperstown, a rustic town set among the lakes and green mountains of central New York State. Ten thousand fans packed the place. At first Cobb did not appear. The centerpiece of the show was missing. Group photographs shot before he appeared showed one empty space. He blamed his late arrival on crowded roads leading to Cooperstown and a flat tire. In 1956, at a dinner honoring him at the San Francisco Press Club, Cobb declared that he had been late at Cooperstown to avoid having his photograph taken with Kenesaw Landis. Landis was on his "shit list," he said, for taking so long to clear him in the Cobb-Speaker-Leonard case of years earlier. "Landis has been dead for a dozen years and he's still a rotten bastard," Tyrus assured the Press Clubbers. "He made me look guilty."

COBB'S MARRIAGE bounced up and down. After Charlie withdrew her divorce suit of 1931 in Georgia and set up housekeeping in Atherton, she filed again within two years. That action, too, was dropped. Then within months she was back in court with a third divorce request. Upon each occasion Charlie had gone through expensive preliminary procedures aimed at a permanent division of their assets. Each time she was either talked out of it or changed her mind.

No one in Atherton or nearby Palo Alto evidently knew what went on behind the doors at Cobb's Hall. Gossip supposedly obtained from household staff had it that Cobb blew up about small things, drank a quart of milk—mixed with a quart of scotch—almost every day, and flew into a rage each time his wife took him to court. Charlie was believed to be asking, under California law, for a substantial part of his millions. "Nobody ever threw so many changes-of-pace at Ty," cracked Lefty O'Doul at the Geary Street pub he ran in San Francisco.

By the late 1940s, Charlie meant what she said, and in 1947, on the fourth time around, actually divorced Cobb. It was town talk that he had hit her across the back with the handle end of a baseball bat—not a crippling blow, but painful and terrifying.

Atherton neighbors filed other reports of violence. According to the local San Mateo County Sheriff's office, on one occasion Cobb played host at Cobb's Hall to his neighbors. Throughout the evening he drank heavily and during dinner used foul language. One of the ladies objected. He called her an "old whore." She broke into tears. Her husband, a former football player and a husky fellow, invited Cobb outside. The host attacked with fists, at which the guest seized a chair, shattered it over Cobb's bald head, and opened a gash. Blood poured down his face. While Cobb lay on the floor, unconscious, the husband called the sheriff.

"I think I just killed a man here," he reported by phone to a deputy.

"What's his name?" asked the deputy.

"Ty Cobb. He lives at this address."

The officer was not surprised. "Yes, we know all about that son of a bitch. It's a wonder somebody hasn't killed him a long time ago."

No charges were pressed by anyone in the case.

Sedate Atherton was scandalized by its celebrity resident on other occasions. Someone remarked at a pool party that Cobb hadn't bothered to mow the lawn around his pool. Cobb shoved him into the water. The Domino Club, a night spot, asked him not to return after he punched a former Pacific Coast League player over a disagreement. The player sued and collected $2,500.

Charlotte "Charlie" Cobb's delayed divorce of 1947 was messy and complicated. At the age of fifty-five she accused her husband, sixty, of treating her with "extreme cruelty" from their marriage day onward, a thirty-nine year period. She asked for $7 million in settlement, or about one-half of what she claimed was his overall wealth in bank deposits, stock and bond shares, rents, autos, jewelry, real estate, and other holdings. In addition Charlie wanted five thousand dollars per month in alimony and sixty thousand dollars in legal fees. Cobb and his lawyers avoided revealing in court the facts behind her cruelty charges.

The case was dropped in California and switched to Nevada with its advantageous both-party divorce and tax laws. Fortunately, Cobb had bought a fishing lodge at Lake Tahoe, near the hamlet of Glenbrook, Nevada, and he qualified as a Nevada resident. "He went on mainly living in Atherton and for a long time got away with claiming Glenbrook as home," explained Elmer Griffin. The amount awarded Charlie was never disclosed. Insurance-bonds expert Griffin's estimate was $6 million outright to Charlie, plus thirty-five hundred dollars monthly in alimony.

Griffin himself doubted that his client was entirely sane. Yet he regarded him as extremely shrewd in financial matters. Despite poor eyesight from age sixty on, Cobb could still scan the small type of the *Wall Street Journal* by using special high-magnification glasses. His "feel" for how a stock or bond issue would fare in the future was extraordinary, and sometimes phenomenal. A Wells Fargo bank official revealed that Cobb made a $385,000 profit in one six-week period of trading. "I know good stuff when I see it," said Cobb. "Also sucker investments."

The elderly Cobb became expert at tax loopholes, while also aiding hard-up ballplayers. Each month he mailed support checks to some three dozen men who had once faced his spikes and not backed away. Johnny————had been admired in the American League for planting a ball in Cobb's face in a sliding situation, loosening some of his teeth. Johnny was one of "my boys" who received support checks. Their names were kept confidential. Another beneficiary was Mickey "Black Mike" Cochrane, a future Hall of Fame catcher. Near-fatally beaned by a pitch in 1937, Cochrane afterward could not function. The Cobb fund helped support him for the rest of his life.

In zany contrast to this thoughtful generosity, the Georgian had telephone service cut off at his Lake Tahoe lodge, suspecting that the lines were tapped by Internal Revenue spies or divorce lawyers. When leaving his Atherton property for the day, he hung bedsheets on the backyard line with an attached note: "JOE—WILL BE BACK IN 15 MIN-UTES." His presumption was that thieves were thereby deterred from breaking in.

Socially, he could be brutal. At a Hall of Fame banquet, Cobb brought as his guest a well-known writer, John D. McCallum. Cobb was seated at the head table; McCallum was seated with the working press. Suddenly rising, Cobb snapped at McCallum, "When you go somewhere with me, you sit where I sit!" Then he dumped the writer's roast beef dinner into his lap. Observers were speechless.

The act reminded sports editor Harry Grayson of the day at the Detroit Athletic Club when he and Grantland Rice hosted Cobb and one-time Cleveland catcher Jay "Nig" Clarke at dinner. Clarke, laughing, mentioned how he had tricked umpires by "fast-swiping" at a runner coming in, missing him, but then tossing his mitt into the air and trotting away, thereby convincing umpires that he had made the inning's third out. That included some outs on Cobb of twenty-five or so years earlier. Grayson and Rice found it funny. Cobb arose from his chair, his face darkening. Fuming, he called Clarke a "dirty SOB" and struck him. "You cost me runs!" he yelled. Clarke escaped, while Grayson and Rice restrained a man gone out of his head.

The ranks of ballplayers he had competed against were narrowing. Every few months he was made aware of the threat of advancing age. In the 1950s came the deaths of Tris Speaker, Eddie Collins, Honus Wagner, Harry Heilmann, Connie Mack, and Grover Cleveland Alexander; in the 1940s it had been Babe Ruth, Joe Tinker, Walter Johnson, Mordecai "Three-Finger" Brown, and Lou Gehrig. He sent flowers, but rarely attended a funeral. He was afraid, thought Lefty O'Doul, that he might be seen weeping in public.

Within the Cobb family, son Herschel died in 1951 at age thirty-four of a sudden heart attack. He had been a good schoolboy athlete, to his father's pleasure. Less than two years later, Tyrus Junior had died at forty-two. After clashes with his father over his poor academic showing, he had obtained an M.D. in obstetrics from the Medical College of South Carolina. Ty junior had been in practice for only a few years when an inoperable brain tumor killed him.

Partially because of the high cost of divorcing Charlie in 1947, Cobb had intended never to marry again. Two years later, however, he took as his bride an attractive divorcée of Buffalo, New York, named Frances Fairburn. "I'm just a lonely old man, sitting around a big, empty house," he had been telling reporters. "And my wife is a real sportswoman. We may go hunting in Africa."

Instead of going on safari, he went to divorce court again, once

more cha
was told
when h
she lo
touch
fied
to h
be
t

~treme cruelty. As associate of Cobb reportedly
Cobb that she felt physically threatened
·le. a steady occurrence. Often
'056 had comic-opera
stalled electri-
seeking access
s guard dogs had
story, had forgot-
one night and took

er Lane in Atherton,
tning fastballs for the
astards found anything

rds with me even when I

ment, 1951, two connected
ation. He enjoyed the public-
th events enabled Cobb to hit
that had denied him a league
y, the House of Representatives
Power resumed hearings held in
on baseball's possible violations of
ears after a raw left-handed rookie
ed in the big league with a pancake
glove and ᵤ ᴶ. Congress continued to argue over
whether or not the ᵣᵤ ᵤe of the standard baseball contract violated the individual player's right to bargain freely for his services.

Cobb's opinion hadn't changed: "Hell, yes!" The reserve bound a player to one team, season after season, in perpetuity. The restrictive practice could be helpful to a career, but only—argued Cobb—if it included the compromise that if a player had spent five seasons with one team and wished to move elsewhere, he could apply for and receive free agency. Even in 1951 this was decades ahead of baseball's mood. What he suggested would come true as part of the overall reformation of the 1970s, when free agency did arrive and created a class of entertainment millionaires.

His congressional testimony led to a 1952 offer from *Life* magazine. *Life* offered him $25,000 to write under his byline two articles exposing the alleged sorry state into which baseball had fallen. For a long time, Cobb had been saying that the game's quality since the late 1920s and onset of home-run mania had been poor. Such team owners as August Busch in St. Louis and Phil Wrigley in Chicago urged that he not lend his name to such an accusation. Coming from him and with *Life*'s huge circulation, it could be bad for business. Cobb signed with *Life*.

His long essay—titled "They Don't Play Baseball Any More"—was powerful stuff. In his opinion:

- The game had declined so far that "only two players today can be mentioned in the same breath with the old-time greats." These two were not Ted Williams or Joe DiMaggio. They were Phil Rizzuto, Yankee shortstop, and Stan Musial, then St. Louis Cardinal's versatile outfielder. Rizzuto and Musial were the last of the smart, scientific players. Men who could beat you many ways were vanishing.
- The game had degenerated into a home-run slugging match: "it's as if two golfers decide to forget all about the course, with its many traps, dog-legs, roughs and greens—and instead just went out to see who could hit the ball the farthest at a driving range."
- If a base runner of Cobb's day could return, he would "run wild against today's inept pitchers and catchers."
- "There are too many joke teams . . . who fall behind 12–2 around the fourth inning." They rob the paying public.
- Players were vastly overpaid, robbed of their incentive, and deprived of spirit before their time.

To knock Ted "Splendid Splinter" Williams, who would retire with a lifetime .344 batting average, and DiMaggio, three-time most valuable player of the American League, was heresy. Cobb didn't care. "It has been a crime the way Williams let managers neutralize his power with odd defensive shifts," he wrote. DiMaggio was an "outstanding example" of how stars stupidly neglected to keep in shape and play to their full ability. His commentary ended with the suggestion: "I think we should throw them all [modern big-leaguers] a bag of peanuts."

Life promoted the diatribe heavily. Most reviewers found Cobb guilty of comparing the streamlined baseball of the moment with a deadball, low-scoring era long phased out. Everything had changed with the arrival of booming bats, relief pitching, development of night play, the impact of television, and the end of the racial barrier. And yet some critics agreed with Cobb that pro football and golf for the masses were catching up with baseball as a draw. Behind all this, they held, was the failure of the 1950s big leagues to produce players in a class with Tyrus Raymond Cobb.

BETWEEN THAT, and threatening to write a book picking up where the *Life* article stopped, Cobb occupied himself with taking bows at old-timer games held coast to coast—a sure box-office feature—attending the Olympic Games at Rome, building a third retirement home at Chenoocetah Mountain, Georgia, near his boyhood home at Royston, and founding the Cobb Educational Fund for young scholars who needed help to complete their college-level education. The CEF kept dozens of boys and girls in the classroom to graduation. Qualifications were that they be needy, unusually bright, and natives of the state of Georgia. Once accepted by the CEF, students had a full ride. But to be chosen was difficult. The founder was asked what sort of young person he wanted to endow. "We want stars—stars in medicine, in law, teaching, in engineering, in life," Cobb told the *Saturday Evening Post*. "We want the Lincolnesque characters from the mountains and the fields." He earmarked $1 million for his foundation. He also donated $100,000 and helped establish the Cobb Memorial Hospital in Royston, Georgia.

"The only time I saw Ty lose control of himself," said George Maines, a longtime friend, "was when some of the kids he had put through school came around to thank him. They broke into tears and Cobb cried along with them." Maines felt that the students Cobb supported filled a void in his life after the death of his two sons.

He was seventy-three in 1960, and heavily addicted to twelve-year-old malt whiskey, when he flew east to be honored at a banquet by the New York Baseball Writers Association as "sportsman of the ages." Through his career he had been General Douglas MacArthur's favorite ballplayer. MacArthur, indeed, gushed about Cobb. That January he invited Cobb to visit him at his retirement home in the Waldorf Towers of New York City. The visit turned into a dull occasion for Cobb. He left the apartment not long after he arrived, claiming that he felt ill.

"Stay a little longer, Ty," urged MacArthur.

"No, I'm not feeling well," said Cobb shortly.

"We probably won't see each other again, Ty," said the aged MacArthur, emotionally.

I had driven Cobb to the famed old soldier's residence, and I watched as MacArthur put his arms around Cobb in a parting embrace. Cobb did not like to be touched. He shrugged free and said, "So long, Doug." Going down in the hotel elevator, Cobb remarked of his number-one fan, "Sentimental old bastard, isn't he?"

Claiming poor health to MacArthur was not an evasion. A year before their meeting, while hunting quail on the flats outside Reno, Nevada, Cobb was hit by sharp pains in his lower back and legs. He collapsed and wound up in the Scripps Clinic near San Diego, California. After his first thorough checkup in several years, the verdict was that he was suffering from an enlarged prostate gland, failing kidneys, dangerously high blood pressure, and diabetes. He never saw a hospital that he fully trusted. He transferred to Emory University Hospital in Atlanta, where he knew the staff and where the finding differed. His prostate was not just enlarged, but partially encircled by a large, mushy growth. The substance was cancerous and spreading to nearby areas.

Aside from a routine directive that he stop drinking hard liquor and smoking, the first thing needed was a prostatectomy to remove the cancer. Emory surgeons were fairly sure that he was strong enough at seventy-three to withstand such an operation. How well he could handle the high-powered radiation treatments to follow, however, was impossible to predict.

EPILOGUE

I n a lengthy operation on December 10, 1959, Cobb's diseased
prostate gland had been removed. Although he withstood the
surgery well, Dr. Hugh Wood of Emory Hospital was concerned
with his uneven heartbeat and a degenerative kidney problem.
"Mr. Ty is worn out—he has been dying for two or three years,"
Wood told Cobb's cousin, Harrison Gailey. "If had come in for regular
checkups, we would have found the cancer. Now it's in the runaway
stage."

Doctor Wood broke the news that was tantamount to a death sentence to Cobb. "He had no comment," reported the surgeon. "He just
insisted that cobalt treatment be started right away."

Emory doctors tried to curtail his activities after a series of cobalt
radiation treatments was completed, and failed. Although the cancer-
attacking treatment was a drain upon his remaining strength, Cobb
caught a plane late in December for Los Angeles to attend meetings
concerning the autobiography that he had long intended to write.
Flatly ordered not to take another drink, he remained friendly with
bartenders from New York's Algonquin Hotel bar to Shanty Malone's
groghouse in San Francisco. He traveled coast to coast three times on
sheer willpower.

After I joined him at Atherton in March of 1960 to continue putting his autobiography on paper—*My Life in Baseball: The True Record*—we sifted during research through several dozen boxes of baseball records dated to the early century, including such yellowed journals as *Police Gazette, Sporting Life, Tip-Top Weekly, Reach Guide, New York Clipper*, and *Cap'n Billy's Whiz-Bang*, unboxed more than fifty of his handwritten diaries dating from 1905 through the 1920s, and located tattered scrapbooks of game clippings. We found letters to him from Presidents Theodore Roosevelt, Woodrow Wilson, and Warren Harding. And a bale or so of correspondence with such fans as Mark Twain, Thomas A. Edison, Will Rogers, Connie Mack, Damon Runyon, Douglas Fairbanks, William Randolph Hearst, Ring Lardner, Ernest Hemingway, Bobby Jones, Toots Shor, Grantland Rice, Knute Rockne, and Al Jolson. There were oddments of many kind, including poet Ogden Nash's alphabetizing of great players, among them:

C is for Cobb
Who Grew Spikes and Not Corn
And Made All the Basemen
Wish They Weren't Born.

One of the best-preserved framed artifacts, an obvious Cobb favorite, was an excerpt from a Damon Runyon memoir for the *New York American* concerning a night with the boys at Toots Shor's celebrities' saloon:

The guys but none of the dolls were there on this night and who ups and saunters through the door but Tyrus R. Cobb. He hasn't played for a long time, but in the company of maybe a dozen Hall of Famers, what does Joe DiMaggio softly say but, 'Here comes God.' And everybody there nods his head.

The Georgia Peach had about $12 million to dispose of—the *Sporting News* placed his wealth at $11.8 million at the least, while sources within his family estimated anywhere from $6 to $13 million, depending upon stock market fluctuations. He would not name a figure to me—"the hell with it, leave what I've got out of my book"—and a mystery existed to the end. He tore up several versions of his last will and testament before turning over a version that satisfied him to the executors, the Trust Company of Georgia. That came on May 22, 1961, only fifty-six days before his death. According to his financial counselor, Elmer "Ticker-Tape" Griffin, three-quarters of his holdings went to his two married daughters, Shirley Beckwith, operator of a Palo Alto bookstore, and Beverly McLaren, a well-to-do Atherton resident, his remaining son, James "Jimmie" Cobb of Santa Maria, California, a successful businessman, and more than one dozen grandchildren. One-quarter of his riches was left to his Cobb Educational Fund for poor but gifted college students of Georgia.

THE PREVIOUS September, while at the Tahoe Lodge working on the book with Cobb, I came across a 1946 press interview with the retired Charlie Gehringer, one of the great second basemen, who had endured Cobb's management at Detroit from 1924 to 1926. Gehringer described him as "a real hateful guy" and verified the story always denied by Cobb that he filed his spikes to razor sharpness. Said Gehringer, "He was a spiking fool—he'd cut you to pieces if you gave him any trouble on the bases." Gehringer was specific, adding that in his eighteen big-league seasons, he never knew anyone so hated by so many players as "Butcher" Cobb.

"What do you want me to do with this Gehringer incident?" I asked Cobb. It was a legitimate question.

"Flush it down the crapper!" he responded, enraged at the reminder that he had been confirmed by an expert to have been a dirty ballplayer. As with a good deal of similar anti-Cobb material, Gehringer's opinion was deleted by order from My Life in Baseball. In the volume he came through as the wronged person, a Caesar knifed in the back, a martyr.

During his final months of life, as cancer invaded deeper, he fought death with dogged determination. But he also spoke of suicide. He ranted at society for persecuting him and showed fear that he might not be properly remembered. His last-gasp hell-raising in the spring of 1961, when we made the rounds of gambling casinos, bars, hospitals, and spring-training camps, could not be wholly attributed to illness and pain; weak as he was, Cobb was repeating himself.

Before he departed my Santa Barbara home in May of 1961, he witnessed a few innings of his last game of baseball. On April 27, I drove him to Los Angeles for the Los Angeles (now California) Angels–Minnesota Twins season's opener. He made it with difficulty to his box seat. Players of both teams wanted to meet him; the game was delayed while such current stars as Harmon Killebrew, Albie Pearson, Ted Kluszewski, and Rocky Bridges shook his hand. Cobb was to throw out the first ball. Players crowded in close, mindful of his weak old arm, to catch it. He threw the ball over everybody's head, almost to home plate. "He crossed us all up to the very end," said Fred Haney, general manager of the Angels.

TOWARD THE very end he grew sullen and silent. He had little to say to the few visitors allowed to see him and returned to the pathetic time killer he had used at home in Atherton—tossing wadded-up paper balls into a wastebasket. Eventually he lacked the strength even to do that. Yet when he checked into Emory Hospital for the last time on June 5, Cobb had a surprise for the medical staff. He undressed under his own power, placed a brown paper bagful of stocks, bonds, and other securities worth some $1 million on a bedside table, and atop that placed his Luger pistol. He gave no explanation for this act. My belief is that he was telling people that a man had lived who was both the greatest in the game and the brainiest outside of it—a combination no one but Cobb had achieved. He was demonstrating with irrefutable proof that he had surpassed everyone. The black gun made his nurses nervous, and Dr. Wood persuaded him to store the documents in a hospital safe.

Nobody was with him at 1:20 P.M. on July 17, 1961, when he died, five months short of the age of seventy-five. Emory announced that death was "peaceful." Insiders said that he looked ghastly.

His foremost rival, Babe Ruth, had died in 1948 and an estimated quarter of a million people filed by his coffin at Yankee Stadium. The beloved Babe packed St. Patrick's Cathedral and every major-league club was represented at the two-day services. Ty Cobb drew just three men from big-league ball to his funeral. They were Mickey Cochrane, old-time catcher Ray Schalk, and Nap Rucker from his minor-league days. Other than these and several hundred Little Leaguers of the Royston area north of Atlanta who lined the path to his twelve-foot-high marble mausoleum, the funeral of the most shrewd, inventive, lurid, detested, mysterious, and superb of all baseball players went unattended by any official representative of the game at which he excelled.

APPENDIX

Ty Cobb's Unbroken Record of Home Plate Steals

(Numbers in parentheses indicate first or second games of doubleheaders.)

Date of Game	Teams and Score	Opposing Battery	Inning
July 22, 1909	Bos 0, Det 6	Wolter & Donohue	7
Aug. 16, 1910	Det 8, Was 3	Groom & Ainsmith	4
May 12, 1911	NY 5, Det 6	Caldwell & Sweeney	7
July 12, 1911	Phi 0, Det 9	Krause & Thomas	1
Aug. 18, 1911	Det 9, NY 4	Killalay & Carrigan	1
Apr. 20, 1912	Det 6, Cle 5	Gregg & Easterly	1
May 1, 1912	Det 2, Chi 5	Benz & Block	1
May 13, 1912	NY 15, Det 4	Vaughn & Street	1
June 21, 1912	Det 2, Cle 6	Blanding & O'Neill	6
July 4, 1912 (1)	StL 3, Det 9	Baumgardner & Krichell	5
May 18, 1913	Det 1, Was 2	Johnson & Ainsmith	7
May 20, 1913	Det 8, Phi 7	Houck & Lapp	3
Aug. 25, 1913	Det 6, Was 5	Bedient & Nunamaker	5
Sep. 15, 1913	NY 5, Det 7	Warhop & Sweeney	5
June 9, 1914	Phi 7, Det 1	Shawkey & Lapp	4
Apr. 28, 1915	StL 3, Det 12	James & Agnew	3
June 4, 1915	Det 3, NY 0	Caldwell & Nunamaker	9
June 9, 1915	Det 15, Bos 0	Collins & Carrigan	3
June 18, 1915	Det 5, Was 3	Boehling & Henry	1
June 18, 1915	Det 5, Was 3	Boehling & Williams	5
June 23, 1915	StL 2, Det 4	Lowdermilk & Agnew	8
Aug. 23, 1916	Det 10, Phi 3	Sheehan & Picinich	8
July 9, 1918 (2)	Det 5, Phi 4	Perry & Perkins	5
Aug. 23, 1919	Bos 4, Det 8	Hoyt & Walters	3

Date of Game	Teams and Score	Opposing Battery	Inning
May 18, 1920	Phi 2, Det 8	Martin & Myatt	8
Sep. 19, 1920 (1)	Was 7, Det 9	Bono & Gharrity	4
Oct. 2, 1923	Det 7 Chi 5	Castner & Crouse	7
Apr. 22, 1924	Chi 3, Det 4	Bayne & Collins	3
Apr. 27, 1924	Chi 3, Det 4	Lyons & Crouse	5
Aug. 10, 1924	Det 13, Bos 7	Ross & Picinich	7
July 3, 1927	Det 5, Cle 7	Uhle & Sewell	1
Apr. 19, 1927	Phi 3, Was 1	Crowder & Ruel	6
Apr. 26, 1927	Phi 9, Bos 8	Welzer & Hartley	7
July 6, 1927	Bos 1, Phi 5	Lundgren & Hartley	1
June 15, 1928	Phi 12, Cle 5	Grant & Sewell	8

World Series

Oct. 9, 1909	Det 7, Pit 2	Willis & Gibson	3

Bibliography

Alexander, Charles. *Ty Cobb*. New York: Oxford University Press, 1984.

Allen, Frederick Lewis. *Only Yesterday*. Rev. ed. New York: Harper & Row, 1964.

Astor, Gerald, and Joe Falls. *The Detroit Tigers*. New York: Walker & Company, 1989.

The Baseball Encyclopedia, 8th ed. New York: Macmillan, 1990.

Beasley, Norman, and George W. Stark. *Made in Detroit*. New York: G. P. Putnam's Sons, 1957.

Bingay, Malcolm. *Detroit Is My Own Home Town*. New York: Bobbs-Merrill, 1946.

Cobb, Ty. *Busting 'Em and Other Stories*. New York: Edward J. Clode, 1914.

———. *My Life in Baseball: The True Record*, with Al Stump. Garden City, N.Y.: Doubleday, 1961.

Einstein, Charles. *The Baseball Reader*. New York: Lippincott and Cromwell, 1980.

Gallico, Paul. *The Golden People*. Garden City, N.Y.: Doubleday, 1965.

Honig, Donald. *Baseball America*. New York: Macmillan, 1985.

———, ed. *Baseball When the Grass Was Real*. New York: Coward, McCann & Geohegan, 1975.

Hornsby, Rogers, and Bill Surface. *My War with Baseball*. New York: Coward-McCann, 1962.

James, Bill. *The Bill James Historical Baseball Abstract*. New York: Villard Books, 1986.

Lieb, Fred. *Baseball As I Have Known It*. New York: Coward, McCann & Geohegan, 1977.

———. *The Detroit Tigers*. New York: G. P. Putnam's Sons, 1946.

Mack, Connie. *My 66 Years in the Big Leagues*. Philadelphia: John C. Winston, 1950.

MacFarlane, Paul, ed. *Daguerreotypes*. St. Louis: Sporting News, 1981.

My Greatest Day in Baseball as told to John P. Carmichael. New York: A. S. Barnes & Company, 1945.

Oliver, Thomas. *The Real Coke, the Real Story*. New York: Random House, 1986.

Rice, Grantland. *The Tumult and the Shouting*. New York: A. S. Barnes & Company, 1954.

Ritter, Lawrence. *The Glory of Their Times*. New York: Macmillan, 1966.

Ruth, Claire Hodgson, and Bill Slocum. *The Babe and I*. Englewood Cliffs: Prentice-Hall, 1959.

Seymour, Harold. *Baseball: The Early Years*. New York: Oxford University Press, 1960.

———. *Baseball: The Golden Age*. New York: Oxford University Press, 1971.

INDEX